This book is dedicated to Mari, brightest star of all.

Table of Contents

Preface	7
Introduction	9
Maps	11
1. A Small Model Nation	13
2. The Age of Revolution	19
3. Arm Yourself and Wait	29
4. The MLN-Tupamaros	43
5. Confrontations	63
6. The Robin Hood Guerrillas	83
7. The People Passed Through Here	115
8. Maximum Tension	139
9. A Number of Dreadful Things	173
10. Reset	201
11. Rise of the Centurions	229
12. The Final Round	245
13. The Napoleonic Twist	285
14. The Last Days	305
Epilogue	327
Acknowledgments	359
About the Author	361
Endnotes	363
Index	397

PREFACE

This book benefits from both primary and secondary sources. The primary ones include interviews conducted by the author with individuals involved in the events narrated here. Among these are a former police inspector and intelligence officer, as well as three top leaders of the MLN and a key politician of the time.

The other primary sources are transcripts of interviews conducted by other researchers, as well as original documents from all sides of the conflict. These interviews were mostly published in Uruguay in the past decade, and contain extensive accounts by the Tupamaros of their ideology, organization, and operations. Other important players in the period also figure prominently in said interviews. As for the documents, they include original MLN propaganda, manuals, and doctrinal materials, as well as press reports and government documents. Thousands of pages' worth of United States government declassified documents, from entities such as the Department of State, the embassy in Montevideo, and the Central Intelligence Agency, are also essential sources.

Secondary sources are mostly books published in Uruguay about the MLN insurgency, the government response to it, and the general context of the period. This collection of books has a varied spectrum of authors: some were committed participants in one side or the other; others are academic or journalistic in origin. A combination of all yields a remarkable overview of the period, with the possibility of crosschecking for bias multiple times.

INTRODUCTION

PUNCHED FURIOUSLY IN the gut. Electrocuted. His head dunked repeatedly in the filthiest of waters. Shot multiple times.

Sitting in his cramped, humid cell, José Mujica thought he had already been through the worst - but he had not. His hair was falling. Most of his teeth were gone. His nervous system was a wreck. He was also losing his mind and was starting to realize it: there was a constant noise of static keeping him permanently perturbed. He was convinced he was being remotely monitored. There was no one to talk to, nothing to read, and no sunlight to see: all he had was himself.

Pepe, as friends and family called him, had plenty of time to reflect on the events that had taken him there. Was it all a mistake? He had risked his life and lost, badly. Was it all in vain? Did his defeat mean that his cause was wrong, or that the wheels had gone off an otherwise worthy enterprise? Defeat - that was a concept to meditate on.

The imprisoned Mujica did not know it, but after over four thousand nights in solitary confinement he would emerge into the light of day and know freedom again. The man that came out was battered but decided never to be bitter. He concluded that in life everyone must carry a backpack full of pain - but that no one should live their lives looking at that backpack.

Pepe Mujica has made many mistakes throughout life. Nevertheless, people around him have always found his capacity for self-reflection attractive. He left prison convinced of trying new methods towards the same pursuit that had landed him there, and succeeded at it. Decades after leaving jail, his body and mind fully healed, at the moment when he rose to prominence Mujica emotionally reflected on the quest he and his comrades had been through: "We have spent a lifetime struggling. This is the game now. Not even the greatest novelist could have imagined what happened".

Now the president of his country, Mujica has also said something else: "I am still a Tupamaro: someone who rebels against injustice". In other words, his essence is to be found in the events that took him to that dank, claustrophobic cell. This is the story of what happened.

Argentina
Bella Unión
Brazil
Salto
Paysandú
Uruguay
Nueva Helvecia
Buenos Aires
Pando
Montevideo
Punta del Este
Argentina
River Plate
0 25 50 Kilometers
0 25 50 Miles

Montevideo, 1968-1973
Prado
Bay of Montevideo
Port
Old Town
Downtown
Tres Cruces
Pocitos
Buceo Port
Malvín
Rivera Park
Golf Club
River Plate
River Plate
0 25 50 Kilometers
0 25 50 Miles
1- CIM raid of May 1970
2- Independence Square
3- Jewels heist of November 1970
4- Monty bank heist of February 1969
5- Military Region I HQ
6- Legislative Palace
7- U.S. Embassy
8- Universidad de la República
9- Punta Carretas Prison
10- People's Prison, 1972
11- Mailhos mansion, April 1970
12- Operation Star 1971
13- Park of the Allies
14- José Mujica shootout, 1970
15- People's Prison, 1970
16- Dan Mitrione found
17- Soldier's Day, May 1972
18- Almería incident
19- Dan Mitrione kidnapped
20- Incidents of April 14 1972

Chapter One:

A Small Model Nation

BEYOND THE WARM waters of the Caribbean, the vast jungles of the Amazon and the frozen peaks of the Andes lies a region of South America that has no meaningful name. Given its shape in a standard map of the continent, it is most often called the Southern Cone.

The twentieth century saw many unfortunate events take place there, although indubitably it was far better off than some of the planet's more troubled places. There was no trench warfare, no industrial-scale genocide, no carpet bombings, no nuclear strikes, no Pearl Harbors, no missile crises, no famines, and no religious or ethnic strife, anywhere. In fact, it is frequently said that countries in the area benefited from their neutrality during the two world wars and part of the Cold War. Revenues from agricultural exports to feed those wars, as well as needy immigrants, flowed in for many decades.

The smallest member of the region, which includes southern Brazil, Chile, and Argentina, is Uruguay. It is remarkable for its moderation in all respects. The climate is temperate; it never snows and is rarely too hot during the summer. The landscape is gentle: there are no mountain ranges, no large rivers, no jungles or large forests, no deserts, and no fault lines to cause earthquakes. Uruguay is, in fact, often associated with an enormous grazing ground.

A country of approximately three million people, the Oriental Republic (as defined in its official name), is one of the smallest states in all of the Americas in both size and population. It also has one of the least populated capitals, Montevideo. Despite its size –or possibly because of it-, Uruguay fared well in political and economic terms for much of its history. As a society made up predominantly of European immigrants –particularly from Spain, Italy, and Portugal-, with solid levels of social integration and a tradition of republican liberalism and democracy, Uruguay never faced many of the systemic problems other countries in the Americas did (and do to this day).

The nineteenth century was a generous time. Liberal governments created a strong state-run educational system, a democratic and accountable government, a strict separation of state powers, a tradition of freedom of expression, and other republican structures. Montevideo was at the end of the century the third most important city in South America after Buenos Aires and Rio de Janeiro. Living standards were above those of Mediterranean Europe, and roughly on parity with global imperial power France.[1]

As the century reached its end, Uruguay adopted progressive ideas such as state-run public utilities, social welfare subsidies, large government expenditures on public works and jobs programs, and other initiatives. In fact, the country's great modernizer, early twentieth century president José Batlle & Ordóñez, consciously set out to "build a small model nation".[2] By the 1950s Uruguay was one of the most heavily "socialized" democracies in the world, with roughly half -and possibly more- of the adult population either working for the state or otherwise receiving its income from it.

A Social Welfare State

The key aspect of Uruguayan history in the years immediately following the Second World War is the economic decay the country endured for the rest of the century.

The invaluable statistics collected by British economic historian Angus Maddison demonstrate this clearly. In the first decades of the twentieth century, Uruguay was a world-class economy. Living there was preferable -by far- to living in most other countries on Earth. However, after 1945, when the post-war recovery began in Europe, Uruguay permanently diverged from its previous path.

At the time, the economy operated as follows: the fertile countryside produced beef and other products that were exported for the consumption of hungry wartime and post-war markets. Those exports were taxed, and with said taxes the government financed state-run utilities, social welfare programs, free housing, large expansions in government payrolls, and so forth.

With *el campo*, or the countryside, providing the main engine, the rest of the economy plunged head-first into socialism. The method was to put most of it under the direct control of the state, which now had multiple companies under its management: railways, electricity, sanitation, an airline, telecommunications, fisheries, a slaughterhouse-meatpacking concern, gas provision, gasoline refinement, an insurance company, banks, and all other "strategic" activities. Some of these, like the petroleum refining monopoly, became symbols of corruption and clientelism.

Politicians

Uruguay had two main political parties since its foundation, each with roughly half of the electorate: the Partido Colorado and the Partido Nacional. They remain some of the oldest continually functioning parties in the world. The Colorados became unbeatable with the achievements of José Batlle & Ordóñez, the most important politician in Uruguayan history. It was his term in office that inaugurated, beginning in 1903, major social and economic reforms ranging from the separation of church and state to labor regulations. As a consequence, the largest wing of the Colorados, the progressive one, began to call itself Batllismo, and its members Batllistas.

Five decades of Batllismo meant that in 1950s Uruguay everything depended on the state. An automobile insurance dispute depended on the state insurance company. The delayed installation of a telephone line was the responsibility of the state telephone company. Even much of the beef supply was in the hands of state-owned companies. All were run by party officials designated by the Parliament. The expectation for citizens became that the legislators they voted for would personally take care of their everyday concerns by telephoning or otherwise prodding the appropriate government entities. It was thus the job of politicians to write down the demands in their *libretitas* or little notebooks and relay them through the party network so that something could be done. When results came through, re-election was likelier. The nationalists in the opposition were out of power, but always retained representation in the Parliament and even in the executive branch, which Batllismo turned into a nine-member collegiate institution rather than a presidential one.

Uruguay was thus an egalitarian democracy with a socialized economy - and it was free of the strife and penury so prevalent in the rest of the world. From a Marxist perspective, this situation was distinctly un-revolutionary. In the words of historian Hebert Gatto, "What is (...) most surprising is not that Uruguay lacked some of the conditions for revolution (...) but rather, it lacked all of them".[3] Gatto recognized a solitary exception, and that was in the intellectual climate. In the 1960s, that single factor would burst with explosive energy.

Bolches & Yankees

In the 1950s Uruguay began to see some Cold War activity. In fact, Montevideo served as a regional espionage center. One CIA case officer serving there beginning in 1956 was Everette Howard Hunt, of later Watergate fame. According to his memoirs, when assigned the destination Hunt had to look Uruguay up on a map; "I was at first deeply concerned that I was being demoted for some reason to this tiny, innocuous country way down in South America (...) Washington cabled me back that this was an important station (...) Argentina and Brazil had evicted the Communist ambassadors, so they were all now concentrated in Montevideo".[4]

The main target of anti-Communist attention in Montevideo, be it local or American, was the Uruguayan Communist Party (PCU) which had been politically quite insignificant since its founding. As all proper Communist parties worldwide, it was subordinated to the letter to the dictates of the Communist Party of the Soviet Union.

A key problem the Communists faced in acquiring more votes was that their ideology had little breathing room in Uruguay. This was not because people were aware of the totalitarian horror that lay behind the Iron Curtain. Those revelations, despite the best efforts of minds like George Orwell's, were still to come. Rather it was because the "social justice" and "people's" agenda the Communists relied on for their campaigns was already in the hands of Uruguay's socialist democrats. With such formidable government activism in place, the Communists' alignment with the Soviet Union, flirtation with street violence, and lack of political innovation caused them to be unwelcome in national politics.

Party officials like Tibaldo Rodney Arismendi would change that, but first they needed to get rid of corrupt Secretary General Eugenio Gómez. They did so in an internal coup in 1955, which left Arismendi in charge. While he and others had in previous times effusively praised Gómez and even his son, overnight they had become evil incarnate and were cast out forever from the Communist herd - and accused of belonging to "the imperialist intelligence services".[5]

Arismendi remained in his position as master of the Communist Party for decades. His first proposal for the new era was weaving a coalition of all Marxist and some non-Marxist parties. The coalition would present its name in elections as a single political option. By pooling all of their votes, members would stand a better chance of defeating the *partidos tradicionales*, the historically dominant Colorados and Nationalists.

While work began on the political alliance front, Arismendi took other steps to expand the influence of his party. First, in 1957 he rebooted the PCU's newspaper. Justicia became El Popular; what before had been an internal party rag became a full-blown daily newspaper.[6] El Popular was designed for mass consumption and to compete with regular newspapers. In the coming decades, it would reflect the viewpoint of Arismendi, of the Party, and of the Soviet Union in every issue. This applied not just to editorial contents and biases, but also to where the news was placed in each issue, or to whether they were included at all.

Next came the Communist youth organization, the Unión de Juventudes Comunistas. The UJC was designed to attract young, socially conscious and promising Uruguayans who could later become party cadres. It targeted university students in particular. In a country with a single, state-owned, and free university, the task was logistically simple. The field was fertile in any case, since social change is invariably a popular concept in academic environments.

As the only provider of higher education in the land, and one that had significant international prestige considering Uruguay's size, the Universidad de la República was one of the most important institutions in the country. Every lawyer, medical doctor, architect, engineer, or economist had studied there, save for the few who might have done so overseas. Generation after generation of

Uruguayan politicians, both from the traditional parties but also from the Marxist ones, had gone there – meaning they often knew each other from early on. Matriculation was increasing: it grew 54% between 1955 and 1966.[7]

A great Communist triumph in this front came as early as 1958, only three years into Arismendi's tenure. The Party and its affiliates were the main backers of a successful campaign, with plenty of protests and demonstrations in between, to change the legal status of the university. The proposal was simple, yet contrary to every principle of republicanism and fairness. The state would keep on funding the university by collecting taxpayer money and allocating it to the institution. Enrollment would remain free. Therefore, the university would generate very little revenue of its own. In exchange for the funding, however, there would be no accountability on the part of the Universidad. Instead, a new system called "co-government" would be implemented, in which the university was governed by councils composed of professors, students, and graduates. It was they who would now decide how the money could be spent, what classes would be taught, what professors would be hired, and so forth.

While the new law was supposed to guarantee the school remained independent of political influences, practice was the opposite. It was the end of the University's independence. The reason was that the Communists, thanks to their oversized presence among the professors and the students, quickly dominated the governing councils - all without the need for political power in the executive branch or in the Parliament.

The 1950s ended with increasing Communist successes thank to street mobilizations, a decaying economy, and a change in government from the Colorados to the Nationalists. It was then that an event took place that shook everything up: the Cuban Revolution of 1959, and its heralding of violent revolution in the Americas.

Chapter Two:

The Age of Revolution

THE DEFINING CONCEPT of the 1960s was *revolution.* There were attempts at achieving one everywhere, in all continents and in all languages. Uruguay was not the exception.

The most comprehensive method for securing a political revolution is often called insurgency. At the time, the works and acts of Chinese revolutionary (and dictator) Mao Zedong were the gold standard for pursuing an insurgent path towards "national liberation".

According to Mao, a proper insurgency mixes political activities that degrade the existing legal order with armed attacks that increasingly get at the government's nerves. In other words, an insurgency combines military operations with political work in a single, cohesive effort: "guerrilla operations are but one aspect of our total or mass war (...) guerrilla warfare must fail (...) if its political objectives do not coincide with the aspirations of the people and their sympathy, cooperation, and assistance cannot be gained".[8] By becoming one with the population, Mao's insurgents become impossible to single out and destroy.

In his writings, Mao also emphasized the role of geography. He established that the countryside ought to be the fighting grounds of the insurgent, and also that specific types of terrain (such as jungles and mountains) should be the primary shelters of a struggling insurgent force. He had readers in every continent anxiously devouring his manuals, each studying the maps and landscapes of his own country to see if they matched what Mao said.

Mao's was a 1930s Chinese theory of war. There was margin for additional thinking, and that came with the 1959 triumph of the Cuban Revolution. Shortly after victory, Argentine revolutionary Ernesto "Che" Guevara wrote a book called "Guerra de Guerrillas", in which he presented the guiding principles of the successful uprising conducted in the island. They deviated from what Mao and the other great Marxist strategist, Lenin, had written. Guevara attacked, in particular, the necessity of having an established political party serving as the nexus of the revolutionary campaign.

While these parties were supposed to generate Karl Marx's "conditions for revolution" through their propaganda and other activities, in the very first pages of his manual Guevara said "It is not always necessary to wait for all the conditions for revolution to be in place". In other words, it was possible to start guerrilla activities right away, conditions or no conditions. In Guevara's theory, attacking the government would create the revolutionary climate that Mao believed could only come as the result of long-term developments and political work. Guevara called this exemplary revolutionary spearhead a "*foco*", and thus his was the doctrine of *foco* guerrilla warfare.

In addition to this, Guevara also identified the right environment for the *foco*, this time in full agreement with Mao: "In the underdeveloped Americas, the terrain for armed struggle will fundamentally be the countryside". The reasons for Guevara's lack of interest in cities were clear: those were "exceptionally unfavorable terrains, where the enemy's vigilance will be far greater and the possibilities for retaliation enormously increased". In fact, Guevara's guerrilla army was predominantly a peasant one: "The banner for the struggle during the entire effort will be agrarian reform".[9]

Guevara visited Uruguay precisely while he was writing his manual on guerrilla warfare (1960-1, according to the preface). On August 17 1961 he appeared at a packed auditorium in the main hall of the Universidad de la República. Chilean senator Salvador Allende was a fellow panelist, and the topic for discussion was revolution. Guevara addressed the rapt audience as follows: "I can assure you that in our Americas, under current conditions, there are no countries like Uruguay, where the expression of ideas is permitted (...) You have something worth preserving, which is precisely the possibility of expressing your ideas; the possibility of advancing through democratic channels as far as one can go".[10] In case his message was unclear, Guevara added "once the first shot is fired, you never know when the last one will be".

This was meaningful because Guevara and the Cubans had become icons for growing numbers of people, particularly youths, all over the continent. The warnings about democratic governments were thorns in an otherwise blooming rose. They were especially disappointing to aspiring revolutionaries in countries with heavily urban demographics. Why should they be condemned *not* to have a revolution only because they happened to have been born in cities?

Be it rural or urban, the Guevarist *foco* model was both a product and a cause of the romanticism of the time. Revolution was not just a political cause, but also a personal quest. The selfless intellectual who took to the hinterlands to lead a peasant army for national liberation became the ultimate symbol of 1960s self-realization.

Along with revolution came terrorism. While the tactic of terrorism had ample precedents before the 1960s -for centuries, in fact-, it was in that decade when it acquired its present-day, agenda-hijacking qualities.[11] A loaded word in many discussions, terrorism is essentially violence targeted at noncombatants in a conflict. The terrorist pursues a far shorter path towards victory than the patient Maoist insurgent.

Being separate concepts, there are thus differences between the tactics of guerrilla warfare and terrorism. The former is targeted at the forces and the infrastructure of the enemy - the practice of war by the weak. Terrorism attacks non-participants in the conflict whose suffering can psychologically influence the enemy's conduct. As noted by terrorism expert Bruce Hoffman: "Terrorists (...) do not function in the open as armed units, generally do not attempt to seize or hold territory, deliberately avoid engaging enemy military forces in combat, are constrained both numerically and logistically from undertaking concerted mass political mobilization efforts, and exercise no direct control over a populace at either the local or the national level".[12]

The major practitioners of revolutionary insurgency considered the issue of tactics as well. For example, in his book Guevara wrote that terrorism was a "considerably ineffective measure, in general; it is indiscriminate in its consequences because in many cases it makes victims of innocent people".[13] In contrast, the Brazilian Carlos Marighella, who raised the flag of urban *foco* guerrilla in the second half of the decade, wrote "Terrorism is a weapon the revolutionary cannot abandon".[14] Overall, insurgents had a choice: nothing except their own decisions could stop them from being guerrillas, terrorists, or both.

The Cold War in Uruguay

Meanwhile, Uruguay was still living mostly on a holiday from history. Although society was well informed of developments overseas, the country had such little participation in world affairs that it was mainly concerned with internal issues. The economic battle for the spoils of the state-run economy was the dominant issue, followed closely by football and other quaint aspects of life. For Uruguay and its people, talk of revolution, peasant uprisings, protracted wars in rugged terrain, or acts of mass violence was distant and rare.

In 1964, a group of Brazilian military officers staged a coup d'état that removed João Goulart from the presidency. Goulart was the spiritual successor of Gétulio Vargas, a dictator with nationalist-socialist origins in the 1930s. Both were populist authoritarians who flirted significantly with Marxism. Once the military got rid of Goulart, he fled –along with his rather large entourage- to neighboring Uruguay.

A situation then existed, as of April 1964, in which tiny Uruguay was hosting the number one enemy of Brazil's new military regime: a potential government in exile. Indeed, Goulart and acolytes like Leonel Brizola, his brother-in-law and deposed governor of Rio Grande do Sul state (the only one that bordered Uruguay), remained publicly in opposition to the new regime in Brasília.

The issue of Brazil breathing down Uruguay's neck over the activities of the exiles, including the possibility of a military invasion to capture them and "stabilize" Uruguay, became a source of concern and intrigue for close to a decade. The pronouncements of the Brazilian government and its embassy, of Brazilian newspaper editorials, and most sensitively the maneuvers of its army across the border, generated considerable anxiety in Uruguay. The CIA station in Montevideo noted these events as well. To its spies, the threat of Brazilian aggression was real enough to warrant reporting it to Washington.[15]

For their part, the Uruguayan Communists entered the 1960s with increasing strength, intent on continuing to accumulate political, social, and cultural forces. The consolidation of the labor union movement was the next major victory for Arismendi. A unique achievement following decades of absorption work, union by union, it was announced in 1966. The result was that there would be a single confederacy of all unions in Uruguay, and it would be called the Confederación Nacional del Trabajo (National Labor Confederacy), or CNT.

The CNT was extremely powerful: it had hundreds of thousands of affiliates, including the all-powerful employees of the state. By 1969 more than half of Uruguay's population continued to depend on state income, either as employees or beneficiaries of social welfare.[16] By owning the key leadership positions in the CNT through its patient committee work, the Communists had once again fetched a power vector significantly beyond their actual votes (2.7% of the total in 1958 and 3.5% in 1962). It was a repeat of the triumph at the university years earlier. Beginning in 1966, the Communist-controlled CNT became one of the top political and economic actors in Uruguay. Its general strikes were frequent, paralyzing, and damaging to each government.

The Years of Crisis

For the other political parties the 1960s were eventful but problematic. The Nationalists governed since their victory in 1958, but they were increasingly divided. The party's great leader from previous decades, Luis Alberto de Herrera, died just as the new government started in 1959. The Nationalist delegates to the Swiss-inspired, rotational executive branch were truly a mixed bag. They could be led one year by a conservative CIA liaison like Benito Nardone, and the next by the Soviet-aligned Eduardo Haedo. The party was simply too heterogeneous. Although the Nationalists won re-election in 1962, they did so with significantly eroded support.

The Nationalists fared feebly because the economy entered a downturn in the late 1950s. In the new decade it only deepened. One of the many reasons was that Uruguay was growing old at breakneck speed. Its birth rate was one of the world's lowest, while its population had one of the highest average life expectancies. To top that off, during the crisis years of the 1960s, for the first time

Uruguay witnessed net population losses, due to emigration. The situation was so dire that as early as 1963 the U.S. embassy reported to Washington that "social security funds (...) are short of liquid assets and will have difficulty meeting their payments in the coming months". Uruguay may well have been the first country in the world to grow so old and so financially wasteful, so fast, that it drained social democracy of its funds.[17]

The economic decline came fast and hard. In 1959, only a year into a period of soft liberal reforms, inflation reached 49%. The reforms were reversed in 1962, and soon after recession struck Uruguay's excessively large banking sector, which comprised over three hundred branches in Montevideo alone, across fifty different banking institutions.[18] A financial crisis exploded in 1964-5. The country's top bank, the state-owned BROU, halted withdrawals from clients' accounts, and the largest private banks collapsed in financial and ethical scandals.*

Popular unrest over these events was so intense that banks did not open for a month. The economy was ravaged. U.S. diplomats noted how "Checks circulate from hand to hand, and five or six endorsements on the back of a check are no longer rare (some enterprises have received their own checks back in payment of debts owed to them)".[19] To top it off, the government botched the solution to the crisis: the BROU bailed out the bad loans of the largest private bank, the Banco Transatlántico, which immediately went out of business while its management was tried for malfeasance.

The rot continued. Inflation in 1965 reached 88%, and it peaked at 136% in 1967. As CIA case officer Philip Agee recognized, by November of 1965: "not a day has passed without an important strike by government employees, schools, banks, the University, the postal and telecommunications systems, printers, port workers, the central administration and others".[20] The demonstrations became a central part of life in the 1960s.

Fixes took years. Only in 1970 -a decade into the downturn- did the infamous Frigorífico Nacional (National Meatpacker), a particularly excessive product of Uruguayan socialism, finally close down. A stunning nine hundred people had worked there, with a

* BROU stands for Banco de la República Oriental del Uruguay. It is often referred to as "Banco República".

monopoly on the beef supply to Montevideo and a quota of free beef for its employees. Many re-sold it for profit among those who did not enjoy such privileges. While the company was dismantled there was a period in which Montevideans had to travel outside of the city limits to purchase beef, the most traditional and sacred of all Uruguayan goods.

With every year that passed, street tensions increased. Union and student rallies ended in riots with increasing frequency, often thanks to Communist orchestration. The PCU's youth militia, the UJC, had cadres specifically trained and dedicated to causing unrest. There was little spontaneous about the labor militancy that increased with each year of the 1960s: there was a "special encouragement coming from the direction of the PCU and the UJC (...) for the staging of violent protests and small-scale attacks already during 1964 and the years that followed".[21]

The strategy was always to demand more from the government, and as soon as it acquiesced, to take to the streets again to demand more benefits, salary increases, entitlements, expropriations, and so forth. The more salary demands were granted, the more inflation increased - and shortly afterwards, those salaries became insufficient and needed to be raised again.

As the disturbances increased in intensity, so did the street tactics of the protesters: barricades, caltrops (known in Uruguay as *miguelitos*), Molotov cocktails, and the wanton destruction of private and public property. By the late 1960s, in student occupations of the main building of the national university (the same where Che Guevara had spoken), the security services were facing debris-lobbing catapults. Passersby had to endure the collection of "tolls" from student groups that resembled paramilitary organizations.[22] In response there was a minor flare in conservative violence directed against Communists and aligned rioters.

Almost all of this was a novel development. Up until the 1960s, violence in Uruguay had been limited mostly to robbers, and was rarely directed at third parties. The police was technologically and professionally limited, but it was effective. Local detectives, except when dealing with non-Uruguayan or uncommon criminals, usually got the job done and managed to capture wanted delinquents.

A Bet on Public Safety

Nevertheless, the increase in political street brawling caught the attention of the United States, which offered Uruguay assistance for the police through its Office of Public Safety (OPS), a subdivision of the Agency for International Development (USAID).[23] At the time, OPS had a key program in Viet Nam, and its advisers were ready to deploy to countries like Uruguay to assist the police. From the American perspective, particularly the CIA's, "the Uruguayan police were an unending source of amusement – their ineptness, the hopelessness of ever making them efficient".[24]

Uruguayan politicians resisted these entreaties for many years, despite the allure of American funds, and for a good reason. Strictly speaking, Uruguay's police forces were doing as good a job, if not a better one, than their American counterparts. U.S. cities like Los Ángeles or Chicago were not exactly known for their successes in public safety. Furthermore, it was the police of southern U.S. states and cities that violently upheld a system of ethnic segregation that was still in the process of being dismantled. Lastly, American security had failed its own president, allowing him to be shot by a mysterious sniper, who in turn got assassinated while in police custody, in a case that remains unsolved to this day.

In turn, from an American perspective, Uruguayan police were too lightly armed. Very few patrol cars in Montevideo had radios, and record keeping was inexistent. These would be the main points of interest of the limited OPS mission authorized for Uruguay.[25] Its first chief, Adolph Sáenz, arrived in January of 1965. In his mind, the main threat was the persistent growth and intensity of Communist-inspired unrest in the streets of Montevideo.

Sáenz arrived just in time to witness the public theater of "street action", in heavy use by Communists to reject the presence of Americans. In 1965 Secretary of State Dean Rusk was visiting Montevideo and presenting a floral homage at the statue of Uruguay's founding father, José Artigas. In the middle of the well-attended ceremony, a member of the Communist youth militia, named Jesús Rolán Rojas, attacked Rusk. The young UJC radical got dangerously close, but was tackled both late and in time by the ineffectual police detail. Rojas did not get to touch Rusk, but he did spit violently at him – and hit his target's face. The incident was particularly unfortunate. In 1964, only a few months earlier, an internal Department of State memorandum placed the "preservation of democracy in Uruguay" as the top U.S. priority in bilateral relations. It carried Dean Rusk's signature.[26]

As the decade wore on, young radicals could easily draw on a perspective of the world that had them under siege by malevolent forces. There was a revolutionary model in place: Cuba. There was an individual revolutionary model as well: Che Guevara. There was a clear-cut enemy: the United States. There were pleasant-sounding objectives like "social justice" and "liberation". All that was needed was leadership and the sparks to set the wheels of conflict in motion.

Chapter Three:

Arm Yourself and Wait

THE FIRST URUGUAYAN radicals thinking of engaging in violent action came together in 1962 in a secret entity called the Coordinador.

The Coordinador was an informal organization set up by multiple Marxist parties for the purpose of training militias away from the main party offices. Many who joined conceived their role as defensive: this was where Uruguayan *izquierdistas* would plan resistance actions against the government's forces and their allies, particularly if the country underwent an authoritarian coup. Others saw the Coordinador as the place where plans for revolution were at last to be discussed. Militants from the different parties exchanged ideological viewpoints and tips on how to acquire weapons, discuss the latest news from Cuba, and make plans for *acciones*, or operations. The first meeting consisted of a group of less than ten men, all distanced to some degree from their organizations.

The Coordinador brought together Socialists, Maoists, Trotskyists, Anarchists and others who not only did not identify with the Colorado and Nationalist parties, but also felt that the parliamentary politics of traditional Marxist parties -the PCU included- were increasingly irrelevant. There were plenty of these small groups, for it was a fertile period for left-wing political organizations. A young radical could pick and choose parties "as if he were browsing supermarket aisles".[27]

The Coordinador was more a confederacy than a real entity. Almost everyone there was part of a contingent representing an existing party or movement. Each cell applying to join had to perform an armed operation to gain full acceptance. Meetings consisted of long sessions in a run-down but safe location in the working-class Montevideo neighborhood of La Teja, with music in the background and wine on the table. Each individual put forward his own ideas about the best path for revolution. The discussion covered everything: basic purposes, potential insurgent tactics, the recent anti-imperialist successes in Cuba and Algeria, the objective and subjective conditions for revolution in Uruguay, and more. Some arguments ended in fistfights and renunciations.[28] Some key introductions were made at the modest dwelling, including that of a man named José Mujica.[29]

Raúl Sendic

At the same time as the Coordinador gathered these militants in Montevideo, a man named Raúl Sendic was organizing the most radical labor union in Uruguay, in the far north of the country. The half-Basque, half-Italian Sendic had been raised in a small rural community in the department of Flores, in central Uruguay, in the 1920s and 1930s.[30] His childhood was full of memories of a make-do lifestyle that he practiced for life. To listen to football matches on the radio, he and his brothers needed to urgently recharge its batteries by spinning the wheels of the mill. The first sight of a train, many years into his childhood, was a scary experience. Young Raúl milked the cows at four in the morning, rode a horse to school, and in general lived the life of a child of the *campo.*[31] As a teenager in high school, he had an early interest in politics. The student newspaper he founded was named *Rebeldía.*

During the late 1940s Sendic studied law at the only possible venue: Montevideo's Universidad de la República, where he was classmates with, among others, Colorado scion Jorge Batlle. He joined the Socialist Party and reached a fairly high position in its youth wing. Ideologically, Sendic was famously independent. At a time when the Communists were still praising the master of totalitarian monocracy, Stalin, Sendic was a free thinker with his own interpretation of the Marxist canon.

As an adult, Sendic became a solicitor. Shortly after finishing his coursework -one exam short of becoming a *juris doctor*- he quit his job at a local law firm and moved to the north of Uruguay. He first worked with beer brewing and leather tanning unions in the city of Paysandú, but Sendic really made his mark in the poorest and most remote part of the country: Bella Unión, right on the border with Brazil and Argentina in Uruguay's northernmost tip.[32]

In Bella Unión, in the department of Artigas, Sendic liaised with a group of disorganized sugar cane workers. The union he founded for them, in a decrepit whorehouse in December of 1961, was called UTAA: Unión de Trabajadores Azucareros de Artigas, or Union of Artigas Sugar Cane Workers. It was the smallest, least prepared, and most militant of all in Uruguay. Sendic let loose with UTAA, planning occupations and strikes at various cane plantations, which got their owners –in some cases, American companies- to make greater concessions to the workers.[33]

For Uruguay's *izquierda*, Sendic's actions in the north were a complete novelty. As the heavily Europeanized parties that they were, and given the strong influence of Marxism-Leninism, they were virtually Montevideo-exclusive organizations. Working in rural Uruguay, where revolution-prone peasants were but a mirage, had always made little sense to them – and they would have felt uncomfortable outside of Montevideo anyway.[34] As fellow socialist and future Tupamaro Efraín Martínez Platero put it, "what politician with a future like the one Raúl had before him would have thought of getting involved with rural unions in Uruguay? No one, absolutely no one. Nobody was thinking of going to where the truly deepest poverty existed".[35]

Sendic, however, was different. He was at ease in the *chacras*, the rice fields, the cane plantations, and in rural establishments and small towns where people like himself dwelt. His years in Montevideo turned him into a well-read Marxist, but in most ways he was the same Raúl everyone had known before. He never adopted the *bourgeois* lifestyle. Contrary to the opinion of essentially everyone else, Sendic was convinced that the urban Marxists would get nowhere, and that the future was in radical action started from the depths of Uruguay, among the rural poor. His jump to the north in 1961, just as Montevideo Marxist circles blossomed in excitement over the Cuban Revolution, pointed towards a different, less chatty path.

In the early 1960s UTAA marched a number of times to Montevideo.[36] It was then that they met the men and women of the Coordinador. Sendic already knew many of its key members from his own years in the city. Despite his passion for the north, it was impossible to ignore the importance of Montevideo, as his UTAA marches toward that city implicitly recognized.

All who met Sendic, both friend and foe, agreed he was an extraordinary man. One of the reasons for this was his pioneering mindset: Sendic was discussing a hypothetical revolution as early as 1955, when the exiles Fidel and Raúl Castro had yet to meet Che Guevara in Mexico for the first time. In addition to his originality, another major aspect of Sendic's leadership qualities was his humility. The founder of UTAA was a man of few, uncomplicated words. According to one associate, "He was influential despite being laconic and succinct; his personality involved extended, very significant silences (...) he had an almost animal-like ascendancy over others".[37] Prominent Tupamara Yessie Macchi agreed: "Sendic is one of the most austere people I have ever known".[38]

This shy appearance obscured a man who had read copious amounts of revolutionary theory and literature. As future MLN leader Eleuterio Fernández put it, "People confused his simple manner of dressing, of carrying himself, and of talking, with theoretical ignorance - when in fact Sendic was, among all of them, the greatest theoretician".[39] He had a peculiar and understated way of conducting himself: temperamental in outbursts, but quiet as a norm. Lapidary in his verdicts on politics, philosophy, lifestyles, and the contradictions of life, when Sendic spoke somehow everyone listened. He was born with a unique form of charisma. Years later, when due to clandestinity and compartmentalization the average Tupamaro did not know the identities of his own organization's leaders, there would be one exception, one name *everyone* in Uruguay knew: Raúl Sendic.

Gearing for Action

In April of 1962, after the first UTAA march reached Montevideo, Sendic was taking his *cañeros* around the city to meet as many allies as possible. It was at one such gathering, in a cold basement mess hall provided by a friendly union, that he first met a young member of the Coordinador named Eleuterio Fernández Huidobro.

At the meeting, Sendic revealed an idea he had: an armed occupation of private rural properties in the north, for UTAA to possess lands as a *fait accompli* before the government could react.

Fernández Huidobro was game: he wanted to hear more of what Sendic had in mind. Their friendship would reside at the core of the Tupamaros for as long as they lived.[40]

Days later, Sendic drove his battered Harley-Davidson, with Fernández on the back, westbound towards the small town of Nueva Helvecia. During the ride, they discussed all sorts of revolutionary topics, and found they were in agreement in nearly all of them. Most importantly, they developed an idea: the Coordinador would collaborate, by providing manpower, in the first revolutionary act in Uruguay's modern history. They would steal several rifles from Nueva Helvecia's Club de Tiro Suizo, or Swiss Shooting Club. The guns would be handed to UTAA, which in turn would use them to stage its invasion of the target *estancias* in the north.[41]

In the meantime, some action was to take place in Montevideo, where one organization considerably bothered Sendic and UTAA: the CSU, or Confederación Sindical del Uruguay (Uruguayan Union Confederacy). It was a rival labor confederacy to the main one the Communist Party was organizing; virtually every Marxist in Uruguay excoriated it as fabrication of the business elite and of the United States embassy.

CSU had publicly questioned the real significance of the *cañeros*' march. Outraged, on May 5, 1962 UTAA went to the CSU's headquarters, and attacked it with sticks and rocks – ultimately torching the whole place. The episode was confusing and violent. There was an exchange of gunfire and an innocent woman named Dora López, a passerby, was struck and killed.[42]

Meeting the Police

Police officer Alejandro Otero arrested Sendic and interrogated him at police headquarters. Both men made a similar impression on each other, as capable and different from the rest of their colleagues. To Otero, Sendic was no ordinary street rioter – here was a man with clear talents, and who gave the impression of being genuinely interested in improving the lot of others.[43] To Sendic, Otero was not just another bumbling policeman. He displayed calmness and the capacity to actually analyze a situation.

Normal police procedure for questioning violent detainees was straightforward: "You either talk or I'll beat you up". Otero's divergent technique was simple. He would ask questions, take statements, type them down, and have the detainee sign them. He would then try the same thing again, and later on again and again. The sheer repetition and bureaucratic dullness of the proceedings, combined with a talent for the actual interrogation, usually produced excellent results.[44] In Sendic's case, the UTAA leader was released, but he and Otero would cross each other's paths again.

Otero behaved differently from other policemen because of his personality, but also because he was benefiting from training that few of his colleagues enjoyed. It started when the police hierarchy recognized his talents and capacity for handling sensitive security tasks. First, in 1962 he was sent to Buenos Aires to study intelligence, counter-intelligence, and investigation techniques under the Federal Police of Argentina. Upon his return and later promotion to *comisario* in 1964 –at age 33 the youngest one in the force by far-, he was appointed head of the section known as Inteligencia y Enlace, or Intelligence and Liaison.[45] It was as the head of that unit that Otero became the most famous policeman in Uruguay, not just during this period but also arguably in history.

The First Steps

The Tupamaros are the result of fusing Raúl Sendic's UTAA with a plurality of members of the Coordinador who wanted to start armed revolution immediately. The first armed action that is usually attributed to this group, before it called itself Tupamaros, took place on July 31 1963. Little did Sendic know upon leaving Montevideo for Nueva Helvecia that it was the last time in over twenty years he would be in the city as a regular citizen, able to see his siblings and parents.[46]

The actual robbery was, according to leading participant Eleuterio Fernández, "a theft proper of a chicken thief".[47] It was a straightforward nighttime breaking-and-entering that transpired with no surprises.[48] Once complete, the team of ten or so members of the Coordinador split into two. One, using the automobile of Fernández's clueless father, was to take some of the weapons to Montevideo. In another vehicle, a van, Sendic was to take the rest to the north.

During that latter ride, driver Jorge Abella lost control of the vehicle and clumsily tilted it sideways. Sendic was sent flying out the back and into some thorny bushes; the guns were dispersed around the roadway. After hastily gathering the weapons and walking kilometers to call for help, they managed to escape the area, but it was already too late.[49]

The police's detective work quickly led to famed troublemaker Raúl Sendic, and to a warrant for his arrest. While all other participants in the operation whom the police identified either gave themselves up or were arrested, Sendic remained at large. His colleagues advised him to surrender as well, or to run for legislative office in a Socialist Party ballot in the next election, so he could benefit from immunity from prosecution. In order to make that easier, he was generously offered top billing in an electoral list, to ensure he would be elected.[50]

This was a critical moment for the birth of the Tupamaros. The reason is that Sendic rejected the offers and chose to remain a wanted man. He would rather start living a clandestine life. Upon learning of his decision many members of the Coordinador left in protest. They felt the move risked everything and attracted enormous attention to the shadowy organization. The members that remained began to work on preparing a secret apparatus to support Sendic, who fled to the north, began wearing disguises and adopted a fake persona as a "healer" –not a veterinarian- of animals on the Brazilian side of the border. Raúl Sendic was now the talk of the radical underground. He cared little about the utter loneliness of hiding for weeks on end in remote parts of Uruguay's *campo*, among reeds and bushes nobody visited. Sendic also made little fuzz of it: his associates recall meeting him hiding in filthy barns, reading Marxist books "plunked in between some crates".[51]

The Coordinador was thus forced into a process of change. Fortunately for Sendic, many of the Uruguayan *izquierda*'s sharpest minds had just joined. One of them was Jorge Manera, an engineer who led the all-important Socialist Party cell that had more than doubled the Coordinador's membership. The Socialists were a decisive contingent: they brought in names like Amodio, Marenales, Martínez Platero, and many others to what was now nicknamed *la orga* (short for "*la organización*"). They also demonstrated formidable security protocols.[52]

The boldest Coordinador operation was staged right in time for Christmas 1963. Its men, armed only with knives, scheduled a delivery of various holiday meals to a phony address in a poor neighborhood. Once the delivery truck arrived, the militants hijacked it in broad daylight. They immediately distributed all its contents among the locals, a task that took only minutes once the neighbors were summoned. According to participant Efraín Martínez, "There was no one to impose order into the whole affair. It was chaotic; five-kilogram flour bags were just thrown about. Later the police came and beat up those who had taken the bags, and their families". The creators of this mix between propaganda and guerrilla warfare, which for now was a one-time occurrence, called it "*comando del hambre*" (hunger commando).

Very few people in Uruguay, even among the police, paid attention to these events. Thus, the Coordinador continued its existence, half as a revolutionary discussion forum, half as an organization performing occasional violent actions. At one point in September of 1964, none other than Régis Debray, the French intellectual most in vogue at the time in revolutionary circles, and also an unofficial representative of Fidel Castro and Che Guevara, visited Montevideo.[53] He attended a meeting of the Coordinador and debated various aspects of insurgency doctrine with its members - particularly with Jorge Torres, a Communist who was developing strategies for a revolution in Uruguay.[54]

There was no agreement between the parts: Debray insisted that any attempt at urban guerrilla was doomed to fail, and that Uruguayan radicals ought to model their revolution on Cuba's Sierra Maestra *foco*. Torres would have none of it.[55] As if that was not enough, Coordinador member Rubén Navillat told Debray that Guevara was "a dunce" for his dismissal of urban approaches and obsession with the rural *foco*.[56]

Something new was brewing, and once it took form it was based on three pillars. First, there was nothing defensive about the new project: the new *orga* would launch a Cuban-style offensive uprising, rather than wait for a hypothetical coup d'état.

Second, guerrilla warfare in Uruguay would be urban. This was based on a simple appraisal of geography. As the Tupamaros later wrote in an internal document, "In this country there are no impregnable geographic locations, nor any with characteristics that facilitate the installation of a rural guerrilla foco that can endure"[57]. In addition to this, Uruguay's two far larger neighbors fell successively, in 1964 and 1966, into the hands of anti-Communist military dictatorships. That meant a cross-border sanctuary for the insurgents, a classic factor that increased the chances of revolutionary success, was out of the question.

Both Mao and Guevara had suggested that the lack of a formidable rural hideout was equivalent to a crippling disadvantage for the insurgent. Nevertheless, the strong voluntarism of the young militants prevailed. They recognized this themselves: "We cannot reduce the objective conditions for revolution to mere geographic conditions. Uruguay lacks geographic conditions for rural guerrilla warfare, but that is not a reason why revolution should wait".[58] Therefore, as simple as a process of elimination of other possibilities, if the revolution had to happen, but it could not be rural, it had to take place in the urban space of Montevideo. There would be no need to descend from the mountains and trek to the capital, because they were already in the capital.

The third and final pillar was that given the many disagreements and estrangements with the established political parties of Uruguay, the new group would follow the theory of *foco* guerrilla warfare. Unlike said parties, they "believed it was possible right now. The hour had come. Che's example had to be imitated. Right here, right now".[59] It was a strategy that prioritized action over theory, propaganda, and other traditional types of political action.

The End of the Coordinador

All these changes proved too much, for they required the Coordinador be something it was not. The events of 1964 proved it was too disorganized to be an actual operational group. The greatest risks came when several member cells, each according to their own ideological purposes, got involved in operations that compromised the security of all others.

The most problematic incident came from UTAA: a botched bank robbery by three of its *cañeros*. Sendic, still faithful to his brusque and action-focused personality, failed to resist the urge to fire a pistol during the incident, from the balcony of the apartment belonging to Violeta Setelich, his girlfriend. As it turned out, the UTAA cell in Montevideo had come up with the brilliant idea of robbing the bank that occupied the ground floor of Setelich's building. They thus risked Sendic's hiding place, but got lucky and the police was none the wiser.[60]

In another of these botched robberies the unaffiliated José Mujica was captured and jailed for several months. He was caught trying to rob a manager of the American-owned textile company SudAmTex.[61] Having learned the lessons of the jailed UTAA bank robbers, Mujica claimed his attempt was for personal profit rather than for a political cause. He thus had to spend eight months in a prison in the Montevideo slum of Miguelete and face a degree of marginalization and scorn from friends, colleagues, and other members of the *izquierda* underground.[62]

There were more failed bank robberies. The protagonists of the most important one came from the Socialist cell of the Coordinador. Jorge Manera was in command, and additional participants included Héctor Amodio, Julio Marenales, Tabaré Rivero, and others. Marenales, an arts professor at the time, entered the bank with two other militants. The robbers were nervous, and the security guard noticed the intentions of the three men in time. A standoff ensued, and the customers panicked. In the confusion, amidst the cries of children, one of the robbers left and boarded the waiting escape vehicle, which quickly sped away and left behind Marenales and a militant named Giménez.

After a violent arrest, Marenales was taken into custody and subjected to beatings and an electric cattle prod, all set to a background of the tango music he liked so much. Detective work led to the driver of the vehicle, the engineer Manera, who was also captured.[63] Both claimed at their trial that they were gathering funds for social services for the poor. They spent several months in jail, although one man never believed their story: Alejandro Otero.[64] In the meantime, Héctor Amodio replaced Manera as the chief representative of the Socialists at the Coordinador.[65]

Upon liberation, there was little for these men to return to. The group had proven half-baked; formal in that it required a partisan affiliation for each cell to participate, and informal in that there were no actual principles or leadership to guide its actions. It had been aimed at radicals who were toying with the game of revolutionary action but had no real plan to go about it. It could also be seen, on the other hand, as a trial balloon.

In 1965, members who chose to remain in contact with each other despite the dismantling of the Coordinador began to talk of reviving the organization, but with a new identity. The purpose of the new entity would no longer be to combine the armed apparatuses of existing political parties. Instead, it would unify efforts and launch a proper campaign for revolution in Uruguay. Whatever came next was meant only for those who had the greatest commitment. The greatest contingents who decided to stay came from the Socialists, from Eleuterio Fernández's group, and from UTAA.[66]

Before any new organization was properly formalized, these men began to call themselves Tupamaros. Early operations were small affairs, like placing explosives at empty banks or foreign-owned factories. For years these would be two of the favorite targets of Uruguay's revolutionaries. The former, according to bank employee Eleuterio Fernández, were "dedicated to stealing".[67] The latter were representatives of foreign countries, or rather of distorted notions of said countries. Bayer was bombed for being a "Nazi" company. Moore-McCormack, a shipping line, was attacked for being American and therefore "imperialistic". However, a planned bombing of an Esso facility was rejected for being too "terroristic" - the group had its tactical disagreements early on. In the words of Eleuterio Fernández, "It was tempting to many superficial and lightweight minds to resort to 'the bomb' at any opportunity".[68]

These were the first occasions in which pamphlets or graffiti were seen at the crime scenes hinting at a new phenomenon. How obscure all of this was is captured perfectly in a U.S. embassy telegram sent to Washington right after the attack on the shipping company: "Painted on outside wall of building appeared words 'Gringos Piratos' [sic] and 'Tupamaros'. Neither we nor Mormac yet understand significance latter word which appeared in quotes".[69]

While a few cells performed those isolated acts, the Tupamaros dedicated a secretive one, led by Efraín Martínez Platero, to exploring the sewer network of Montevideo. Members entered it every Friday for months on end between 1965 and 1966. They navigated the underground with caged canaries in tow, so that just like in the mining industry, the birds' bodies would serve as warning signs for the presence of noxious gases. Entry would take place late at night, with handkerchiefs and other fabrics covering the noses and mouths of the infiltrators. Often, they would have to walk in sewage up to their chests, or to avoid the massive cockroach colonies that burst forth upon moving the manhole covers.[70]

Avoiding these and other obstacles, the Tupamaros mapped everything they saw, from doors and barriers to manholes and other exit points. The explorers also learned that a minimum of three people was needed any time a sewer operation was being conducted. It was the only way to ensure that if one fainted there would be two to exfiltrate him or her. The prospect of being alone in that vast and tomblike network of brick walls was truly intimidating.

The Birth of the Tupamaros

In January of 1966 an essential gathering took place: the top-secret Convención Tupamara. For the first time, only confirmed members of the new organization attended. They were fewer than those who attended the Coordinador meetings, but they were far more in harmony than they were before. They had an objective (revolution), a strategy (an urban guerrilla *foco*), some experience in action, and a high level of motivation.

One of the first steps the new organization took at the Convención was electing a leadership, although most decisions would still be taken democratically. The chosen members were Raúl Sendic, Eleuterio Fernández, and Tabaré Rivero. The Sendic-Fernández partnership was also tasked with crafting a number of internal documents that detailed the organization's identity. The initial propaganda slogan, tailored for a group still looking for its first members and trying to establish a meaningful identity, was "Ármate y espera" (Arm Yourself and Wait).

It took some time for the Tupamaros to gain track. The number of confirmed participants in the revolutionary project was quite small: fifty-two at most.[71] On top of this, there was little operational "work" actually being done. Many of them still clung to forms of parallel militancy, or a legal work life. In the case of Sendic, he was still organizing UTAA marches –even though, as a wanted man since 1963, he obviously could not partake in them himself- as late as 1968. Fernández was still employed in a bank.

Despite this slow start, there was no question that the international situation, as well as Uruguay's, was heating up. 1966 would *not* be the most intense year of the decade, and yet it was filled with major developments. China launched its Great Proletarian Cultural Revolution, which heralded a decade's worth of madness and mass murder. Revolutionary priest Camilo Torres, soon to become a Latin American icon, died in combat in Colombia. Che Guevara himself, after a brief African adventure, emerged clandestinely in the very heart of South America, starting a rural *foco* in remote parts of Bolivia. To top this off, there was a military coup d'état in Argentina, and the American chapter of the war in Viet Nam escalated substantially.

The Uruguayan election of 1966 placed before voters the matter of keeping a parliamentary system of government or replacing it with a presidential one. They chose the latter, and the winner of the election was retired Air Force general and Colorado politician Óscar Gestido. It was Gestido and his vice president, Jorge Pacheco, who presided over some of the first days of open subversion in Uruguay in a long time.

CHAPTER FOUR:

THE MLN-TUPAMAROS

THE TERM "TUPAMARO" is an obscure historical reference. It emerged as a contraction of Tupac Amaru II, the name of an Incan leader also known as José Gabriel Condorcanqui, who in the eighteenth century fought in the Andes against the Spanish. In the nineteenth century, when pro-independence revolutions sought to cast away Spanish rule, imperial troops took to calling all the rebels, Incan or not, "Tupamaros". The name later appeared sporadically in South American literature, notably in Uruguayan writer Eduardo Acevedo Díaz's 1888 novel "Ismael".[72] The Uruguayan revolutionaries of the 1960s revived the term in an attempt to self-identify as the next generation of fighters for national liberation. The name also helped frame their revolution in a continental scale, establishing a kinship with resisters against imperialism elsewhere in the Americas.

Founding member Tabaré Rivero had been toying with the name "Tupamaros" since 1964, around the same time when his fellow subversive Navillat was telling Régis Debray that Che Guevara was a "burro" for insisting an urban guerrilla was unthinkable. Eleuterio Fernández Huidobro pushed for the adoption of the name, as well as a symbol for the group: a five-pointed star with a "T" inside.[73] In 1965, with the Coordinador dead, the name stuck as the title for the new group. Some complained that few outsiders would even know what the foreign-sounding term meant, but Fernández wanted it that way purposefully: "let people go through the trouble of finding out".[74]

The main slogan of the Tupamaros was "Habrá patria para todos o no habrá patria para nadie". It meant "There shall be a fatherland for all, or there shall be a fatherland for none". The phrase was also not their own, but at the same time it was not in wide use. Their specifically lifting it from the annals of history -in this case a history of a 1904 civil war between Colorados and Nationalists- was a statement of nationalist, rather than Soviet or Cuban, inspiration.[75] It encapsulated the insurgents' socialist justice mindset: the resources and opportunities of the Uruguayan homeland would be available to all, or the Tupamaros would ensure the few could not be the only ones to benefit from them.

At a meeting in Parque del Plata in early June of 1965 -which was conducted under compartmentalized conditions, with everyone wearing hoods- the organization formally adopted the more complete name Movimiento de Liberación Nacional – Tupamaros. It is important to note who these founding men and women were, for they remained important for the rest of the MLN's existence. The best-known and most respected of the founders was Raúl Sendic, who was discussed in the preceding chapter. Sendic turned forty years old in 1965. As such he was old compared to most of the others.

The Old Men

Eleuterio Fernández Huidobro was far younger: he turned twenty-three in 1965. Nevertheless, he was an unquestioned Tupamaro leader, and a decisive member of the MLN all the way to the end. A man of high intelligence and superb rhetorical skills, with a witty and sarcastic sense of humor peppered into almost everything he says and writes to this day, Fernández Huidobro did not come from a politicized, much less a Marxist, family. His parents arrived from Castile in 1930; he was born in Montevideo in 1942.[76]

Fernández Huidobro approached radical politics during his time as a high school student. He enrolled in Uruguay's top school for high achievers, the state-run Instituto Alfredo Vásquez Acevedo, or IAVA. The institute was only a few steps away from the Law School of the national university –the same one Raúl Sendic had attended-, and shared many of its professors. Fernández became a rabid reader of Marcha, Uruguay's top publication for intellectuals, inevitably with varying degrees of Marxist bents. However, after graduating in 1959 young Eleuterio -known as Ñato to friends and family- took a job at a branch of the very capitalist Banco Popular. During Fernandez's time there, his participation in union and political activities led to an early liaison with the Coordinador. On the occasion of the Nueva Helvecia gun heist of 1963, he handled a firearm for the first time in his life.[77]

Fernández became the Tupamaro closest to Sendic. In fact, both men complemented each other well, for Sendic was a man of few words and stubborn, chaotic habits. Ñato, who was an exceptional writer, had just the right skills to translate Sendic's ideas into proper political manifestos. He himself recounts how he saw Sendic during the period: "He wrote in an old Underwood typewriter, sitting on the dirt floor, in between the chickens that shat over his papers (...) He was lazy when it came to writing, but when he felt like doing it he was brilliant".[78] In addition to this key synergy with Sendic, and his foundational role in the Tupamaros, Fernández would be the author of a majority of the MLN's documents and propaganda. All of that would come later. In the mid-1960s, he was so young that he began storing MLN propaganda and weapons in the bedroom he had in his parents' house. Fernández loaned his father's car for the Nueva Helvecia operation.[79]

Julio Marenales was a man with equal umbrage within the MLN as Sendic and Fernández, meaning he was one of the founders or "viejos". A man of extraordinary strength of mind, stubbornness, and physical fortitude, Marenales could always be counted on to demand more of himself than all the other Tupamaros. As the type of person who woke up before everyone else and took it upon himself to do repairs, build weapons, and dig tunnels, Marenales was a natural leader. Born in 1930 of Galician and Neapolitan stock, his origins were in Montevideo's lower middle-class. His father died when he was only ten years old. As an apprentice sculptor in his teenage years, young Julio developed a talent for the arts and crafts, as well as considerable bodily strength.[80] In 1964, at the time of his first arrest, he was a professor at the national School of Fine Arts.

More often than not, Marenales's partner in arms was Jorge Manera. Known as "El Inge" –shorthand for El Ingeniero or The Engineer-, Manera was the most technically competent of the founding Tupamaros in all issues having to do with his profession: vehicles, electricity, weapons, explosives, construction, and so forth. Aged thirty-six, in 1965, Manera was low-key compared to Sendic,

Fernández, and Marenales. He often preferred to be the driver in operations, but was nevertheless a bold man to the point of ill-thought bravado. Manera knew Sendic and Marenales –as well as many other founding members of the MLN- from their days together at the Socialist Party.

Manera's successor as leader of the Socialist cell in the Coordinador upon being arrested in 1964 was Héctor Amodio. The young socialist, born in 1937, had a background as a printer at a newspaper press, where he gained a reputation as an efficacious union leader. One of the earliest organizers of Uruguay's illegal Marxist underground, it was Amodio who used his Socialist Party connections to recruit individuals like Marenales into the Coordinador. Amodio had a complex personality, but his most defining characteristic was his talent as an urban *guerrillero*.

When it came to being out in the streets, Amodio was one of the MLN's best assets; certainly the top one of its early period. This was curious, given that he did not look the part of an agile commando, given his height and gait. Nevertheless, he had no qualms about stealing a parked vehicle by popping open its hood in broad daylight and working the engine, while authoritatively dismissing the owner who complained from the window of his house.[81]

Amodio had a steady girlfriend in Alicia Rey, the female Tupamara who perhaps reached highest in the organization's hierarchy. She had a close relationship with her boyfriend, and both were described as ugly by their peers -possibly because of a personal dislike. Alicia Rey was also one of the better shots in the almost completely amateur group of initial MLN members, which meant she was initially tasked with teaching marksmanship to new recruits.[82]

Efraín Martínez Platero was yet another founding member of the Tupamaros who came from the Socialist Party. Much like Eleuterio Fernández, he was on the younger side of the equation -but was nevertheless sharpening machetes in preparation for an imagined rural guerrilla campaign as early as 1962. Joining in 1964 at the behest of his oldest brother Leonel, Martínez remained fully committed to the cause of revolution despite the collapse of the Coordinador, and maintained his membership into the new MLN.

Like all other Tupamaros except Sendic, Martínez Platero retained a "legal" life -in his case, studying to be a veterinarian- and did not fully plunge into the reality of an insurgent until the first arrest warrant in his name came out. In the meantime, many of these part-time *guerrilleros* had to co-exist with their families, friends, acquaintances, schools, jobs, and more. At one point, after learning of his son's activities, Martínez's father arranged for young Efraín to meet a prominent government minister at the time. The official promised Martínez Platero a job, but the Tupamaro rebuffed him on ethical grounds. With a clear aversion towards personally practicing violence and essentially his entire family involved in the MLN, Martínez was a showcase of the group's capacity to attract intelligent and talented individuals.

Not all the Tupamaros had such access to the halls of power.[83] José Mujica's Italian-Uruguayan mother became a widow when her son was a schoolchild, so she raised him mostly alone. The boy grew in a lower-middle class home, more often than not helping her cultivate and sell flowers in various markets of Montevideo's growing working class belt. As Mujica remembers it, "We endured a dignified poverty (...) Uruguay still did not know what penury was". Young José got started at an early age, working at a bakery and learning floriculture from the best cultivators in the area, the immigrant Japanese family Takata.

Mujica was exposed to the experiences typical of the outer neighborhoods of Montevideo. One of them was classically Uruguayan. During the 1950s, Prime Minister Luis Batlle owned property near the Mujica home. During his years of bicycling to the flower markets, young José -known as all Josés in Uruguay as "Pepe"-, often crossed paths with Uruguay's leader and glimpsed the entrance to Batlle's home, flanked only by two policemen. On several occasions, Batlle stopped Mujica to buy flowers from him: they were intended for his wife, an Argentine woman named Matilde Ibáñez, and the mother of up-and-coming politician Jorge Batlle. In his time as a lawmaker, Luis Batlle had also boarded the trolleybus a few times with Mujica's mother, Lucy Cordano, and helped with her bags.

Like Fernández Huidobro, Mujica attended the prestigious IAVA high school, but never graduated. Instead, he linked up with small-time criminals from Montevideo's shadier neighborhoods. It was around that time that Mujica met the most radical politician of the Partido Nacional, a man named Enrique Erro. While Pepe's academic career drowned in student riots, alcohol, and various escapades, his ties to Erro allowed him to gain a steady income from the party. He also developed a network of political connections, and traveled to see some of the world. Mujica helped organize Erro's youth wing, and operated as part of a "price monitoring squad" when Erro briefly served as minister. He was a constant presence in Montevideo's bars, chatting, networking, drinking, and organizing continued political struggles in favor of populist socialism.

As with many other Marxists of the early 1960s, Mujica's trips took him to Cuba and the Soviet Union. Referring to the latter, where he visited Moscow and Armenia, he said "That trip was absolutely decisive in my never belonging to the Communist Party (...) I was able to easily see the bureaucratic authoritarianism and the buddy networks (...) To me it was incomprehensible that people went to the Soviet Union all the time and nobody saw any of that". Flying from Moscow, Mujica also got to visit Communist China. The greatest contrast, however, was "The vision I brought from my trip to Cuba (...) It was wonderful, the budding revolution was full of poetry". Mujica met Che Guevara and visited the Sierra Maestra, only a few months after the triumph of the insurgent Movimiento 26 de Julio.

After a paltry showing at the 1962 elections, Mujica addressed prophetic words to his political mentor, Erro: "I feel that this will not be the path," and quit party politics. The 1964 episode in which he tried to rob a Montevideo businessman remains poorly explained. After serving almost a year in prison, Pepe drifted away from a Maoist group he had associated with, and thus from the Coordinador. In 1966 Julio Marenales recruited him back, now with the MLN formally constituted. Mujica had missed the organization's founding, but he approved of its *foco* approach over the party-based infrastructure the Maoists and the other Communists insisted needed to be created. It was thus that he became a Tupamaro.

Another man soon to join the MLN was Mauricio Rosencof.[84] His personal history was quite different from that of most of the MLN's founders. His parents, Yitzhak Rozenkopf and Rajzla Zylberman, had left a small Polish town near Lublin in 1931. Yitzhak found a job as a tailor in a small town in Uruguay, a move that saved his family from the *Shoah* a decade later. Like many immigrant Jews from a bleak time in Western history, the Rozenkopf couple had certain political sympathies: Republican Spain, the Communist Party, and later on, Zionism. Young Mauricio began his work as a precocious writer for the Yiddish-language Marxist publication Unzer Fraint. Later, he joined the Communist Party and became a writer for its publications. It was also around that time that he met Raúl Sendic.

As one of the deepest thinkers the MLN had, Rosencof's ideological journey is reflective of the one his generation of radicals went through. Just like Mujica, two international trips changed his life. First, in 1962 he traveled to Cuba, where he also met Guevara. Just as important was the 1964 trip he undertook to the promised land of Marxism-Leninism, the Soviet Union. It left distasteful impressions. The young Uruguayan writer, whose passion was often more for literature and theater than party politics, also got to visit places outside of Russia. He witnessed the Soviet suppression of non-Russian culture in Samarkand, and got the distinct impression, when visiting Budapest, that perhaps the 1956 uprising in that city was not purely a CIA concoction.

Upon returning, Rosencof split amicably from the Communists just in time to shift his gaze to what his old friend Sendic was organizing. It was exactly what he was looking for, although he became a full member only a few years later.

Che Guevara's "New Men" - and Women

The social makeup of the early Tupamaros was heavily middle class. Few came from humble origins like Mujica's, but none came from a rich family either. This was a typically Uruguayan makeup, reflective of the moderate society the decades of Batllista Socialism had built. While many had had access to high education and were of above-average intelligence, none had benefited from luxurious lifestyles.

Ethnically the Tupamaros also represented Uruguayan society in ways that did not single them out easily. There was a logical prominence of Spanish and Italian names, but there were also Basque, Portuguese, Polish, Ashkenazi Jewish, German, English, Lebanese, Russian, and other backgrounds in the mix.

Both genders were well represented. In fact, the MLN was one of the first rebel groups in history to heavily integrate women in its operations and in certain levels of leadership, although no Tupamara ever made it to the small committee that ran the organization, known as *el ejecutivo* and *la dirección*. According to historian Alfonso

Lessa, by 1969 39% of the MLN's ranks would be made up of women.[85]

Although there were disputes over the issue of women not making it to the top leadership, many Tupamaras believe that "Accession to the MLN was equal for men and women",[86] or that "there was [no] more discrimination against women than there was in other spaces in our society".[87] Indeed, women participated in all MLN activities. They guarded VIP prisoners, worked in the services divisions crafting fake documents and explosives, and led cells in important guerrilla operations. Years later, Rosencof would famously say that "women are never more equal to men than when they have a .45 in their hand".[88]

Yessie Macchi was the most prominent Tupamara. The daughter of a retired military officer who had served as military attaché in Washington, Macchi was a beautiful young woman. Once the MLN gained publicity, many inevitably commented on this fact. It would also have a decisive impact in her life years later. Even the official government history of the war against the MLN, published years after the fact, noted her looks.[89] Macchi also had some of the most radical views among the Tupamaros, particularly in favor of using violence. In the early days of agitation in Uruguay she was already in the midst of the fray: "I felt happy as I lobbed stones; I thought it was wonderful to be throwing rocks instead of theorizing all the time".[90] She proved a formidable *guerrillera* multiple times.

The MLN was not nearly as open to homosexuals as it was to women.[91] That was one barrier the group did not breach. In fact, there were homophobic aspects to MLN propaganda, targeted at specific individuals, which emerged later.

The Principles and Strategy of the MLN

During the MLN's preparatory years of 1966-7, Sendic anonymously published an article called "30 Questions for a Tupamaro". It was the group's first disclosure of its name and way of thinking.

The article faithfully reflected the deep doctrinal influences the Tupamaros had absorbed in previous years: "revolutionary action in itself, the very fact of arming oneself, of preparing, of acquiring supplies, of violating bourgeois legality, generates revolutionary consciousness, organization, and conditions (...) it is revolutionary actions that beget revolutionary situations". In other terms, "instead of revolutionary words, we propose to change people with revolutionary acts"[92]. This text constitutes a prime exposition of *foco* thinking. It is as representative of the theory as anything Guevara or Debray wrote.

In order to bridge some of the doctrinal gaps with those who thought differently, the MLN decided to be an unusually open organization. Thus, one conciliatory "finding" circulated around this time entitled "Foco o Partido, Falso Dilema" (Foco or Party, False Dilemma). That way, Leninists and Maoists had an open window to join the revolution. Additionally, a slogan that went "Action unites us, words divide us"[93] sought to patch any disagreements - and it worked. There was room for everybody, as long as the goal was "national liberation" through armed action.

All of the MLN's efforts were designed to pursue the objective of violent revolution. What was left mostly unsaid was that the Tupamaros were planning an uprising against a liberal democracy, one that Che Guevara himself had advised them not to attack. This was the most important judgment call the Tupamaros had to make, the mother question of all: was there a situation ripe for revolution in 1960s democratic Uruguay?

The MLN's analysis, focusing on the economic crisis and the wealth of certain families, answered yes. In other words, the democratic system was a sham. This political diagnosis was highly warped by an obvious desire to conduct revolution no matter what. It served to answer the mother question in the affirmative, despite the opinions of Uruguay's top Marxist intellectuals who openly said there was "objectively no possibility of revolution".[94]

The MLN's strategic analysis was somewhat smarter than its political analysis. Observations on Uruguay's weak military and police, as well as the debate on rural versus urban guerrilla warfare, carried on from the days of the Coordinador. The group was aware of the scarce successes in the history of urban guerrilla warfare; that could not be encouraging. Still, they saw themselves as having no alternatives. If urban guerrilla was the only way, then it would have to be the way.

The budding Tupamaros' preparatory considerations extended into tactical methods. A key fact the group identified early on was "the low rates of violence in existence in Uruguayan society for decades now". This led the group to "delay the start of what it called 'unlikeable' or violent acts".[95] The Tupamaros fully agreed with Guevara that the insurgent fighting for social justice was the harbinger of the New Man, the mythical figure of utopian socialist thinking. Once again, the MLN summarized its resolutions with a slogan: "Illegality is one thing, and brutality another".[96]

Despite all this, the MLN was a violent organization and knew it would be unable to avoid the act of killing. In Guevara's guerrilla, only notorious criminals were to be executed; the enemy's soldiers were to be kept prisoner and later released.[97] According to the MLN's rules, assassinations "will only be conducted after a conscientious, exhaustive, and detailed analysis. They will only be justified in defending very important components of the revolution". Terrorism, which was mentioned but undefined, was out of the question in the group's official rule book: "This type of attack is rejected on grounds of inhumanity, for it harms innocent lives and has negative political effects".[98]

The MLN rulebook was thorough. One important set of instructions was for cases when a member was captured by the security services: "There is only one way to behave when confronted with such a situation: hold on to the agreed cover story, and then...silence".[99] In fact, the document said, it was preferable to die than to betray one's comrades. Captured *guerrilleros* must always deny being Tupamaros or having participated in *acciones* of any sort.[100] This preparation worked significantly well for the MLN for many years, for its highly motivated cadres proved adept at resisting police interrogations and beatings or acts of torture.

The Buildup and the Baptism of Fire

The "Arm Yourself and Wait" phase was slated to end with the year 1966. A national election was to take place on November 27 of that year. The Colorados were expected to defeat the Partido Nacional and return to power; the economic crisis had simply been too debilitating. For the first time in their lives, the individuals who made up the Tupamaros did not have their mind in electoral politics. They had given up on them years ago. Rather, they were focused on a place called El Cazador: an arms shop in downtown Montevideo.

Fifteen Tupamaros, combining men and women, formed a task force to rob the store late on election night, while the city was emptier than ever. The group was careful; the men wore suits and ties, so as to become impeccably inconspicuous to the police. As Eleuterio Fernández notes, "whenever a comrade saw another with that look, he would invariably be apprehensive. It was like a combat uniform".[101]

The robbery went well: Julio Marenales led a group that took "some twenty long guns, about 50 handguns with a lot of .22 ammo, as well as 7.65 ammo, knives, and lanterns. There were Remington rifles, Brnos, Spanish shotguns".[102] To top this off, the group stumbled into a number of police uniforms that could have obviously advantageous uses.

The weapons stolen at El Cazador were not meant for long-term storage. Rather, they were to be used days later in the MLN's first guerrilla operation, a moment of extreme anxiety for its members. No Tupamaros outside of Montevideo knew about it, and only half of those in the city were in on the secret. As a security measure, the participants destroyed all the pictures they could find of themselves.[103] If there were any contingencies, the police would only be able to base its detective work on the photo in their national identification documents.[104]

The operation consisted of raiding the rubber tire manufacturer FUNSA. The salaries for the month of December, as well as the yearly bonuses, were to be there for the taking. The loot disclosed by the MLN's informants promised to be fruitful. Sendic, by then nicknamed El Bebe, expressed misgivings about stealing from the working class, but the tipsters suggested the company would pay no matter what. Due to various reasons, he, Marenales, and Manera were kept out of the operation. This meant Eleuterio Fernández and Héctor Amodio, from among the core MLN members, took the lead.[105]

From a strategic perspective, this was a pivotal moment for the MLN. According to the theory of counterinsurgency of French military officer and Algeria veteran David Galula, the Tupamaros were still in their "cold" revolutionary period, meaning they had not yet started violent operations. The group was unknown, or barely known, which meant the enemy could not yet target it. For liberal democracies it is hard to detect these threats, for there are civil rights considerations impeding governments from performing intelligence work on civilians who are innocent until proven guilty. If the emerging insurgents are careful and make little or no "noise," they will be almost impossible to detect. However, once the MLN or any such group goes through its baptism of fire, it loses the protective shield of anonymity, and the counter-insurgent's own strategy will then be activated. If the insurgent has not prepared for this response, he will not survive for long.

In the days preceding the FUNSA operation, the group stole vehicles for use as transportation. One was a Chevrolet truck for which the MLN switched the number tags for fake ones. A small cement barrier was also built adjacent to the tailgate, so those who rode on the back could use it as cover in any shootout. The truck was not given a new paint job.

The Chevrolet would carry five people in total: two in the cabin, including the driver, and three on the bed. The driver would be an Argentine member of the group, with Eleuterio Fernández riding shotgun. Of the three men on the back, two would be Argentine and the third would be the young Tupamaro Carlos Flores. The Argentines, exiles from their own country and temporarily joining up with the MLN, were thus providing the backbone of the operation. Following the truck would be the overall supervisor of the raid -Héctor Amodio riding a Vespa- plus an additional van with two backup Tupamaros.

On the night of December 21, just hours before the operation was to begin, the MLN was finishing the preparations for the attack in a Montevideo apartment. At two in the morning of the 22nd, a Tupamaro handling a firearm accidentally fired it. No one was hit and the noise went unnoticed, but it nevertheless left many on edge. Eleuterio Fernández adeptly describes the mood in those final hours of waiting before an event that would change their lives, one way or the other, forever: "The operation has been studied and discussed a thousand times. Each member knows his role by heart, repeats it to himself and to others like a kid with a list heading to the grocery store. The more he repeats it and thinks it over, the more nervous he gets (...) The combatant is submerged in a world plagued with unreality, where even the most trivial things acquire a disproportionate importance".

On the morning of the operation, the truck picked up each Tupamaro from designated collection points. When the time came to fetch the young Carlos Flores, the Tupamaro -son of a retired police officer- was late, so the truck had to idle and go around the block. While this was happening, a friend of the owner of the stolen Chevrolet happened to spot it and report it to a police patrol car that also chanced to be passing nearby. Patrolmen José Bonaudi and Carlos Vega, plus driver Santos Fernández, approached in their vehicle just as the convoy restarted its route, with Flores on board.

The police signaled for the Chevrolet to stop for an inspection, but the vehicle refused and continued. As the sirens went up, the men on the bed fired their weapons at the police, and a chase ensued. Before even reaching their target, the Tupamaros were engaged in their first combat operation in the busy streets of Montevideo. The *guerrilleros* on the back of the vehicle fired Uzi submachine guns and Mauser rifles at the police car. They threw grenades at it, although they failed to explode. Meanwhile, the MLN van and motorcycle chased the pursuing police car, ready to go into action as soon as they had an opportunity. In the crossfire, a woman named Damiana Tejera was shot in her left knee; one estimate counts over two hundred rounds fired in the chase.

As the police were able to summon reinforcements, and the situation was turning too chaotic, the riders of the truck decided to abort the operation. They drove the vehicle into a large, empty lot with few trees or features other than grass and dirt. The occupants quickly dislodged and continued firing at the policemen, who had followed the Tupamaros, stopped a few meters away, and opened fire from behind the protective cover of their car. A majority of the *guerrilleros* escaped, some hijacking civilian vehicles to flee the scene. Before Flores had the opportunity to escape from the bed of the truck, police officer Bonaudi shot him directly in the forehead and killed him. The Tupamaros later learned the shooter had been a "champion police marksman".

The arriving MLN pursuers in the van and the motorcycle saw the disarray, and were not identified by the police as fellow participants in the criminal activity taking place. Therefore, they cut their losses and escaped as well. All that remained behind to illuminate what happened, apart from bullet holes and casings, was the body of Carlos Flores. Working that same day off his identity and running checks on his family, friends, and acquaintances, police investigator Otero's detective work produced major results.

Even before noon that day, the La Teja neighborhood house that was the birthplace of the Coordinador and home to its many preparatory meetings in years past, fell. Multiple arrest warrants were put out for probable accomplices of Flores, and the news broke out that a few dozen Uruguayans were wanted by the police for belonging to an armed, subversive organization. As predicted by Galula, the MLN was about to be stamped out.

Otero enjoyed talking to the Tupamaros when he had them in his office. On one occasion, he explained how he conceived the MLN's strategic situation. According to the *comisario*, the group could be visualized as a rectangle, with one corner shaded to represent the Tupamaros. The rest of the rectangle was the MLN's security, the collection of mechanisms and precautions that prevented it from being captured. If the shaded section grew to bring in additional members, the quality or amount of the security array would inevitably decrease; "He claimed to be waiting for us to make that mistake".[106] Mastering this balance was to be the essence of the competition between the MLN and its pursuers for years.

Five days after the failed FUNSA raid Otero's detective work led to an additional MLN safe house. A single Tupamaro, Mario Robaina, was holed up there. Upon arriving, the police called on him to surrender. The commander, Antonio Silveira Regalado, "kicked open the door and entered the house brandishing his .45 caliber Thompson submachine gun (...) But Comisario Regalado froze in astonishment when he pulled on the trigger of the Thompson but nothing happened".[107] In the confusion, shots were fired and the policeman was gunned down and killed.[108] During the ensuing shootout, Robaina committed suicide. Thus, in only two days Uruguay's peace had been shattered by incidents that surprised almost everyone: there were armed rebel cells operating in the country, and they were already clashing furiously with the police.

The immediate days after these two operations were the riskiest ones in the history of the MLN. Like most insurgent organizations, they were finding themselves closest to extinction at the very outset. Their first clashes with the security services had proven ineffectual and were revealing to the enemy much of the organization's extent. The wanted Tupamaros endured many weeks of severe risk, spending nights in the sewers, entire days inside the wooden stalls beach-goers used to change clothes, crashing with friendly but wary acquaintances, and anywhere else shelter might be found.[109]

The year ended days after the shootouts, with Otero briefing the press on the connections he had verified between Argentine terrorists and the incipient Uruguayan subversive movement. He also uncovered evidence of the mysterious group's survey of the

Montevideo sewer network, which he inspected himself for clues.[110] As it turned out, the Tupamaros had developed the best blueprint of the Montevideo sewer network that anyone, including the government, could have.

Back to Basics

The year 1967 thus began for the MLN in emergency mode. The entire country was talking about the Tupamaros, who had vanished into thin air after the shocking incidents of December. A savior arrived in the form of old Sendic acquaintance Mauricio Rosencof. The former Communist propagandist and playwright got the group an apartment to function as a safe house until the coast was clear, so the entire fugitive contingent moved into that single dwelling. They would have to live there for the first weeks of January.[111] Few were allowed to leave, and only rarely. Security was paramount.

As part of this carefulness, the leadership decided the MLN would not publish anything to comment on what had just happened. There would be complete silence from the organization, so as to dry up the trail of evidence and information the police fed on. This directive applied for most of the year, which the group smartly took up as a time of careful reconstruction after a debacle that had almost smothered it.

Co-existence in that situation was difficult. There was an obvious climate of impending doom; news came of the manhunt that had them as targets. Furthermore, sharing an apartment among twenty people was a nerve-wracking experience. Minimizing noise was essential to the point where the toilet was not flushed during the day.[112] Disputes erupted, particularly between those with the strongest tempers.

For example, in one occasion, as Marenales tells it, "Everybody decided that the one who had to go out grocery shopping was me, because I was unrecognizable from my newspaper pictures. I went out and bought ingredients to make a nice stew. Before I was done cooking El Bebe approached the pot and tried to dip a piece of bread on the juice. I told him 'Bebe, wait until I'm done, it's only a little more, then we'll serve it and all eat together.' He got pissed off! He said all sorts of things to me and added that he wouldn't eat anything. I was untroubled: I served the stew for everybody (...) and he didn't eat, he didn't eat! Beginning that day, whenever food was scarce I would ask him 'Bebe, why don't you pull another hunger strike so we can have enough?'"[113]

Soon after, an UTAA *cañero* who was not yet wanted by the police checked out a makeshift ranch Sendic had assembled years earlier in the sleepy beach town of Solymar, not far from Montevideo. Upon verifying it was clear, some of the *clandestinos* -the name used to refer to members who were wanted by the police-moved there, thus relieving pressure off the apartment. A new situation developed: now Sendic was the only one who could be visible, for he had secured a false identity that allowed him to navigate the streets with relative ease. It was he who literally fronted the modest Solymar house, sitting on the porch sipping Uruguay's traditional mate drink behind a sign that read "Luis Martínez, Constructor".[114]

Sendic's fellow Tupamaros liked to have fun at his expense. His brusque manners, his unburdened lifestyle, his temperament and the few words he had for virtually every matter were a frequent source of amusement. Sendic did not explain himself; he just did things. Talented craftsmen like Marenales and Manera teased him for the "house" he had built, which at one point was so unstable the leader of the *cañeros* simply tied one of its ends to a tree.[115]

El Bebe insisted on doing things his way; unpretentiousness and austerity were his signature traits. For instance, he was a terrible bicycle rider, but during 1967, after things calmed down, he insisted on visiting newly purchased MLN lots of land by riding one. Numerous injuries followed. It was like that with everything: Sendic made his own cigarettes –of the lowest possible quality, according to his fellow *guerrilleros*-, built his own hovel-like living room with a fireplace on the floor (which resulted in a permanent smoky haze that reached up to people's waists), and so forth.

The MLN had scarce resources, and most were invested in acquiring properties in Montevideo's suburban areas, to the east and the west. Therefore, little money was left for food. As Fernández recalls, "for a long period of time we were subjected to a permanent diet of cow entrails, particularly chunchullos, acquired at pitiable prices from a seedy butcher". Many of those food products were wrapped in newspapers, from which the Tupamaros' own mug shots looked back at them.[116]

The cell Efraín Martínez and his brother Leonel shared with other Tupamaros, including María Elia Topolansky and Aníbal De Lucía, was the only part of the Montevideo MLN that remained "legal" (the opposite of clandestine in MLN jargon). Its members were not wanted by the police and could therefore avoid the hardship of living as fugitives. Because of this, they also had the sensitive task of helping the rest survive this riskiest of periods, particularly by acquiring new safe houses and legal documents. According to Efraín Martínez, "It was called Cell 'E' (...) Every member of the cell had names that started with 'E' (...) My brother was named Emiliano, after Emiliano Zapata. I was Eugenio, after no one in particular. Aníbal De Lucía's name was Eros".[117] Cell E's basement functioned also as a photographic studio and laboratory, where each of the clandestine Tupas had his picture taken. The shots were used in new false identification documents.

The year 1967 turned out to be one of transition and recovery for the Tupamaros, after a birth that was almost aborted. According to Martínez, that whole year of gestation "must have been the richest year for those inside the MLN in terms of reading and discussing among the comrades, in bases and shelters. We discussed Debray, Che Guevara, socialism, the realistic possibilities of pursuing a guerrilla in Uruguay, the general outlines".[118] It was also then that the method of armed propaganda, soon to become the main MLN operational effort, was conceived. If they survived without being detected and taken out by the police, the Tupamaros would come back smarter and stronger than before.

That year, with the MLN mostly out of business, saw various events taking place at the national level. After his November 1966 victory, Óscar Gestido became president in March; in April he received Lyndon Johnson and the rest of the heads of state of the Americas –save Cuba, naturally- for an Organization of American States summit in Punta del Este. Uruguay's economy continued to sputter; there were frequent cabinet shakeups and nobody knew whether Gestido's economic policies were liberal, socialist, or anything in between. Most likely, the president himself did not know either.

The Communist Party continued its strategy of accumulating forces and staging large-scale strikes and protests to increase tension and debilitate the system of government. Outside of Uruguay, the situation was increasingly tense: the American war in Viet Nam was reaching its peak. Student agitation everywhere was on the rise. Next to Uruguay, Brazil and Argentina continued to make noise, week after week, annoyed at the continued activities of Communists and other Marxists in the small republic. Throughout all of this, the MLN maintained its policy of staying under the radar.

Incredibly, after an entire year of protecting the organization in its cradle, 1967 ended much like 1966. In December, with Sendic visiting Cuba, a cell of Tupamaros was staying at a safe house in the small seaside town of El Pinar, a few kilometers east of Montevideo. Among others, Eleuterio Fernández, Efraín Martínez, and top MLN medical doctor Ismael Bassini were staying there. As it turned out, an Argentine family had its personal belongings stolen from their car while they were at the beach; witnesses described to the police a motorcycle on which the culprits sped off.[119]

While looking around the neighborhood, the police spotted a similar bike parked in the house the Tupamaros were staying in. Completely oblivious to this latter fact, they knocked on the door to question the owners. Martínez opened it, and upon being recognized as a wanted man he was asked to come with the agents. Immediately, Fernández appeared by the half-open door with a pistol in his hand, and told them "don't move or I'll ice you".[120]

The two policemen raised their own weapons; Martínez disarmed one of them, Víctor Bentancor, with a martial arts move. Shots were exchanged at close range. Crisis beset the MLN once again: one of the policemen was shot in the chest, as was Fernández in one of his legs. Bentancor fled the scene, leaving his partner behind. The Tupamaros agreed: an evacuation had to take place immediately. The doctor Bassini hurriedly healed Fernández's leg as best he could, and also looked after the fallen policeman. As explained by Martínez, "we assisted him. We gave him good care, we calmed him down, and said 'Don't worry because now we're leaving, but your people are coming any minute - that's why we're leaving. You just rest easy here'. We assisted him, placed his head on a pillow, put him in covers, gave him a bunch of stuff".[121]

After that, the Tupamaros fled separately so as to better lose the police pursuers set to arrive at any moment. Martínez walked long stretches of beach, with bags and backpacks full of firearms. Fernández underwent a difficult trek, trying to simultaneously stay away from any human beings while suffering from a fresh, bleeding bullet wound. He ended up walking twenty-five kilometers to the closest MLN safe house, hounded by the sounds of helicopters and police sirens flooding the area. The Tupamaro codenamed Jesús later made it to the opposite end of the Montevideo metropolitan area -from the eastern suburb of El Pinar to the western side-, successively by foot, taxi, and bus.[122]

This time, however, the MLN had better luck than in the previous year. The police was unable to trace the Tupamaros who had evacuated the house, and no new arrests were made. In fact, after some time had passed the group felt confident and released propaganda carefully explaining its account of the incidents, including how one of them had "asked" the policemen to stand down before raising his weapon, as well as noting how they provided medical care to the fallen policeman.

The text, which reached all the major newspapers, partly read "we are not common delinquents; our struggle is not against police officers. Our struggle is against those who use armed institutions, as well as those who lead them, to repress the people while preserving their own privileges (...) We have started a struggle in which our lives are at stake. It will only end with victory or death (...) For us the hour of rebellion has definitely come, and the hour of patience is past us. The moment for action and for a commitment right here, right now, has arrived. The time for conversation, theoretical announcements of purposes, and promises that will never be kept, is over. We would not have dignity as Uruguayans, nor dignity as Americans, nor dignity for ourselves, if we did not listen to the dictates of conscience, which calls us day after day to the fight".[123] It was a dramatic statement of principles, of revolutionary intent, and of passion for the cause. The stage was set, and now everyone in Uruguay knew what the stakes were.

The group's security situation at this juncture was paradoxical: it was vulnerable to random incidences like the police visit, but it was also upgrading the way its members handled personal security. Losses had been significant but manageable: a safe house, a motorcycle, a truck, three handguns and ammunition. The formerly legal Efraín Martínez Platero now became a clandestine fugitive: arrest warrants were always major blows. The MLN's final meeting of 1967 took place days later with Sendic visiting Cuba, Fernández in recovery, and Marenales and Manera chairing. The goals for the following year would be further protecting the organization, growing cautiously, and launching the first significant operations not designed simply to acquire weapons and money. In other words, true insurgent actions.

Sendic returned earlier than expected given the urgent news of the El Pinar incident. His reports were not encouraging. There would be little money coming from Havana; almost no firearms were on offer either. The Cuban Communists did offer training courses in guerrilla warfare -Sendic took one in assembling mines-, although the Uruguayans would naturally have to travel all the way to the island to partake in them.[124] In fact, Sendic heard from his Cuban liaisons that it made sense to fuse the MLN with the Communist Party, or with the Argentine terrorist organizations that were slowly emerging again in that country. In other words, although for the MLN those had been months of extreme significance, to the outside world the Tupamaros had been largely a non-factor. The incident at El Pinar had worried some, mostly in the police, but that was about the extent of the Tupamaros' impact. The MLN existed, but it had yet to make its voice truly heard.

Chapter Five:

Confrontations

ÓSCAR GESTIDO, THE ineffectual president inaugurated in March of 1967, died on December 6 of that year. The succession to vice president Jorge Pacheco coincided with the MLN's incident in El Pinar. When the press published the Tupamaros' propaganda detailing their version of events, Pacheco reacted swiftly and surprised everyone. Just a week into his term in office, he signed executive decrees that banned the Socialist Party and a series of Marxist publications over the crime of "subversion".

Although some politicians and historians like Julio Sanguinetti have defended the measure, since it was technically contemplated in the Constitution, there is no question it was an unprecedented turn of events. Never before in Uruguayan history had a political party been banned, even in previous eras of civil war. The same went for the press, particularly in a country with one of the richest traditions of media liberty and diversity in the hemisphere. From any perspective, Pacheco's was a brash, foolish maneuver, a disproportionate spike in the government's intolerance. The Socialist Party and its cousin publications had indeed justified subversive actions, but there was no evidence they were involved in helping them take place.

Policemen and Spooks

The new president came into office bent on combating the increasing sense of lawlessness spreading in Uruguay at the time. When combined with the endemic economic crisis the country had proven unable to overcome, his administration was bound to be a complex one. The state Pacheco commanded had two main instruments of power for dealing with security problems: a Ministry of the Interior and a Ministry of National Defense. As is the norm in free republics, the military was normally barred from operating inside the country. Due to the small size of Uruguay, the Ministry of the Interior controlled the police forces of all districts in its territory.

During the previous years of sporadic MLN actions, the police failed to understand what it was dealing with. The Ministry of the Interior had only one man in a command position who correctly understood the threat. Alejandro Otero, who held the rank of *comisario* and remained the chief of the police intelligence division, weaved together the propaganda and the incidents to conclude Uruguay was facing an incipient but organized insurgency. For years afterwards he was the main reference in the government's anti-Tupamaro efforts, and thus his name became permanently associated with that of his enemies.

Individuals on all sides of the conflict have recognized Otero as a smart, efficient and humane detective. Born in 1931 to immigrant parents from Galicia, Otero joined the police in 1951. His superior skills, complemented with his special training, led to his becoming the police's star officer. He became a famous, easily recognizable figure in 1960s Uruguayan society. Everyone knew who "Comisario Otero" was. Youthful and media-savvy, Otero was always mindful of his image and ready to provide a press conference or briefing on the latest exploits of the police.

With the dual responsibility of fighting armed subversion and managing the government's counter-intelligence efforts -and roughly fifty men to accomplish both missions-, Otero was a key official for foreign governments to liaise with. Of those, the United States was Uruguay's greatest ally in security and economic terms. In January of 1965, a new U.S. player arrived in town: the Office of Public Safety, or OPS.

OPS programs were focused on augmenting local police capabilities. One effort consisted of sending promising Uruguayan police officers to OPS academies in the United States and Panama. USAID also provided Uruguay with grant money to purchase advanced police equipment, like vehicles and radios. Last but not least, OPS officers stationed in Uruguay provided on-the-ground advisory, examining Uruguay's capabilities and providing tailored assistance to mend gaps in the country's efforts.

While OPS and the CIA were separate efforts, there was a connection between them. According to both the CIA's Philip Agee and Adolph Sáenz, the New Mexico policeman tasked with heading OPS in Uruguay for its first four years, an agreement between the two entities allowed the CIA to post one of its case officers as an OPS advisor.[125] That advisor would thus work mostly out of the OPS offices and benefit from the many contacts with the Uruguayan police to be found there, rather than from the CIA station under diplomatic cover.

In the overall picture, Otero has acknowledged "This country's intelligence services were practically non-operational. They were clueless about what was going on, and what consequences it could have for the future".[126] The most important event both the Ministry of the Interior and the CIA station missed was the creation of a secret militia within the Communist Party. As early as 1967 this clandestine force was smuggling rifles from Communist Germany; throughout the years it would assemble an impressive arsenal. The objective of this unit, whose existence was known only to top-ranking members like Secretary General Arismendi, was to provide a decisive armed backbone for the moment when the Communists took over. It would also serve to protect the party, both when outside of government and in case it did take over, from the backlash of its enemies.

The 1966-7 incidents in which the Tupamaros appeared in the police's radar piqued Otero's attention far more than the espionage work. However, in pursuing that mission he faced even more hurdles. One was the problem of a democracy facing an urban guerrilla or terrorist group. Distinguishing its members from innocent civilians imposed strong limitations on police actions and tactics.

In addition to this, Uruguay's police had further handicaps. They had no experience at all in dealing with armed groups, much less of the political variety. Its members were often individuals of humble origins, who were poorly paid and trained. To top it off, according to Otero, "Weapons were another problem: they were scarce, and several were in a state of disrepair. I remember we did not even have paper to type on". Furthermore, unlike the police, the Tupamaros had a carefully thought-out strategy. It is because of this austere context that Otero is most remembered for his refusal to beat up or otherwise hurt his detainees.[127]

The Stars of the Political Intrigues

For virtually every single day of Pacheco's term in office there were bitter political intrigues taking place. A number of characters appeared on the scene at this time, all of who would have decisive roles to play in deciding the country's fate. As of 1968, Uruguayan politics -still before the coming spike in MLN activities- was a rollercoaster of scandals and tension.

One major written product of the American embassy is useful in navigating the period. It was a periodic report to Washington of the situation in Uruguay, with a compendium containing biographical information on all the major figures involved in local politics. Within its pages appear the infamous nationalist general Mario Aguerrondo ("currently refraining from coup activities due to his admiration and support for President Pacheco personally"), Communist boss Rodney Arismendi, or top Marxist intellectual Eduardo Galeano ("highly intelligent; anti-US; not a Communist"). Other individuals, who were comparatively minor then and became more important in recent times, were also in the U.S. radar: José Mujica ("Presently he is being sought by the police"), Julio Sanguinetti ("extremely intelligent and able"), Luis Lacalle ("politician with great promise; of distinguished and wealthy family, ambitious, attractive and intelligent"), and others.[128]

Galeano deserves a special mention. His 1971 book, "Las Venas Abiertas de América Latina" (The Open Veins of Latin America), was the most important work of non-fiction published in the region during the period. It opened with a series of banner statements: "The international division of labor consists of some countries specializing in winning and other countries specializing in losing (...) The more liberty is given to business, the more prisons it becomes necessary to build for those who suffer from business (...) [the imperialists] who profited did so because [Latin America] lost".[129]

Galeano's work was a prime contributor to a "Latin American narrative" blooming in the region at the time, whereby every single ill that hurt its societies was the fault of the Spanish, the British, or the Americans, usually in collusion with "sepoy" home oligarchies.

What Galeano wrote defined the political ideology of Latin American radicals to this day, and is a prime example of the *weltanschauung* of the Tupamaros. In closing with "Years of revolution are sweeping by; years of redemption (...) the perpetuation of the current order of things is the perpetuation of the crime", his book summarized the call to arms that Che launched in the 1960s.

Another figure of interest was a general named Líber Seregni. The Uruguayan military may have had little importance nationally, but its highest-ranking officers were growing in prominence. The Nationalists had promoted Mario Aguerrondo to chief of police for the years 1959-63, and he thus became a well-known national figure. Former Air Force general Óscar Gestido served as president for the Colorados. He in turn placed Seregni, of known Colorado social-democratic persuasions, in charge of the country's top operational military command.

Officially called Military Region I, this was the Army post tasked with the defense of Uruguay's core, meaning the south-central region that included Montevideo. Military Region I was in charge of repelling any foreign aggression –an impossible prospect-, and also of protecting the government from domestic insurrections. It was only natural that Gestido placed a man of his own party, like Seregni, in such a sensitive position. Following his retirement in 1968, Seregni grew into a major political figure - just like Gestido himself.

Gestido's successor became even more important. Jorge Pacheco turned out to be a stern and heavy-handed president who polarized Uruguay's political climate like never before. He was a man of few words, with modest experience in Colorado print journalism, high school teaching, and as an amateur boxer. He rose thanks to vast family connections in the party. At the time he became president, according to top fellow Colorado Sanguinetti, "he had little relevance. He had been a representative with almost no record of accomplishment, and had never been a minister. He was not a well-known figure".[130] Pacheco hated public exposure and to explain himself to the public.

The new president rarely if ever changed his mind, and had a strict vision of the rule of law that brooked no challenges. In the fight against the Tupamaros that would take place in the coming years, he would never make a single concession - a remarkable fact when compared to the records of other leaders facing similar confrontations. At a time of enormous upheaval, Pacheco was a pillar of stability.

The presence of such a gray and "tone deaf" figure drove many young radicals into concluding the new president was the incarnation of conservatism and subservience to imperialism they had long feared. According to Eleuterio Fernández, "Pacheco was the greatest creator of Tupamaros Uruguay ever had".[131] In fact, for years he was the number one target of the MLN, the one man they would hit if they had the opportunity. The American embassy knew this was a potential scenario. However, like everything else in Uruguay, the presidential security detail was unprepared for an armed challenge: "The unit has no internal communications equipment (neither mobile nor fixed) and has only two ¼ ton trucks".[132]

Pacheco did not make things easy for supporters like fellow Colorados Jorge Batlle and Julio Sanguinetti. After the taboo of censorship was broken with the newspaper closures of late 1967, it became common practice for the government to censor newspapers, even though the legitimacy of any such authority remained questionable. At one point, the executive branch decreed the temporary closure of a newspaper for captioning a photograph of Pacheco surrounded by military officers with the words "Pacheco surrounded by his base". This arbitrary criterion extended to economic news: the government censured newspapers that reproduced currency exchange data from the Buenos Aires Herald, for the "crime" of disputing its own, centrally mandated values.[133]

Both of Uruguay's main political parties, the Colorados and the Nationalists, reached their greatest degree of internal ideological division in the late 1960s. For instance, the Colorados under Pacheco generally followed a lukewarm pro-business, anti-inflation line, although they rarely considered privatizing state companies or other market-friendly measures. Nevertheless, this was still too much for factions such as that of Senator Zelmar Michelini, a man of deep socialist convictions.

Similar gaps existed in the Partido Nacional, then reeling from its 1966 electoral defeat. After the end of the second Nationalist administration, the unquestionable leader of the party became Wilson Ferreira, a fiery speaker with heterodox views. The hardest politician of all to pin down, and a man venerated by the

Nationalists to this day, Senator Ferreira seemed to have it every way on every issue. He was the man of the rural constituencies that traditionally supported the Partido Nacional – but was also, much like the Socialists and Communists, in favor of a so-called "agrarian reform". Ferreira was thus a question mark, a man who played all sides of the growing conflicts with the ultimate intention of establishing their unpopularity and becoming the only viable alternative for the next election.

Other Nationalists had virtually nothing to do with Ferreira. For instance, Enrique Erro continued in his position as a hardcore Cuban-aligned radical who frequently expressed support for the Tupamaros and their actions. He remained close to former aide Pepe Mujica. Yet other Nationalists, like the retired general Aguerrondo, were diametrically opposite and hoped for a conservative government that destroyed all Marxist influence in the country. Naturally, men like Aguerrondo would hear nothing of state takeovers of private property, rural or otherwise.

The Communist Strategy

The Communists were looking with interested eyes not just at these political rivals, but also at the mavericks of the MLN. Relations between the PCU and the Tupamaros were always singular. Each saw the other as a fellow traveler with the wrong strategy; one misguided for being too outdated in its outlook and the other for the inverse reason. The Tupamaros called the Communists "bolches", in reference to the Party's heavily pro-Soviet (or pro-Bolshevik) identity. The Communists, in turn, nicknamed the Tupamaros "ultras", as in "ultra-radicals" guilty of childlike adventurism.[134]

In 1967, during the MLN's hiatus year, it emerged that living legend Ernesto Guevara was deploying to Bolivia to jumpstart an insurgency against the military dictatorship that ruled from La Paz.[135] Since this coincided with the MLN's disarray following the failed FUNSA raid, the Communists offered the Tupamaros a deal: they would be spirited out of Uruguay, away from police persecution, and given the opportunity to join Guevara in Bolivia. The Tupamaros declined the offer.

Later that year, in October, the announcement of Guevara's death was a "bomb of freezing water dropped on our heads"[136] for the Tupamaros, and a moment of celebration for anti-Communists throughout the region. Adding *détente* with the Soviets and an economic downturn in Cuba –by 1970, a decade into the revolution, the country was back to basic agriculture-, it appeared like the 1960s upsurge in revolutionary subversion died with Che, symbolically in the very geographical heart of South America.[137]

To compound this, when that year Uruguayan journalist Carlos Gutiérrez asked Fidel Castro specifically about this issue, the Cuban dictator answered: "Your country lacks the geographic conditions for armed struggle. There are no mountains, no jungles. No guerrilla can be conducted there (...) an armed insurrection, right now, would not last two days in your country".[138]

While the Tupamaros pondered how to proceed, the main PCU effort at subverting the Uruguayan government, and at sowing a state of permanent tension, peaked in 1968. Unionized employees of virtually every public service continued to paralyze life in Uruguay. In fact, the Communists managed to radicalize the unions of Uruguay's few private industries, so for instance banking employees were constantly on strike. At one point, the frustrated national government militarized the banking industry and used the Army to force bank employees to work - which later led to more strikes and protests.

Beginning in May, roughly around International Workers' Day, Montevideo's main avenues were in flames and constant occupation. Bolstering the demonstrations and riots for 1968 were high school and later university students. Both were organized by subsidiaries of the Communist Party's UJC, whose membership had grown by six thousand members since 1965.[139] It was during this period when Arismendi famously stated that no country in the world had more strikes per year than Uruguay, and he was probably right. For instance, "On November 25 the CNT staged a gigantic general strike. Over 500,000 workers struck. Bombs exploded (...) several buses were torched and the streets were sprinkled with caltrops. On November 27 (...) laws were passed addressing some of the demanded raises".[140]

The situation was so drastic that a "militant" union emerged among hospital patients, who were protesting –or rather, *demanding-* food, money, and jobs upon leaving their state-funded beds.[141] A news item only months earlier noted how Uruguay boasted the largest number of official holidays per year, worldwide: twenty-three.[142] Although Uruguay had never had an entrepreneurial culture, what little there was reached its nadir during this period, when a veritable assault on capitalism, profit-making, and business culture in general became mainstream. The Communist vision was one of complete disarray in the government to the point when resignations and a "need for a pact with the workers" brought the PCU into the government. It was slowly becoming real.

The Return of the Tupamaros

During the second half of 1968, however, this Communist campaign found itself flipped around. That was when the MLN returned to insurgent operations, a full year and a half after the botched FUNSA raid. The Tupamaros, safely watching the many disturbances and riots of 1968 from their newly built safe houses, decided it was time to strike again. Otherwise, the moment of revolution might pass them by.

One of the main targets for the unions' crippling strikes was UTE, the state-run power and telecommunications company founded by José Batlle & Ordóñez at the turn of the century. The president of the company was a man named Ulysses Pereira Reverbel, a personal friend and political ally of President Pacheco. A universally disliked man, alternately spotted at nocturnal parties and at strikebreaking incidents, Pereira Reverbel even had a murder in his background for which he had only served six months in prison.

The Tupamaros decided they would kidnap the president of UTE, and ransom him in exchange for the company's concessions to its striking workers.[143] The codename for the operation, and for the target Pereira, would be "Pajarito", or "Birdie". Pereira was to be kidnapped upon leaving his apartment building in Montevideo's seaside *rambla*, on the way to the government vehicle that drove him to UTE every morning. The car had two men posted to it: a driver named Nicolás Galdós and a secretary named Miguel Rey. An operation in Montevideo's *rambla* was risky but feasible; many things could go wrong. The Tupamaros practiced the attack so many times that the one who played the Pajarito usually ended up bruised and beaten.

On the morning of the operation, Julio Marenales -in command, dressed as a policeman- approached the target just as he left the building and walked to his car. With the help of Mujica, in the role of a well-dressed civilian Marenales had been trying to "arrest" moments earlier, he overpowered the prominent politician while the other Tupamaros swooped in and dealt with Pereira's aides. In the official MLN telling, while his assistants resisted, "the 'birdie' remained quiet, inundating the scene with a penetrating perfume".

Blows were exchanged as Marenales and Mujica subdued Pereira and forced him into the back of the vehicle. The MLN driver who boarded it immediately tried to speed away, but Rey pushed his way into the car to extract his boss. To remove him, Mujica shot him in the shoulder at point blank range. Once the vehicle started, Galdós the driver -who had been shot in the hand- commandeered a vehicle to pursue the Tupamaros. Moments later the MLN's backup car rammed his sideways, and with a visual display of firepower intimidated him into abandoning the chase.

During the getaway, the Tupamaro with the most first aid expertise, medical doctor Ismael Bassini, injected Pereira with powerful sedatives. Bassini repeated the procedure twice, seeing that Pereira was still pumped with adrenaline and making the ride unmanageable. However, the doses were excessive, and the opposite happened: the hostage went into a convulsive state of shock, vomiting on himself and on the car, and quickly turning purple. Bassini had no choice but to assist him, trying to pull his tongue out and providing mouth-to-mouth breathing assistance. The MLN's official history emphasized the alleged bravery of this act, given that Pereira had just been vomiting - but omitted it was the Tupamaros' own actions that almost killed their victim.

Pereira was held hostage for a number of days. Upon hearing from his masked interrogators the truthful accusation that he had murdered a young man years before, he supposedly cried. His makeshift cell was completely covered in newspaper sheets, and secretly wiretapped with audio recording equipment. Pereira was also forced to perform basic human needs in front of his guards. The Tupamaros made a point of mocking his homosexuality throughout his "stay" with them, and most humiliatingly, in their propaganda. The MLN's accounts of the operation, most likely written by Eleuterio Fernández, placed constant references to Pereira's mannerisms, tone of voice, choice of words, cowardice, and so forth, to paint a picture of a "marica": "Normally and invariably prim, at that moment and for a few minutes his voice and his gestures turn into those of a woman, an old hag enraged to the point of hysteria".*

The kidnapping of Ulysses Pereira was a shock to the population, and it immediately became the breaking news event of the year. Everyone talked about this new appearance by the mysterious group of subversives that refused to go away, and was now demonstrating upgraded capabilities by performing an audacious operation. The government's response was furious; with police deployments and raids everywhere suspects could be found - all to no avail. One raid, conducted without a judicial warrant, into the premises of the national university resulted in a "veritable battle".[144] In the end, Pereira was released after five days in captivity because the MLN realized it could not hold him indefinitely. The Tupamaros did not -yet- have an adequate structure to keep hostages for extended periods of time. Nevertheless, the operation dominated local headlines, made it to the international press, and introduced a greater segment of the population to the name of the Tupamaros. It was a preview of things to come later.

The Fires of 1968

Beyond the MLN's kidnapping, 1968 continued to be a year of enormous tension, for on the day following the liberation of Pereira an event took place that is still remembered every year in Uruguay. The centers of student agitation -the most violent of all- were always by the Universidad's major schools, such as Law or Medicine. Rioting students would typically barricade the avenues around them, as well as the entrances, in their fights with the police.

Oftentimes these turned into combat situations, with the entrenched students catapulting various objects and Molotov cocktails at the riot police. The American advisor Sáenz describes what it looked like for an outside observer: "To thwart the use of horses in controlling civil disturbances, mob leaders threw petards (firecrackers), Molotov cocktails and rocks to frighten the animals. Marbles were thrown on the street to cause the horses to fall when they stepped on them. Horses were often shot at and stabbed with knives, large pins and other sharp objects. Barricades constructed

---

* The term "Pajarito", or "birdie" was partly a reference to this. So was the case with the first mention of the "penetrating perfume".

with planks, debris and automobile tires blocked the main streets in Montevideo and were set on fire during riots".[145] The Internationale was typically heard at one point or another, in respites before renewed clashes with the police.

The few remaining private homes in these areas soon succumbed to this climate of tension, and the downtown zone in particular was depopulated of anything but commerce and the university. Combat extended to the bars across the street; chairs and tables became parts of the barricades and the bonfires. The Communists were not playing around, and there was little spontaneity to their protests. Each of the incidents was carefully prepared; rioters were trained, briefed, supplied, and commanded to ensure maximum effects at a minimal cost. Recruiters prowled the various schools of the university, identifiable by the color of their shirts: Communists, Tupamaros, Socialists, and so forth.

However, the violence was too great, and thus uncontrollable. Even the Communist organizers thought the risks, particularly of provoking the government, were too great. During the riots of August 12 a man with the impossible name of Líber Arce was shot and killed by policeman Enrique Tegiachi. The name Líber Arce sounded exactly the same as the Spanish word "liberarse", which means "to free oneself" - a trendy concept in 1968. A "martyred student", Arce was transformed into an icon of youthful resistance against the dark, helmeted forces of fascism. His funeral procession across Montevideo was enormous; large parts of the press and the Catholic Church came out with strong statements against the national government and the police.

In reality, Arce was not simply a "student", but rather a member of the Communist UJC militia. He was twenty-seven years old, and although technically in the University his real purpose was recruiting others to the Communist cause, and organizing occupations and riots. During the investigation, the policeman Tegiachi claimed he did not intend to kill anyone but was rather acting in panic at a situation that was out of control.

Arce's cause was a classic example of how the Communists could take a single incident, carefully prune it of inconvenient facts, and turn it into a *cause célèbre*. Today in Uruguay few if any people know that Arce was twenty-seven, and that he was working as a professional Communist rioter attacking the police. In the continuing streak of Communist propaganda victories, only days after these events the Soviet Union launched its greatest military campaign since 1956, when it annihilated the Prague Spring with armored vehicles and bullets. The Uruguayan Communist Party was naturally enthusiastic in its support - for the Soviets.[146] Communist doublethink and doublespeak reached their peak: rioting youths in the free world were the expression of discontent with the evils of capitalism, and were authentic. Rebels in Communist lands, on the other hand, were manufactured and unworthy of any sympathy. Millions in the free world, most of whom were not ideological Communists, fell for these propaganda traps.

To worsen the situation, in subsequent days, the police killed two more student rioters in Montevideo; both were also members of the UJC.* Given the commotion caused by the killing of Arce, the police's usage of live ammunition -when the protesters, despite their boldness, never employed firearms- was an enormously foolish decision.[147] These events came in the midst of a dramatic period for the Western world. Che Guevara had died the previous year. In death he became the mythological icon of generations of young radicals. Martin Luther King Junior had been assassinated in April by a white supremacist. A month later Paris was rocked by its own student uprising, as were many other cities around the free world. The Soviet propaganda machine had a veritable worldwide banquet to feast on.

There were few years in history, even for the very eventful twentieth century, that were as packed with such a succession of major occurrences as 1968. This was reflected in what the United States embassy in Montevideo reported to Washington, itself rocked by racial riots: "The world is going through a period of accelerated change under which almost all previously accepted values and traditional attitudes are under question".[148] Very few diplomats have had the opportunity to write such reports in their entire careers.

Polls showed that a majority of Uruguayans rejected the government's emergency security measures, and placed the responsibility for the deaths of the rioters not on the rioters themselves, but on Pacheco and his cabinet.[149] According to Eleuterio Fernández, in mid-1968, as Montevideo burned with riots, strikes, and barricades, "people were banging on the gates to join" the MLN.[150] The group performed isolated actions, including armed

* Their names were Hugo De Los Santos and Susana Pintos.

robberies and the nocturnal bombing of the empty offices of highly symbolic targets. On one occasion, José Mujica and Leonel Martínez Platero placed explosives at the headquarters of the Colorado newspaper Acción.[151] There was also plenty of reading and especially recruiting. Each Tupamaro visited the social circles and environs with which he or she was well acquainted, and hinted strongly they could be the conduit towards joining "los tupas". More importantly, after feeling secure enough in their feet following the Pereira operation and the lack of a forceful police response to it, the Tupamaros prepared to launch their first sustained operational campaign.

At the time there were still only about fifty members. They were all committed to the cause and had many months, in some cases years, of experience avoiding or confronting the police. Hiding mostly in safe houses in the western and eastern outskirts of Montevideo, the MLN functioned under the leadership tetrarchy of Raúl Sendic, Eleuterio Fernández, Julio Marenales, and Jorge Manera. After securing a total of ten safe houses, the *dirección* agreed to split the organization in two for the first time. It was the birth of the MLN's columns.

Organizing for Action

Sendic and Fernández would jointly run Column 1. They would operate from the eastern outskirts of Montevideo, an area comprising beach towns like El Pinar, Shangrilá and Solymar where the group had based itself since the FUNSA raid. It would also be in charge of non-guerrilla tasks like managing contacts with unions and political parties.

Column 2 went to Marenales and Manera. It based itself west of Montevideo, in a safe house baptized Marquetalia in honor of a major insurgent base of the Colombian FARC. Column 2 would focus first on guerrilla operations, and therefore got the best operators for the coming fights. This did not by any means signify that Column 1 would not conduct operations. Efraín Martínez worked as liaison between the two columns. This groomed him for later positions of leadership, and allowed him to serve in a key function for the MLN: "I was the coordinator for the entire leadership (...) I would meet Marenales and Manera in their truck, in the Pajas Blancas area, and there they would hand me things for Bebe or Ñato. There would be documents, letters, or money".[152]

Marquetalia was a key MLN facility. Its functions included shelter, storage, planning center, workshop, academy, meeting hall, and more. Marenales and Manera ran it as a tight ship. Their favorite deputy was top female Tupamara María Elia Topolansky, a highly motivated radical who responded better than everyone else to the emergency drills the leaders conducted. The Marquetalia Tupamaros all slept in the same space, on the second floor of the structure, directly on the wooden floor. Marenales, always first to rise and impose order, rested his head on a brick. It was no hippie community, but rather a militarized cell working on firearms, improvised explosives, and other guerrilla instruments. One of the incorporations to this wing of the MLN was José Mujica, who graduated from a peripheral Tupamaro to a full member in 1967.[153]

Although the MLN still had the upper hand against Otero's pursuers, the downside was the permanent sense of paranoia about things that could be amiss, odd, or out of place. What if the safe house, the apartment, or the agreed meeting place had already been detected and was being staked out by the police? What if there was no way to ensure the police was not observing from a window, from across the street in civilian clothes, from inside a vehicle, or perhaps remotely? The urban *guerrillero* could melt in the city, but he could also begin to see crowded environments as a problem.

The most important security measure the Tupamaros adopted was compartmentalization. They called it "the organization's main defense recourse" and its "general security principle". It consisted of treating knowledge like an object, and carefully allowing it only in the minds of those who absolutely *needed* to have it. Knowledge meant anything related to the MLN: the real names of team members, the addresses of safe houses, the telephone numbers of contacts, the dates and times of activities, and so forth. In fact, "as a general principle, no one must say anything to anyone else unless it is functionally necessary".[154]

Compartmentalization was one of the Tupamaros' greatest achievements, for they took it seriously. Years would pass in which *guerrilleros* who worked closely together never knew each other's real names.* The key was that they did not *want* to know said names. Meetings often required using hoods, so that participants did not know what the others looked like. Messages, both spoken and written, were coded. Members and associates were driven to secret locations blindfolded or otherwise oblivious to their path and location.

The MLN practiced compartmentalization vertically and horizontally. The former meant the leaders of a column would know the guerrilla identities -a name and contact information- of the column sub-chiefs, but each sub-chief would not know the identity of those parallel or subordinate to him. The militants of each of these cells knew nothing of the activities, identities, or locations of others. Horizontal compartmentalization worked too: leaders were deprived of information as well, if there was no need for them to know it. The *dirección* insisted on this being applied to themselves: each member of the tetrarchy would be involved only with certain columns, and therefore know little about the activities of others. The leader tasked with supervising Column 1 knew next to nothing of Column 2's infrastructure, membership, and so forth.

No Respite for the Police

The Pereira kidnapping increased police attention towards the MLN more than ever. Information was still hard to come by, for the Tupamaros had done a good job -especially considering they were amateurs- of hiding themselves. In his memoirs, OPS's Sáenz recalls how the U.S. country team in Uruguay -combining the embassy, the CIA station, and OPS- estimated the strength of the MLN around this time. The station chief, Richard Sampson, estimated there were about five hundred Tupamaros in action. The diplomats thought they were facing "the best organized, most determined, and most effective urban terrorist organization thus far".[155] Sáenz, closer to the police, believed the organization had demonstrated having sufficient resources for a "combat army" of close to 2,000 "Tupes", as the Americans had taken to calling them. In reality, although

---

* In some cases, they *never* learned the real names. Some Tupamaros still refer to others automatically by the *nom de guerre* rather than by the real name, even when they know it well.

recruitment was speeding up, in late 1968 the Tupamaros were less than a hundred men and women.[156]

After more than four years in Uruguay in which he had seen the birth of the MLN and its attempts at jumpstarting an insurgency, Sáenz returned to Washington in mid-1969. This was just as the Tupamaros' main armed campaign was escalating. His replacement as head of OPS in Montevideo was Dan Mitrione. The former policeman from Richmond, Indiana, who had become a police advisor in Brazil's OPS program for a number of years, was a father of nine who "did not believe in carrying a gun". This applied not just to his time as a government advisor in dangerous South American cities, but also to his time as a police officer back home.[157]

Following the Pereira kidnapping, the Tupamaros opted not to conduct additional operations in 1968. Instead, they concentrated on robbing more banks and weapons, on recruiting new members, and on organizational matters. A number of differences emerged during these debates that led to a new split into columns. To many members, a dichotomy between two leading pillars emerged: Raúl Sendic and Héctor Amodio. The latter was not a member of the tetrarchy that made up the *dirección*, but was doubtlessly the next one in line in importance. Amodio had been present at most actions the Tupamaros had conducted so far, had proven his operational qualities, and was now recruiting increasing numbers of people.

On September 24 of 1968 two significant disputes were tabled at a plenary of the organization. First, Sendic complained about having being kept out of the loop of the Pajarito operation: Pereira had been freed without consulting him. Furthermore, he wanted more autonomy for groups such as the one made up mostly of his UTAA cane workers. In contrast, Marenales, Manera, and Fernández preferred a more centralized structure.

The other complaint came from Alicia Rey, Amodio's partner and the most important female Tupamara: she had been bypassed for leadership consideration in the initial split in two columns. What lay behind that, according to her, was the *machismo* of top MLN leaders, specifically Manera (who missed the meeting because he was in Cuba) and Marenales. Important members of the MLN, like Tabaré Rivero and Rey's own partner Amodio, argued strongly in her favor, and by extension in favor of greater equality for Tupamaras.[158]

Both disputes were solved amicably with a Solomonic decision. Amodio and Rey were provided with their own Column, which was given the number 15. Sendic and the UTAA contingent of *cañeros* also got an entire column created for them to fill: Column 20.* Both would have significant degrees of autonomy, as was the rule with all columns. In fact, the Tupamaros chose to end 1968 with a total of seven columns.

Just weeks after these meetings, the MLN suffered a major blow to its security. One of Amodio's newer recruits, Alberto Candán, had been in charge of transporting photo ID-ready portraits of each of the fugitive Tupamaros, in order to craft new documents for them. Candán lost the roll containing those pictures, and to compound the error failed to notify the MLN of the loss. Once the roll was found and made its way to the police, a valuable intelligence trove appeared in Alejandro Otero's hands.

Based on that and other clues, the police under the *comisario's* command picked up the trail of the Tupamaros and traced it to a vehicle that Manera, the usual trusted chauffeur, drove around the Montevideo metropolitan area. No one in the MLN detected this close police surveillance, which in October of 1968 was getting closer and closer to determining where the group's safe houses were. However, the enormous disturbances and chaos of 1968 made the government anxious to show concrete results, fast. Once the Minister of the Interior learned that Otero and his men had a confirmed MLN vehicle tracked down in its daily routine, he ordered an arrest rather than a continuation of the surveillance.

Otero, despite his correct instincts in favor of netting a bigger catch, complied. On October 8, a police car rammed the MLN vehicle and immobilized it. Inside was Julio Marenales - the same man who had been arrested four years earlier after a failed bank robbery. Once under interrogation, Otero showed him the photographs from Candán's lost roll. It turned out, said the policeman, that they had made the foolish mistake of all wearing the same tie, which they handed from one to the other during the speedy photo session in the MLN's secret basement. It was one more giveaway that essentially made the false identifications useless. Policemen simply had to look out for that particular tie.[159]

---

* Beyond 1 and 2, column numbers were non-sequential.

With Marenales out of the picture, the tetrarchy lost one of its members, and thus another Tupamaro had to be brought in. The choice was clear: Amodio became the newest member of the *dirección*.

Apart from this reorganization, the MLN tried to establish good relations with the friendliest regime it could find in the world: Cuba's. Many, including Sendic and Manera, traveled to the island to train as *guerrilleros* and to establish useful connections. Visits were handled clandestinely: the Uruguayans traveled to Prague via Buenos Aires and Paris. After spending some days in the Czechoslovak capital undergoing security checks, they were put on a flight to the island; the return leg traced a similar direction. Throughout, the Uruguayans' handler was a man known only as Veitías.

Among the training programs various Tupamaros took in Cuba were aircraft piloting, heavy weapons, clandestinity, communications, underwater demolitions, target practice, improvised rifle manufacturing, the counterfeiting of U.S. dollars, and more. Despite this close cooperation, according to Eleuterio Fernández, "in general relations were poor. The Cubans did not understand the issue of urban warfare".[160]

All Hands on Deck

Uruguay had known years of enormous agitation in recent times: 1958 featured massive demonstrations for the autonomy of the national university. In 1964 there were endless intrigues and tensions over the Brazilian coup d'état and the exiles that arrived in Uruguay. In 1965, the country's banking system shattered, and it had not yet recovered. Nevertheless, 1968 had been the most tension-filled year in recent memory.

In the last days of December, the Tupamaros staged a novel act of propaganda. They placed a series of boxes with hidden springboard mechanisms at a public fair in Montevideo. Once the timers in the devices were activated, the boxes suddenly burst open and began to shoot out hundreds of MLN propaganda leaflets, claiming that the hour was arriving when the Tupamaros would avenge all injustices in representation of the Uruguayan people.[161] The next phase of their insurgency, the one that would make them world famous, was coming.

Chapter Six:

The Robin Hood Guerrillas Armed Propaganda in 1969

IN MONTHS PRIOR to January of 1969, the MLN recruited a young architecture student named Lucía Topolansky. Her identical twin sister, María Elia, had preceded her in joining the ranks of the "subversives". They came from a half-Polish and half-Spanish family, in the latter instance from one of the first to immigrate to Uruguay long before its independence. Lucía was a woman of few words, with a melancholic and low-key tone. She often dressed in the latest fashions, including colorful miniskirts - the opposite of a rugged *guerrillera*.[162] In her time as a Tupamara she would consistently demonstrate discipline, efficiency and fortitude.

The Monty Bank

Lucía worked at a downtown Montevideo investment bank named Monty. The president of the firm was the powerful Carlos Frick, also Pacheco's Minister of Livestock and Agriculture at the time. Although Topolansky was barely 22 years old, she quickly came to realize that something was wrong in the business the company did.

Once recruited, she revealed to the MLN that she was privy to Monty's secret double accounting system, which hid the illegal dealings in foreign currency conducted by the bank on behalf of multiple VIPs. After decades of regulations and years of crises, most transactions in foreign currency were banned. Topolansky demonstrated Monty was violating these laws.

The Tupamaros decided to stage a small raid, in the midst of the summer when few people were in the area, to rob the bank and unravel its operations. It was executed late in the afternoon of February 16; only a handful of employees, including some of the owners, were present. The Tupa in charge of the assault was Héctor Amodio, dressed as a policeman. Among those present was María Elia Topolansky, who looked to the employees just like the colleague they knew, her twin Lucía.[163]

The *guerrilleros* were swift, and barely had to use their weapons in taking over the firm. They took the roughly $116,000 (in 2014 dollars) they found, but most importantly went straight for the accounting ledgers Lucía had described. After only a few minutes inside the facility, they left without firing a shot or harming anyone.

The MLN's next moves were notoriously different from the norm for bank heists. First, upon noticing that the owners of the firm did not notify the police of the robbery, the Tupamaros themselves did so. In other words, they called the police's attention to their own crime. Second, they notified the press of these facts, and announced they were conducting an analysis of the stolen Monty books. Later on, in their masterstroke, they left the original ledgers, as well as the MLN's study of their contents, at the home of a state prosecutor tasked with financial crimes.

The ploy worked: the newspapers were filled with accounts of the unusual robbery. The prosecutor started an investigation that confirmed the MLN's accusations, and a judge sentenced some of the illegal financial operators to jail. As a consequence of the uproar, President Pacheco banned all non-banking investment firms from operating in the market.[164] Lucía Topolansky joined her sister in the MLN's underground network: she was now a wanted person, and had sacrificed her "legal" status for the life of a fugitive. She would later excel at weapons maintenance and the crafting of improvised ammunition and explosives.

The Monty raid was a prime example in what the MLN called armed propaganda. The thinking behind it lay deep in the minds of leaders like Raúl Sendic, Eleuterio Fernández, Efraín Martínez, or Mauricio Rosencof. Fernández coined a straightforward allegory to represent the origins of the stratagem: "Uruguay was a china shop and we could not afford to be an elephant on skates".[165] In other words, a destructive revolution in a country like Uruguay had to be approached, paradoxically, with an extremely judicious use of violence. After years of debating these matters, the Tupamaros at last had arrived at a fresh yet logical solution to this problem.

The Invention of Armed Propaganda

MLN doctrine on armed propaganda was strict. The key was that armed operations had to be tied to the political cause the organization was advancing: one had to be symbiotically associated with the other. Upon learning of an operation, the target audience – the population- had to immediately process it as an act of justice.

Historically propaganda had been a *tool* of political activities, including revolutions. It was not an operational tactic because it did not involve true action on the part of the insurgent, except for the dissemination or broadcasting of its contents. To propagandize was, essentially, to speak and write.

The *armed* propaganda of the Tupamaros was different because it conveyed the message through the application of direct, coercive action. Seen from the outside, an armed propaganda operation might look much like a guerrilla raid, for it involved a number of armed insurgents launching some kind of attack. The difference with a conventional guerrilla strike was that the purpose of the action was not to degrade the capabilities of the enemy, but rather to transmit a message about the MLN's cause.

In order for an act of armed propaganda to not be terroristic, it had to avoid projecting violence against the innocent as gallantly as possible. The purpose of armed propaganda could not be terror, but rather admiration and sympathy. Therefore, the Tupamaros' methodology avoided certain techniques, such as bombings: "This kind of operation is unlikely to deliver political results for the guerrilla. Timed explosive charges in public places may cause needless victims among the population".[166] Operations would be designed to humiliate the government, display the tactical superiority of the group, and awaken admiration in the population.

A typical example was how the Tupamaros hijacked civilian vehicles for use in their raids. While some *guerrilleros* drove off in the stolen car, others kept close to the civilian victim and strolled with them around the city for the duration of the operation. According to accounts from the time, "In those long walks there were people who, while held prisoner by a girl young enough to be their daughter, expressed their sympathy for the MLN or provided fatherly counsel to their kidnapper".[167] Taxi drivers were the most frequent victims. Sometimes the Tupamaros got requests for a previous kidnapper to appear, in order to resume an interesting conversation from a previous hijacking of the same taxi cab. Later, the Tupas returned the cars. In the case of the taxi drivers, they were given an amount of money equivalent to a day's work.[168]

San Rafael

These principles took years to develop, and were first tested in the Monty raid. The Tupamaros were barely getting started. Just four days after robbing the bank, the group staged another major operation: an assault on the country's most important casino, the San Rafael. This time, it was Raúl Sendic who commanded the cell that hit the major Punta del Este tourist hotspot. They came from his "column of the interior", the nickname Column 20 got because a majority of its members were not from Montevideo. One of the members joining the raid was Jorge Zabalza, one of the newest and most motivated recruits.

The scion of a half-Basque, half-Jewish family,[169] Jorge was the son of Pedro Zabalza, a top Partido Nacional politician who earlier in the 1960s presided the National Council of Government. A bully and a brawler in his teenage years, Zabalza left his native town of Minas to study in Montevideo, but did not fit well there either. He was a frequent feature at the student riots that shook the Law School in previous years, but never actually studied anything. Instead, he tried his luck traveling. He wound up in a kibbutz in Israel, carrying boxes of produce in the Les Halles market of Paris, and sipping champagne at the Moulin Rouge.

His true calling came on a trip to Cuba. Zabalza went there for nine months' worth of instruction, aiming to join Che Guevara's adventure in Bolivia. Weeks into the training program he learned of Che's death. With that, all that was left was returning to Uruguay. His preparatory regimen had been intense and had turned him into an efficient *guerrillero* –particularly by the MLN's amateurish and inexperienced standards-, but the focus had been exclusively rural, in the tradition of the Sierra Maestra. Lessons on foraging and camping in the woods would be of little use in Montevideo.

The Cubans arranged in September of 1968 for Zabalza to meet a clandestine contact who could hook him up with revolutionary elements in Montevideo. The contact turned out to be none other than Ricardo Zabalza, Jorge's younger brother by five years. During Jorge's adventures overseas Ricardo had joined the small but growing MLN; now the brothers were reunited under the same revolutionary banner.

When Zabalza finally got to meet Sendic for the first time - already a famous figure in Uruguay-, he was disappointed: "The leader of the MLN was soft spoken, with a reedy voice and the mannerisms of a drab hick. How could this guy lead the country's toughest guerrilla organization?" Sendic, in contrast, was enthusiastic: he took Zabalza under his wing and asked him numerous times about his experiences in Cuba, about the lessons from the Sierra Maestra and the Vietnamese guerrilla, and about his advanced technical knowledge of operational planning.

Sendic tasked Zabalza with upgrading the UTAA group into a proper MLN column, and also with chaperoning a Brazilian named Roberto Manes. An officer of the Brazilian Army who had fled to Uruguay along with deposed dictator João Goulart and governor Leonel Brizola, Manes was friendly with the Tupamaros. They in turn sheltered him from the police's attempts to detain and extradite him. More often than not, Manes proved to be careless and an annoyance rather than a contribution.

The MLN cell in Punta del Este in February of 1969 was a motley crew that could not contrast more with the fanciest town in South America.[170] Sendic, as always, led by example: "Sky-blue pants, a Cuban guayabera shirt, and white espadrilles to walk the coastline of the Rough Sea Beach, while at the same time burying supplies, water, and weapons in various strategic points" Also bunking there was José Mujica, although he was not in town for an operation, and much less to enjoy the many qualities of *Punta.*

Rather, Mujica was in hiding because the police had detected him. The Tupamaro had been sitting on his toilet one day when he heard an excited radio broadcaster announcing he was riding with the police to arrest Mujica at his home. The Column 10 Tupa immediately fled and became a wanted man. It turned out Mujica had asked an acquaintance to hide some guns for him, but a maid had found them. Once the police became privy to this most exigent of favors, the man pointed the finger at Mujica, whom he knew as a "contrabandist". The demands of clandestine life proved too much for the amorous relationship Mujica had at the time with MLN beauty Yessie Macchi, which ended right around this time. On the flip side, the turn to clandestinity granted him an upgrade, whereupon he became the guerrilla commander for Column 10.

Meanwhile, in Punta del Este, the MLN deployed many of its "legal" cadres in surveillance of the target casino-hotel, including in the park across the street and in the form of couples strolling inside the facility. The objective was straightforward: fund-raising to increase the MLN's resources. The plot began thanks to a man named Honorio Grieco who worked at the complex. Grieco informed the Tupamaros of the best time to assault the administrative office and safe, and the MLN set up its cell to attack at precisely that moment.

The first half of the plan centered on the key-holder for the safe, a man named Sunhary. On the day of the operation, as he left for his lunch break at home, the team followed him from a safe distance. At a certain moment, two "policemen" approached the manager and said it would be necessary for him to accompany them because a robbery had taken place at the San Rafael. The policemen were in fact Tupamaros Lucas Mansilla and Ataliva Castillo, and providentially for them there indeed *had* been a disturbance in the San Rafael earlier in the day.

With the manager on board, Zabalza drove the van towards the hotel. He knew the area well because he and his family had traditionally vacationed in Punta del Este every summer. During the ride, Sunhary became nervous and the ruse was revealed: Castillo pulled out his Luger and subdued the frightened employee. During the confusion Zabalza almost crashed the van head-on into the car carrying none other than the Zabalza-Waksman family: his parents. Apparently, his cap and sunglasses did the trick and successfully hid his identity from his own relatives.

Upon arriving at the casino, three men got down and entered the premises: Sendic, sporting a business suit, and the two "policemen". Immediately upon breaching the entryway -thanks to their disguises- and revealing their true intentions, the Tupamaros saw a cleaning lady going into a nervous breakdown. The Tupas calmed her down by explaining who they were, what the objective of the operation was, and that no harm would come to her or any of the employees. With the crisis solved and the remaining staff (plus one addicted gambler seeking to play at noon) tied down, the Tupamaros used the manager's keys and emptied the casino of all $12 million in 2014 dollars of summertime revenues. Thanks to a strategically calculated long weekend, five days' worth of gambling was now in MLN hands.

Even before the group announced this operational success, it reaped the credit through the press. Reporting on the incident reflected the reputation the Tupamaros were acquiring: "There are very suggestive indicators pointing towards the possibility that this hit was the work of a commando team of the so-called MLN. These include the perfectly falsified police identification documents, the presence of an individual disguised as a policeman, the decent treatment of the victims [and] the adequate appearances that did not raise any suspicions".[171] The American embassy, doubtlessly in contact with police liaisons, could not help but report to Washington that "Sendic (...) is a master at covering his tracks. Even police officials show a grudging admiration for his skill in setting up the assault".[172]

There was more to the robbery. Sendic, noticing the Robin Hood image the group was acquiring, found out that part of the money they had stolen was destined to pay the casino workers' salaries and tips. Therefore, he decided to announce the MLN would rectify its actions and return the money belonging to the employees, and thus steal only from the "oligarchic" gamblers.[173] It was a brilliant propaganda coup, and it brought the Tupamaros a great amount of international attention. The news media in the United States, Canada, Britain, France, West Germany, and Italy began to cover the feats of the Tupamaros with increasing frequency. TIME magazine titled an article "Uruguay: The Robin Hood Guerrillas". In colleges and meetings of radicals, the MLN became a favorite topic of discussion, solidarity, and potentially of emulation.

The You-Know-Whos

These successful armed propaganda operations were accompanied by an epic wave of bank robberies. In just three months in early 1969, the MLN robbed at least fourteen of them, each time vanishing without casualties either on its side or among civilians and policemen. The Tupamaros justified their raids with pamphlets they left behind and handed to the customers briefly held hostage. The flyers partly read "Bourgeois property is our natural lifeline, and we reserve the right to expropriate it without any kind of compensation. The revolution helps itself to what the privileged have in excess".

A major casualty for the MLN of early 1969 was that of a second member –after the fall of Julio Marenales in October of 1968- of the leadership tetrarchy: Jorge Manera, the engineer. Manera was captured when visibly monitoring a police raid on an MLN safe house. A number of policemen surrounded him and the Tupas he was with; the Army's Colonel Ramón Trabal, detached to the National Police School, personally grappled Manera to impede him from pulling out his pistol.[174]

Hours later, the first policeman to interrogate Manera was an inspector named Conserva. When the Tupamaro refused to respond to his questions, the inspector began to beat him up. Alejandro Otero soon interrupted the session and shouted at Conserva: "'Inspector, in my department no one gets hit!'" The officer resisted and promised retaliation, but Otero prevailed and saved Manera from further violence. The Tupamaros, in turn, replaced the engineer with Efraín Martínez in the leadership, and operations continued. At the time, the four leaders of the MLN met once or twice a week to jointly decide on operations, statements, finances, and other matters.[175]

At the time the Pacheco government was still focusing much of its reaction to national instability not on the MLN –which remained mostly a police concern-, but rather on those who publicly spoke in their favor or appeared to be taking their side. Thus began a veritable escalation in the government's use of *medidas prontas de seguridad*, or prompt security measures.*

The measures enabled the executive branch to enforce limits on freedom of association and expression, as well as government interventions in the education and services sector. There was also an insistent use and abuse of censorship decrees. Newspapers like Época, El Popular, Extra, and even Pacheco's own Colorado Party's publications began to be banned temporarily over certain articles or words, including "Tupamaros". Other contents were also prohibited, notably the Gillo Pontecorvo movie "The Battle of Algiers", which accurately documented the insurgency of the Algerian FLN. Given

---

* An alternate translation is "limited state of siege".

the number of words banned from publication, people began to refer to the Tupamaros by various names in colloquial conversations: "the nameless ones, the bang-bangs, the you-know-whos".[176]

Politically, Pacheco was increasingly isolated from the Parliament and from important factions of his own party. A key driver of the split was that the Parliament adopted a greater oversight role of his tenure. In particular, the legislative body began to investigate -and verify- stories of police abuse of detainees, particularly among rioters and Tupamaros. The Parliament also voted to lift Pacheco's prompt security measures. The president, however, reinstated them each of the many times the lawmakers overruled them. This counterbalance to Pacheco helped the careers of many lawmakers, but the showdowns also built up the president's anti-subversive image.

The Tupamaros were undeterred by all of this. In fact, Pacheco's decrees only swelled their ranks, for they removed the legal platforms that many radicals and Marxists possessed to publicize their views. To many, this was proof of the truthfulness of the MLN perspective: a dictatorship was coming; the "system" was in its last reactionary throes, and it was time to push full speed ahead with the revolution. Aside from this recruitment boon, the government measures did complicate the MLN's operational range. According to Tupamaro Marcelo Estefanell, when prompt security measures were in effect, "There was no chance of meeting, it was impossible to gather groups of more than three people".[177]

The Most Effective Propaganda

The MLN maintained its ingenious approach to insurgency for a long time, thus solidifying its image as a witty organization. The spring-box devices first deployed in 1968 continued appearing throughout the city, to the annoyance and fright of some who were startled by the suddenness of the mechanism, and the delight of others who were beginning to spectate these events like a movie, playing out before their very eyes.

The messages the Tupamaros were disseminating were ambitious, with slogans like "The power of the people speaks through the muzzles of the clandestine rifles of the Tupamaros".[178] The Tupas' next major armed propaganda operation happened in

May of 1969. A hint lay in Che Guevara's manual on guerrilla warfare, where he wrote "The most effective propaganda (...) is that which is delivered orally by radio".[179] The Tupamaros took that statement and twisted it in a rather spectacular way.

The target for the operation was the transmitter for the popular radio station Sarandí.[180] Unbeknownst to anyone else, Tupamaros had quietly hovered around the bus stops and farms adjacent to the antenna. A Tupamara had entered the facility with a pretext to befriend the caretakers who manned the mostly automated installation. These reports confirmed there was minimal human presence inside.

Twelve Tupamaros (ten men and two women) arrived on the night of May 15 in a single Ford truck, with Sendic in command. The moment for the attack was chosen with special care: the broadcast of a key match of the world's oldest international football tournament, the Copa Libertadores. One of Uruguay's top two clubs was playing that night, so everyone was listening. The MLN's preparatory efforts went beyond actual necessity: the few people inside surrendered with barely an attempt to block the entryway. The Tupamaros did not need to pull out their weapons to get what they wanted. Thus were quickly subdued the caretaker and his family.

The MLN had done its homework: one of the Tupamaros present was a radio technician, who immediately set out to work on the station's systems. There were also attempts to gently calm the caretaker's family. Jorge Zabalza brought the man's wife a glass of water, while Sendic pulled out the musical toy he brought to keep the couple's son distracted.* By the time the technician got the MLN's recorded tape rolling, the first half of the match had already ended.

Suddenly, all those tuned in to Sarandí heard the signal change to an MLN announcement played on a loop. It was getting the greatest attention possible from a football-crazed society. An untold number of people was hearing, with full clarity, the group's propaganda. It was one of those moments when people looked stunned at their radios, and then at each other, simultaneously understanding what was happening and yet unable to believe it. The Tupamaros struck again; they were everywhere and nowhere.

---

* The child was not there; the toy was left anyway.

The recorded message, read out most likely by Eleuterio Fernández Huidobro, spoke against the Pacheco government, against his Minister of Foreign Affairs (top banker Jorge Peirano), against the United States, the International Monetary Fund, and a similar litany of ills.* Most urgently, the Tupamaros had a message for the Uruguayan population so aching from multiple political, economic, and social ills: "Uruguayans, those of you who suffer from penury and hardship because of a bad government should not lose hope". Help was on the way.

In total, the propaganda was broadcast for over forty prime time, maximum-audience minutes. The message looped six times before it was stopped. The police, Otero included, became so anxious at the lack of progress on the explosives the Tupas left blocking the door that they cut the power to the entire neighborhood. Soon after, ignoring the MLN's warning sign, they charged directly into the transmitting station.[181] The booby trap the sign had warned about was indeed there: "A few harmless fireworks".

The MLN continued to perform this kind of action, taking over radio stations to condemn the visit of United States Special Envoy Nelson Rockefeller and other major propaganda magnets, for years. Monitoring all of this, the U.S. Embassy was underwhelmed by the actual statements in the message. Nevertheless, it drew a comparison for Washington staff to understand what had taken place: "It is roughly as if the Students for a Democratic Society were to interrupt the broadcast of an NFL championship game in the U.S."[182]

My Theory!

The late 1960s continued to be a time of enormous upheaval and eventfulness for humanity. The Tupamaros, as busy as they were with their burgeoning insurgency, were not oblivious to that. On July 20 1969, NASA's Apollo 11 was about to achieve one of

* The International Monetary Fund has for decades been a favorite target of anti-capitalist thinking. What critics failed to realize was that in cases like Uruguay, the IMF's loans were a better deal for small Uruguay than for the governments that loaned the money. Without the IMF's funds, Uruguay could never have paid the generous salaries and benefits it had promised legions of state employees, retirees, and so forth.

mankind's greatest accomplishments: landing men on the moon. Naturally, even the Tupas were glued to their television screens for the occasion. That day, Zabalza, the action-hungry and Cuba-trained radical, was holed in a safe house with the exiled Brazilian Colonel Roberto Manes.

Visiting Zabalza was the leadership's Efraín Martínez Platero. The latter had recently been injured by another Tupamaro who had accidentally discharged his weapon and left him with a .45 caliber bullet lodged in his leg. The MLN performed clandestine surgery on Martínez, which left him temporarily walking on a cane. While in recovery, and obviously relegated from operations, Martínez was providing training and guidance to various members. His visit to the house where Zabalza and Manes were staying happened just in time for them to pause, sit down, and watch Neil Armstrong, Edwin Aldrin, and Michael Collins's own adventure take place on the television.

Manes was an odd character: "he was a strong guy, of strong build, but rather pint-sized; deep blue eyes, with a white beard (...) He was always clutching a revolver and a cat, with his hands pressed against his chest".[183] The colonel sat on his chair stroking the cat and providing live commentary on what was happening on the television. Neither Martínez nor Zabalza were particularly fond of the Brazilian, who was offered protection for reasons of ideology and solidarity. It made sense for the MLN to have powerful allies, particularly because no one knew who would be in power in which country in the future. Manes' name was in the newspaper as someone the Brazilian military regime wanted extradited due to his seditious dangerousness: they belonged to the same side.

The commentary Manes provided was, to say the least, disconcerting. Just as the Eagle landing module started its final descent towards the lunar surface, the colonel announced he had a "theory" he was eager to prove. His theory, as told to Martínez and Zabalza, was that there was oxygen on the surface of the moon. In fact, Armstrong and Aldrin should be capable of removing their helmets and breathing normally, an image Manes was anxious to see beamed back on the television. The mood was inevitably lightened when the Americans walked on the Moon and no such experiment was forthcoming. Manes despaired: "My theory! My theory!" he said grabbing his head and pacing the room. Martínez and Zabalza rolled on the floor, laughing at their wacky Brazilian friend.

After the broadcast ended, it was back to business for the small subversive cell. Martínez turned to Zabalza and began to introduce the new improvised grenades he had brought. Upon overhearing this from his couch, Manes interjected and asked for the whole lesson to restart, for he was fascinated by what was being said. As he put it, there was much he could learn from the Tupamaros on handling grenades and firearms. Once again puzzled by the colonel's interest in the most basic of military drills, Martínez resumed his lesson.

Manes interrupted again with a question. His concern was whether some kind of grenade could be assembled with two fuses. Why would he want two fuses, Martínez asked. Manes gave a bizarre explanation about having one fuse for "the people" and one for the "army". The grenade was to be simultaneously symbolic and real: it made no sense in either case. Martínez and Zabalza were outraged: here was the great hope, the experienced Brazilian colonel the Tupamaros could rely on to upgrade their combat capabilities, spewing lunacy on every topic imaginable. The cold, hard truth was that the Tupas would have to rely on themselves and themselves alone.

Just six days later, thanks partly to Manes' insistence on careless outings, the police raided the house. Otero's forces entered and captured the Brazilian only minutes after Sendic left the premises. Lying in wait for arriving Tupamaros they did fetch Zabalza, who lost his shootout with the cops and was promptly jailed.[184] Manes's rather unique personality remained on display, with police reports indicating he "described himself to arresting officers as 'supreme commander of the national army of liberation' of Brazil".[185] Under interrogation, Manes also gave away details of the Tupamaro, codenamed Álvaro, who wandered through safe houses teaching courses on explosives, and walking on a cane. It was one more clue for Otero and his detectives.

More captures slowly happened during 1969, although the structure of the MLN remained intact. One arrest that splashed across the front pages of the newspapers was that of Yessie Macchi, "an attractive young woman who was distributing MLN flyers".[186] Her physical attractiveness resulted in singular press coverage and further contributed to drawing a picture of the MLN as a diverse group. What was this organization exactly about, with members ranging from the engineer Manera and the political scion Zabalza to the daughter of retired colonel Macchi? All had diverse (and promising) backgrounds, and yet were members of an organization dedicated to revolution. With such people in the ranks, it was proving to have formidable capabilities.*

A Warm Welcome for Rockefeller

One non-armed propaganda operation in 1969 displayed an incipient terrorist deviation in the MLN: the nocturnal takeover of the General Motors complex outside of Montevideo.

The attack was timed to coincide with the visit of Nelson Rockefeller to Montevideo, as a symbolic double rejection of two major icons of American capitalism. The famed American company had invested in an automobile factory in Uruguay, but the Marxist discourse so insidious at the time saw anything American – particularly large corporations- as toxic and inherently vile. The company was also accused, more specifically, of supplying patrol cars to the Uruguayan police. As for Rockefeller, at the time he was the Governor of New York, and newly inaugurated president Richard Nixon's special envoy to the Americas.

Despite the high degree of intelligence the MLN displayed in its strategic and tactical plans, the attack on General Motors made little sense. After all, the classical complaint by top radical voices like Eduardo Galeano, Rodney Arismendi, Mario Benedetti, and others who shaped the thinking of the Tupamaros, was that Uruguay was a victim of international capitalism, as evidenced by its export-dependent economy. According to this ideological viewpoint, the country's prosperity flowed exclusively to a few families who owned most of the agricultural and cattle-breeding land. Those families exported the goods to "the north" and thus took for themselves the totality of Uruguay's cash riches. In other words, they sold out the country's resources to the empires of the world. In the meantime, the urban poor, the landless, and other disadvantaged classes were left without anything.

Per this manner of thinking, the better alternative was an independent path, in which industrial production rather than

---

* The loss of Macchi was a bitter blow for the MLN. She was a valuable *guerrillera* trained by Cuban professionals who fell in a minor, leaflet-distributing propaganda operation.

agricultural exports became the driver of value-added economic growth. In that sense, Uruguay's Marxists should have welcomed a factory producing automobiles, employing Uruguayan workers and managers who were in turn gaining essential technological knowledge – if only it had not been named General Motors. However, because it was, it had to be destroyed.

Once again in disguise, a small team of three Tupamaros made its way to the plant on the night of June 20. The chosen ruse was Air Force officers searching the premises for suspicious activities. The guards waved the Tupamaros in and were promptly subdued. Once free to "work", the three *guerrilleros* bathed the entire office complex in fuel oil and set it on fire. Although they were supposedly careful not to destroy the manufacturing plant itself (an indication that there were internal debates and compromises), damages were massive. It was the greatest catastrophic loss in the history of Uruguayan industry, equivalent to $6,500,000 in 2014 dollars.[187]

While the MLN shook the country with its raids and robberies, other groups, particularly among students, maintained their own radical "activism". Their acts of sabotage further contributed to the escalation in chaos and tension that now dominated Uruguay. In some educational institutions images of Che Guevara replaced national emblems, and the flags of Cuba or Communist Viet Nam replaced the Uruguayan one. The police were called in every day to respond to one disturbance or another. Tension and uncertainty became an everyday sensation, especially in Montevideo.

Another Kidnapping

In September of 1969 –a year after the Ulysses Pereira or "Birdie" operation- the MLN staged a second major kidnapping.[188] The target was wealthy Italian-Uruguayan businessman Gaetano Pellegrini Giampietro. A prominent banker and newspaper owner, Pellegrini was the son of a minister who had served under Benito Mussolini. A hardcore believer in that "cause" himself, Pellegrini is one of the few people to openly call themselves a fascist in an interview.* In Uruguay he was mostly associated with the Colorados.

---

* "Mussolini is one of the greatest men who have lived in this world", he maintained decades later.

Pellegrini appeared in the MLN's radar during consultations with the banking employees' union, AEBU, on how to help them prevail in a strike. The idea was that by abducting one of the top representatives of the business side of the labor dispute, they would be able to break the banks' back and force them to yield to AEBU.

Pellegrini was taken prisoner without incident; the squad that kidnapped him included a Tupa named Raúl Bidegain, to whom the media and police gave increasing prominence. The overall commander was once again Amodio, who by then had earned his own Sendic-bestowed nickname: *traca-traca*, after the sound a sub-machine gun makes when fired. The kidnappers took Pellegrini, just as had been done with Pereira, to a safe house with a hidden compartment (or in MLN jargon, "*berretín*") inside.

Conditions in the narrow *berretín* were terrible; Pellegrini was subjected to hostile treatment and minimal personal space, although he was not directly hurt. His space was limited to a tight, grave-like ditch on a dirt floor; conditions "could not have been worse". His interrogators, wearing hoods, saw in him a member of the "oligarchy" who was incapable of feeling solidarity towards the common man or worker. The hostage offered to leave the country forever if he was freed.[189] In the darkest moments, his kidnappers led him to believe his father and two of his children had died.*

Just three days after the banker was kidnapped, the Communist Party's top-ranking labor leaders decided to call off the banking strike, for reasons of strategic pacing.[190] This compromise removed a key component of the political-labor imagery behind the Pellegrini kidnapping. The Tupamaros thus had the choice of freeing their hostage, or of doing something else with him. They chose the latter, and turned the kidnapping into as much of an armed propaganda operation as possible.

The MLN's new demands were soon announced. Pellegrini would be freed without any ransom or labor demand. All that had to happen was that his bank make two generous donations: one to a public school in an impoverished area of Montevideo, and another to the medical clinic of a union cooperative.[191] The Tupamaros would not take a dime.

---

* Pellegrini says this was a personal form of torment on the part of the guards. Once the MLN leadership learned of this, the guards were reprimanded.

After months of intrigue and wrangling over these matters, and in defiance of orders beamed down by Pacheco, the MLN's demands were met: Pellegrini's associates wrote the required checks to the two institutions. The Tupamaros had indicated they would keep Pellegrini for only a month; they instead released him seventy-two days after his kidnapping.

The victim emerged emaciated and eager to leave Uruguay. He did just that, and did not return for decades. Journalist César Di Candia, who interviewed him immediately after his release, saw that "He had lost so much weight that his body wiggled inside his impeccable Italian-made cashmere suit. His eyes were bulging and lost, and he trembled constantly". Pacheco, on his part, ordered the members of his government who had helped in the negotiations to resign, and for Otero to debrief them.

Pando

Operations like the torching of General Motors and the kidnapping of Gaetano Pellegrini reflected the MLN's capability to act outside the confines of its armed propaganda doctrine. In October of 1969, with the organization on a roll of unstoppable actions, came the largest guerrilla operation in the history of the MLN.[192]

The occasion was the second anniversary of the death of Che in Bolivia, and the place was a small but strategic city thirty-two kilometers northeast of the capital called Pando. Although its permanent population was barely twelve thousand, Pando saw a permanent traffic of people and lorries passing through, given its position as an industrial satellite town of Montevideo. At the time, the MLN had a few hundred Tupamaros in activity and many more in its support network. The plan was ambitious: to take over the city for a short period of time. The operation would be a demonstration of insurgent power in a country that had rarely seen major breaks in law and order, much less of that scale.

Given the logistical requirements of the operation, for the first time all columns of the MLN participated. Almost all Tupamaro leaders would be present in the city. Only Efraín Martínez, still wounded after the friendly fire incident, stayed behind in Montevideo. Mauricio Rosencof of Column 10 came up with an idea for the insertion of a large number of armed men and women into town: a funerary procession, riding in five vehicles from Montevideo behind a hearse. The remaining half of the assault force would arrive in Pando by bus or other means of transportation. The overall commander, Amodio, would ride a motorcycle around the city to coordinate the actions of the different cells.

Pando was a comparatively simple target in that all of the MLN's objectives were close to each other, in or close to the main street. There would be six teams in total, one for each target. The police and fire stations -the main sources of government resistance- were the first two. Then came the telephone exchange, to guarantee the town lost its main communications with the outside world for the duration of the raid. Finally, three banks, including a branch of the large, state-owned BROU, were to be robbed. All would be taken at gunpoint; an unprecedented forty-nine Tupamaros would show themselves at the same time. To identify each other in the chaos to ensue, the Tupas operating in Pando would wear special white bracelets.

The operation began on the morning of October 8 with the arrival of the nine "bereaved" plus a "priest" at Martinelli, Montevideo's most reputable funerary home. From there, they boarded the rented vehicles to ride towards Pando. On the way, next to a parked blue Volkswagen Kombi, they picked up a total of ten "nephews" of the deceased, who would also be attending the burial, all carrying heavy bags. José Mujica was one of them. Each played his part, discussing the life of the deceased man, and firmly gripping their concealed weapon.

Six kilometers later, along the road leading to Pando, a signal was given and the drivers of all the vehicles were subdued. Once they were removed from their positions and placed in the MLN Kombi van, some Tupamaros changed into their disguises. The procession continued the short ride into Pando, with the Kombi following slightly behind.

While this meant twenty Tupamaros arrived in the procession, a further twenty-nine did so on their own means. Among them were two commanders dressed as sharply as possible: Sendic and Fernández Huidobro. They and others coming by bus or car brought their weapons disguised among fishing rods, briefcases, and other implements.

The main use of Rosencof's processional plan lay in that it provided a fast and camouflaged *exit* for all forty-nine, once each objective was completed with lightning speed. They would leave together in the black cars, and once outside of Pando the procession would be difficult to pin down as an MLN attack force. All entry, displacement, and exit times had been studied and timed.

The funerary convoy entered the city shortly after noontime without encountering obstructions. From inside a bar, sets of attentive eyes watched as the procession slowly drove by. Amodio, however, was late. He and his partner, Manuel Menéndez, were unsuccessful in hijacking a vehicle in time, so they ended up arriving in the city with the attack virtually underway. They had stolen a gray Peugeot automobile instead of a motorcycle, with a consequent loss of mobility once in Pando.

The attack on the city took a total of twenty-five minutes. It began with the most important of all the targets: the police station. In the minutes before 13:00, a series of people began to show up at its front desk. A psychologist and a sociologist were conducting an opinion survey; two bickering individuals had been in an accident in the street, and three were officers of the Air Force in full uniform. Each had a different errand or request to make of the police. In reality, all of them were Tupamaros from Column 15, secretly carrying sub-machine guns, and at the agreed time pointing them directly at the faces of the startled policemen.

Among this critical group of assaulters Amodio had placed his partner, Alicia Rey, and his successor at the helm of Column 15 since moving to the leadership, Alberto Candán. As the policemen were neutralized, one of the Tupamaros smashed the station's radio, and a smaller group went inside to capture whoever else remained; no shots had been fired yet. In the last room one officer resisted; shots and grenades were exchanged. Rey panicked and thought the operation had been ruined due to the loss of the surprise factor, but Candán steadied her, barking "Nobody's leaving this place, damn it!". Outside, a support squad waited in case it was needed. Inside, the cops were locked inside their own cells and had their weapons looted. Only one officer, named Tejera, escaped and ran towards the telephone exchange to call for help.

Once the police station was captured, Amodio, who had just arrived, drove by the designated operational area holding a white handkerchief out the window. It was the go sign. The other squads immediately got off their vehicles and assaulted the five remaining targets.

The crucial attack on the telephone exchange befell to Column 10, whose operational commander was Pepe Mujica. It was also staged from the inside: some of the customers already within the facility, perusing pay phones in booths, were Tupamaros hiding guns in their clothes and bags. At the appointed time, they came out and joined those just entering; a total of six men and one woman were there to neutralize Pando's communications.

Just then officer Tejera rushed into the telephone exchange intent on transmitting an alarm, only to find the Tupamara Ledis Castro, who hours earlier had been performing brilliantly as a grief-stricken daughter, pulling out her rifle and forcing him to surrender. The telephone operators were so stunned that they froze in their seats; they had to be shouted at and shoved away from their posts, and secured along with the clientele. While some *guerrilleros* disabled the communications systems, others prepared a fake explosive device to delay any restoration of communications once they left. Mujica himself briefly explained the operation and the usual MLN assurances, and requested technical assistance to disable the facility. His squad was early to leave after completing all its objectives; on the way out they subdued another policeman.

The largest bank in the city, the BROU, was the main fund-raising target. The task of robbing it fell on Column 20, under Sendic's personal command. Thirteen men and one woman made up the assault team.

Sendic, dressed as a bank executive and sporting a poorly accomplished blond dye -it looked carroty-, began by walking up to a sleepy guard, oblivious to what was about to happen, and forcing his entry into the bank with another Tupamaro. While the rest of the team assaulted the facility, Raúl Bidegain, dressed as a policeman, moved outside to provide some degree of cover for the operation, his sub-machine gun fairly visible. Pacing back and forth on the sidewalk by the bank's door, he stopped all individuals trying to enter the building or pass by it, and told them to keep their distance. As part of this effort, he helped an elderly lady and two schoolchildren cross to the opposite sidewalk to continue their commute: the charade had to be complete.

While being tied down, the civilians inside learned from the Tupamaros about the affiliation of the robbers and the reasons for their actions. One *guerrillero* named Solsona launched into a planned speech on Guevara and Latin American revolutionary thought for the benefit of the twenty-seven hostages.

The BROU attack suddenly went wrong when a gunshot was heard inside. As it turned out, a young Tupamaro named Fernán Pucurull had dropped his bracelet. The Tupamara in the team, Nybia González, had picked it up and, while clumsily handing it to Pucurull and holding her weapon, accidentally discharged the gun and hit her *compañero* in the spleen. Combining this with the insistent passing of the minutes, Sendic aborted the raid. With only half of the bank's money bagged, the team activated the evacuation plan. Pucurull was taken to the vehicle designated as the medical emergency center: the hearse, with the coffin still on top. The BROU team evacuated inside this "ambulance" and an additional vehicle at 13:14.

That was not close to being the only accidental shot in the Pando attack. At the Banco Caja Obrera Popular de Pando, the Column 5 assault team started with Alfredo Cultelli jumping over the counter and Ricardo Zabalza -brother of the imprisoned Jorge- shouting "this is a robbery, we are Tupamaros". Moments later, while bagging money, Cultelli accidentally discharged his Luger, although this time the bullets only hit the floor.

Nearby, Column 1's target was another bank only a few meters away, a branch of the Banco Pan de Azúcar. Commanding six Tupamaros there was Alfredo's father, Andrés Cultelli. This bank, as well as the fire station tasked to Column 15, was taken without incident.

With the gunfire coming from the police station and various other points, the police in the street prepared themselves for combat, and a shootout ensued. At roughly 13:15 almost all the Tupamaros in Pando were on the street, herding civilians, directing traffic, and rushing their return to the evacuation vehicles. Then the main firefight began. Most found cover behind cars or inside buildings, as the bullets flew and provoked a scene of massive chaos and shouting. People were shoved, windows were shattered, crowds burst about, all in response to the thundering of the firearms taking place along the street.

Although a number of policemen flinched from fighting, many responded to the MLN attack in spite of its intimidating dimensions: eight vehicles and close to fifty well-armed *guerrilleros*, all dressed as civilians, in a small area. One brave officer stood directly on the sidewalk to shoot at the Tupamaros robbing the Banco Caja Obrera Popular. They fired back and struck him in the head, blowing off his cap. The *guerrilleros* left him behind, but in reality only his hat had been shot off. The policeman recovered and rushed into a bar, from whence he resumed firing at the Tupas who were now boarding their vehicle.

With multiple cells having shootouts with the police, it became close to impossible for the MLN to coordinate actions or to determine who was where. An additional policeman named Heber Roncio followed his colleague's lead and entered a bar to benefit from cover while firing from the window. His was the same target: the escape vehicle under Eleuterio Fernández's command. The car was severely damaged.

Moments later, a third policeman named Ramón Britos engaged the same vehicle in the middle of the street. In the crossfire, in which Ricardo Zabalza loudly fired his sub-machine gun at his enemies from inside the moving vehicle, an innocent civilian named Carlos Burgueño was struck and killed. He was the first such casualty in the MLN insurgency.* Burgueño's wife had given birth to their son the day before, and he had stopped at a bar for a drink before heading to the hospital to visit. The Tupamaros have always held that policemen firing from the windows of the bar shot Burgueño, who by pure coincidence carried the same last name as the false dead person in their procession.

There were more civilians than usual in the sidewalks: dozens had grown curious about the various noises coming from the MLN operation, or had heard about what was happening and could not resist the idea of taking a look at the Tupamaros in action. Others, over forty in MLN estimations, had walked furiously to the telephone exchange, demanding their service be restored. The Tupamaros yelled out for them to stay away and remove themselves from the street, but the scene was too chaotic and events were moving too fast. In Mujica's recollection, "We had a crowd in there, people we had to subdue inside the facility, including some women going into hysterical fits, whom we managed to calm down (...) They were too many; near the end we must have had something like a hundred people in there. They were raining from every direction. Of

---

* The death of Dora López during the torching of the CSU union happened in 1962, years before the foundation of the MLN.

course we had not foreseen it! We did not think that when the phone lines were cut, people would go and protest at the exchange!"

According to Fernández, "My group was the most shot up of all during the evacuation; the car looked like a colander. Bullets flew everywhere. We told people to stay indoors, because they went out to have a look; guys were leaving the pubs with glasses in their hands. Uruguayans are somewhat careless, possibly because they do not have mandatory military service and thus do not know what a ricocheting bullet can do". Eleven days after the attack, policeman Enrique Fernández died of wounds sustained from MLN gunfire during the shootout.

Escape From Pando

To close the operation, the Tupamaros dropped various leaflets around the targets, raised the MLN's flag, and re-boarded their vehicles, with the crowds spreading apart to let them sprint. Throughout, numerous witnesses later reported supporting the police and helping them single out Tupamaros. The *guerrilleros*, in turn, recall demonstrations of support from the populace. Behind, one Tupa concentrated in propagandizing about Comrade Che forgot to evacuate, and the others in turn forgot about him: he was left behind for the police to capture easily.

The vehicles left in a slow convoy formation; Amodio drove his stolen Peugeot in front, and had to swerve at the last moment to simultaneously avoid running over the policeman Britos and to furiously ram the vehicles placed as obstacles, thus punching a way through for the others. With the way cleared, the rest of the vehicles took off, although gunfire crippled three of them. The sound of gunfire, bank alarms, and furious car horns to clear the streets enveloped the getaway of the Kombi van, five funerary vehicles, and Amodio's car.

The convoy rode painfully slowly: no more than 60 km/h. It briefly stopped at a cemetery to restore the order of each column. There was tension, excitement, anxiety, and glee over the successful raid. Amodio fired his pistol in the air to summon his group, while everybody rushed towards the correct vehicle per their instructions. Meanwhile, the national police had learned about the raid and raced to the city. Alejandro Otero was among them, rifle in hand. Close by were detachments of the police's best combat units: the Republican and Metropolitan Guards. The Tupamaros attempted to reconstruct the funerary procession, but that critical part of the plan failed: the vehicles left the cemetery at different times, and thus three of them (two cars and the Kombi) took the wrong route.

The Kombi and the vehicles from the BROU and fire station raids, which took the wrong rural path, met two police patrol cars on the other side of a small bridge. It was around 13:40, and thirty Tupamaros were now temporarily blocked from escaping. The *guerrilleros* abandoned their vehicles and a furious firefight ensued. While many of the Tupas at the scene, including Raúl Sendic, stayed to shoot back and later flee by riding a suburban public bus, twenty others ran cross-country to escape.* One Tupamara had to do so in heels and a skirt. She recalls Sendic seeking to put some order, but the situation was too frantic: "Don't run, god dammit!"

As sirens blared and helicopters approached, a few Tupamaros escaped. Many others, despite their attempts to use tall grasses and trees as camouflage, were progressively cornered by a force of one hundred members of the police Metropolitan Guard. Crossing creeks, undulated terrain, fields, farms, and woods, the dispersed Tupamaros were increasingly alone, tired, and in panic. According to one *guerrillera*, being in a furious shootout made her realize "fear has its adrenaline component, I did not know that before. Your mouth turns into a paste of sorts".

Ultimately, three Tupas met their end in a final stand in the fields outside of Pando, shot and killed by the "Metro". The first of them, Jorge Salerno, had participated in the opening assault on the police station. He was twenty-four years old. Before being gunned down he opened fire and threw a grenade in the proximity of a school packed with children, causing nearby windows to explode and the students to dive for cover. Shortly afterwards, four Tupamaros burst into the school, engaged in a shootout with the police, and ended up surrendering.

During these chases MLN founder Eleuterio Fernández was wounded and captured; in his recollection, "I had never felt so many bullets buzz by above my head (...) you could hear gunfire and sirens

---

* Sendic made it out, just barely, in a small truck the MLN had deployed to transship the loot.

everywhere". In total fifteen more Tupamaros joined him in police custody; it was the greatest catch since the start of the conflict.

In contrast to the incidents in the fields of Pando, the vehicle carrying Column 10 had sped by itself through a longer route, and had fared best of all: it escaped to Montevideo without incident. After transshipping into a vehicle and a safe house, where they celebrated with the wounded Martínez Platero, the squad members followed Mujica's orders and sat down at a bar to hear the news over the radio, to which everyone in Uruguay was now glued.

In Punta Carretas prison, the main one in Montevideo housing virtually every Tupamaro captured, the large number of jailed MLN members also learned of the operation through the airwaves. Once the radio announced the city of Pando was under attack, the celebratory shouts from the many cells occupied by Tupamaros became deafening to the worried guards. The mood changed when, later in the day, the announcers broadcast the names of those killed in action. In his cell, powerless, Jorge Zabalza heard the name of his younger brother Ricardo added to that of Salerno. He was "left in shock, like a sleepwalker. He spent the night in silence, reviewing the cascade of images and voices that plunged him into the mental state closest to madness". The third dead Tupamaro was Alfredo Cultelli. He fought alongside his father Andrés in Pando. Both Alfredo Cultelli and Ricardo Zabalza had been in the initial funerary procession that entered Pando. Before the day was over, the senior Cultelli saw a picture of his dead son in the evening newspapers.

The Pando raid electrified the country, but not in the same way as the previous MLN operations. The deaths of the civilian Burgueño and of the policeman Enrique Fernández, not to mention the massive shootout in the middle of a busy city, scared the public. The MLN insurgency was the central fact of political life; to many it was a matter of constant attention. Some in the police thought Pando was so violent that it stopped the MLN's series of successes. After all, of the close to fifty Tupamaros who had partaken in the operation, nineteen had been taken out: sixteen captured and three killed.

The U.S. country team in Uruguay, internally, felt the same way: "Public Safety advisors pleased with sure direction of operation and cooperation of all forces involved".[193] However, Alejandro Otero of police intelligence firmly believed "the Tupamaros were not done (...) ours had been a partial victory (...) and we had not yet won the war".[194]

The captured Eleuterio Fernández joined fellow MLN founders Julio Marenales and Jorge Manera in prison. With Fernández out and replaced by Lucas Mansilla, Raúl Sendic was the only remaining member of the original leadership tetrarchy, which was now made up of himself, Héctor Amodio, Efraín Martínez, and Mansilla.

Clues gathered from the identities of the Tupamaros killed in Pando allowed the police to track down some of their support networks and safe houses. Otero's forces successfully netted many *guerrilleros* during the subsequent weeks. To compensate for the unexpected loss of most of the Pando bounty, Mujica's group conducted a couple of robberies to sustain the MLN's finances. One of them, on October 15, was at another financial investment firm, named Etcheverrigaray-Petcho, which once again failed to call on law enforcement for help. Therefore, the Tupamaros themselves denounced the hit: the *financiera* had been involved in illegal dealings and was trying to hide it even after being robbed.[195] In the days after Mujica and his colleagues ensured the newspapers learned of the illegal investment banking activities, and also launched more robberies to strengthen the MLN's strained finances.

The Blows Are Absorbed

The Tupamaros were well prepared for anything the police might throw at them. They provided members with training in counter-interrogation techniques, in resisting beatings and torture (to the stern Marenales, the former could not qualify as the latter), and in carrying plastic tubes with money and other items inside their anuses. Furthermore, there was a whole array of clandestine MLN resources becoming increasingly available to them, as their recruitment numbers exploded: safe houses, hideouts, multiple false documents (and facilities to produce new ones), medical clinics with surgery and ambulance capabilities, psychological therapy services, plastic surgery services, aerial transportation, lawyers, and more. One internal message making the rounds read: "The health service requests the following information from each *compañero*: tetanus vaccine, typhus vaccine, diphtheria vaccine, smallpox vaccine, and blood type".[196]

As Leonardo Haberkorn has noted, "that creativity, those resources put in the service of the group, contributed to generating the sensation that the MLN was invincible".[197] The Tupamaros could excel at their trade: the owners of safe houses could house a Tupamaro for week, recovering in one of their children's beds, and not see his face once.[198] Not seeing, hearing, or knowing was a cardinal security principle, and according to all accounts the highly motivated MLN followed it brilliantly.

Historian Clara Aldrighi, a Tupamara herself, suggests that the Pando raid reinforced the MLN's recruitment; "It seemed like the flame of revolution was lighting up Uruguayan society, judging by the number of volunteers knocking on the doors of the organization".[199] Some of the new recruits were being deployed in an operational track different from armed propaganda: Line H, for "hostigamiento" or harassment. Line H was the urban equivalent of classic guerrilla warfare: striking directly at the enemy's forces by surprise, and fleeing before any response was possible. Examples of Line H included the assassination of a policeman riding a city bus and of another one who was trying to arrest Tupamaros. Two more policemen were shot and killed, each with over ten bullet wounds in his body, by Tupamaros robbing banks.[200]

A lighter form of Line H involved disarming policemen in the street and in their homes: in those cases they were more humiliated than hurt. Disarming operations also revealed the MLN had access to the personal information of individual officers, with the consequent psychological and morale implications in the ranks. At one point these were combined with sabotage against the country's power company UTE, with a series of planned "hits" against hapless cops using the distraction of the blackout. Perhaps no one has better summarized what it was like to live through such incidents like the Colorado politician Sanguinetti, who wrote "Every day there was news that shook the Uruguayan populace".[201]

A Bank Caper

There was one more spectacular MLN operation before year's end. The target was the Banco Francés e Italiano, another bank right in the midst of Montevideo's financial district.[202] There were twenty days' worth of intelligence collection and analysis ahead of the attack. The commander was the group's most capable: Amodio, who led it himself. The plan began around 19:40 on the evening of December 27, when the bank was already closed to customers but the employees were still inside, wrapping up the day's affairs. As the agreed hour approached, a series of individuals began to appear near the bank: lurking in bus stops, circling the block to park vehicles, chatting on the sidewalk. In total, there were eight men and two women gathering for the operation. At one point, in a very Uruguayan scene, one of the *guerrilleros* ran into an acquaintance that happened to stroll by. A conversation about bus routes and various things began to take place, naturally causing the Tupamaro to become anxious – although he could in no way show it.

The main doors to the bank were long closed, but the plan was for a "delivery man" to come to the service entrance with a tray of pastries –a typical gift from grateful business associates during that time of the year- that needed a signature from the doorman. However, the MLN was unable to steal a proper bakery delivery van in time, so instead a bomb threat became the ruse. The person knocking on the door was thus a "messenger" from a well-known postal agency, sporting its familiar uniform. Once the bank's guard opened the door for the messenger and they started talking, two policemen from Otero's Intelligence and Liaison division interrupted: there was an emergency. The police had detected an MLN attack on the bank, and it was necessary for the officers to check to determine whether there were timed explosives or infiltrators inside. The messenger became a suspect, so he was told to get in as well.

Once inside, the policemen –joined by four officers from the police's bomb disposal squad- gathered all employees and announced an MLN attack was set to take place against the bank. They would have to stay within the facility and cooperate while they investigated various potential entry points. The officer in charge told the employees to "Please not touch anything; do not press buttons nor pick up your telephones, because the bomb might go off". The employees then examined the main floor with some of the policemen, while the rest checked the building for potential loose ends.

Naturally, the messenger and the policemen were Tupamaros: they themselves were the threat. After some time they abandoned the conceit for the benefit of the thirty hostages. In the MLN's telling: "'Well, gentlemen, the bomb thing was a joke' –mumbling, relieved smiles-, 'but what is not a joke is that we are Tupamaros and we are here to take the treasury and some documents' (...) A secretary faints, but most people remain calm". The employees far exceeded the Tupamaros in number but had been tricked into a captive situation. More Tupamaros arrived through the side door and set for their big prize: opening the main safe.

There was, however, a problem: three keys were needed to open the vault, and only one was then at the bank. The other two were in the hands of a manager who had already left for home. A decision had to be made: the operation would be abandoned, or the vault would be opened one way or another. Amodio, the "messenger", chose the boldest option: to directly seek the manager with the two missing keys, and bring him over to open the safe. A major obstacle emerged: the man in question, named Baracco, was not at home but rather at a social event attended by hundreds of people, eating dinner.

Despite these difficulties, the Tupamaros went there and, always as policemen, gently notified the man that his colleague –the manager still at the bank- had committed suicide. It was necessary for him to come with them, with the keys, to perform routine security checks. Baracco had a surprise for the Tupamaros: he did not have the keys either. He had in turn given them earlier to a third manager, named Brunetto, who was at home. Improvising, the MLN "police" team drove to Brunetto's home, knocked on the door, and explained the situation once again. More obstacles appeared: "He does not pose any objections, but because his wife is quite jealous she demands the policeman show identification that proves this is not a ruse for his husband to go out for a night of merriment. It would seem like the man was a specialist in pulling tricks on his poor wife".

In the meantime, the employees of the bank were subjected to propaganda speeches, and the raiders used a list provided by union contacts to separate and reprimand employees who were anti-union. The telephone calls of relatives worried over their excessive tardiness had to be screened. Excuses had to be made up, although in one case the wife of manager Franco Berri personally went to the bank to verify her husband's story – and joined the ranks of the hostages. One of the Tupamaras took special care of Victoria Rey, the female employee who went through a nervous breakdown. Another employee, who was carrying a large sum of money among his personal effects, was allowed to keep it, for that was not the target of the MLN's operation. The Tupas mostly tried to soften an inherently tense situation: if for some reason the police found out about the attack, a standoff could result in the unimaginable.

In the end, close to three hours passed with the bank under MLN control - and no one in the outside world noticed. When Brunetto the manager arrived with the keys and saw the bags filled with the documents lying on the floor, he became pale, and the cops revealed the truth. Despite their best efforts, the *guerrilleros* were unable to get the keys working, and in frustration broke the safe's lock. With no alternatives left, they locked the employees behind a barred door, with the keys in full view of anyone who walked in, and called the police. The operation was abandoned, although the MLN counted it among its clearest demonstrations of operational capacity against hard targets. The big loser was Federico Repetto, the employee who conceived the operation and "sold" it to the Tupamaros in exchange for 80% of the money inside the vault. Instead, the yield of the operation was only fifteen bags' worth of sensitive bank documents.

Rendez-Vous With Glory

The year's end augured well for the MLN. It had accumulated increasing material resources in the form of money, weapons, safe houses and support networks. Its operations spoke for themselves, particularly in their public impact and humiliation of the government. Even among the military there were individuals amused and intrigued by the spectacular armed propaganda actions of the Tupamaros.

The MLN also received some positive press coverage and reasonable measures of public support and tolerance as measured by opinion polls and accounts from the time. Nevertheless, in the overall picture the vast majority of Uruguayans was still outraged and wary of a group that was, after all, robbing and bombing banks, killing policemen, and pulling off acts like Pando that endangered the working folk in their daily business. According to one Gallup poll, 48% of Uruguayans thought the Tupas were "highly dangerous".[203] The MLN's degree of success was thus in comparison to a year and beyond before, and the Tupamaros were mindful of this.

The death toll for 1969 was five Tupamaros (three in Pando plus two in separate incidents), five policemen (four in combat, one murdered in cold blood) and three civilians (Burgueño in Pando plus a private arms collector and a bank guard) killed in MLN operations. It was completely unprecedented in Uruguayan history. Virtually all of it was taking place right in the midst of the city's capital, day in and day out. The question on everyone's mind was first, where might the Tupamaros strike next, and second: will I be there when it happens?

In its typically analytical and self-reflective style, the group produced a private written review of the year. There was obviously a great degree of satisfaction; few organizations in history could point to a more productive and successful twelve months. In the telling of hardline Tupamaro Samuel Blixen, it was easy to imagine Pacheco being "lonesome, chewing on his envy over the ratings his hated enemies were reaping day after day".[204] In internal deliberations many Tupas were already talking of reaching the stage of the insurgency equivalent to Mao and Castro's final descent from the mountains and into the capital cities. The revolution seemed to be at hand; the Viet Nam-like foco Guevara had requested was finally burning.

The authors of the yearly review had a more sober look they wanted to impose on these anxious ranks.[205] In their view there was also no question the MLN was on a roll, but victory was not imminent: "Many expected a 'rendez-vous with power' for 1969, a 'rendez-vous with glory' for the year that just passed (...) To play the card of the masses, to be the *foco* of the size that everyone discusses, is not child's play (...) This [next] stage will thus be harder than the previous one, for it has superior objectives".

The strategic picture was also clarified: before January of 1969, the struggle had been "for the organization". In other words, the MLN had fought for the sake of its own existence and growth. Since then, with the armed propaganda campaign, the struggle for the people themselves had truly begun. The results were positive: with over one hundred operations, of which the MLN counted seventy-seven of significance, the leadership concluded "In the current Latin American outlook, we appear to be the guerrilla with the best military pace and with the greatest impact".

It was not a minor statement to make: from Mexico to Antarctica, there was no other insurgent organization active in the

Americas with an equal degree of operational success, efficiency, public acceptance, and international renown. In neighboring Brazil, the radical Marighella was also hijacking radio stations,[206] and more famously publishing his "mini-manual" for urban terrorist and guerrilla operations in June. His uprising met its demise before year's end.

The MLN leadership, like a board of directors at a major corporation, identified mistakes, successes, emerging challenges, and recommendations for the future. That very issue of international success was a priority: the *dirección* recommended the creation of a subdivision dedicated exclusively to international liaison. Given its growing contacts with fellow radicals in Cuba, Brazil, Chile, Bolivia, and Argentina –with many more to come-, plus the attention of the media in North America and Europe, the MLN was in need of a dedicated diplomatic corps of sorts.

A more immediate obstacle was the increasing efficiency of the police. The MLN was still far ahead of it, but the Metropolitan Guard was becoming a more impressive combat force: encounters with them were likely to go badly for the Tupamaros. The detectives were also not letting up: Otero and his men hunted the Tupas relentlessly. There had been casualties; security had been lax in many cases. Every fall of a Tupamaro rippled beyond the individual: he or she could lead, willingly or not, to the names and locations of other people. Weapons, documents, and other resources could be lost. Furthermore, fallen Tupamaros were difficult to replace with a fresh recruit as experienced as the original, particularly when referring to the founding generation.

In order to tackle these problems, the leadership also proposed the creation of a service dedicated to overseeing intelligence and counter-intelligence. At the same time, compartmentalization was to be tightened to protect the security of the organization. Even unpunctual Tupamaros were to be reprimanded for risking the security of others.

With these fixes in discussion, the MLN found itself fully primed to repeat and improve on its feats in 1970. Late 1969 propaganda was typically poetic: "we are inspired by nothing other than the possibility of ending the enormous injustices of this regime, whose limousines and palaces we see next to malnourished, school-less children, of this regime of bungalows and hovels".[207]

Chapter Seven:

The People Passed Through Here
Armed Propaganda in 1970

WITH THE SUCCESSES of 1969, there was no question that many Uruguayans approved of the Tupamaros' actions. Some joined or helped the group, and others admired them silently. A neutral observer at the time, independent and democratic socialist Hebert Gatto, has observed how during this Robin Hood period, "the populace enjoyed [the group's] capacity to make a mockery of the government (...) The solemnness, the elegance, and the wit on display in some of these first operations became veritable legends, particularly when contrasted with the clumsiness of a police force scarcely prepared to face an insurgency of a far superior cultural level".[208]

The internal MLN review of 1969 acknowledged this, and summarized plans for 1970 with the slogan "More Monty, less Pando".[209] In other words, more armed propaganda and less guerrilla warfare was the optimal strategic path.

In spite of said plans, the new year began with the police forces feeling the heat of the Tupamaros' *hostigamiento*. There were attacks everywhere. One officer was shot in the neck while defending his house from an MLN raid.[210] The police were furious, a fact verified by increased reports of violent interrogations –the detainees invariably called it torture- taking place in their facilities.

The Police Reshuffle

To top this off, on January 14 the star detective Otero was transferred out of the police's Intelligence and Liaison division. The reprimand was over an interview he granted an Argentine magazine in which he spoke absent-mindedly of entering politics and of moving to Brazil to become a football referee. Otero had also acknowledged police brutality.

The famous *comisario* has always blamed the United States country team in Uruguay for this removal, in particular the CIA's William Cantrell. The reason for this enmity is that the United States, through the OPS program, was fostering the creation of a new unit within the Ministry of the Interior to replace Otero's. He had repeatedly fought back against such efforts, and blocked American advisors from gaining too many inroads into his work.

There was no love lost on the other side: "Police officials tired of his headline hunting at expense of intelligence officers who do real work (...) Otero has been long-time source of friction in intelligence unit because he seeks personal publicity (...) and has incorrectly become identified in public mind as the official responsible for Tupamaro defeats (...) there are several capable police officers able to take over intelligence division".[211] One of them was Víctor Castiglioni, a former bodyguard of President Pacheco.

With Otero out, and thanks especially to OPS's efforts, a new detachment was created under Castiglioni: the Dirección Nacional de Inteligencia y Enlace. A *Dirección* was an upgrade over the previous *División*, and it was given most if not all of its predecessor's activities. However, successful police work was about more than shuffling personnel: at least one member of the unit, Raúl Zuloaga, turned out to be working for the MLN – and he would not be the last.[212]

Police techniques were another focus, although not as prominent as the organizational reforms. A preferred tactic in the fight against the Tupamaros was nicknamed the *ratonera*, or the mousetrap. It was a classic urban feint: tracking down an MLN safe house, breaking and entering once it was empty, and then waiting for the Tupamaros to arrive and arrest the entire cell. That was how Jorge Zabalza had been captured the previous year, as had many others. This forced the Tupamaros to design a system of "alarms" that would prevent them from falling into a *ratonera*.*

While the police continued to have the occasional success, particularly when it came to headline-grabbing arrests, in the overall picture the MLN was progressing at stunning speeds. As Tupamaro Luis Nieto explains, during this period "When [the police] conducted raids, we already knew they were coming, because every afternoon we had meetings with MLN members who worked in the courts, and got us a list of search warrants"[213]. The historian Aldrighi further explains this dramatic intelligence capability of the Tupamaros: "some members were placed in nerve centers of the state bureaucracy, in the Judiciary, in the Civil Service, in the Police, in the military and in large private companies; others were related to legislators or politicians from both the traditional parties and from the left".[214] The Tupas had eyes and ears everywhere.

The Pacheco administration faced more than just the armed siege of the MLN. Partisan politics were growing red hot. By 1970 it was clear that the increasingly estranged Parliament had one star legislator in its floor: Senator Wilson Ferreira of the Partido Nacional.

Ferreira was a master at grilling the government's ministers in hearings, who often felt compelled to resign afterward. He was also relentless in his attacks on the government and its policies in general, beyond specific gripes with one minister or another. Toeing a populist line that combined nationalism and socialism, Ferreira had his eyes set on the 1971 election that would produce Pacheco's replacement. The terrible results of the Colorado government so far bode well for his aspirations.

Meanwhile, on March 31, Parliament passed a symbolic but unnoticed law: the state at last took over the rural lands the UTAA marches of the early 1960s had demanded be "expropriated".[215] The *estancias* became part of the government's "colonization" program, one of the favorite institutions of Uruguay's proponents of state-driven collectivism. The expropriation was an indication that the country's political-economic system was far from being "oligarchic" or overly capitalistic. It also provided clear evidence that a

---

* MLN alarms consisted of agreed-upon decorative arrangements, or object placements, to indicate whether it was safe to approach or not.

progressive Parliamentarian path could get UTAA and others to their initial objectives, although by 1970 this was long in the past.

Opening Moves

One MLN operation after another proved how formidable the Tupas had become. In February they robbed the main branch of the BROU in the northern city of Salto, 420 kilometers from the capital. The heist yielded a substantial sum, for the time and for the size of the bank, of $140,000 in 2014 dollars. It was vintage MLN logistics: an insider had "given away" the target, and enabled the entire operation to be minimally violent. The punchline was that the insider was no bank teller: he was the branch's deputy manager.[216]

More importantly, early 1970 saw a daring raid entitled Operación Paloma, or Operation Dove.[217] The date was March 8 – International Women's Day, an unplanned coincidence-, and the target was the Montevideo prison facility where captured Tupamaras were held. The commander of the operation was, once more, Héctor Amodio Pérez. His plan was surprisingly simple, thanks to the incredibly permissive conditions at the facility.

The prison housing the Tupamaras was nominally under the aegis of the Ministry of the Interior, but in reality nuns ran it from an adjacent convent. Naturally, the sisters did not carry firearms, and their guardianship regimen was not exactly tough for the Tupamaras. Although most if not all of the *guerrilleras* were non-believers, they were nevertheless helping with services and other activities in the main chapel. The temple had a door that led directly to the street.

Operación Paloma was concordantly straightforward. A total of eleven men, two women, and four vehicles made up the team executing the plan. It started by feigning an injury, summoning an ambulance, and hijacking it. Adopting the identities of the medical staff, they drove to the prison and parked outside the chapel doors. The rest was simple considering what the MLN was capable of: "There were ten minutes left before the start of mass when the phony male nurse entered the church. Almost immediately two additional parishioners entered and, mingling with the others, resolutely made their way to the altar. Once there they pulled out their firearms –so did the nurse- and with them subdued not just the stunned attendants, but also some guards standing by the barred door that connected the nave to the prison facility (...) in five minutes the patient [police] work of one year had been undone". All the women had to do was walk out the front door and be driven away.

Thanks in part to this operation, Amodio's reputation increased significantly. In fact, his Column 15 was fast becoming an outsized component of the MLN. Amodio, always its supervisor from the *dirección* apart from being its founder, imposed a clear set of criteria for the unit. Famed for his studiousness and methodical conduct in the planning of every operation, the former printer rarely made a mistake when it came to operational security, counter-intelligence, safety procedures, and contemplating every potential contingency in advance. His safe houses were always tidy; his weapons were clean and loaded; everyone under his command knew where they were supposed to be and what they were supposed to do.

New recruits often asked specifically to be sent there. The unit's allure lay in its high frequency of operations and its remarkable rate of success and impact. Fresh Tupamaros who wanted to see a lot of action often joined to operate under Amodio and his lieutenants, which included his partner Alicia Rey and his chosen successor at the helm, Alberto Candán. Eleuterio Fernández has said that at the time Amodio's prestige in the MLN was greater than Sendic's. Others recall a "legend" around him: "that he was a daredevil, that the cops were afraid of him".[218]

Amodio may not have made it to the original leadership tetrarchy, but he had been the first to join it after the capture of the sculptor Marenales. His importance was underlined with the creation of a new position for him. It was called Inter-Columns Coordinator, and it granted him a say in the actions and decisions of every part of the MLN. The post functioned like a commanding height with a unique view of the secretive MLN. At the same time, a gap emerged between Amodio and the rest of the leadership.[219]

The Consolidation of the Columns

In particular, the contrast between Sendic and Amodio grew over time. According to one Tupamaro who remains anonymous, "Amodio was very efficient and *El Bebe* was a genius, although administratively he was not efficient (...) *El Bebe* mixed up his contact papers, he could have forty of them in his pocket (...) He had everything mixed up and his rustic condition as a *paisano* could not be overlooked".[220]

There were key lifestyle differences at stake. Sendic was representative of a unique breed of *gaucho* mindset, a man with an automatic low profile, a soft, almost thready voice, a modest personal appearance, and yet an enormous self-confidence and decisiveness of action. The column of the interior was almost purely under his aegis. At the same time, as usual, "he himself asked not to be taken as a figure of reference".[221] In the recollection of Tupamara Cristina Cabrera, "If there was cleaning to be made he would do it himself. If there was a need to 'squeeze' [MLN jargon for hijacking] a car he would go first".[222] Sendic remained the fascinating leader by example, the man of few words and significant actions.

On the other hand, Amodio was a creature of the city, of the industrial working classes and their unions, cheap leather jackets, motorcycles, and desires and expectations for a certain quality of life. Many would come to notice how these small contrasts manifested themselves: Amodio dressed better, drove better vehicles, drank better liquors, and smoked better cigars. Sendic was often mistaken for a lowly *peón de estancia*. Yet, the latter came out as the deeper and more sophisticated of the two. As one Tupamaro explained, "Sendic was the one who thought the most, but he did not look the part. It is one thing to plan the game, and another to plan the full championship. Amodio was important for one match, but *El Bebe* was essential for the championship. He was a guy who was somatically stricken with strategy".[223]

Other columns associated with neither Sendic nor Amodio had different reputations. For instance, Column 10, where José Mujica and later Macchi herself operated, was known as a more easygoing column. According to member Celeste Zerpa, "We were more humane, more sensitive. The news that arrived from Column 15 was scary. They thought we did not pull off enough operations, they dismissed us as 'pub-dwellers' (...) On the other hand, we looked at them with a certain envy, as the strong column, the 'heavies'. Sometimes we prepared something and after a month it was yet to be executed, so the leadership would take it away from us and two days later Column 15 would pull it off. No matter how it needed to be done, they did it. They were overachievers. They would perform up to four operations per day, while we did one per month".[224]

These leadership and column dynamics became increasingly important as the MLN grew in size and status. Just as in 1969, in 1970 the main campaign was armed propaganda. However, new developments caused an increase in the number of non-armed propaganda actions. One of them was the breakneck rise in new recruits, particularly in Column 15. The MLN's youngest and freshest Tupamaros were also some of the most violence-prone.

Another factor enlarging the range of MLN activities was the necessity of "responding" to the group's armed opponent, the police. The deaths and torments of Tupamaros necessitated, in their mind, a violent response to demonstrate the organization was capable of fighting a real war. Many thought escalation would speed up the advent of the revolution. Lastly, the Tupamaros' own founding documents had contemplated that sooner or later they would have to move from "feel-good actions" to more traditional guerrilla-style operations. It was, they thought, the only way to become more than a group merely nibbling at the edges of Uruguay's political and social structure.

A Stern Warning

One of the most dramatic and decidedly non-armed propaganda operations of this period was the Tupamaros' first targeted assassination. The objective was high-ranking police officer Héctor Morán Charquero, head of the police's Brigada Especial and "one of most effective police agents against terrorist MLN-Tupamaros".[225]

The MLN's case against Morán was plain: the man was a brute, a torturer, and a thief.[226] He had allegedly used an electric prod on captured Tupamaro Rodebel Cabrera for over an hour, not to mention his beatings of common criminals as reported to Tupas through the prison underworld. This was not just hearsay: Morán did have a voluminous file in the courts, with plenty of paperwork on previous complaints and disciplinary measures. He had also stolen repeatedly from crime scenes and partaken in contraband. To top all this off, Morán had more than once bragged about his actions, and responded with bravado to the notion that he could become a target for the enemy.

The cop had been lucky lately: an MLN safe house had fallen to the police, and in it were found dossiers and draft plans for a strike against him. The Tupamaros had never conducted a targeted hit before, but Morán did change his routes out of precaution. This did not stop the Tupamaros: their many eyes were already set on him.

The attack was to take place at a point in Morán's daily commute. It was in a bend in the famous kilometric *rambla* or seaside promenade, one of Montevideo's finest areas. Vehicles there often traveled at high speeds, but to compensate for this there were few escape vectors, and even less in this particular section in the Parque Rodó area.

The MLN deployed two vehicles with three Tupamaros each. Every *guerrillero* was carrying a powerful gun, and some brought grenades. The designated killer would use a nine-millimeter Star sub-machine gun to fire directly at Morán.

The cars waited for the target, looking in opposite directions, as he left his home and drove in the foreseen route. Soon after, in the *rambla*, the kill vehicle sped up to Morán's side. The policeman was driving a German-made Opel, not one to be outrun easily. His trained eye immediately noticed what was happening before a shot was fired, so he began to engage in evasive maneuvers; a high-speed chase ensued.

Shooting at each other in the *rambla*, the two cars continued for some time until the MLN's managed to position itself beside the Opel. At that point the killer placed half of his body outside the window and fired directly at Morán, who was hit. Once the Opel stopped, the policeman was finished off with a few more bursts, and the team evacuated the area. Witnesses recognized famous trigger-puller Raúl Bidegain at the scene – quite possibly as the killer.

The attack was stunning. It fed a different vision of the MLN, as an organization undertaking justice by its own hand and capable not just of entertaining armed propaganda operations, but also of somber ones like assassinating prominent members of the security services. According to Adolph Sáenz, the U.S. Public Safety delegation "felt a deep sorrow because Moran Charquerro [sic] was a patriot and a good man". Crucially, the Morán hit served to intimidate the police out of further prisoner abuse. All that was needed was for the name of the abusing agent or officer to come out of the prisons –and it would-, for them to fear a similar fate.

The law of casualties applied to both sides.[227] As an operational leader in Column 10, the normally tousled José Mujica wore appropriate MLN attire for meetings and other activities: "Suit, white shirt, a dark, thin tie per the latest fashions, coat, and a small business executive's briefcase". He had to be careful: he was wanted by the police since the detection of his MLN affiliation and gunrunning activities the previous year.

On March 23, Mujica was meeting with Walter Sanzó and other Tupamaros at a bar called La Vía in the depths of Montevideo. They were sharing a bottle of *grappa* and discussing various aspects of what would later be known as the Mailhos raid. A policeman named José Villalba was also at the bar, and despite the business attire he recognized Mujica from his mug shot. A patrol in the area arrived soon after he made the call, so Mujica opened his bag, reached for his weapon, and started a shootout.

It was a bloody incident: two policemen were wounded, one of them severely. Mujica was shot twice. One of the cops, in a state of shock and outrage over a fallen comrade, shot Mujica again while he was lying on the ground, bleeding. Soon, an ambulance fetched him and took him to the nearby Military Hospital; his life was very much at risk after a total of six bullet wounds.

This was not the first time Mujica had been shot. Earlier, much like Efraín Martínez, he had been in a domestic MLN accident when a gun had accidentally discharged and hit him. Now his life was pending by a thread, but Pepe got lucky: in typical MLN fashion, the surgeon on call at the hospital turned out to secretly be Tupamaro Óscar Guerrero. He was in safe hands and his life was saved.

It took Mujica two months to recuperate before being sent to Punta Carretas prison, although he faced multiple complications with his stomach and experienced hair loss. For the foreseeable future, Pepe -whose *yuto*, or codename, was Facundo- was out of the game. There was, however, an act of vengeance: in January of 1971 the MLN murdered Villalba, who had foolishly confirmed his role in Mujica's downfall on a radio show.* They did so right outside the same bar where Facundo almost died.

* This is by Mujica's own admission.

Mud and Gold

In April of 1970 the next major armed propaganda operation took place.[228] The Tupamaros had successfully recruited a man who worked in the mansion and office of a wealthy family named Mailhos. The clan owned land throughout Uruguay, including multiple *estancias* and tobacco concerns. The employee, named Roberto Barbeito Filiponne, revealed that the owners had a secret vault stashed with gold ingots and coins that had never been disclosed to Uruguay's financial regulatory authorities.

The family had acquired the bullion in 1939; they were known as King George V Gold Sovereigns and represented two hundred kilograms' worth, for a total of $1.9 million in 2014 dollars. Only five people knew this secret: two members of the family plus three employees. Barbeito had not accessed the safe in the past two years, but had never forgotten about this most seductive of secrets.

Eighteen Tupamaros, led by Efraín Martínez from the *dirección* and Mauricio Rosencof from the Column 10 command, staged a complex nocturnal raid during a weekend on the semi-empty house. In order to accomplish the mission they had to build and transport a special machine to help them open the 1,500 kg vault. The device was similar to those used in automobile repair shops to unload heavy engines, with a lift mechanism.

Behind all of this was the key man in the operation: Juan Almiratti, the MLN's top engineer along with the then-imprisoned Jorge Manera. Almiratti was still a legal Tupamaro: he had been the owner, since 1958, of a construction company with up to one hundred workers in the payrolls.

The first step was, as usual, a stealthy infiltration. In order to achieve this, Barbeito performed a ruse. First, he caused a pretext to summon a "plumber", who was in fact Almiratti. Once the engineer conducted his survey of the premises, the plan proceeded. Barbeito purposefully left a bottle of fine wine at the house, telling the house's caretaker, who would be on duty on the night of the operation with his wife and fifteen year-old daughter, that he would return to pick it up. Upon arriving that night, Barbeito told the caretaker the "truth": he in fact had a side business as a bootlegger and was using the empty house, that same night, to unload a shipment for distribution. The caretaker would be given a small cut if he agreed to turn a blind eye and let Barbeito and his men do their business in peace. All was then agreed, and Barbeito was able to make the calls that green-lighted the operation.

A large truck arrived and backed deep into the grounds of the house. Inside was a large group of Tupamaros, as well as the machine that would be used to extract the safe. Other Tupamaros arrived on foot. Once inside, some stayed in the kitchen guarding the caretaker and his family, while the rest navigated the enormous mansion to look for the safe.

It turned out, "just like in the movies", to be behind a picture of an *estancia*, in the office of one of the family members managing the business. It was no ordinary safe: comparable in size to a refrigerator, it had its own walk-in space. In an unexpected complication, it was built into the walls of the room. It was also impossible to crack on-site. There was no choice but to dig the whole thing out, under Almiratti's supervision.

While this was tackled, others took the time to explore the place. Rosencof broke an MLN rule and stole something for his own benefit: a Limoges ceramic plate for his girlfriend, who had suspected him of being involved in a different variety of late night adventure. The Tupas saw many indicators of luxury: plenty of cash, radio transmitters to the various *estancias*, firearms encased in glass, and more. The *guerrilleros*, at the peak of their ideological conviction, were outraged: "the upper floor (...) is an outpouring of luxury. It shows lavish luxury, proper for an Asian palace, and it leaves the *compañero* stunned: a billiards room, a drawing room, an enormous dining hall, a kitchen, bathrooms and other spaces for various uses. Chinese vases, innumerable porcelain and silver objects. Fireplaces, pianos, corduroy-upholstered sofas, Persian rugs, mirrors, crystal cabinets, hundreds of wine glasses (...) Tens of fine chairs, two refrigerators stocked with select spirits, closets stuffed with fine china (...) three electrical stoves next to each other (...) The Tupamaros do not know how to conduct themselves in such a palace: where our curious man treaded, over waxed floors and delicate rugs, he left traces of his shoddy, muddy shoes".

It was later than planned when the box was finally removed and wheeled to the awaiting truck. Before the MLN cell left the premises, it left a piggy bank in lieu of the massive steel safe. Barbeito turned to a blackboard the family used to indicate when one of the members was out of town, and if so where he was and how long he would be there. Typical messages were "Gustavo -

Punta del Este, until March 2" or "Germán - Paris, from the 4th until the 7th". Below this, Barbeito wrote his own status update: "Roberto - Until victory, always", a play on Che Guevara's famous send-off. Barbeito also left instructions saying his car was to be sold and the money given to the poor. Nearby was an unmistakable signature: the star logo of the MLN.

The group left the premises at 5:30, just as the new day was dawning. The raid took far longer than expected, given the logistical complexity of removing the box: all the more a satisfying success. Barbeito immediately sank into the MLN underground. Martínez and others, holding the bullion in their hands, were ecstatic.

The Mailhos raid was a stunning success for the Tupamaros. The press covered it thoroughly, and reflected on the care displayed during the operation, on the pinpoint targeting of an "oligarchic" family whose wealth was partly illegal, on the propaganda messages Barbeito left, and on the many curious details.[229] The American embassy, a trusty barometer for the MLN insurgency as witnessed by professional analysts, titled its report "Tupamaros Stage Largest Robbery in Uruguayan History".[230]

The stolen assets financed the organization to the point where there was money to spare, and Mailhos gold to send to friendly insurgents in Chile and Bolivia - but that was not all. Once again, the Tupamaros had stolen the firm's accounting books and delivered them to the judiciary. The result spoke for itself: the head of the firm, seventy-five year-old Luis Mailhos, "was arrested for failing to declare his ownership of the gold, and for having dodged the corresponding tax on his assets".[231] Mailhos had desperately contacted Tupamaros imprisoned at Punta Carretas and sought to buy back the damning documentation, but the MLN refused to do so: he was left to the judges.[232]

Mailhos was the prototypical MLN operation with profitable public relations results. Many young radicals inspired by such actions, from all over society, flocked towards the group in response. It promised to be the adventure of a lifetime. As many members explained, being a Tupamaro was acquiring connotations of glamour and power.[233] Neither non-violent nor ultra-violent, the MLN was trying to forge its own path towards revolution.

By mid-1970 the Tupamaros were the dominant topic of conversation in Uruguay, and were increasingly well known in neighboring countries, in the United States, and in Europe. They were not done with spectacular operations by any means.

The Ultimate Raid

It was May 28 of 1970. The waves of new recruits brought the MLN a man named Fernando Garín. He was a twenty-three year-old cadet at Uruguay's Centro de Instrucción de la Marina or CIM, the national naval academy. Working with Raúl Sendic's column of the interior, Garín proposed a plan bolder than anything attempted before.[234]

Once again, the key to the raid was audacity, creativity, and unmatchable intelligence assets. As Mao had said, "Intelligence is the decisive factor in planning guerrilla operations".[235] This dictum would clearly be on display in this latest nocturnal raid.

The stakes were high. One of the largest MLN teams ever assembled, totaling twenty-two Tupamaros (of which two were women) was to undertake the most dangerous and ambitious mission since Pando. In fact, it was arguably more difficult than the latter, for this involved going directly into the lion's den with a force less than half as powerful. The objective was the headquarters of the CIM itself.

The night opened in a safe house in the residential neighborhood of Pocitos, where some participants were taught how to handle weapons for the first time. Others, like Bidegain and Macchi -now free thanks to Operación Paloma-, were there to provide a more experienced finger on the trigger. Unlike in previous operations, most of the team would arrive all together in a single vehicle: a large truck, with most of the Tupas hidden in the back.

On the way to the CIM, the truck stopped while Tupamaro Fernán Pucurull telephoned Garín to provide the green light. As the truck idled, a policeman approached and asked the driver for his identification documents, leaning on the cargo beneath the tarp without realizing he was touching the arm of a Tupamaro, and that all around him were over a dozen heavily armed men and women.

The entrance of the CIM looked directly to a part of the *rambla* that was desolate late at night, right by Montevideo's port. Nobody lived anywhere near the area, so aside from the occasional car and passerby, only the base's sentries would be on the street. The truck approached and stopped at a safe distance, waiting for the signal. There were three armed guards posted by the door and an additional one on a balcony directly above them.

The green light came when the Tupamaro cadet Garín, who was conveniently in charge that night, emerged to supervise the guards. For a brief moment he removed his helmet, threw it in the air, and caught it: it was the sign Sendic and his men were waiting for. Almost immediately, a car arrived with two policemen explaining that a sailor on leave that night had been involved in a bar fight in town, and that they needed to address it with someone in charge.

Garín, as the ranking guard, asked to discuss the matter inside, so he and two of the guards accompanied the investigating officer inside. The other policeman agreed to provide temporary sentry duty along with the remaining naval guard. Immediately after crossing the door, Garín and the "policeman" disarmed the two soldiers that had entered with them, along with an additional one posted at the front desk.

Meanwhile, outside, the remaining cop, plus the guard next to him and the sentry on the balcony, watched as a truck arrived and parked right by the CIM front space. The young couple driving it got off and walked towards the building, so the policeman approached and ordered them to stop: no civilians were allowed. He asked for their documents and an argument ensued: one of them was a student at IAVA, so he might be a radical bent on some kind of attack. Suddenly, Garín emerged from behind the balcony sentry's back and swiftly disarmed him. Now while he aimed the guard's rifle below, the "policeman" and the couple -made up of Bidegain and Macchi- disarmed the last sentry, who was powerless to act.

With that, the way into the building was clear. Four Tupamaros took the uniforms of captured soldiers and led the way into the facility. Once inside, and led by Garín, the MLN teams went dormitory by dormitory, and room by room, quietly subduing the cadets in small groups. In some cases there was trouble waking up the sailors. One group was playing the card game *truco* on a small table. As the official MLN narration of the story goes, suddenly one of the Tupamaros dressed as a soldier entered and surprised everyone by producing his weapon: "'I win: I scored 38 - and we are Tupamaros'. And indeed he had a long .38".

All the cadets, save one who hid beneath his bunk, were made to walk to the *plaza de armas* or internal courtyard. There were sixty-four in total. Most were in their underwear, and were made to hear the inevitable propaganda speech, straight from the mouth of none other than their classmate Garín. Later, some who started to feel the cold of the late autumn night were given blankets. The MLN team dispersed to fetch every weapon it could find. Sendic, despite being the commander of the raid, kept silent.

To preserve appearances, there were still "sentries" posted outside. A vehicle packed full of soldiers arrived: it turned out ten cadets had been granted an evening out in the town, and were returning to base. In a merry state following a good night, their first question to the sentry reflected concern: was the commanding officer on duty in a lenient mood? Oblivious to what was happening inside, their preoccupation was disciplinary action due to their inebriated state and late arrival. The sentry played his part and told them not to worry, so they walked into their home base, relieved.

Inside, another Tupamaro feigning guard duty raised his weapon. The leader of the revelers smiled back, winked, and "drew" a weapon with his hands: "bang, bang" he gestured back, and continued without stopping. The look of dismay on his face once he arrived at the main courtyard and saw what was happening must have been priceless to the Tupamaros.

The operation wrapped up with the MLN loading every piece of war-making equipment in the facility into their truck and an additional one they commandeered, courtesy of the Navy. Not a single shot was fired, and no alert ever reached the outside world. Before leaving, "they raised their flag (...) in the central courtyard, they photographed the emptied arsenal, graffitti'd slogans, cut the telephone wires, and placed a false explosive device on the sealed front door, with a sign that read 'The people passed through here'".

The MLN's quick-reaction networks distributed the stolen weapons throughout Montevideo, across every column. They did so in broad daylight, wrapping the guns in tarps, at the busiest intersection in Uruguay: 18 de Julio and Ejido. The bolder the urban guerrilla got, the better it performed.[236]

These weapons were different from the ones the Tupamaros had been haphazardly acquiring before. They included brand new, military grade, U.S.-made AR-15 rifles, ammunition, and other supplies. In total, according to official MLN tallies, the yield included 190 Springfield rifles, 120 M-1 Garands, 50 .45 caliber pistols, 180 .38 revolvers, 6 AR-15s, 90 fragmentation grenades,

70,000 rounds of ammunition and multiple radios, gas masks, shovels, and other pieces of equipment. Some guns belonged to private collectors who, fearful of frequent MLN raids on their homes, had relied on the Navy to safeguard their arms.

The American embassy was inevitably stunned by what happened. In its message explaining the operation to Washington, the diplomats noted in brief but telling statements that a "spectacular Tupamaro raid" had taken place. It went on: "There is much anger and considerable embarrassment in military over naval center raid (...) Morale in Navy has fallen very low over loss of equipment and lack of any resistance to Tupamaros (...) Tupamaros removed virtually all arms and equipment in center, used as headquarters for GOU naval security forces (...) Operation exceptionally well planned and executed".[237] To top this off, some of the looted equipment had been "MAP supported", meaning purchased under the American-funded Military Acquisition Program. In conclusion, it was "the most successful Tupamaros operation to date and reflects its growing capability for active subversion".[238]

The House of the Witches

There was still more armed propaganda in the MLN's arsenal to come. The last front-page raid in the campaign, staged in late 1970, targeted a uniquely Uruguayan place: the Caja Nacional de Préstamos Pignoraticios, or National Bank of Pignorative Loans.[239] The Caja was essentially a state-owned pawnbroker. Its business consisted of appraising and taking citizens' valuables as collateral for loans. It was one more way for the Uruguayan state to provide cash to its citizens, and it was an enticing target for the MLN.

The Tupamaros, as usual, had benefited from formidable intelligence assets. Through insider tips they had learned about specific safe deposit boxes containing the jewels of wealthy families, which came to be known as "las brujas" or the witches. Therefore, this was to be the attack on the Casa de las Brujas. The chosen date was November 12. The location of the target was, in classic MLN fashion, brazen: directly across the street from the headquarters of the Ministry of the Interior – in other words, of the national police force. A Tupamaro named Pedro Guinovart had infiltrated the Caja over six months in advance, and joined the ranks of the nighttime guards.

The operation could not take place during the day; it would have been too busy with customers anyway. At night the managers who had the keys and passwords for accessing the valuables would be absent. Therefore, an ambitious plan was once again hatched: Column 15 would simultaneously assault the private home of each of the three managers of the Caja, and upon their arrival each would fall into an MLN "mousetrap". Once captured, they would be robbed of their keys or taken to the bank and forced to open box forty-three, which was supposed to contain over a billion pesos' worth of valuables.

Such an ambitious operation required a formidable deployment; in fact, it was larger than both Pando and CIM with sixty-two Tupamaros in action. The logistics were vast. The managers' homes were spread out across separate neighborhoods in Montevideo; coordination had to be superb. If one part of the plan failed, the entire operation had to be canceled. If failure was not adequately communicated, oblivious teams would proceed and fall into a trap or a confrontation with the police – who were obviously right across the street.

The Tupamaros crafted intricate plans to avoid violence in executing their mission. Each of the three home targets was given to a special task force. In the first one, the manager's wife worked as a dentist, so a Tupamara sought her services a month in advance. The *guerrillera* cultivated the relationship as much as she could, and told the agreeable dentist everything about her life with her boyfriend. Although the Tupamara often felt badly about deceiving this genuinely interested person, there was no room for softness in the MLN: "There are worse things that squeeze the heart, that can hurt and outrage a person even more [than deceiving the dentist]. For example, a billion pesos in superfluous luxuries locked for years and years, while thousands upon thousands of men, women, and children suffer from endless hunger and penury". With time, it became easy for the infiltrator to contact her dentist outside of office hours.

The next task force chose a different approach. The home of the second manager was an apartment in a building with no easy entrance. MLN intelligence reported the man owned a newsstand as a secondary business, so the plan was to ring the intercom downstairs and claim a couple was there to give him a gift. They had won the lottery after purchasing the winning ticket at his newsstand, so they wanted to give him a token of their appreciation. They would just drop a few pastries and leave, on to their next stop in the "thank you" tour.

In the case of the third house, a female doctor would ring the bell and ask to see a sick child, for a scheduled house call. Upon being told that she had the wrong address, she would ask to use the telephone in the house to call the clinic and find out what happened.

The targets were struck successfully during working hours on November 12; no resistance was posed. The dentist's heart was broken when her "patient", accompanied by her boyfriend, broke off the social engagement by pulling out a Luger and announcing she was a Tupamara. "Why did you keep on deceiving me, on lying to me for so long? Why did you do that? How perverse!" were the woman's words according to the MLN itself.

In the apartment, the celebrating "couple" successfully made it inside, only to find there was a social gathering with ten people in the living room. There was no choice but to subdue all of them; as usual some time was spent on explaining the operation and what the Tupamaros stood for. The final target was also taken successfully, and thus the first half of the operation was complete.

Throughout his six months in the job, the bank infiltrator Guinovart had worked his charms and lies to accommodate things for the night of the operation. He had introduced his three fellow night watchmen to his "brother", who bootlegged alcohol from Argentina. Due to his profession, the brother always had a nice bottle of quality liquor to provide, so his increasingly frequent visits were always welcome in those long, boring nights in the empty halls of the bank.

On the night of the raid Guinovart opened the door to the assault group of Tupamaros commanded by Aurelio Fernández. The sentries, who did not even have time to reach for their weapons, were captured easily. Even as they were being tied down, they told the Tupamaros it would be an impossible hit, given the facility's security protocols. In response, the MLN had its own ace up its sleeve: the triple home assault from the previous hours, and the resulting keys.

Later in the night, the sentries from the next shift arrived. Upon being told to stand down because a robbery was taking place and they were now prisoners of the Tupamaros, they failed to believe it. Some laughed and joked around, pretend-chasing each other around a table saying "Tupamaros...Oh, the Tupamaros will eat me!" It stopped being funny once the weapons and the ropes came out.

The loot from the *brujas* was once again spectacular; it amounted to fourteen bags packed with jewels worth $5 million 2014 dollars in the estimation of the Uruguayan government. The Ministry of the Interior, right across the street, never learned about what was taking place before its very gates. In fact, it only found out when Aurelio Fernández, the commander of the operation, telephoned to alert them.*

Once again, the Uruguayan government and its security services were thoroughly humiliated. The press called it "the heist of the century". To complete the armed propaganda impact, the MLN publicly stated the following: "We shall keep the jewels of frivolity and big capital. But we also expropriated other jewels, simple ones, belonging to people of modest means. They are in the minority. A mistake led to them being added to the expropriated lot. These jewels will be returned".[240] Accompanying this statement was a method for citizens to prove their ownership and recover the goods. Later, the Tupamaros gifted one of the jewels to Kim Il-sung, the dictator of Communist Korea and arguably the world's greatest oppressor at the time.

Attrition...

By the time the armed propaganda campaign wrapped up in mid-1970 –the jewels, in November, were an outlier heist-, the MLN had grown from about fifty core Tupamaros to more than a thousand. An increasing number was receiving combat and intelligence training in Cuba. An additional two thousand individuals volunteered to help in the support network known as Comités de Apoyo a los Tupamaros (Tupamaro Support Committees), or CATs, tasked with providing logistical help at various moments of need.[241]

The Uruguayan military, writing a history of the period years later, recognized that the years of armed propaganda represent "the

* Fernández even told the police where he had parked the hijacked vehicles, so that "you don't waste time looking for them".

stage where the seditious group makes itself known and acquires notoriety, both inside and outside of the country, due to the spectacular nature of several of its operations".[242] As Macchi put it, "The operations seemed so perfect. Seen from the outside they were being undertaken in such a spotless way".[243]

Furthermore, new Tupamaros joined from across a wide range of social backgrounds and positions that helped improve its operational potential some more. For example, the induction of multiple medical students allowed the MLN to develop a network of field hospitals, with ambulances, surgery capabilities, and even a team of psychologists for frail Tupamaros – all in the clandestine underground of Montevideo.[244]

The MLN also strived to notify the population of its motives. For instance, once it learned of social skepticism over the amounts of money it had acquired in the spectacular robberies, a flyer spread to tackle the issue: "The Tupamaros seek justice, not charity. They do not distribute handouts. They are not fighting to give the needy and humiliated bread today and hunger tomorrow. No, the Tupamaros, the MLN, are not fighting so that things will remain as they are (...) the millions that it expropriates are poured, completely and to the last cent, to the struggle, to the revolution that is forging that country, that society".[245]

At the closing of the armed propaganda campaign, the Tupamaros had perfected to a great degree the art of operating within the urban confines of a city like Montevideo. *La clande* (or "being clande") became a way of life. Great care had to be taken, for example, with the unavoidable recognition of faces, vehicles, houses, and other traces of their activity. In essence, *anything* could turn out wrong when operating as an urban guerrilla: an acquaintance could be present at the locale where an operation was taking place; civilians might get in the way of a raid; police patrols might be in unexpected places - or off-duty but still armed, and so forth. All of this and more had to be taken into account every time the Tupamaros took to the streets. Sometimes, people like Sendic resorted to sleeping on the beach rather than a safe house that might not actually be so safe. There was also a toll on personal and family matters: El Bebe, now also known as Rufo, learned of the death of his mother through the newspaper.[246]

Attrition took form mainly in the "*caídas*" of prominent Tupamaros, all of which became mass media news events. In June of 1970, a police patrol recognized and arrested none other than master operator Héctor Amodio Pérez. The Tupamaro alternately known as Antonio, Ernesto, Ricardo, and especially Gustavo denied having any leadership role in the MLN, despite having planned and commanded most of the major hits, including the raid on the Monty financial firm, the kidnapping of Gaetano Pellegrini, the attack on Pando, the failed robbery of the Banco Francés e Italiano, the Operación Paloma prison escape, and many more. In other words, Amodio's capture was of a symbolic importance surpassed only by the potential arrest of Sendic, but in operational terms his loss was the greatest the MLN could suffer.

At the time, the public and the press lacked an understanding of who was *truly* important among the Tupamaros. For instance, Raúl Bidegain had a great degree of publicity around him despite his never commanding an action team, much less a column. He was rather a talented and fearless shooter. Because of this, the other Tupas teasingly called him "Coca-Cola", meaning he was all publicity.

Following Amodio's arrest, Alberto Candán, like Amodio before him, was elevated from leading Column 15 to the leadership tetrarchy. Now it would be made up of Sendic -still standing, clandestinely, since the Nueva Helvecia incident of 1963-, Efraín Martínez Platero, Lucas Mansilla, and Candán. Such changes had inevitable consequences. Candán, in contrast to Amodio, was more of a *gatillero* or trigger-puller, an action-oriented radical who displayed a little too much enjoyment in acts of physical intimidation and violence. Amodio had godfathered him in the organization, but nevertheless there were rifts between them.[247] Differences in style and temperament could account for widely divergent decisions taken at the top of the MLN.

...and Escalation

After four years of existence and close to two of applying armed propaganda tactics, the MLN was becoming the central political fact in Uruguay. It had achieved this without recurring to foreign assistance or sanctuaries. Sympathy for the MLN was so widespread that it was not limited to one social class or to the *izquierda*. For instance, former military officer Luis Agosto noted how on hearing of operations like the Mailhos mansion, "I felt a certain joy (...) I do not know if it was sympathy that we felt for the Tupamaros, but we had an expectation that they would make the country change".[248]

The Tupamaros' international significance as revolutionaries was clearly the greatest in the continent since the days of the Castro brothers and Ernesto Guevara, and was at the time one of the two or three best-known revolutionary organizations in the world. All of this happened so fast that the individuals in charge of responding to the insurgency were mostly unable to keep up with events. According to former army colonel Sergio D'Oliveira, the government's main mistake in stopping the rise of the MLN was a "complete lack of psychological operations directed at the population (...) to jolt it from its apathy and convince it to choose sides in favor of the state. On the contrary: if there was any coherent psychological action at the time, it was always on the part of the Tupamaros".

In other words, it was only the MLN that was truly attempting to change the opinions of the population from opinion A towards opinion B. The Pacheco administration was content to pursue its police operations, often haphazardly, without exploiting the many negative sides of the MLN. One obvious example was the attacks on the private homes of those very policemen. As D'Oliveira explained, "After some time they had to abandon this procedure, for not only did it detract from their popularity but they also met the firm and energetic reaction from the relatives of the policemen, as well as from neighbors who on several opportunities successfully repelled assault attempts".[249] Others included the bank robberies -which almost always involved civilians-, the Pando shootout, the torching of General Motors, and the assassinations of Héctor Morán Charquero and other policemen. There were plenty of unsavory MLN operations to propagandize about.

Mid-1970 saw a major and irreversible change in gears for the Tupamaros. With the approval of new operational plans at the top, armed propaganda would never again be the main type of action the group engaged in. An internal document said the following about this interplay of tactics: "A guerrilla movement that abuses propaganda actions in detriment of significant military operations loses value in the popular conscience".[250] In other words, the MLN had successfully used armed propaganda for the purpose of becoming a full-fledged insurgent organization. Its doctrine suggested the tactic had to be abandoned in the next phase of the revolution, for it could not be employed indefinitely towards a final victory.

There was clearly a climate of cruder violence anyway: the strikes, riots, occupations, barricades, and other forms of "popular resistance" continued every day, as if the MLN's campaign was not enough. In one particularly sad incident, a band of student fanatics assaulted the offices of the director of the famed IAVA high school, shoving and slapping him out into the street.[251] Violence, as the expression went, was *instalada en la sociedad*, or pervasive in society.

It is in this context that the new MLN plans began on July 28 1970 when the group kidnapped a judge named Daniel Pereira Manelli. They interrogated him about various aspects of his investigations and rulings in cases involving them, and held him, according to Alejandro Otero, "in a small bathroom, which could only be accessed through a hole in the wall; a truly deplorable place. If this had happened to a subversive detainee in police quarters, it would have been considered a violation of human rights".[252]

Efraín Martínez's recollection focuses on another aspect of the kidnapping. As a member of the leadership, he was standing right in front of Judge Pereira as Sendic interrogated him. Martínez objected to having the hostage hooded during the interrogation, but Sendic told him to trust his methods. Then, Sendic told him: "You are here in front of a revolutionary court that wishes to ask you a series of questions concerning the rulings you have served. We want to know what answers you will give now, because we know the ones you have given in the past". According to Martínez, "Then we started asking questions. For every correct answer he gave from a judicial point of view we lifted the hood just a little. We pulled on the hood until in the end we took it off. So *El Bebe* said to him: 'You see? Justice needs to be blind, but not hooded' (...) And then we released him!"[253] The judge admitted that his verdicts had been influenced by political pressures and, soon after his release, resigned from his post.

What nobody knew was that the MLN was about to directly impose its own brand of justice on its enemies.

CHAPTER EIGHT:

MAXIMUM TENSION

BY MID-1970, attrition from police operations had taken a toll on the Tupamaros, particularly on their leaders. Three quarters of the original leadership tetrarchy were in Punta Carretas prison: Julio Marenales, Jorge Manera, and Eleuterio Fernández Huidobro. Héctor Amodio joined them in June, and the list went on with lesser-known names. Eleuterio Fernández thus hatched a plan to escalate the insurgency and force the government to free the prisoners.

What came to be known as Plan Satán consisted of kidnapping important foreign officials off the streets of Montevideo. They would be held as hostages until the government released *all* Tupamaros, who were called "political prisoners" in MLN propaganda. More than one hundred were on the list. The plan sought to force the Pacheco government into an uncomfortable situation with powerful foreign governments, and ultimately into an institutional crisis. According to a RAND Corporation study of the case, the demand was, at the time, "the largest prisoner ransom ever demanded for kidnapped diplomats".[254]

The security situation for foreign officials in the Americas, particularly for U.S. personnel, had grown worse because subversive groups like the Tupamaros were increasingly targeting them directly. The situation was so dire that in April of 1970, three months before the launch of Plan Satán, the CIA distributed an analytical report entitled "Kidnapping as a Terrorist Tactic in Latin America".[255] The note recounted in detail a series of incidents: just between 1968 and 1970 there were kidnappings and murders of U.S. government officials in Guatemala, the Dominican Republic, Argentina, and Brazil. In the latter case, the ambassador was ransomed in exchange for captured insurgents. The tactic was new, but it was spreading like wildfire. The risk of kidnapping for American officials in Latin American countries with active guerrilla or terrorist organizations was high.[256]

That same month, the Department of State's intelligence division, the Bureau of Intelligence and Research, produced its own report. It dealt specifically with Uruguay and was even more prescient: "A combination of factors exist in Uruguay which make a terrorist kidnapping likely (...) The identification of the US with the training of police in Uruguay possibly increases both the chances of an American being chosen as a potential victim and the danger that he or she would face if kidnapped".[257]

Plan Satán was launched on the morning of July 31. It was a remarkable demonstration of the MLN's capabilities.

Plan Satán

One cell, belonging to Column 15, kidnapped the consul of Brazil in Montevideo, Aloysio Dias Gomide. The Tupamaros targeted him both for his nationality and for his alleged connections to extreme conservative-nationalist elements in Brazil, supposedly guilty of human rights abuses against local activists and insurgents. Two teams deployed to extract Dias from inside his family's home in the exclusive neighborhood of Carrasco. The first, led by Henry Engler, waited outside ready to provide backup. The other, led by Adolfo Wasem, invaded through the front door. The Brazilian locked himself in the bathroom to avoid the Tupamaros, while they variously dealt with, and allegedly pointed their weapons at, his wife and child. Ultimately, Dias surrendered and was taken hostage.[258]

There were two more kidnapping teams active in the city at the same time, and both were targeted at United States officials. The first deployed to the residential neighborhood of Pocitos, and staked out the apartment building where two diplomats lived. Their names were Gordon Jones and Nathan Rosenfeld, and at the time they car pooled to the drab building where the embassy was newly housed, a short drive away in the *rambla*. The Tupamaros knew this, and thus prepared an operation to kidnap two victims in one strike.

That morning the MLN squad infiltrated the building's garage and waited for the diplomats to approach their vehicle. Rosenfeld was seized first, and the Tupamaros immediately asked for Jones. Upon the latter's arrival, both men were struck and forced into vehicles.[259] Rosenfeld managed to get away almost immediately by jumping off the moving vehicle after leaving the building.

Jones wasn't as lucky, but had also been alert. He had been tied, wrapped in a carpet-like tarp, and put on the bed of a truck. The fast-thinking recent father of two had puffed his chest as much as possible, and was thus able to wiggle his body to loose the constraints.[260] With the vehicle idling at a rest stop, possibly waiting for a contact to arrive and transfer the victim, Jones managed to climb the tailgate, drop to the ground, and hop on his bound legs towards a nearby store. As locals assisted him, the MLN squad sped off.

The third kidnapping cell in action that day -also from Column 15- turned out to be the most important. The leader of the cell was Olga Barrios, an experienced Tupamara. In Pando, she had been in a shootout with the police at a rural school. More recently, she had escaped from the women's prison as one of the thirteen "Palomitas" and joined the raid on the naval academy. Days before his arrest in June, Amodio had personally handed her the instructions for this operation. Barrios led a team of seven Tupamaros, using three vehicles stolen that same morning.

The target was Dan Mitrione, the head of the USAID-OPS program advising the Uruguayan police. As in the other two kidnappings, Mitrione would be attacked directly in his home or its environs, rather than risking action downtown or near the embassy. On the morning of July 31, an unarmed Mitrione boarded the vehicle sent to drive him to the embassy. His chauffeur was an armed policeman. Soon after driving off, while still in the residential neighborhood of Malvín, a pickup truck with Pando veteran Andrés Cultelli on the wheel drove from the opposite direction and rammed Mitrione's car, pushing it into the sidewalk. Immediately, Barrios rushed towards the vehicle, rifle in hand, smashed the passenger's window, and subdued Mitrione, pulling him out. The driver-bodyguard was completely immobilized, stuck in his seat and surrounded by weapons pointing at him.

While shoving Mitrione into the back of the transfer vehicle, a Tupamaro codenamed Darío shot him. The universal MLN claim was that it was an accident, although there is no way of verifying it. The wound to the American's shoulder was not life-threatening; the Tupas quickly evacuated the scene and sped off with their prize.* After several transfers, Dias and Mitrione were taken to an underground compartment in a safe house in the northern outskirts of Montevideo.[261] Since the kidnappings of Ulysses Pereira, Gaetano Pellegrini, and Daniel Pereyra, the MLN had been publicly calling this place the "Cárcel del Pueblo", or the People's Prison. In reality, there was more than one of these facilities; Judge Pereyra, who was about to be released, was held in a separate one.

Dan Mitrione

Dan Anthony Mitrione became a central figure in the history of the period. At the age of forty-nine, he had spent most of his career as a policeman in his hometown of Richmond, Indiana. According to New York Times journalist AJ Langguth, who published a thorough account of the case, police work in the town of 44,000 was "undemanding – drunk drivers to book, breaking and entering cases to investigate". Since the town was so small -even by Uruguayan standards- Mitrione moonlighted in other jobs, such as washing automobiles, to make ends meet. Mitrione was remembered in Richmond for being in favor of reducing police violence: he reprimanded excessively violent agents, and advised his force not to use blackjacks during arrests.[262]

Mitrione joined OPS in search of career opportunities. His first posting, in September of 1960, was to Brazil; he spent seven years there. Work ranged from inspection tours and speechmaking to the details of laboratory work and changes to police uniforms. There was a lot of justified criticism of police abuse and torture in Brazil, which meant that Mitrione emerged from his years there with valuable experience, but also damages to his reputation. By being present in abusive countries like Brazil and South Viet Nam, OPS exposed itself to criticism as an accomplice.†

After his seven-year Brazilian tour, Mitrione spent the period 1967-9 in Washington, as an instructor at the International Police

---

* The Tupamaros soon healed Mitrione and divulged reports on his physical examinations by the MLN's medical team.

† In turn, OPS claimed to be designed precisely to undo abusive practices.

Academy. Located in the Car Barn building that today belongs to Georgetown University, the IPA brought together students from police services from around the world, and employed professors like Mitrione to teach them modern police work. Upon requesting a new overseas tour, Mitrione was designated to become Adolph Sáenz's successor in Montevideo. His intent was practical: he badly needed to support his large family.[263] Mitrione arrived in Montevideo in the depths of the winter: July 18, 1969. It was just two days before the Moon landing, and in the midst of the first year of MLN armed propaganda operations.

The main American targets for an organization like the MLN were prominent officials, beginning with the ambassador. Right after him, or possibly above the ambassador, would be the chief of the CIA station in Montevideo, whose identity the MLN most likely never knew. Other CIA case officers would also be most interesting to the MLN: the agency was, by far, the boogie man of all anti-American activists and insurgents worldwide.

After the CIA, the next tempting target was the Office of Public Safety. Sáenz had fended off a possible kidnapping attack in 1968, and now Mitrione had taken his place.[264] The Richmond policeman preferred to move around without a personal firearm and with little police protection; he did not speak Spanish and was new in town.[265] That made him an easier target than his predecessor, than anybody from the CIA, and of course than the ambassador.

The MLN did not come up with the notion of targeting Mitrione on its own. The Tupamaros themselves have revealed it was Cuban intelligence that both initiated the MLN's Mitrione file and contributed to the actual kidnapping. The tip came from Manuel Hevia, who had fled Communist Cuba to the United States, and had arrived in Montevideo in 1964 as an aide to the CIA station.[266] In reality, Hevia secretly served as a spy for the Havana regime.

In his secret contacts with the Tupamaros, Hevia fingered Mitrione as a particularly valuable target.[267] He claimed the American had been in charge of training Dominican and Brazilian policemen in torture techniques, as part of the wars those regimes waged against subversives comparable to the Tupamaros. In fact, Hevia later claimed in a book that in Montevideo Mitrione personally kidnapped hoodlums off the streets, practiced torturing them in his basement, and later murdered them. Hevia filled his writings -and presumably his claims to the Tupamaros- with lies, including that

Mitrione spoke Spanish and that he instructed policemen that it was advisable not to know anything about a prisoner before questioning him –exactly the opposite of what every detective is supposed to do. For good measure, Hevia added grotesque scenes, such as the mass murder of the hoodlums and a torture session with a cackling Uruguayan policeman electroshocking a victim, while the victim foamed from his mouth and Mitrione looked on approvingly.[268]

Hevia was not the only one who contributed to the Mitrione black legend. For instance, later in 1970 a Chilean Communist senator stated he knew "for a fact" that Mitrione was a CIA officer. Major writers aligned with the MLN's cause, like Uruguay's Mario Benedetti, wrote matter-of-factly of Mitrione as a CIA "agent", as is the case today in countless sources a simple Internet search will yield.[269] This is curious given that Hevia acknowledged in his memoir that OPS personnel were mostly policemen and FBI agents ("they are policemen; they do not hide it nor could they"). Other sources that built up the idea at the time include the Cuban intelligence front Prensa Latina, as well as statements by a policeman who had secretly joined the MLN, Miguel Ángel Benítez.[270]

The scriptwriter for the movie "État de Siège", which dramatized the Mitrione case, was also told in full confidence by a Dominican Communist official that Mitrione had operated in Santo Domingo as a torture instructor – when in fact Mitrione never set foot on the country.[271] Later, other authors have added literary flair to Mitrione's alleged sessions, luridly depicting the American's silent satisfaction from the pain of his helpless victims and even his collection of victims' eyes and nails - all without evidence.[272]

Mitrione's engagement in torture, in any country, has yet to be documented.[273] Even the most important study of the case, by the MLN historian María Clara Aldrighi, fails throughout 424 pages of text to prove that he was a torturer or a CIA officer. In his strongest argumentation on the subject, New York Times journalist AJ Langguth noted that Mitrione most likely witnessed harsh interrogation or torture sessions that, given his position, he had the opportunity to stop – and chose not to.[274] That is the greatest extent of the accusation.

The MLN saw the internationalization of the conflict as a way of cornering its top enemy, the government of Uruguay, into an untenable position. The tactic had worked in other countries, particularly Brazil, where dictators Artur da Costa e Silva and Emilio

Garrastazú had previously liberated *guerrilheiros* in exchange for hostages, including the American ambassador. This suggested the MLN would be able to recover a large number of Tupamaros with a single operation.[275] Although there was no guarantee that the Uruguayan government would do the same, they expected it to be unable to resist the pressures coming from the United States and Brazil, whose officials were now in its custody.

The Hostage Crisis

In order to leave little time for speculation following the kidnappings, the MLN told the press it was behind the kidnappings. Its press release demanded the liberation of all imprisoned Tupamaros, and did not set a deadline for the government to carry this through.

In the first hours after the attack, the U.S. embassy denied that Mitrione was an employee of the CIA. Brazil, through its government and the multiple newspapers and radio stations sympathetic to it, made it clear that it expected Uruguay to fully yield to the MLN to preserve Dias's life. Early in the crisis, one of those newspapers editorialized as follows: "Brazilians remain hopeful that President Pacheco will not use the father of six children as a guinea pig in testing the principle of not negotiating with terrorists, which radical factions in Uruguay defend".[276]

Hours after the first MLN communiqué, with the government still in shock and beginning to organize the greatest manhunt in the country's history, the group released the preliminary victim of Plan Satán, Daniel Pereyra. The judge carried with him an additional MLN statement, which reported on Mitrione's status. There was great detail in the description of the hostage's gunshot wound and his recovery; the Tupamaros had brought a medical doctor to assist him. Meanwhile, in Punta Carretas prison, the jailed MLN contingent performed drills in the courtyard, preparing for the moment of their liberation and renewed guerrilla campaign.[277]

The kidnappings threw the country into crisis mode. Emergency measures were taken to sweep Montevideo with police and military patrols in search of the diplomats. A record twenty thousand security agents of both forces (roughly Uruguay's entire military today) were out on the streets, conducting over one thousand raids in a single day and detaining dozens of suspects.[278]

Efforts included house-to-house searches of specific areas, roadblocks, strict identification procedures at points of entry (and exit) to the country, and inspections of medical facilities.[279] None of this provided a clue to the hostages' whereabouts. Unfortunately for the pursuers, the safe house where Mitrione was being kept was fifteen blocks north of the outer limit of the perimeter being combed.[280]

As predicted, the governments of the United States and Brazil pressured the Jorge Pacheco administration into negotiating with the MLN in order to secure the release of the hostages, but Pacheco was adamant: there would be no negotiations with the subversive Tupamaros. For this reason, the days between the kidnappings on July 31 and the partial resolution on August 10 were of maximum tension in Montevideo.

There were at least two problems with the MLN's demand of freeing every Tupamaro serving time in prison. First, in Uruguay the powers of the state were separate, as in any proper republic. It had been the judiciary that had sentenced those Tupamaros to jail, each time finding them guilty of one or more crimes. That meant the executive branch was incapable of simply opening the cells and liberating prisoners. Aware of this, the U.S. embassy sounded out key members of Uruguay's Supreme Court, including its president Hamlet Reyes: "they would not accept any kind of pressure to liberate prisoners in exchange for hostages".[281]

The second problem was just as important: Pacheco would never consider the possibility even if he had that power. Knowing this, many hoped he would resign the presidency to enable a reduction in tensions. The sensation was that if Pacheco resigned, the MLN would be so satisfied that it would release the hostages. Groups of Pacheco's closest friends and allies, according to fellow Colorado Julio Sanguinetti, met with him in the darkest hours of the crisis to suggest precisely that. However, according to the latter, "Pacheco never considered resigning under any scenario".[282] The president felt particularly strongly about this point when considering who his vice president was.

Alberto Abdala was playing a discordant note. During the first hours of the crisis, the vice president spoke to reporters about how it was time for reconciliation between Uruguayans, and potentially for "amnesty". Pacheco could not have been more outraged. The contradictory messages helped fuel the MLN's belief that the president was running out of options and growing increasingly isolated. Upon learning of this speculation about a potential amnesty for subversives, common criminals banded together and wrote to the government asking to be included in any amnesty law. They had a point: their crimes were often of less gravity than the MLN's, and they were not involved in any blackmail with hostages.[283]

In addition to this, a majority in the Parliament was dismissive of the notion of passing a law to free the jailed Tupamaros. That meant each of the three branches of the Uruguayan state was on the record against amnesty. The Tupamaros continued to hope that a political sequence was in the cards: Pacheco would resign, Abdala would take over the presidency and decree an amnesty, and then the Partido Nacional's Wilson Ferreira –who was illegally in contact with the MLN- would spearhead an effort to legalize the Tupas and bring them into the political process.[284]

Unbeknownst to the Tupamaros and to some of his closest allies, Pacheco was doggedly determined to defeat the MLN without yielding one centimeter of ground. As revealed by former presidential bodyguard Víctor Castiglioni, now the police officer in charge of Intelligence and Liaison, "Pacheco Areco had given us orders to the effect that, in case he was kidnapped, no one should negotiate his liberation".[285]

Meet the Tupas

As hostages of the MLN, Mitrione and Dias were subjected to interrogation and to a strict regime of complete isolation from the outside world. They were in the hands of Column 15, the strongest and most radical of all the subdivisions of the MLN. The safe house where they were kept was well compartmentalized: it never came close to be found by the police.

The custodians of the fifty year-old Mitrione saw him as a James Bond-like figure.[286] One Tupamaro told Aldrighi how "We knew that he gave a demonstration of his abilities at Police Headquarters. He was able to disassemble and reassemble a pistol while blindfolded and cuffed (...) we examined him in case he was carrying a hidden transmitter". Tupamaro Rodolfo Wolf also recalls instructions given to Mitrione's guards: "he was a trained individual, capable of killing with his bare hands. They must never lower their guard. Even though he was not young, he was CIA, with their martial arts skills and everything else".

The interrogation of the hostages was a significant event for both parts. The victims adopted different approaches: Mitrione was conciliatory, while Dias oscillated between desperation and outrage. On August 2 Mitrione's captors held a long session with him, which they recorded and later shared in part with the press. The two Tupamaros spoke in intermediate-level English, something that put the American at ease and moved him to speak in what must have been his natural tone of voice. The two hooded Tupamaros talking to Mitrione were Adolfo Wasem and Armando Blanco - both close to the top of the Column 15 hierarchy.

The transcript of the conversation serves as a window into the mindset of both sides. The tone was always laid back; there was chuckling, side quips on the conditions in the cell, and joint reflections on the inherent sadness and strangeness of the situation.

The Tupamaros asked Mitrione two categories of questions. The first concerned his work, and the second his opinion on various topics. When talking about Mitrione's work, it became evident that the MLN did not have accurate information as to who the American was, and much less what he actually did. The focus of the hostage's answers was on the advisory work he had performed with various police forces in Uruguay, particularly on the usage of vehicles and radios in the field. As documented by the New York Times' Langguth, the truth was that Mitrione's work had started with the basics, such as advising the police to change rules of engagement that forced agents and officers to fire their weapon in the air before pointing it at an armed suspect.

Mitrione's answers annoyed the main interrogator, Wasem, who responded with zingers and sarcasm. When asked for his opinions on the Tupamaros and their country, the advisor was careful to praise them: "I believe young Uruguayans are very intelligent. I think here is better than anywhere else in Latin America, because there is a better education system, you have schools. The only negative side is the scarce aspiration to work more, to have better jobs".

A top obsession of the interrogators was the CIA: would Mitrione confess to being one of its "agents"? Would he tell them everything he knew about it? Here Mitrione spoke a slight untruth, stating that he knew nothing of the CIA. In reality, as head of OPS he necessarily had to know the workings of the CIA, details about its station and its officers in Montevideo, and its usage of OPS itself as a cover for case officers like William Cantrell. Mitrione protected these sensitive secrets.

The conversation continued with the same back and forth: the interrogators attacked, complaining to Mitrione about Pacheco's newspaper closures, police corruption, and so forth. The U.S. advisor responded in an accommodating manner, and then the threatening tone returned: "We do not enjoy killing at all, but we will do it if necessary. We killed Morán Charquero with a smile on our faces. We knew we were doing something our comrades would congratulate us for. He was a torturer. There are many of them and we are going to kill them all". The threats continued: Wasem expounded on his wish to kill "Monsieur Fleury", referring to the Rio de Janeiro police force's most infamous commander, Sergio Fleury. He also discussed the MLN's number one objective, Pacheco: "I would like to meet him too. Under the same circumstances I met you. Or even worse, really".

Near the end of that exhausting session, Mitrione said that no matter what happened, "The only thing I regret about all this, which I do not like, is the suffering of many innocent people. My wife and children have no reason why they should suffer". The response was frosty: "I have a wife and children too. But you know, you do it for money and I don't". One of the last statements Mitrione made in this conversation, according to the MLN's own transcript, was "the Tupamaros are smarter than other groups. They only kill when it is necessary. There are others who kill indiscriminately and ask questions later".

Two days later, Dan Mitrione turned fifty years old. He did not tell anyone and no Tupamaro said anything. MLN instructions were to speak to him continuously to prevent the hostage from falling into a bout of depression. One guard who never left the facility during the crisis admitted that the American was increasingly anxious and tormented by his situation: "He talked to me multiple times about his wife and children, and in those cases he became emotional". According to another guard, Mitrione's later days of incarceration had him "very scared".

There was a second interrogation session days later. Conducting it was a single Tupa: Alberto Candán. In a surprising – or suspicious- breach of MLN efficacy, the audio recorder failed to register the conversation, and therefore only written notes were published. Candán was at the time a member of the *dirección*, and its supervisor-chief for Column 15. A veritable incarnation of the MLN action man of the time, he had a taste for violence and for exercising power over other individuals. Twenty-eight at the time of Plan Satán, Candán had been at the most dangerous of the Pando objectives (the police station), and also participated in the high-speed assassination of Héctor Morán.

Candán's interrogation of Mitrione focused on operational affairs that might be of interest to the MLN in undertaking future operations. In truth, it appeared the organization was not well prepared to ask the right questions and adequately process the answers of such a high-level source. Once again, some of the questions reflected a conspiratorial way of thinking that was simultaneously naïve and ideological. For instance, Candán asked Mitrione about "a storage area for weapons and foodstuffs, as well as a submarine-based escape system" at the embassy.

The hostage rejected, on the record, Candán's accusations that he had been involved in torture, both personally and indirectly through his students in Brazil and Uruguay. The fact that Mitrione did not speak Spanish, and the obvious limitations that fact imposed on him for any such work, did not occur to Candán. Some of the guards at the People's Prison admit to having observed Candán treating Mitrione violently during the interrogation of what was already a broken man. Candán "treated him with scorn and told him to stop lying, because we knew he was a bad person". Aldrighi, the MLN's semi-official biographer, used the code term "interrogating with severity" to refer to this.

Almería

A few days into the crisis, polls conducted by organizations such as Gallup produced a significant indicator for this midway point in the MLN's insurgency. A third of society thought the kidnappings were legitimate; a third thought the opposite, and the final third was neutral. 60% thought the Tupamaros would return Mitrione safe and sound. In the meantime, the police –with the advisory of OPS, now more urgent than ever- set up a special task force and a hotline for civilians to provide intelligence tips without fearing MLN retaliation. One solitary success was the takedown of the safe house where Candán was most often staying; he and Alicia Rey watched from a safe distance as the police raided it.[287]

With a climate of tension and emergency restrictions in place, it was difficult for the MLN's compartmentalized cells and columns to operate. Nevertheless, the significance of the situation meant the *dirección* thought it worth the risk to meet in one place.[288] There were many things to discuss, not least how to deal with Mitrione, reconsidering the demands made of the Pacheco government -a full week had passed since their publication-, and most sensitively, what advances were being made in secret contacts with politicians that might help the MLN undermine the administration.

The police had secretly tracked down a ground-level apartment in the Malvín neighborhood where high-ranking Tupamaros could sometimes be seen. It was clear that it was an MLN safe house, but the detectives had held back, preferring to deploy surveillance until the right moment. On the rainy morning of August 7 the police sprung its trap, on the occasion of the *comité ejecutivo*'s meeting to discuss the fate of the hostages. Since then, the incident became known simply as "Almería", after the street where the apartment was.

At eight in the morning, top police inspectors Óscar Delega and Hugo Campos -in civilian garb- knocked on the door and, upon it being opened by an MLN operator, forced their way inside. They subdued the Tupamaros guarding the apartment, Edith Moraes and Asdrúbal Pereira, and sprung a classic "mousetrap". The two officers were so swift that Moraes was unable to place a visible alarm signal for arriving *compañeros*.

As depicted in the Costa-Gavras film "État de Siège", after breaching the apartment Delega and Campos sat down on the couch and forced Pereira to open the door normally as attendants arrived for the meeting. One by one, they were welcomed to the sight of a police arrest and incorporation into the mousetrap. Outside, in complete stealth, more policemen awaited as backup.

One after the other, the members of the MLN who were slated to attend the meeting arrived and fell into the trap. Two women were the first to fall. One was Nelly Jorge, wife of top MLN leader Eleuterio Fernández. The other was Alicia Rey, partner of Héctor Amodio and, as the leader of Column 15, the MLN's highest-ranking woman. Next came two male Tupamaros: Diego Piccardo and, to the great delight of Delega and Campos, Raúl

Bidegain. At last, one of the best-known Tupamaros, the one his colleagues called "Coca-Cola" due to his notoriousness, was in the hands of the police. As a confirmed murderer, he would most likely be given the maximum sentence and become a permanent loss to the MLN's ranks.

The Almería safe house kept on giving. Two more Tupamaros showed up, and these were truly big fish. One was Efraín Martínez Platero: he had been a member of the MLN leadership for over a year, and was one of its top armed propaganda strategists. He had been in the police's radar for years, particularly after the incident at El Pinar of late 1967. More recently, he had commanded the raid on the Mailhos mansion. Described as "arrogant" upon being arrested, Martínez Platero became the highest-ranking MLN capture since Amodio.

To top this off, another Tupamaro falling that day at Almería was none other than Alberto Candán. Just weeks after taking out Amodio, here was his successor first as commander of Column 15 and later in the leadership, not to mention one of the most dangerous of all Tupamaros. Candán had noticed something was off with the apartment and had turned around and left. The officers in the street detected him and after a brief shootout Campos captured Candán and took him inside the apartment. With him and Martínez, half of the MLN leadership had fallen in a few moments.

This was not close to being the ultimate catch of the day. After seven years on the run from the police, since the days of the Nueva Helvecia robbery prior to the foundation of the MLN, Raúl Sendic was supposed to be at Almería to attend the meeting. The police did not know this, and by late morning there had already been a few incidents in the street with Candán, and also before that with the arrest of Bidegain and Piccardo. Small groups of people were gathering in doorsteps and sidewalks, attentive to the strange incidents.

As Sendic arrived alone in his Volkswagen, he witnessed part of the incident with Candán, and rushed to the apartment to fetch a weapon in order to take Campos out. It was thus that he walked in to Tupamara Nelly Jorge sitting stiffly on the couch directly in front of the open door, and to Delega's gun trained directly on him. Sendic was immediately disarmed and pushed against the wall. While being frisked and asked who he was, he answered "one more soldier" of the MLN; his identification document was obviously false.

Once he sat down, cuffed, on the back of a police jeep, someone noticed familiar features in his face, and asked him who he was. That time, he answered with the truth. What was possibly the most satisfying radio message in Uruguayan police history came soon afterward: "I have Sendic!". Capturing him completed a remarkable feat: three quarters of the MLN leadership taken out in a single day. The organization's entire decision-making apparatus was eliminated, and crucially, the location of Dias and Mitrione could at last be obtained from the new captures. The last remaining member of the leadership –and also its least experienced-, Lucas Mansilla, detected what happened and successfully avoided the entire scene.

The capture of Sendic inside the Almería safe house was the greatest coup for the police since the start of the MLN insurgency, for he was its main symbol and very first clandestine *guerrillero.* Upon recognizing the long-sought subversive, the policemen remarked on how chubby he seemed. The Tupa leader was not yet in the mood for wisecracks, and retorted that whatever they said, they knew what he fought for. Later on, as he, Martínez, Alicia Rey, and Nelly Jorge were taken to the police station on the back of a jeep, the high speeds of the convoy and the heavy rains from earlier in the morning caused splashing water to soak the prisoners. Sendic used the opportunity to complain to his captors about torture starting even before they reached the station – a line everyone in the vehicle laughed at, including the police officers.

The announcement of the yields from the Almería raid took Uruguay by surprise, and immediately became the breaking news subject of every discussion. The police's reputation was at its peak: in the press conference describing the raid, it was revealed that the intelligence services had been monitoring the Almería apartment for two months. The mood in police quarters was "euphoric". This time, the urban environment had favored them: eight weeks of surveillance had gone undetected. A similar feat on a rural hideout would have been close to impossible.

The victorious mood in the police did not last: the captured Tupamaros were not cooperating. Harsh treatment had only gone as far as hosing the prisoners -naked and hooded- with freezing water. In interrogation, Sendic only said he was a prisoner of war, no longer an MLN leader. Since none of the other captured Tupamaros spoke to their interrogators, the latter appealed to the judiciary for permission to employ sodium Pentothal (a truth serum) to learn the location of the People's Prison. At the peak of the tension and the rush to free Dias and Mitrione, a judge denied the request, alleging that Uruguayan laws did not allow an investigation to clash with the physical and psychological integrity of an individual. Police ranks dropped from euphoria to dejected shock: once again, they felt overly restrained in the tools they could use to fight the MLN.

There was an additional issue to consider: no one except the Tupamaros themselves was cognizant of which of them actually knew where the hostages were being held. The MLN took its compartmentalization seriously. Efraín Martínez, for example, did not know: "They could have tortured me as much as they wanted. I was simply unable to tell them". It is likely that Sendic did not know either. In contrast, although the police was unaware, Candán knew everything, for he himself had personally interrogated Mitrione at the "Cárcel del Pueblo".

Despite these facts, Pacheco faced intense pressure from the governments of Brazil and the United States. Both, in particular the former, wanted him to do more to ensure the lives of the hostages were preserved. The language employed by the MLN's recent statements, talking of revolutionary tribunals and the urgency of a response to their demands, had made things tense. However, the president –in a clear refutation of the notion that his country was an imperial dominion, colony, or puppet of those two countries- doggedly refused to address the MLN at all, or to order an illegal "squeezing" of the prisoners. Pacheco's steady line in the face of powerful allies shattered one more aspect of the MLN and Communist narrative of Uruguay as a subservient country.

As for the MLN ranks, Almería was devastating: "we heard Sendic had fallen. It was the worst thing the 'Orga' could go through (...) It was as if the heavens collapsed". The one remaining leader of the Tupamaros, Mansilla -who had robbed the San Rafael casino dressed as a policeman along with Sendic, Zabalza, and others- was forced to pick three others to join him in forming a new tetrarchy for the *dirección.* All that he chose belonged to the newer generations, who were less experienced in the development of the MLN's organization and identity, but who were tested in operations. The chosen ones were Samuel Blixen, an ultra-violent Column 15 journalist, Manuel Menéndez -Amodio's partner during Pando-, and

Juan José Domínguez. Meeting for the first time on August 8, the new leadership had two burning issues to discuss.

No Way Out

The first decision was the MLN's retaliation over the Almería raid, which was launched before the arrests were over. The target was inside the downtown headquarters of the Ministry of Livestock, Agriculture, and Fisheries. It proved to be the MLN's oddest: a sixty-five year old American named Claude Fly.[289]

Fly was a soils specialist. In the past, he had performed fieldwork in Afghanistan, Sri Lanka, Ivory Coast, Ghana, Egypt, Jordan, and Peru. Uruguay should have been, by far, the easiest of these assignments. He had landed in Montevideo on January 15 1970, barely six months after Mitrione and another six months before he became the target of the Tupamaros. At the time of his first diplomatic reception at the U.S. embassy, the notion of being targeted by subversives had been a source of nervous laughter among attending Americans.

On the morning of August 7, Tupamaros Jorge Torres, Andrés Cultelli and Armando Blanco appeared at the ministry disguised as repairmen. The target was working in one of the offices inside. A soft-spoken man of gentle manners, Fly was not an employee of the United States government and was not a member of the embassy. His work was purely technical and it often involved visiting various parts of the country. Funding for his contract came from the Ministry, although its origins were in a USAID agricultural development grant.

Fly did not speak a word of Spanish, and was often disoriented about various aspects of Uruguay in general. When he saw the Tupamaros burst into the office and manhandle him, he managed to yell "Tupamaros, help!" a few times before being immobilized and wrapped in a large rug in which they took him to the waiting vehicle. Like every kidnapping victim of the MLN, the geologist was kept blindfolded and physically restrained as he navigated the streets of Montevideo, changed vehicles a few times, and finally arrived at a maximum-security MLN safe house. A trap door on the floor was opened, and "down I went into a dank, dark, and smelly crawl space under the house".

The shocked scientist spent that night in the freezing Montevideo winter "in terror and loneliness". In the days that followed, Fly was treated to a surprisingly harsh regime of isolation and psychological torment. As a wholly innocent man in retirement age, who constituted zero political or security threats to the Tupamaros, he was nevertheless denied all possibility of communicating with his family, not to mention access to decent living spaces, bathrooms, and human contact. To the scared Fly, the Tupamaros were simply young and silent sentries, staring at him from behind homemade hoods day and night. From Fly's perspective, gazing intently at those hooded figures, "the top corners stood up like the horns of Satan. Glaring black eyes, made eery by the varying gleam of flashlights, shone out through the roughly cut slits". The Tupamaros surely imagined themselves as humanist and harmless kidnappers, but their failure lay in not conceiving of how an innocent victim like Fly might see them. He could not know what would happen to him, and his thoughts were with his wife, as well as his family back in Fort Collins, Colorado.

In addition to kidnapping Fly, the second decision made by the new leadership was to publish a statement radically changing the course of Plan Satán. Upset over the collapse of Almería and the enormous burden of leading the organization, and thinking it likely that the captured Tupamaros would be tortured and murdered, the decision was to establish a forty-eight hour deadline for the release of all imprisoned Tupamaros. If the deadline was not met, the hostages would be judged by a "People's Court" for their crimes, and the sentence would be carried out.

That statement worried many in the public, the press, and the governments involved, and with reason: it adopted a harder tone, and referred to both men as representatives of "murderous" governments. The charges against Mitrione were the worst: he was accused of being a spy, a trainer of forces that later killed people, and a facilitator of weapons. Before deciding on establishing this deadline, the new MLN leadership had consulted with the various columns. The majority was in favor of executing Mitrione; according to historian Aldrighi, virtually the entirety of the MLN "demanded" the American's death. In fact, according to Rosencof, some Tupamaros wanted to murder Mitrione, Dias, and even Fly at the same time.

There were still more twists left. On the very same day when the new leadership published its deadline, it fell to a spectacular police raid. Detected at their meeting house in the placid Parque Rodó neighborhood, Mansilla, Menéndez, Blixen and Domínguez were arrested with less than 24 hours as the MLN's *dirección.*[290] Their latest press release threatened there were twelve hours to go before the deadline for Mitrione's life expired (nothing was said of Dias or Fly), and now the MLN once again had no leadership. In fact, it was in worse shape than after Almería, for on that occasion Mansilla had survived and reconstituted the top command. Now there was no one left.

Despite these advances, the lack of contact with the MLN and the publication of the deadline maximized tensions among the Uruguayan, Brazilian, and American governments. A disgraceful moment for the latter came when the Secretary of State, William Rogers, cabled the following to Ambassador Charles Adair: "We have assumed that GOU [Government of Uruguay] has considered use of threat to kill Sendic and other key MLN prisoners if Mitrione is killed. If this has not been considered, you should raise it with GOU at once".[291] According to Uruguayan journalists who investigated the issue, Pacheco supposedly retorted to his Minister of Foreign Affairs Jorge Peirano, who was conveying the unusual American proposal, what follows: "This guy is either drunk or off his rocker! What does he think Uruguay is? Viet Nam?"[292] The response from Montevideo to Foggy Bottom, as reported by Ambassador Adair, was humiliating to the hierarchy of the Department of State and the National Security Council: "I showed [Peirano] text of message (...) [Peirano] stated his type of government did not permit such action".[293]

According to the sentries who guarded his cell, Mitrione became increasingly depressed.[294] His main interrogator, Candán, had disappeared. He was informed not of his capture, but rather of the MLN's decision to establish a deadline for their demands to be met. One letter he was allowed to send to his wife, via MLN liaisons with the press, reflected this: he underlined the words indicating his life was at risk, and dependent on the actions of the Montevideo government. According to his guards, things got progressively darker: "he broke down and said he knew he was going to die".

After the passing of the deadline, the MLN leadership published press release number nine, which announced the People's

Court had reached a verdict and that the sentence for Mitrione's crimes was death. The ruling would be executed within twenty-four hours. Everything went into a tailspin. Brazilian consul Aloysio Dias's wife, Aparecida Leal, was a constant media presence. Fearing for her husband's life, she was loudly taken to the prison where Sendic and the others were being held, to beg for her husband's life. Efraín Martínez witnessed her confront Sendic, face to face, and receive as response a calm explanation: "Madam, from the moment we go to jail we are incapable of doing anything at all, because we have a pre-existing protocol that says imprisoned Tupamaros lose all decision-making authority".

The government also maximized its efforts. The largest security sweep in the country's history was announced as a desperate measure to rescue the hostages: every available policeman and soldier was deployed in a block-by-block search of the city of Montevideo. There was little time: the press release was found at 14:00 on Saturday August 8, and the execution was announced for noon the following day.

In the hours before the deadline was met, Montevideo was abuzz with tension, intrigue, and tumultuous police operations often resulting in arrests boisterously saluted by people in vigil at their doorsteps. Everyone was on edge. Just twenty minutes before the deadline, U.S. Ambassador Adair took to the airwaves and pled for Mitrione's life. The anxiety-filling deadline passed, and only later was the MLN heard from again: it simply announced that the next statement would appear on Monday, August 10, at noon. In effect, the Tupamaros had delayed their execution of the sentence by twenty-four hours.

The American and Brazilian governments were breathing down Uruguay's neck: for once, Marxist propaganda about imperialism was real. As disclosed in the RAND report on the Mitrione case, "Conversations between U.S. officials and Brazilian generals on August 9 confirmed that the Brazilian Army was on a major alert posture in Rio Grande do Sul garrisons and on modified alert as far north as Rio de Janeiro (...) All the Brazilian generals interviewed were pessimistic over the outlook for Uruguay and were somewhat disdainful of the Uruguayans and their system of government".

Mitrione was in the custody of Column 15, and it was that column's crippled command that decided his fate. Amodio, Rey,

Candán, Blixen and others captured in the past days and weeks had all been in its leadership. Now three radical but efficient students were improvising how to run it. They were Henry Engler, codenamed Octavio and leader of the talented guerrilla cell "The Mexicans"; Rodolfo Wolf; and Armando Blanco. The latter served as one of Mitrione's two interrogators the first time he was questioned. In the early afternoon of that Sunday, August 9, they met to decide what to do with the life of a man whose death sentence had already been decreed and whose scheduled time had already passed.

The fateful decision was made then and there: Mitrione would die. Engler was the leader of Column 15's combat division. After the fall of Candán and Rey at Almería, he became the overall commander; he would therefore be managing the execution.

Henry Engler Golovchenko had moved from his hometown in the north of Uruguay to Montevideo in 1964, aged eighteen, to study medicine. He and other "militants" at the School of Medicine provided medical support to union protesters and rioters in emergency situations. Engler approached the MLN during the fires of 1968. As he put it, "What was decisive for me was when the police opened fire on the demonstrators. That changed the situation radically". Engler called his accession to the MLN "the most glorious thing that happened in my entire life".

In 1970, he and others like Rodolfo Wolf took over Column 15 and the Mitrione decision. Wolf later recalled "We saw it with the rigidity of young and inexperienced people. A certain day and time had been given as deadline, and if the exchange was not accepted he was going to be executed. When we were left leaderless, we stuck to the wording of our press release".

The men Engler chose to conduct the execution were Antonio Mas Mas, Aurelio Fernández and Esteban Pereira. According to Engler, upon being given the order to kill Mitrione, one of the chosen hitmen "grabbed his head and said: 'This cannot be!' (...) he thought it was a horrendous situation".

The operation began on the afternoon of Sunday August 9, hours after the deadline had passed, with the robbery of a Buick automobile. In the evening, approximately at 21:00, Mitrione's guards informed the hostage that negotiations were taking place and he would be moved to a different location. To make the transfer easier for everyone, he was given an intravenous dose of valium. He was then bound, blindfolded, and transferred to the stolen vehicle.

The Tupamaros present that night narrated for MLN historian Aldrighi what happened afterwards. The dose given to Mitrione was the strongest he could take; that way he would sleep through the ordeal. He was moved into the house's garage in a dizzy state, and from there into the back seat of the Buick, with his tied hands behind his back. His alleged last words as an MLN prisoner were "I feel like I am in paradise".

After driving for some time across the unlit and winter-emptied streets of the Puerto Rico neighborhood, they arrived at a parked MLN vehicle. After changing cars, the three Tupas at the scene were the driver Esteban Pereira and the two trigger-pullers, Antonio Mas Mas and Aurelio Fernández.* Still inside the parked car, the moment of truth arrived. Mas Mas and Fernández pulled out their weapons, aimed them at Mitrione, and, as they screamed "For Viet Nam and Latin America", opened fire: two rounds in the chest, one in the head. According to Pereira, "Mitrione was asleep, but at the moment when the bullet hit him in the chest we heard a soft gasp".

Hours later, at around 4:15, a police patrol found the parked car. The officers noticed the body of a man stretched out on the back, and immediately called for reinforcements. The information did not take long to reach the OPS advisors posted to the national police headquarters: Mitrione's subordinates. Ambassador Adair deployed them immediately to the scene to determine whether the much-feared outcome had taken place. In the meantime, the national government learned the news while Pacheco presided over an early morning cabinet meeting.

The End of an Era

The reaction in Uruguay and around the world to this shocking incident was a major turning point in the insurgency of the Tupamaros. In a country that had been little used to crime and violence, much less to the revolutionary variety, the cold-blooded

---

* Mas Mas was, according to top police officer Víctor Castiglioni, "the cruelest assassin the Movement ever had. He was involved in approximately ten [lethal] crimes".

murder of a bound man shocked the population. Support for the MLN plummeted among the general populace, something that the Tupamaros themselves have recognized and that was widely reported at the time. The "man on the street" suddenly saw a different face of the conflict, as compared to the earlier days of armed propaganda.

Virtually all accounts of the insurgency agree on the gloomy quality of this incident. One Tupamaro told journalist Alfonso Lessa "That was one of the most terrible days I can recall in Montevideo (...) It was horrible. Horrible. To me, that day was when terror began to spread in Uruguayan society"[295]. Gallup opinion polls agreed: a full 69% of Uruguayans were against the murder of Mitrione, with an additional 10% not expressing an opinion. Barely 18% of the total said the Mitrione murder was not a crime, and that the insurgent group should continue existing. It was approximately half of the amount reported by a previous, pre-Mitrione poll. Even the heavily Marxist newsmagazine Marcha, which was usually pro-MLN, acknowledged how "all" reactions had been negative.[296]

To some high-ranking MLN leaders, the outcome should not have been like that at all. Eleuterio Fernández, the creator of Plan Satán, saw a blunder in the Mitrione case: "the execution was a very damaging political blow for the MLN, which aborted the current of sympathy it had been enjoying among ample segments of society"[297]. Efraín Martínez, who was captured in Almería, told the historian Aldrighi how "In no way did we think of executing someone. It would have been the stupidest thing anyone could conceive (...) If Almería had not fallen, Mitrione would be alive. There is no question about it".[298]

In his first encounter with U.S. ambassador Adair following the murder, Minister of Foreign Affairs Peirano "spoke movingly of deep sense of sorrow and grief that all decent Uruguayans felt with Dan's murder and said yesterday at airport when he saw the whole Mitrione family assembled, his own grief was indescribable. Even the death of his parents had not affected him more".[299]

In Washington the situation was also tense. The possibility of a Brazilian attack against Uruguay had been discussed since 1964: with the fate of Consul Dias in the balance, that scenario was closer than ever. The Uruguayan ambassador to Washington, Héctor Luisi, met with Department of State officials moments after news of Mitrione's death arrived. After discussing an appeal to Fidel Castro to call for an end to terrorism, he noted that "if Brazil were to take aggressive military action as a result of its reaction, the GOU would not fight but instead distribute the weapons of its Army among its people".[300] They were preparing for a complete disaster situation.

Unbeknownst to the Uruguayans, one silver lining was secretly reported days before the murder of Mitrione.[301] In most confidential terms, a Brazilian regime source told an American diplomat that "President Médici as *gaucho* has lived much of his life with Uruguayans, has a high regard for their country, and is reluctant to offend its government".[*]

The Mitrione crisis proved many of the MLN's complaints about Uruguay were false. Much of the organization's propaganda justified its activities on the notion that the police force was packed with brutal torturers. Mitrione himself was allegedly in Uruguay precisely to teach that. Furthermore, Marxist denunciations of "right-wing, paramilitary death squads" following Central American and Brazilian models were increasingly vocal.

Yet, the government of Uruguay and its security forces not only respected the judiciary's denial of a permit to use truth serum on the prisoners. They also abstained from harsh interrogation or torture of men like Sendic, and there were no death squads roaming Uruguay during the crisis, kidnapping MLN or Marxist hostages to counter-intimidate the Tupamaros. Tragically, and as noted before, Mitrione himself had believed this cultural tradition would be reflected in his Tupamaro abductors, when he told them "From what I have read, the Tupamaros are more intelligent than other groups. They kill only when it is necessary. There are others who kill indiscriminately, they kill first and ask questions later"[302].

Around this time a major controversy erupted over statements by comisario Alejandro Otero to a Brazilian magazine. The former chief pursuer of the Tupamaros told journalist Arturo Aymoré that Mitrione's death had been imaginable, and that the American had been involved in teaching torture techniques to Uruguayan policemen. The immediate furor over the statements caused the government to interrogate Aymoré and Otero himself, who decisively rejected the notion that he had said any such words. Otero later said he never told Aymoré anything like that, and that in fact he only met Mitrione once.[303]

---

[*] A *gaúcho* is a native of the state of Rio Grande do Sul, which borders Uruguay.

There were plenty of reactions to the murder of Mitrione, both inside and outside Uruguay. Domestically, despite some outliers, everyone from the Communists to Marcha condemned the murder. Internationally, there was universal outrage – even in the Soviet Union, by then less in favor of violent revolution than ever. The New York Times compared the Tupamaros to Adolf Hitler; The Washington Post, Zbigniew Brzézinski, the Pope, the French press, and many others publicly condemned the MLN.[304]

The romantic Robin Hood warriors of just a few months before had forsaken their reputation. Retired army colonel Sergio D'Oliveira noted how the Tupamaros had until then successfully based their operations in Uruguayan traditions of face-to-face combat and proper respect for combat rules. The cold-blooded murder of the bound American was "the first major mistake" they made.[305] Even the self-proclaimed doctrinarian of urban guerrilla warfare, the Spaniard Abraham Guillén, later wrote that after his interrogation and public humiliation, Mitrione's death sentence "should have been commuted out of respect for his eight sons, but on condition that he leave the country".[306]

Despite these negative consequences, the MLN helped turn kidnappings into a major tool of modern insurgency. There had been plenty of kidnappings worldwide before, but few that had been executed so tenaciously and as part of a sustained campaign. After Plan Satán, many subversive organizations -particularly in Europe in the 1970s- began to emulate the Tupamaros by kidnapping politicians and businessmen from the streets of their cities.[307] The MLN, "the world's most formidable and proficient urban guerrilla movement", became a model for terrorists.[308]

A discordant note in the mournful hours after Mitrione's death came from Vice President Alberto Abdala, a superb representative of the decadent Uruguayan political class of the time. On the morning of August 10, the same one when Mitrione's body was found, an interview with him appeared in a newspaper. The headline was "I want to be president".[309] Whatever Pacheco's faults may have been, he was right in making every effort to keep the excitable and unstable Abdala away from power.*

* One year later, shortly before leaving office but still a serving vice president, Abdala told visiting U.S. Embassy staff "the Embassy should not be surprised in the future to find him assuming highly radical positions and even 'leading mobs in

Pacheco could not trust his cabinet to be helpful either. A great example is the late 1970 visit of high-level Washington official Samuel Eaton. Mitrione had been murdered and Fly was still in the MLN's hands: the situation was dire. Nevertheless, as reported by Eaton himself, upon visiting acting Minister of Foreign Affairs Ricaldoni (Peirano was away), the response he got was that "it would be best for Mr. Eaton first to talk to the Minister of the Interior".[310] A telegram carrying the same date reveals Eaton went directly from one ministry to the other. His report on his talk with Minister of the Interior Antonio Francese, on various options for ransoming Fly, was that Eaton should "pursue it with the Minister of Foreign Affairs upon his return".[311] This was a microcosm of the Kafkian Uruguayan state bureaucracy.[312]

The People's Prisons

Following the tragic end to the Mitrione kidnapping, Aloysio Dias and Claude Fly continued to be the MLN's hostages. The former's wife spearheaded a massive media campaign in their native Brazil to have her husband freed. Although she and her government tried to pressure the government of Uruguay to comply with the MLN's demands, Pacheco's position was beyond clear after what had happened with Mitrione. Thus, a fundraising campaign became the main drive to free Dias: he would be ransomed through a private effort.

The Brazilian consul went through similar moments with the Tupas as Mitrione did. Brazil had been high on the minds of the Tupamaros, since 1964, as a source of militarism, oppression, repression, reactionary politics, death squads and so forth. Dias was in a precarious position as a representative of that regime. His interrogation reflected this, although the consul held his own against the hostile questioners.

The Tupamaros began by asking Dias about torture in Brazil, and in particular about the "assassination" of Carlos Marighella, the urban terrorist killed in combat in São Paulo the previous year. Much of the conversation drifted towards the issue of "fascism" in

---

the street'". In addition, he proudly showed his visitors an arts studio contiguous to his office, where he had painted at least twenty-five paintings.

Brazil, the campaign to liberate Dias, and the death squads that killed representatives of "the people" in Brazil.

At one point in the conversation, the female interrogator managed to express the mainstream line, concerning revolutionary violence, employed by radicals throughout the 1960s and 1970s: "It is important that you know that the violence of hunger, the violence of penury, the violence of oppression, the violence of underdevelopment, and the violence of torture lead to the violence of kidnappings, the violence of terrorism, and the violence of the guerrilla". It was a perfect reflection of the dominant left-wing thought of the time, most on display in Galeano's "Open Veins of Latin America".

Dias was outraged when the guards read him a letter from his wife. The Tupamaros were sufficiently transparent to reproduce his angry response in full in their transcript of the session: "Please end all of this. This interrogation is an exploitation of myself as an individual for you to further your ends, and I do not see any sense in it. If you do not want to release me, then kill me or leave me here, but I think this is an exploitation of human dignity".[313]

Claude Fly underwent similar treatment as Mitrione and Dias: interrogations and complaint sessions about his home country.[314] The list included American imperialism, racism, fascism, the CIA – to which he was ludicrously accused of belonging- and the usual litany of anti-American conspiratorial ideas mixed with a "barrage of questions and insults". To Fly, it was all distressing. If he was seen as belonging to such an evil killing machine, how good might his chances of surviving be?

Fly never knew whether it was night or day; his meals were not identified as lunches or dinners, and the light was always artificial. He acknowledged in his memoirs fantasizing about killing his captors and escaping. The Tupamaros continued to cause psychological harm to their victim for many months, showing him pictures of his wife crying in newspaper clippings that in turned caused him to become afflicted with a terrible, impotent sadness.

Later on in his captivity, Fly's situation improved. He got to read a bit, including intensive readings of the New Testament, and to play long card games with his guards. The police were actually close to him a few times. On one occasion he was rushed to a minuscule *berretín* inside a wall, for the police knocked on the front door with the intent of searching the home. Quietly and literally sticking to the two Tupamaras guarding him, Fly had to hold his breath in the cramped, hot space while the police ended their intervention downstairs.

Later on, at a different underground location, Fly was kept in a cell next to Dias's. It was the Brazilian consul who revealed to him the grisly fate of Mitrione, a fact the MLN had dishonorably yet logically kept from their only other American kidnapping victim. Fly was horrified: "cold fear settled in my chest (...) I wanted to tear down that blue curtain and rail at the guards for their wanton brutality and insensibility to humanity". Oddly, Fly shared conversations with Dias that ended in uncomfortable theological debates between the strongly Catholic Brazilian and the strongly Protestant American.

On February 21 1971, more than six months after being kidnapped by the MLN, Consul Dias was freed. The ransom was a quarter of a million dollars (equivalent to $1.5 million in 2014 dollars), an enormously large sum that contributed greatly to the MLN's coffers.[315] The Brazilian government immediately spirited him away from the country in a military airplane, without giving the Uruguayan police a chance to debrief him.[316] Dias's famous wife told the Montevideo chief of police that since the Uruguayans had not helped at all with their case, the Dias family would not help them either. The American embassy was distraught: Dias could have extremely valuable information for the purpose of rescuing Fly. The Brazilians could not have cared less.

With the embassy pursuing this track with the Brazilian government, the Brasília regime once again revealed its callousness. Not only did it refuse to grant American diplomats access to Dias – which was limited to useless written exchanges-, but it specifically requested that the embassy *not* share any of the information with the Uruguayan government.[317] The U.S. embassy in turn suggested to Foggy Bottom not to honor this request, but it was a stunningly perverse conduct designed to punish Uruguay for not following Brazil's foolish hostage situation policies.[*]

Fly's path to freedom was more complicated than Dias's.[318] By February of 1971, he had been in MLN captivity for seven months.

* Not content with this, Brazil also bullied Paraguay into supporting its position, rather than Uruguay's, on the issue of kidnappings. If not, Paraguay's "trade and commercial relations" with Brazil would "suffer".

He had spent Christmas, learned of the birth of a granddaughter, learned of his son's attempts to trade himself for his father, and never managed to determine whether it was daytime or nighttime, all under MLN captivity. He maintained a Bible- and exercise-heavy routine, although conditions were terrible. He was never allowed to change his clothes, and permission for various acts of personal hygiene was restricted for days on end. Every time the power was cut in the People's Prison, typically due to the proximity of the police, the lights and the electric fans were cut off. All that could be felt during those endless minutes was the funk of confinement, the heat, and the fear and anxiety of the situation. In Fly's recollection, "The blackness seemed to suffocate and strangle us, as though it were a deadly gas. The stench of sweating bodies, rotten, moldy clothes, and stale food mingled with the blackness. It seemed as if we were sinking into a rotten, abysmal chasm with no dimensions". That summer, all those factors combined to make breathing itself "distasteful".

Unbeknownst to Fly, his family and the American government agreed on a creative effort to rescue him. Turning the tables on the MLN, the proposal was that if Fly was freed the United States would send an advanced kidney dialysis machine to Uruguay. Variants included providing direct medical treatment in the United States, free of charge, to a number of Uruguayan children. The plan made remarkable sense, and would likely have placed the MLN in an untenable position. However, it was never tried. The Uruguayan government was more absolutist than ever: it would not allow the publication of an MLN manifesto in the legal press, which at one point was the only demand the Tupamaros had in exchange for the liberation of the soils specialist.

Two days after Dias' liberation, Claude Fly suffered a heart attack while doing push-ups. Immediately after this mishap, one of the MLN's medical doctors, Jorge Dubra, was brought in to see him. The MLN knew that if Fly died in its custody, it would face a backlash that would dwarf that of the Mitrione case seven months prior. For this reason, and possibly also for basic reasons of humanitarian decency, the organization pulled all the stops. Its impressive medical service was brought in force. Fly witnessed the deployment of oxygen tanks, an intravenous feeding solution, and "a nurse, a doctor, and a specialist with electrocardiograph (ECG) equipment working in the little cell outside my cage".

A treatment program was set up, with daily visits, blood samples drawn for laboratory analysis, enemas, catheter tubes, injections, and baths. When it became clear that Fly could be in the throes of a major life-threatening crisis, he witnessed the Tupamaros destroy parts of the hideout to make room for a gurney.

On March 2, 1971, he was freed. The MLN briefly kidnapped a doctor named Jorge Dighiero to check on the hostage and witness the adequate handling of his release. Patient and doctor were dropped off directly at Uruguay's best medical facility, the British Hospital, along with a copy of Fly's electrocardiogram and the diagnoses of the MLN's doctor. Within a half hour of his arrival at the hospital, the American ambassador, Charles Adair, was there to see Fly: "He was the first fellow American I had seen in seven months! (...) I grabbed him and cried and shook with deep emotion!"*

The Indomitable Hostage

The next foreign victim in Plan Satán came in early January of 1971. It was in the depths of the Uruguayan summer, with Montevideo virtually empty, and six months after the Mitrione murder. Dias and Fly were still in the MLN's hands; however, preparations were made to house many more hostages. Obtaining the release of MLN prisoners through pressure on the government was now only part of the reason; another lay in the international significance the Tupamaros acquired after the 1970 crisis, and yet another in the more straightforward benefit of monetary ransoms.

The new target was Geoffrey Jackson, and he was the MLN's most important one yet: the ambassador from the United Kingdom. As the representative of a world power, one of only five nuclear states at the time, and a country with a long history in the region, Jackson was an extremely sensitive figure.

British influence in the River Plate and Southern Cone regions was second to none during the nineteenth century, but waned notoriously with the disasters of the two world wars. Nevertheless, London maintained a diplomatic presence, and Jackson was quite

---

* Fly would have a modicum of revenge in that his debriefing "provided the basis for locating a secret compartment containing a large arms cache in one of the four locations" where he was held.

the representative of a proud line of Foreign & Commonwealth Office professionals. In the summer of 1970-1, Jackson and every other diplomat in Montevideo knew they were at risk of kidnapping, particularly if they came from a country like Britain. In fact, Jackson first arrived in Montevideo on the very day when Mitrione, Dias, Jones, and Rosenfeld were attacked.[319]

In the weeks prior to his abduction, Jackson began to notice small changes in his daily life. Young people were visible everywhere: while he jogged, while he played golf, and so on. Mysterious telephone calls reached the ambassadorial residence at night. There was also "that sensation which needs no explanation to those who have endured the presence of mice, or rats, behind the woodwork, that certainty of an intelligence and strength, always invisible, but always there, present, vigilant, somehow malignant".

Jackson's daily routine began by leaving his official residence, one of the nicest in all of Montevideo, at the appropriately called Park of the Allies, not too early in the morning. He rode with an unarmed chauffeur in the main car, and behind him was an additional car with two guards – also unarmed, per Jackson's insistence. From the Park of the Allies the vehicle rode through the *rambla* of Montevideo, which offered wide open spaces, high speed, and a pleasing view of the water.

After a few minutes, the chauffeured vehicle turned right – north-, up one of the narrow streets of Montevideo's Ciudad Vieja – the oldest part of town, designed mainly as a Spanish colony in the eighteenth century. To this day, its streets remain uncomfortably cramped, with a single lane for traffic, vehicles parked on both sides, and various annoyances on the way. Jackson usually expected to be at his office around 10:15.

On the morning of January 8, the vehicles left the Park of the Allies area –which Jackson knew was under MLN surveillance in the form of too-frequent "picnics"- without incident. The embassy cars also made it through the entire stretch of the *rambla* without encountering any alteration to their daily routine. Upon entering the final portion of the route in the Ciudad Vieja, the usual morning logjams occurred: delivery vans, trucks, pedestrians, and more. Upon doing one of these myriad stops to yield to others, a van hit the second embassy car from behind. The owners got down and began to survey the damage, while the guards inside the car did the same. At the same time, in the front car, Jackson saw a truck emerging to block the way, and simultaneously a fruit-and-vegetable vendor on a street stall just meters from his car pull out an assault rifle.* The MLN was attacking.

While the guards in the back were assaulted, the attackers on the front opened fire directly across the front windshield of Jackson's car. The rounds landed on the upholstery of his back seat; they were targeted at the guards involved in the scuffle behind the car. Once the guards were overpowered, the Tupamaros opened the door on Jackson's side, struck him fiercely, and spirited him away.

The first moments after this, which Jackson recounted in his excellent memoirs, were a mixture of confusion, outrage, worry, and pure English firmness: "I congratulated myself that my wife could count at any rate on a widow's pension [and that] my briefcase contained nothing that could injure or embarrass my government". While being transported to the People's Prison the British ambassador had blood taken from him, and was drugged intravenously so he would not be of concern to the *guerrilleros*.† His first stop was at a safe house containing a *berretín*, or hiding compartment, in the far northeast of Montevideo. Among the first things the MLN guards intended to do to Jackson was to remove his necklace and signet ring, something to which he steadfastly refused.

The ambassador described his time as an MLN hostage in excellent detail. For the first two or three weeks he was "totally" unable to eat, and was simultaneously bothered ("almost physically distressed") by the pop music blaring out of MLN radios. The Tupamaros questioned Jackson about the British presence in Uruguay, particularly that of companies with subsidiaries in the country. Jackson refused to comply with this demand for information; "The reply was that this was an order, to which my reply was that I took orders only from my government, on which stalemate we parted".

Cultural differences often became unbridgeable, thanks mainly to the MLN's deep ideological posture. Jackson's growing beard was referenced to in jest as making him resemble Francis Drake: a great English naval commander in his eyes, but a pirate to the MLN's –

---

* "My captors were very proud of this refinement, of which I was told repeatedly afterwards".

† In fact, Jackson later noted that throughout his time as a hostage "The Tupamaros used drugs lavishly, including truth drugs, and tended to overdose".

and his dismay. Similar things happened with the sport of golf – a clear symbol of oligarchic wealth to the Tupamaros, and a proud sport of the anti-aristocratic Scots to the Briton Jackson. At one point, a Tupamaro asked him if he owned a castle: surely a well-spoken British diplomat *had* to be a blue-blooded plutocrat.

The British government displayed the same level of grit that its representative in Uruguay was demonstrating in his tiny, impossibly humid cell.* According to diplomatic contacts with the American embassy, London was "prepared wait out extended confinement of Ambassador Jackson".[320] Meanwhile, the latter read plenty, exercised as much as he could, complied with mandatory "interviews", played card games, and more. Some conversations oscillated between detailed discussions of the guards' hoods, and his stoic defense of Britain. At certain points, Jackson touched the darkest of all topics: "more than one of them winced when I took my courage in my hands and asked them how they could live with the ghost of Dan Mitrione".

In any case, to Jackson the guards were most disagreeable: boorish, unkempt, and in the case of the women, singularly unfeminine. In one case, "If technically and aesthetically [her] eyes were things of beauty, their habitual expression would have petrified a basilisk". A demographic study was inevitable: only one guard did *not* have a university education. A psychological one as well: "I did not meet one who did not seem disturbed or psychologically scarred". Nevertheless, despite his greater composure than Fly, Jackson was also subjected to the psychological torment of captivity. In one of his nightmares, "my Mephistophelian Tupamaro guard in his cubby-hole would at long last remove his Ku-Klux-Klan hood, revealing a cured face of baked clay, which he would in its turn peel off in sections, leaving just a skull beneath".

Jackson was freed much later in 1971, in circumstances that will be described ahead. He was by far the most stoic of all the hostages. Upon arriving back home ("at last, the hedgerows of England"), he could not help but reflect how "In two hundred and forty-four days and nights I had not shed a tear. Nor would I now. But for five full minutes I could not speak a word".

---

* Jackson later wrote "I would not have believed that in such conditions I could have brought myself when necessary to kill cockroaches with my bare hands; but needs must".

Despite Jackson's stiff upper-lipped presentation of himself in public and in his book, he silently suffered from prolonged imprisonment with the Tupamaros. According to telegrams exchanged between the British and American embassies after his liberation, "his long captivity had had noticeable deleterious effect on him".[321]

Plan Satán proved to be one of the MLN's lowest points, and a very ineffective stratagem. It was not the only disastrous MLN idea of 1970 and the years that followed.

CHAPTER NINE:

A NUMBER OF DREADFUL THINGS

IMMEDIATELY AFTER THE tragic events of Plan Satán in August of 1970, the fresh American deputy ambassador to Montevideo, Frank Ortiz, wrote to Washington: "To an outsider like myself it would seem as though the Government has done significant damage to the operational capabilities of the terrorists. However, those knowing more of the subversive movement tell me that the brain of the organization is still intact and new outrages can be expected (...) Any number of dreadful things could yet take place here".[322] How right he was.

By the second half of 1970, the situation in Uruguay had deteriorated so much that President Pacheco decreed the school year was over by August 28, with almost half of the year's classes left to go. This enormous mistake, a concession to the chaos imposed by others, only deepened the involvement of the by-standing middle classes in the war with the Tupamaros. Virtually everyone in Uruguay was feeling the impact of the confrontation one way or another.

Plan Cacao

In September, with the country still reeling from the terrible Mitrione incident, the MLN launched Plan Cacao, a wave of terrorist bombings against multiple civilian targets. The campaign showed how much the group had changed. Having lost most of its initial members, including the entire leadership, the organization remained militarily strong. It was also more prone to violence than before. The new leaders felt that the insurgency had to be relentless and escalating. It was time for the Tupamaros to impose their presence on society not just through ingenious armed propaganda operations, but through the direct destruction of the "oligarchs" and the representatives of "imperialism". The list was long: Uruguay's wealthy; diplomats of foreign governments and countries; multinational corporations; banks; large *estancia* owners; and others. A vast majority were civilians.

In the Correo Tupamaro (Tupamaro Courier), one of the main propaganda outlets disseminated during this period, the language was clear: "the oppressors, the oligarchs, the landholders, and the people in power are not at war, they are bystanders. They are *balconying* [the conflict]. Fire and gunpowder have yet to reach them. Fear and uncertainty have yet to reach them. But this war is against them - and to them it will come. Let them feel the impotence of the raided worker, let them feel the fear of detained students, let them feel the fear. Let fear rise in their parties, in their fancy places of enjoyment ".[323*] A separate part read "The war must be taken to where the enemy takes it: their homes, the places where they enjoy themselves; it must be made total. The enemy cannot have one minute of calmness".[324]

The Tupas based this plan on many sentiments. One was that attacking policemen (Line H operations) was proving successful militarily, but not politically. After all, the cops were typically lower middle-class individuals with scarce education, who were following orders, and who actually represented Uruguay's "proletarians" to a considerable degree. Another was a sense of retribution: if the homes of union leaders, student rioters, MLN sympathizers, and others could be raided by the police, so would those of the powerful.

To some members, like Celeste Zerpa, this was precisely the appeal of the radical swerve of Plan Cacao: "I liked it. It was good to sneak into the properties of the capitalists, of the shameless. You acted wickedly, you vacated people from their homes, you left children in the streets: well, as revenge we are breaking into your house".[325] Lastly, there was a sense of class warfare, notorious in the

---

* The term "balconying" is coined here as an equivalent of the Uruguayan slang "balconear", which uses the image of someone on a terrace or balcony watching things come to pass to convey passivity.

Tupamaros' disgust with the way the upper middle classes had fun at night and so forth. One internal report held nothing back: "Many of us, given our class origins, do not have the hatred expressed in combat by those who have been exploited. Many of us have compassion for our enemies because of an incorrect political judgment (...) We need to awaken class hatred in ourselves as well".[326] While some Tupamaros had reservations with the plan, their voices were never truly heard.

The phenomenon of revolutionary attacks on civilians was not happening only in Uruguay. Terrorism has existed throughout history, but the twentieth century saw the emergence of spectacular, global attention-grabbing attacks for the first time. Beginning in 1968 in particular, terrorism gained ground at a dramatic pace as the tactic of choice for revolutionaries, most famously when in use by Palestinian organizations.[327] In the words of Brazilian João Quartim, who noticed this increasing fascination with terror, "For certain activists, a week without an attack seemed a week in which the revolution made no progress".[328*] By the 1970s, terrorism was a frequent occurrence in North America, Europe, the Middle East and the Southern Cone. The MLN was a part of this phenomenon.

Some of the government's actions contributed to increasing the MLN's anger. Take for instance one of Uruguay's most demonized families of the 1960s, the Peiranos. A prominent Italian-Uruguayan clan, its members had significant banking holdings and professional prestige as lawyers. In 1971, Jorge Peirano –the Minister of Foreign Affairs at the time- had his Banco Mercantil bailed out by the same government he was serving in. This outrageous act only fueled the flames of the "Cacao mindset" of revenge against the perceived oligarchic ownership of Uruguayan society and its government. In one particularly bold attack, an MLN hit team assaulted Peirano's home while he was out. The staff was taken hostage while a number of objects and furniture was piled in the middle of the house and turned into a large bonfire. Later, the job was finished with explosives, which injured a small child that walked into the scene just as a bomb detonated. The boy suffered burns to his face and scalp.[329]

---

* Quartim was, until January of 1969, a member of the insurgent group Vanguarda Armada Revolucionária Palmares. Along with Marighella's ALN, it was the most important of the Brazilian urban guerrilla groups.

There were innumerable attacks similar to the Peirano bombing, all targeted at the homes or companies of specific individuals. Some of the most prominent included the destruction of a wire news agency, of the country's largest textile factory, of multiple banks, of a bowling alley, of several discotheques and movie theaters, of a golfing club, and of the facilities of American multinationals such as General Electric, Esso, or Coca-Cola.[330] The private homes of Marines who guarded the American embassy also continued to be attacked. One leaflet distributed in Montevideo that year read: "So long as the Uruguayan people are exploited, tortured and incarcerated by the oligarchy and the gringos, the oligarchy and the gringos shall have NO PEACE".[331]

Either Everyone Dances or Nobody Does

In almost none of these attacks did the Tupamaros harm people, but the message was clear. Anti-American conspiracy theories and beliefs were accumulating, and in the age of Viet Nam it was difficult to counter them. The U.S. embassy noted, with justified frustration, "A 1970 Gallup survey showed 67 percent believing the U.S. guilty of economic exploitation of Uruguay. This despite the fact that U.S. economic involvement in Uruguay is small".[332]

The most remembered attack of Plan Cacao was the firebombing of the Carrasco Bowling Club. An MLN arson squad approached early in the morning of September 29 1970, and after breaking in bathed the place with gasoline. The fuel that soaked the wooden structure was supposed to ignite after the detonation of explosive charges the group left behind. However, this latter part was somehow botched and the explosives failed to go off.

Returning on their steps, two Tupamaros went inside to check on them. Just when they were doing so the charges detonated and quickly engulfed the entire facility in flames.[333] Carlos López and Roberto Fernández were trapped inside. That was not all: a cleaning lady was also trapped in the collapsing embers of the facility. A young man named Ricardo Zerbino, who lived nearby and witnessed the scene, rushed and helped Hilaria Quirino out of the debris, thus saving her life.[334]

Emergency responders heard the screams of one of the Tupamaros, who survived the collapse but was trapped by the debris and the flames. Firemen saw him spewing hatred and insults at them, simultaneously asking for their help and excoriating them. Following instructions not to approach the flaming structure because of potentially lethal collapses, there was nothing they could do. The following day, the charred bodies of the two dead Tupas filled the front pages of the newspapers: it was clearly a massive propaganda defeat. On the same day a different MLN squad torched a restaurant named La Rochelle, claiming it was frequented by "many rich people and Americans, something which must end". Material losses were total.[335]

As emblematic of Plan Cacao as the torching of the Bowling Club was the destruction of textile company SudAmTex. It was the greatest loss in the history of Uruguayan industry, at $23 million in 2014 dollars, thus surpassing the MLN's own attack on General Motors a year earlier.[336] The company, which was a subsidiary of a New York firm, manufactured textiles mainly for export.[337] Shortly before the attack, its management had reported it considered "its Uruguayan workers as the all-around best in over 20 company branches around the world".[338]

Other places, from the YMCA to firms like International Harvester and Fleischmann, were also destroyed. One that yielded an enduring slogan for Plan Cacao was the destruction the trendy Montevideo nightclub Zum-Zum. One afternoon in September 1970, a team made up of two men and one woman forced its way into the semi-empty facility. After subduing the staff, they soaked the place in gasoline and torched it. The destruction was massive, and it included some of the best imported audio equipment available nationwide. The slogan, as graffiti'd by the Tupamaros at the premises, was "Either everyone dances or nobody does": either all social classes could dance for fun, or no one could.[339]

All of these places were well known to legions of Montevideans, so the attacks were the talk of the town. A prominent "hit" targeted Montevideo's Club de Golf. Located in prime real estate in the best neighborhood of Montevideo, Punta Carretas –a few blocks from the prison where most of the Tupamaros were held-, the club was used both for the actual sport and for nocturnal parties. On both counts, the Tupamaros dismissed it as a decadent institution representative of the ill-begotten wealth of the "oligarchy". The British ambassador Jackson called the golf course there "one of the most idyllically situated (...) in the world".[340] The attack, on December 22 1971, was timed for Christmas, when the venue was at its busiest. Lots of weddings had to be cancelled.

The New MLN

Before Plan Cacao the Tupamaros, save for the use of ineffectual grenades, had tended to respect Sendic's admonitions about using explosives. As the MLN founder said, "explosives cannot be controlled: from the moment you leave the bomb in place, a neighbor might choose to walk the dog at three in the morning and you will find yourself hurting innocent people".[341] Now, with the founders out of the picture, and more radicalized individuals in charge -particularly from Column 15-, explosives were an acceptable weapon.

Plan Cacao dominated all MLN activities for the rest of 1970. The strategic change was so clear that during a December interview with Mauricio Rosencof -employing his *yuto* Urbano-, a journalist noted the Tupamaros' reputation had clearly been damaged in the public eye. Upon the journalist inquiring whether the MLN had decided to clarify its political-social ideas to the people, Rosencof brushed him off: the Tupamaros already had the support of Uruguayans, he claimed. Armed propaganda operations, he confirmed, "are not being given priority at the moment". Urbano closed the interview by claiming the MLN was "indestructible".[342]

Plans other than Cacao were still active, although fewer resources were devoted to them: the Plan Satán hostages were still at the People's Prison; the heist of the jewels in front of the Ministry of the Interior happened in November of 1970; and naturally Line H, for guerrilla harassment, continued to target the police.

That meant that in 1971 all of the MLN's plans coincided, which makes it the year that best shows the complexity of its insurgency. The official strategic document for the new year read: "PEOPLE'S PRISON, ROOSTER, AND CACAO will be the three military 'cores'". In other words: more kidnappings, a continuation of urban terrorism, and a careful development of Plan Gallo (or "Rooster"), a top-secret operation which will be discussed later.[343]

The new year began with the hijacking of a milk truck and the distribution of its contents among the needy in poor neighborhoods: a classic armed propaganda operation that this time included the looting of a toy store and the subsequent distribution of the toys among impoverished children.[344] At least for a moment, the Hunger Commandos were back.

Spectacular robberies, often easily turned into propaganda coups, also continued to take place. For instance, on July 15 an MLN squad of "heavies", including the former CIM naval cadet Fernando Garín and one of Dan Mitrione's killers, Antonio Mas Mas, robbed the main branch of the state-owned BROU in the northern city of Tacuarembó. The team took hostage all the employees and managers. José Milán was one of the latter; he had "given away" the bank to the Tupamaros, and was acting his part out as one more hostage in order to mask his betrayal.[345] It was a repetition of the robbery of the Salto BROU a year earlier.

Only two weeks later, the police got back by netting a great catch: Mas Mas. The evidence of his starring role in the MLN's most significant kill was not yet publicly known, but the Spanish immigrant was more than just that. He was a bold frontline operator, a man filled with hatred and in a delicate state of mind, who represented Column 15's so-called militarism at its worst. His was a significant loss to the Tupamaros.[346] Curiously, the physical survival of Mas Mas upon being arrested meant that Column 15's heavies were not following one of their own "actionist" slogans, which according to Efraín Martínez went "Better a dead Tupamaro than a jailed one".[347]

Still, the MLN had plenty of men to replace Mas Mas, for it was at peak recruitment. A typical example was Carlos Liscano. In 1970, the Escuela Militar de Aeronáutica or National Aeronautical School had purged him due to his political opinions. Armed with professional training, he became –like the CIM cadet Garín before him- one of the few but very valuable Tupamaros with actual military experience. This singular benefit to the "orga" was reflected, as described by Liscano himself, in how the organization treated him: "in 1971 and 1972 I was full-time at the MLN. I was never clandestine. The organization paid its full-timers a salary: I had a budget. The MLN approved it and gave me what I needed to subsist, to pay for rent, food, and the bus".[348]

Liscano drilled other Tupamaros in combat tactics and helped with managing the organization's increasing arsenal. Naturally, his most important task was guerrilla operations: "I still have in my memory images of scared civilians (...) You could discern your violence in people's faces". For men like Mas Mas and Liscano, hijacking civilian vehicles, robbing banks, invading movie theaters to disseminate propaganda, bombing houses and businesses, and gunning down policemen was a daily occurrence.

In one infamous incident representative of the new MLN, the Tupamaros took over a plastics factory named NiboPlast to rally the workers to their cause (in other words, forcing them to hear the group's propaganda). One of the foremen called the police, and the MLN cell fled the premises. Months later, in June, the Tupamaros murdered the man in cold blood.[349]

At the same time, Line H, with the MLN in possession of more insurgents, weapons, and money than ever, continued relentlessly. On one occasion, the Tupamaros directly assaulted a police station, killing two policemen.[350] In another they gravely injured the Montevideo chief of police. The hits did not relent: at the Hospital Pasteur, a team of disguised Tupamaros killed two more policemen and escaped unscathed. Things were so out of control that Tupamaro Luis Alemañy got to fire an improvised bazooka from a moving taxi at a Metropolitan Guard vehicle.[351]

The fact that many of the men being killed were men in uniform did not make their deaths any less disgusting to society. First, as was explained before, Uruguayan policemen came from the working, lower-middle class. They made little money and there was no widespread hatred or suspicion of the police as existed, often justifiably, in countries like Mexico or Brazil. Second, beyond that general impression, some attacks were obviously too cruel and cowardly. That was the case on the morning of July 30 1971, when at a park in the Cerro area a man was found sitting with his back against a tree, his head sunk below the shoulders. It was the body of Ildefonso Kaslaukas, a young policeman and father of five who had been shot in the back of the neck, execution-style, the previous night.[352] The picture of the "sitting man", splashed across the newspapers, once again proved the MLN had stopped playing around in its revolutionary war.

The MLN's waves of attacks were raising tempers everywhere. Hostility between *izquierdistas* and the rest of society, particularly in opposition parties, was strong. Battles continued daily in the streets, colleges, high schools, unionized companies, and more. A typical example of life at the time was, once again, at the Law School. In mid-1971 a representative for the Partido Colorado's pro-Pacheco wing named Walter Craviotto was assaulted, beaten out of the facility, and had his automobile torched for the crime of studying there while being an anti-subversion Colorado. In another incident, there was a large explosion at the Chemistry School, in what turned out to be an impromptu off-hours MLN laboratory crafting explosives.[353]

Left behind in all of this was the most creative tactic of the MLN, armed propaganda. Some plans to continue that campaign were left behind on paper, never executed but nevertheless preserved in the Tupamaros' and the police's archives. One of these would have targeted one of Uruguay's longest and most important traditions: the Exposición Rural. Similar to its larger version in Buenos Aires, or to the Salon de l'Agriculture in France, "la Rural" is the yearly trade fair and breeders' competition for cattle, sheep, equines, and other categories. The MLN's attack plan, codenamed Ñandú, consisted of kidnapping animals rather than people. The Tupamaros would let them loose in the middle of Montevideo's busiest avenues at rush hour, with clearly readable signs containing witty MLN sloganeering.[354] The plan was never executed, since focus was on the more violent campaigns.

One of the oldest MLN lines of operations consisted of acquiring resources and supplies. Every MLN column had three parts: political, military, and services. The latter saw less action, but was highly esteemed. It was the services Tupamaros who requested the guerrilla cells steal over two hundred high-quality wigs in March of 1971. In a different heist, Services obtained carefully targeted aerial photographs of Montevideo and other parts of Uruguay from a government agency.[355] With that, the insurgents now had privileged intelligence to cover all of Uruguay, something few other non-state actors managed to obtain before the age of online commercial satellite photography.

In addition to this, a large number of people had joined the MLN and its peripheral support cells, the CATs. Almost all of them were eager for action. Languishing in prison, MLN founders like Martínez Platero found this troubling: "they thought this was a two or three year thing (...) They imagined us marching directly to the Palace of Justice and tearing it down, like Lenin did. We [the founders] did not think that way at all". In fact, the MLN was allowing too many people in: "The organization fattened. It's not that it grew: it got fatter!"[356]

The Dark Side of Counter-Terrorism

On the government's side, exhaustion and desperation were setting in. Uruguay was out of control. It was, after all, in April of 1971 when Communist chief Rodney Arismendi proudly repeated that Uruguay was the country with the most general strikes per year in the world. The police often appeared overwhelmed; there was a real possibility that the MLN insurgency could become unmanageable. To top this off, there were criminal gangs robbing banks and posing as Tupamaros to benefit from the MLN's reputation and speed up each heist.[357]

Due to all this, the government sought authorization from the Parliament to maintain emergency measures that allowed the police as much leeway as possible in conducting investigations and arrests. Harsh interrogations had mostly stopped since the assassination of Héctor Morán; the police were on notice about the consequences of torture.

The issue of police abuse had been in discussion in the Parliament and in the media for some time. Unfortunately, it is difficult to confidently assert how pervasive torture was. On one hand, it is unquestionably true that in the late 1960s and early 1970s the police committed abuses against detained radicals, including Tupamaros. That much has been recognized by members of the police themselves. On the other, it is also true that "militants" were instructed to complain about torture no matter what had happened, in order to obtain judicial interventions that exonerated them from their actions.

Diverse observers such as the Tupamaros and the U.S. country team in Montevideo had assessed the local police to be an incompetent, ill-equipped, almost constabulary force. It was thus unprepared for the Cuban-inspired revolution of the Tupamaros and the Leninist strategy of tension of the Communists in full view in Uruguay. Descriptions in MLN and Communist propaganda of a fascist or savagely repressive police could not be true - not when the force lacked, as *comisario* Otero described, paper, vehicles, or handcuffs.

The truth probably lies in the middle, meaning that abuses occurred but were not an official policy or a sustained effort. These excesses consisted of more than physical violence against detainees. Top police intelligence officer Víctor Castiglioni recognized that he did "many illegal things, because that is what intelligence is about. The tasks of intelligence are mostly outside of the rule of law (...) I would, for example, sneak somewhere at night to go through someone's books".[358]

The Parliament's investigations into police abuses often came from unexpected sources. Senator Amílcar Vasconcellos, a Colorado antagonist of Pacheco of strongly Social-Democratic persuasions, often led the hearings and commissions. As he privately explained to the American embassy, "the Commission had uncovered unmistakable evidence that police had employed harsh methods and tortures on prisoners in the past (...) he doubted that there had been any formal police policy or directive on tortures, but thought that it was employed mainly by some lower-level officials with sadistic personal tendencies".

Vasconcellos added that torture had been used mainly against victims "with little or no organizational backing which might take reprisals on police". In other words, the Tupamaros and the Communists, especially after the Morán murder, were mostly safe. OPS verified these findings: "Information from our own sources at police headquarters generally bears out Vasconcellos' conclusions – that there was mistreatment of some prisoners by police earlier this year, but since that time such practices have largely disappeared".[359]

The gravest abuses, however, were the extrajudicial killings of unarmed Tupamaros and their collaborators. The possibility had been in the minds of the *izquierda* since the early 1960s, and in some cases since the 1950s. Talk of "oligarchic death squads", which never made sense in Uruguay, arrived with news of anti-Communist repression in Brazil and Central America. Uruguay's radicals imagined that all the ills that affected "fraternal" countries in the region were automatically possible in Uruguay, from landed aristocracies and monopolistic corporations to Yankee invasions and CIA coups d'état. The killing of protesters like Líber Arce in 1968 had contributed to this false theory of impending massacres.

Nevertheless, a number of appalling murders did take place. The first such case was that of Manuel Ramos, a young "legal" Tupamaro employed in Uruguay's diplomatic corps. His corpse was found on the morning of July 31 1971 on the rocks of Kibón, a major events venue right by the water in one of Montevideo's finest stretches of *rambla*. He had been shot twelve times. Pamphlets left at the scene were signed "Comando Cazatupamaro Óscar Burgueño", named after the civilian victim of the MLN's attack on Pando.[360]

Another case was that of Íbero Gutiérrez, a young Tupamaro who was kidnapped late at night on February 27 1972, taken to a desolate part of Montevideo, and shot dozens of times. Forensic evidence indicated Gutiérrez was tortured, for he was shot in different parts of his body in spaced time intervals.[361] Another young man named Héctor Castagnetto was also kidnapped -there were witnesses the moment it happened- and made to disappear.

The names and youthfulness of the victims suggested they were known to the killers through intelligence work; they had never appeared in newspaper or other media accounts of MLN feats. This also meant they were vulnerable targets. Rather than extermination, the purpose of the killings seemed to be revenge and intimidation. In other words, the murderers were likely to be tied to the police. The Tupamaros were outraged.

This was also the analysis of the United States embassy: "Although MLN has murdered several police officers for no apparent reason over past two years, Ramos is first known case in which MLN member has been executed by counter-terrorist group, and represents escalation in counter-terrorist tactics. It seems to be further major step toward 'Guatemalization' of Uruguay".[362] The terminology was still in its infancy: "counter-terrorist" meant what today would be called paramilitary or parapolice murder gangs.

Before finishing his tour of duty in Uruguay, U.S. Ambassador Charles Adair took up precisely this topic with Minister of the Interior Danilo Sena. Adair tactfully suggested "counter-terrorist tactics generally fail and only lead to escalation of violence". Sena's response, as described by Adair, was sadly less than exemplary: he "said he understood my position but stated that Uruguay now at war with terrorists and in such a struggle it might be necessary to have recourse to all types of actions (...) GOU had to demonstrate that MLN was not all powerful and many different types of action might be required to prove this".

Immediately understanding the implications of what he had just heard, Adair did the right thing: "I agreed with the minister that he had a very heavy responsibility but I wanted him to be sure that US position was also clearly understood".[363] Now, without having directly debated the issue, Adair knew two things: elements in the Uruguayan government had hinted at extrajudicial operations, and they in turn knew the Americans disapproved. In response to this, orders for all Embassy staff, including the Public Safety Program advisors, were to "make it clear that such activity is beyond their competence and they cannot participate in any way with advice, or material or technical aid".[364]

More Men in Uniform

With the police in dire straits, there was a development in the government's counter-insurgent efforts that was little noticed at the time: the rise of an entity called SID. In Spanish, the acronym meant Servicio de Información de Defensa: Defense Information Service. It was the Ministry of National Defense's intelligence agency, created in 1965 but largely toothless until 1971.

SID was tasked with keeping a close eye on foreign powers like Brazil and Argentina, but there were growing domestic aspects to its work. Ties with the police already existed: many of Uruguay's ministers of the interior and chiefs of police had been Army generals.

The Army colonel put in charge of SID on January 5 of 1971 was precisely the kind with an eye for non-military activities. His name was Ramón Trabal, and he had served in 1967 as chief of the Police Academy.[365] Trabal came from a family with a history in uniform: his father had served as military attaché to Britain and France in the 1920s. The Trabals were Catalan immigrants with impeccable academic, social, and military credentials. In Ramón's case these included military training in Argentina and the United States. Each time, Trabal shone and demonstrated superior intellectual qualities.

The SID chief's appearance, with a perfectly polished uniform and a thin, trimmed mustache, exuded the confidence and discipline of the career officer. Like virtually every other military man in Uruguay, he had no experience in war. Still, Colonel Trabal's appointment provided him with a privileged position to witness the conflagration taking place in Uruguay. Per the orders of the defense minister, the service started analyzing a matter of internal, rather than external, security: the MLN insurgency. Nevertheless, SID was still a secondary division of a modest military with little strategic depth. As with everything else in the Uruguayan state, there were scant resources, human and otherwise.

Trabal and other high-ranking officers analyzed the issue of subversion and put their conclusions in a report. Their writings had a different approach from the norm: "it is necessary to attack economic crimes. It is a way to reach down to the causes of sedition and tear down some of its banners".[366] Up until that point, orders from the highest level -Pacheco- said the Tupamaros were to be considered strictly a law enforcement issue. They were delinquents engaged in crimes, and as such should be submitted to the usual process of police persecution and judicial determination of their fate. Discussing the "causes" of their uprising, or any of their political demands, was supposed to be completely out of the question.

While the military slowly started its engines, police operations continued to the point where a stalemate seemed to emerge. The tit for tat of urban guerrilla warfare continued for all of 1970 and 1971. During those long months, both sides perfected their techniques, and the Tupas consolidated their credentials as the most experienced urban guerrilla organization of the Cold War. Part of this capacity lay, as always, in the group's remarkable penetration of its enemies. For instance, policeman Miguel Benítez not only secretly worked for the MLN, but was also a participant in U.S.-hosted training programs.[367]

Despite these crippling weaknesses, the police, under the leadership of Castiglioni, improved on its own. According to the chief of Intelligence and Liaison, "To me there was no greater gift or enjoyment than the moment when a *comisario* came to tell me they had captured a Tupamaro base and were bringing in the documents. On those occasions I would stay there to study all those papers". This was a clear failure on the MLN's side: as early as 1968, instructions were to "keep facilities clear of papers and documents. All documents that are unnecessary or have fulfilled their purpose must be burned".[368]

One example happened on March 2 of 1971 when the police raided an MLN safe house in the Ciudad Vieja that turned out to be a major intelligence facility for the "orga". As explained by army colonel Sergio D'Oliveira, inside were "individual dossiers on practically every member of the Montevideo police force and the armed forces, both active and retired". Later in the year, on the symbolic date of October 8 (Che Guevara's death), the police raided the main building of the national university: the already infamous Law School. Among other things, the raiders found photocopies of government dossiers on Tupamaros - yet one more example of the MLN's long reach.[369]

During all of this, the MLN leadership was made up of newcomers Adolfo Wasem and Donato Marrero, plus Henry Engler and Mauricio Rosencof.* The latter two could not be wanted by the police because their lives as Tupamaros were unknown. As Octavio and Urbano, their covers were holding.

Sewers, Breakouts, and Cubans

With its consolidation as a guerrilla force in Montevideo, the MLN began to use the city's sewer network extensively. Jorge Manera, the MLN's historical "engineer", had come up with the plan years earlier, and called it Plan Gardiol.[370] By 1971 the group had an excellent notion of how to navigate the underground. Now, special passages were dug to connect many *berretines* directly to the sewers, in order to facilitate escapes from surrounded houses.

The MLN also consolidated an indisputable reputation for taking care of its own. Not only were members provided with medical services; the organization also helped out the families of fallen Tupamaros. Nothing was more impressive than the way the MLN looked after the Tupamaros in prison. This included not just the threat that any ill that befell a jailed Tupamaro would be mirrored in retaliation once the culprit walked out of the prison. It also meant striving to free them, both by providing lawyers and, naturally, escape routes.

The message was first sent in early 1970, with the liberation of thirteen Tupamaras from their prison-convent. In July of 1971 two key Tupamaros escaped from the government's hands. First, Juan Almiratti, the engineer behind the masterly Mailhos heist, managed to simply run away during a transfer to a courtroom.

Second, and quite more spectacularly, the infamous Raúl Bidegain escaped from inside Punta Carretas prison. The operation was classic MLN.[371] It began with Bidegain's brother, Gabriel, visiting his sibling. In the meeting room, where the prisoners and their visitors met all together, separated only by a table, Sendic and other Tupas nearby caused a confusing incident. Gabriel and Raúl

---

* Nelson Berreta was briefly in the tetrarchy but was arrested and thus yielded his place to Marrero.

Bidegain were left in the middle of a huddle, where they quickly hugged, turned 180 degrees, and put Gabriel's long trench coat on Raúl.

After a few nerve-wracking moments Raúl Bidegain left, discretely hiding as much as he could beneath the coat. Gabriel, who had committed no crime and was sacrificing himself for his brother, joined the procession of Tupas back into the prison, carefully guided and shielded from guards' eyes. After arriving in his cell, his question was obvious yet surreal: "Now what do I do?"

The plan was for the Bidegain switch to remain undiscovered for a few days, by keeping Gabriel deep inside his cell as much as possible. However, Raúl himself called the police to notify them that he "left prison because he no longer felt like being behind bars". Upon learning this, the guards summoned "Bidegain" to check whether it was true. As Gabriel walked the main corridor, the officer on duty had to swallow hard and realize the stinging truth. As he slapped himself and uttered profanity, the cells all around him thundered victoriously: "M-L-N! TU-PA-MAROS! M-L-N! TU-PA-MAROS!" The brothers did not even look alike.

Two MLN activities that grew considerably in this period were political and international liaisons. The man most in charge of these was Mauricio Rosencof. It was thanks to him that at last the Cuban connection produced some results.

The golden age of the MLN-Tupamaros and other groups in the Southern Cone coincided with a period in which the Cubans were downplaying their pro-subversive actions. With the election of Salvador Allende as president of Chile in late 1970, Havana's interest in the region picked up again.

In 1971 Rosencof traveled to the island and negotiated a training agreement with Fidel Castro. Cuba would also provide weapons and money, although never in great quantities.[372] U.S. intelligence correctly detected this was the case: "There is little evidence thus far that Cuban support for terrorists has amounted to more than training and propaganda; there is no evidence of Cuban (...) cooperation in aiding terrorists".[373] Still, to the Tupamaros it was better than nothing at all.

The transshipment point for trainees and weapons, in both directions, was Allende's newly established Communist beachhead across the Andes. In the months and years to come, Chile became for the Americans, the Cubans, and the Soviets the main point of interest in the Southern Cone. The Tupamaros developed strong connections to the new regime and to its paramilitary organization, the formerly insurgent Movimiento de Izquierda Revolucionaria (Revolutionary Left Movement) or MIR.

Unbeknownst to the Tupamaros, and obviously to the police, there were in fact two streams of weapons illegally entering Uruguay for purposes of subversion. One was Cuba's, and it was destined for the MLN. Many of the weapons were German firearms captured during the Second World War. The Soviets had given them to the Cubans, and now the Cubans were in turn giving them to groups like the MLN.

The second stream went to the Communist Party. Curiously, the guns were much more modern than what the Tupamaros were getting: M-16s, at the time the most innovative combat rifle in the world. The Communists' M-16s came from the hands of American soldiers captured or killed in Viet Nam. Now they were winding up in Uruguay, in the top secret caches of the nameless Communist paramilitary organization.[374] What the PCU refrained from doing, however, was engaging in any action. For the moment it stuck to Arismendi's orders, which in turn followed a strict Soviet *détente* line.

Strategic Aimlessness

A new wave of MLN kidnappings targeted only Uruguayan men, except for the British ambassador Jackson. All of the kidnappings had a political dimension, but in addition to that were designed to extract concessions or money from the victims' families and colleagues.

In March of 1971 the Tupamaros kidnapped state prosecutor Guido Berro, and published the results of his interrogation. It was, naturally, a prosecutorial approach: the *guerrilleros* severely criticized his positions on military jurisdiction for certain MLN actions. Berro was freed shortly afterwards, but more "People's Court" kidnappings were in the cards.[375]

The next target was highly symbolic. It was none other than Ulysses Pereira Reverbel, the same man they had taken as their first hostage in August of 1968. Since his liberation, Pereira had remained a relevant man, with the same close ties to President Pacheco. He continued as president of the power utility UTE, and a stalwart supporter of Pacheco's hard line. His flamboyance was also widely commented on, particularly his appearances at various parties. Naturally, Pereira had upgraded his personal security: he carried a pistol, was driven around by a professional guard, and made his appointments at the last minute so as to not give any potential tipsters the chance to alert attackers to his whereabouts.[376]

On March 30 of 1971 Pereira made one such appointment: a visit to the dentist. Alas, his security measures failed: the MLN learned of the day, time, and place of the visit. Somebody had given him up; Pereira was not exactly popular. During the consultation, a group of men sporting the uniforms of a moving company burst in. One of them, the *guerrillero* Mario Píriz, struck Pereira with an iron bar. They then spirited him out inside a rug. The dentist's office was right in the middle of 18 de Julio Avenue; it was a signature MLN strike in open daylight in the capital's busiest street – and against a VIP target struck for a second time.[377*]

Ulysses Pereira was treated even more violently during his second kidnapping than in the first. He was kept permanently in the darkness at the cramped and humid Cárcel del Pueblo – with the exception of sleep time, when the light was turned on.[378] He was also disallowed to use forks and knives while eating. This was exactly contemporaneous with loud MLN complaints about "torture" of their detainees. The oppressive oligarchs were being at last forced to live the life of humble proletarians: it was classic MLN Robin Hood vengefulness.

In a transcript of Pereira's interrogation revealed by journalist Álvaro Alfonso, the guards are shown alternating between complaints about "Yankees" wanting "Uruguayan petroleum" (something that did not exist) and braggadocio such as "We are the only political force that can flip the country around whenever it wants".[379] The group grew so confident during this period that it invited foreign television journalists to interview its "detainees". Footage of Pereira speaking from inside his cell survives to this day; he is shown saying, on the topic of his treatment, "Treatment has been very good. I have received a humane treatment, which I did

---

* Pacheco was conducting a meeting with ministers Bordaberry and Sanguinetti when an aide whispered the news. The president continued the meeting normally and only once it concluded told them what had transpired. He explained his behavior by revealing that since the uptick in MLN activity he had made up his mind that the group might harm him by kidnapping one of his children. After mentally steeling himself for that scenario, everything else had less of an impact.

not believe would be dispensed to prisoners here". When asked if he was tortured he said he was not.[380]

There was a lot of turnover at the People's Prison. In early 1971 British ambassador Geoffrey Jackson, businessman Ricardo Ferrés, state prosecutor Guido Berro (though briefly) and Ulysses Pereira went in. The Brazilian Dias and the American Fly went out. There was, however, more room in the cells. The next victim was more prominent than Pereira: none other than Carlos Frick, a former minister of Pacheco's and also former president of the Monty firm Lucía Topolansky had given up to jumpstart the MLN's armed propaganda. On May 14 1971 an MLN assault squad appeared directly at his home. Two men and one Tupamara boarded Frick's vehicle forcefully, and when the businessman resisted he was shot directly in the chest. The struggle was so rough that the car crashed head-on into a tree, sending the Tupamara riding in the back flying across the pavement.[381] None of the injured died, and a core member of the "oligarchy" was in MLN hands.

Later on, yet another prominent businessman, named Jorge Berembau, was also kidnapped and taken to the People's Prison. The ransom for Berembau was reminiscent of banker and newspaper publisher Gaetano Pellegrni's in 1969: a total of $1.5 million in 2014 dollars was to be distributed among his employees, and he would then be freed.[382] In some respects, the spirit of armed propaganda was still alive – but it was drowned by an avalanche of cruelty.

Henry Engler was the rising star of the MLN. He continued to be a medicine student while being doubtlessly the greatest *guerrillero* the MLN had after Amodio. This turned him into a *referente* of the Tupamaros and a top member of the leadership. Almost all of the organization's great operations after Almería have his imprimatur. Throughout, he achieved the feat of remaining a legal rather than a clandestine Tupamaro. In fact, according to Engler, his home "had been raided multiple times after neighbors called the police and mentioned certain visits to my house. However, I had pictures of Pacheco, and propaganda and lists favoring Pacheco".[383]

Engler is the main representative of the second generation of Tupamaros, the one that had executed the sentence on Mitrione and was now enthusiastically conducting Plan Cacao. According to a 1972 police report, these young Tupamaros came from all professions and academic backgrounds: medicine, engineering, teaching, banking, journalism, and more. To an older Tupamaro, these youths dreamed of "marching down 18 de Julio sporting an olive uniform, a beret with a five-pointed star, and a machine gun". They were the core of a generation that due to the decay of the country had seen its middle-class ambitions frozen or crippled. In the words of Jorge Batlle, they had been locked into "a beer income with a thirst for champagne".[384]

New MLN leader Adolfo Wasem was also a product of Column 15. An interrogator of Mitrione, and also a prominent second-generation Tupa, Wasem had, according to Efraín Martínez, one of the hardest strategic lines in the MLN.[385] He had gotten started as a revolutionary during the fires of 1968, when a ricocheting bullet fired by a panicking policeman struck him in the leg and catapulted his militant reputation.[*] Both him and Engler considered themselves disciples of Alberto Candán, who had fallen in Almería. While Engler specialized in armed operations, Wasem came from the services section.[386]

Wasem was the third most prominent member of the new leadership tetrarchy, after Engler and Rosencof. He benefited from being in the *dirección* at the Tupamaros' most resourceful moment, with the capacity to fly in an MLN airplane to Paraguay, and from there to Chile to meet Fidel Castro. He was captured on July 2 1971 and thus joined the rest of the male Tupas in Punta Carretas prison.

While there, the MLN debated its strategic aimlessness. Sendic, in particular, complained about Plan Cacao. He rejected it as cowardly and added it was preferable to fight "face-to-face, gaucho style".[387] Writing from prison, his proposed alternative was Plan Remonte. It consisted of reinvigorating the Tupamaros' political message by taking over movie theaters, factories, university classrooms, and buses, where small teams of Tupamaros propagandized to the people. These cells gave speeches, handed out flyers, and often projected slideshows. Sometimes they hijacked up to five movie theaters simultaneously.[388]

Nevertheless, the lines were clearly drawn: the old leadership jailed in Punta Carretas disagreed with the strategy adopted by the clandestine *dirección*. Speaking decades after the fact, many Tupamaros from both sides of the debate acknowledge those behind

---

* According to one friend at the time, Wasem was "brainless" in his action-minded personality.

the Sendic position were right. Efraín Martínez, who was a "dove" in the debate, believes Plan Cacao "was the most terrorist, most fucked-up plan the MLN-Tupamaros pulled off. That's when everything got messed up". Former Tupamaro Luis Alemañy called it "madness". Hugo Wilkins added "We faced massive rejections for that kind of attack". Samuel Blixen, a biographer of Sendic and a leader of Column 15 himself, called it a "failure". Even Engler, the main commander behind the effort, said it was a "monumental mistake".[389]

The goal of revolution was always on top of everything else, but it is clear that many Tupamaros were more interested in the immediate satisfaction of operations. The group's military capabilities were still there -in fact, they were in peak form-, but the same could not be said for their political talents.

It is thus easy to identify a descent, as time passed, into greater permissiveness for purposefully harming or killing people, particularly civilians. There were precedents in the kidnappings of Ulysses Pereira and particularly of Gaetano Pellegrini in 1968 and 1969. Both had been physically and psychologically abused. In 1969, the Tupamaros became for the first time responsible for the death of a civilian who was innocent from any perspective – the Pando bystander Carlos Burgueño. In 1970 came the first targeted assassination: Héctor Morán, the abusive police officer. Under Plan Satán the MLN committed its first certifiable murder in the person of Dan Mitrione. Plan Cacao brought a veritable wave of bombings, arsons, and other attacks.

In April of 1971 a new milestone in the Tupamaros' ethical downfall came with the execution of one of its own people. The case in question is that of a man named Roque Arteche, who was not a real Tupamaro but rather a *gambusa* – a common criminal who joined the MLN in prison through an alleged conversion to the cause. In reality, after leaving jail and linking up with the Tupas, Arteche –a creature of the Montevideo underworld- returned to his old ways. He stole money from the coffers of the "orga" and of friendlies who generously and at the risk of their lives hosted him and others in their home. More worryingly, he stole an MLN weapon and used it to murder a man at a bar, over personal issues.

Arteche was little more than a street rat, the kind the MLN was usually indifferent to. It had been a mistake to allow him in the organization, and it was a huge mistake on his part to violate the

Tupamaros' trust. What none of the sides probably foresaw was that Arteche would be "detained" and interrogated while tied to a chair. Although the thief tried to negotiate his way into exile in Chile, to join the growing MLN contingent in that country, there was no way to make it work. Soon after, Arteche was found dead in a dumping ground; Engler told inquiring Tupamaro Armando Miraldi that the MLN had gotten rid of him. The *gambusa*'s fate was grisly: his head was repeatedly smashed with iron bars.[390]

The MLN was getting away with such killings because individuals like Morán, Mitrione, and Arteche were –either factually or allegedly- morally unclean. None of them counted as a true civilian in the eyes of the MLN or its supporters. In wider society, a majority of people concluded it had turned into a terrorist organization that was making life unsafe for everyone. The Tupamaros were a threat, a revolutionary organization that would not do its work bloodlessly, despite its initial promises.

These contradictions emerged with full clarity in the MLN's official strategic document for 1971, the same one that announced the three plans for that year would be the People's Prison, Cacao, and the Rooster (still to be described later). The text reflected the twin personalities of the MLN. It opened by complaining about a lack of Cacao operations: the leadership expected more.

Oddly, later on the same document said "operations must be ultra-feel-good (...) Distribution of foodstuff in slums. Pure propaganda invasions on the radio. Armed propaganda. The 'Pandos' must for now be removed from the list of viable actions, considering the blood-spilling risks they imply".[391] Upon reading this, field commanders and street *guerrilleros* could not know what to expect: they had to be "ultra-feel-good" terrorists, *guerrilleros* who distributed basic necessities while kidnapping civilians and firebombing buildings.

The Ballot Box Looms

On top of all this, 1971 was an election year. Uruguay had –and still has- a fierce tradition of wariness towards presidential re-elections. When the system of government transitioned in 1967 from a parliamentary to a presidential one, part of the deal was that there would be no presidential re-election. That way, at least one temptation of the newly empowered executive branch –perpetuation- could be checked in advance.

The firebrand Pacheco decided to challenge this. In a risky move given Uruguay's customs, he and his allies successfully got permission to hold a referendum on a constitutional amendment that would allow for the re-election of the president. The question would be posed to the electorate simultaneously with the election for president. Since the reformist drive could fail to gather enough votes, the Partido Colorado required a backup candidate. If Pacheco's bid failed, all of the party's votes would be counted in favor of that candidate - a surrogate of the president. The man chosen for the role was Juan María Bordaberry.

Bordaberry was not one of the most important members of the Colorados. He had not been one of the top ministers in the Pacheco government (he was the Minister of Agriculture and Livestock), nor one of its elected municipal governors, and was never a prominent advocate of the party. In fact, Bordaberry was originally a member of the Partido Nacional, and of its most conservative branch at that. He did not fit well at all with the party's previously majoritarian Batllista, social-democratic bloc.

A Basque-Uruguayan with wealthy rural roots, like many Uruguayan politicians Bordaberry had benefited from nepotism: his father Domingo had been a senator between 1934 and 1947. Although Juan María was not stained by corruption scandals, he was nevertheless a classic product of the political reproductive machine. His political ideas were mainly -but also vaguely- against excessive state intervention in the economy. In the late 1950s and 1960s he was a member of the Benito Nardone "ruralist" movement within the Partido Nacional.

Bordaberry's selection to run for president meant Pacheco felt confident: he was placing an unimpressive political figure as candidate, trusting he would win his re-election drive. The campaign was on: Bordaberry recognized his subsidiary role and pushed openly for the constitutional amendment that Pacheco so wanted. The president framed himself as an indispensable man whose unique qualities required the entire political system to be accommodated around him. Perhaps the combativeness of his time in government, from its very first day, had gotten to Pacheco, who increasingly saw himself as the salvation of Uruguay.

The nationalists fielded a strong candidate in Wilson Ferreira. Although he had served in the semi-liberal nationalist governments of the early 1960s, he saw himself as the champion of agrarian "reform" that included the state takeover of private property. He was the greatest foe the Colorados had in the Parliament, but his ideology was purposefully hard to pinpoint. Ferreira's strategy, particularly his economic platform, fished for votes from all sectors. There also appeared to be many Colorado voters on the fence, particularly non-conservative, Batllista social democrats who were too frustrated with Pacheco.

Gearing towards the 1971 elections, Wilson was the star candidate, the one who could flip Uruguay around. Many questions hovered around him, for his promises were large. How exactly would he restore peace among Uruguayans? Would he make concessions to the rioting Communists and the insurgent Tupamaros in order to calm things down? Would he really initiate a dramatic program of economic "redistribution"? What would happen to Uruguay's credit lines and international relations? Despite all of this, Wilson was not by any means the only novelty of the 1971 elections.

That was reserved for the *izquierda*. For the first time, all Marxist, Socialist and Communist parties in Uruguay joined under a single banner, called Frente Amplio or Broad Front. Founded in February of that year, the Frente constituted a major achievement for the Communist Party, which since the re-emergence of the Tupamaros in 1968 had been relegated to second place, behind the insurgents, in the push for socialism.

Nevertheless, as Communists are wont to do, they had stuck to their long-term strategy of accumulating forces. The Tupamaros were often a problem because they risked the entire *izquierda*'s existence through their provocation of government repression. At the same time, it was clear the "ultras" had radicalized and mobilized many among the young, the intellectuals, and others. Frente Amplio supporters were some of the most energized of all.

The man chosen to be the Frente's candidate for president was Líber Seregni, the recently retired general who until recently had been a Colorado. Seregni provided a friendly face for the Frente, but his proposals and statements did not augur well for Uruguay's political system. In his first speech as candidate, the general condemned the government's violence -meaning the police-, but not that of the MLN's terrorist acts.[392] Seregni was not the only Colorado who founded the Frente Amplio. In fact, he was more of a military officer who had happened to vote Colorado than a politician. Leading the way for actual Colorado politicians defecting to the Frente Amplio was Zelmar Michelini, a socialist of increasingly questionable democratic credentials.

The rise of the Frente put the MLN in a complex situation. It had rejected any such path from its very inception, out of disappointment and ideological rejection of party politics. Now virtually all of its ideological allies, plus other elements, were converging in the Frente Amplio.[393] A number of the Tupamaros themselves argued the group could not stay away from the electoral race. In particular, the former Communist Mauricio Rosencof insisted on having some form of MLN legal partisan organization.

The compromise solution was to not abandon guerrilla operations, but to upgrade the MLN's political efforts with the creation of the Movimiento 26 de Marzo, or 26 of March Movement. The group, which was part of the Frente Amplio, published its platform in March of 1971. A cursory glance at the text suggested enacting the program required a massive amount of violence. The direction was clear: a totalitarian, collectivist society that at least on paper sounded indistinct from Cuba and the Soviet Union.

Among the MLN's ideas were the state takeover of all large *estancias*; of all "large" factories, supermarkets, grocery stores, butcher shops, and other food suppliers. All foreign trade would pass to the hands of the state, as would all banks. Naturally, all "large" foreign-owned properties –not just business investments- would go, and in a sign of the hardline radicalism of the time, "large" private homes would also be looted.

Under the MLN's vision for Uruguay, the entire economy would turn into a planned exercise from the top down; a complete welfare state that guaranteed citizens cradle-to-grave government services of all sorts. This was particularly disturbing because, as the historian Hebert Gatto points out, in 1971 the economic failure of Communism in Cuba, the Soviet Union, China, and other countries was already known.[394]

The list of proposed measures did not end there. There were provisions for the murder of journalists who opposed the MLN or its political allies. This was obviously a reference to men like Jorge

Batlle -someone the MLN dreamed of kidnapping-, Julio Sanguinetti, and any others who published newspapers with anti-MLN lines (a majority in Uruguay). Naturally, there was no mention of preserving freedom of association or of expression. Given this program and its many implications, it is no wonder the U.S. Embassy began forming task forces to propose actions, both covert and overt, to impede a Frente victory.[395] Discussions began in May of 1971.[*]

The 26 de Marzo would have made Lenin and Mao proud, but it also contained the potential seeds of the organization's destruction. It was now easier for a young radical to join without becoming a *guerrillero*. The latter were usually selected and compartmentalized with care. In contrast, the 26 de Marzo began to function as a vacuum for accepting all kinds of people who wanted to be part of the Tupamaros' revolution but were not cut out for real, gritty, urban guerrilla warfare. Orders from the MLN leadership were: "put every CAT possible in the Frente Amplio".[396]

The political parties, their lists, their nominees and their programs were in place early in 1971. The campaign proved to be less than exemplary. The candidates failed to debate each other, and there was more bitterness and violence than in any election in recent memory. There were frequent small-scale attacks on political clubs of all parties. According to a police report, "one hundred and forty political clubs have been targeted in attacks in the first six months of the year. The rates are as follows: one hundred and thirty three of the Partido Colorado; five of the Communist Party; one of the Partido Nacional; one of the Frente Amplio".[397]

Deep Breath Before the Plunge

By September, two months before the presidential election, some thought the Tupamaros were fizzling. Plans Satán and Cacao decreased tolerance for them among the populace. Few in civil

---

[*] On July 20, Ambassador Charles Adair wrote the following to Washington: "I would prefer to see us take actions in advance calculated to assure Frente Amplio defeat in the elections than do nothing and risk a subsequent military coup (...) I prefer to see a traditional party victory at the polls and then work hard to persuade and help them to resolve their basic problems". It is unclear what the White House decided. The ambassador later noted he wanted to investigate "what the CIA group does with its budget in the anti-'Frente' field".

society, including among Marxists, were on board with the notion of a revolutionary guerrilla. The MLN suffered significant losses, and new recruits were either of lower quality or of a more violent, alienating nature. There were few new members who could help the group infiltrate key institutions, as had been the case during the armed propaganda years when it had insiders everywhere. In addition, the government increased its rewards for citizens' anonymous tips in the fight against subversion.[398]

The situation was so complex that for once, the organization recognized that Otero's old allegory of the rectangle with a shaded angle (the larger the shaded angle, representing the Tupas, the less security they had) was true: "We have yet to solve the contradiction between the human potential the people provide us in the form of hundreds of future combatants, and the capacity of the organization to absorb and train them".[399] The MLN had the privilege of self-awareness of its strengths and weaknesses - but apparently little could be done about it.

Meanwhile, down in the ranks, feelings were exactly the opposite. As reminisced by Tupamaro Mario Teti Izquierdo, "what we wanted was to be out on the streets. We were twenty, we wanted to do stuff, not go around pondering anything".[400]

On the night of September 5, 1971, these problems were temporarily left behind, because all of the organization's efforts centered on a single spot. A plan that had been at work for months and that had brilliantly been kept secret was executed, and changed everything.

CHAPTER TEN:

RESET

ALL MALE TUPAMAROS captured in the course of the MLN's insurgency were jailed in a single place: Punta Carretas prison.[401] Thanks to this unusual concentration, which included all of the organization's founders and leaders, a Punta Carretas MLN began to function. The more Tupas who joined as prisoners, the more power they accumulated within the perimeter of the penal complex. With more than two hundred *guerrilleros* in the facility, they reached a critical mass that was virtually impossible for the guards and wardens to contain.

The Punta Carretas MLN was organized around two leadership cells, which were codenamed C1 and C2. The first was essentially a replication of the old *dirección*. Its attributions included all relations with the outside world, from consulting about ongoing operations to political advisory and communications security. The members of C1 were Sendic, Fernández Huidobro, Marenales, Manera, Amodio, Candán, Mansilla, plus two that were less known but had become close associates of these leaders: Diego Piccardo and David Cámpora.

C2 was the directorship behind all prison-related affairs. It managed an influence network that kept most of the guards bribed, the internal supply and communications systems, and more. One of its members was José Mujica, who in Punta Carretas began to acquire increasing levels of importance and access in *la orga*. With him were Jorge Zabalza, Leonel Martínez Platero –brother of Efraín-, Gabino Falero, Pablo Blanco, and top doctor Ismael Bassini.

The interest of the MLN in its imprisoned members had been on display since Plan Satán. Following that failure there had been continued demands for the liberation of the prisoners in exchange for kidnapping victims, and also legal arguments that the Tupamaros were "political" prisoners rather than criminals. Salvador Allende's brief intercession failed to make Pacheco budge on the Geoffrey Jackson ransom case, and few in Uruguay believed the political dissent argument for a second. There would be no amnesty.

The prison at Punta Carretas was located in the middle- and upper middle-class neighborhood of the same name. Only a few blocks from the waterfront, and a short distance from downtown Montevideo, the prison dated from a time when few people lived in the area. However, by the time of the Tupamaros, the jail was in the middle of a residential neighborhood. More than half a century of development had caught up with it.

The New Nest

There were two geographies to describe in Punta Carretas prison: the facility and its inhabitants. The facility consisted of a large, rectangular perimeter wall surrounding a series of courtyards and the main jail structure, which had four floors including the ground one. From the highest cells on the top floor, inmates could see the neighborhood's homes and daily life. Some prisoners wrote letters to families they became acquainted with purely through observation.

Each of the main structure's four floors consisted of two lines of cells separated by corridors and a gap. It was impossible to walk from the north or south row of cells to the other one, on any of the floors, without passing by the guards' station, called the Observation Center. From there, safely locked in case of emergencies, the security team could monitor the entire prison population, as well as communicate with the outside world.

The guards who patrolled these hallways were mostly weaponless: orders were for prison personnel to be unarmed within the walled compound. It was the sentries and snipers on the walls and guard posts who had the firepower. In case of an emergency, protocol was for the guards and staff to lock themselves in secure locations, call for reinforcements, and wait for a police assault squad bringing dogs, gases, and combat equipment to subdue the rioters.

The perimeter walls were thick and designed for surveillance, with walkways on top. There were floodlights, machine guns, and armed snipers ready to fire. Aside from the main cell structure and the walls, the rest of Punta Carretas prison consisted of a few courtyards and smaller buildings housing offices and the visitors' wing.

Gambusas and Football

The Tupamaros were called "Special Prisoners" to differentiate them from common criminals. They were all clustered together, meaning they mostly shared cells only with other Tupamaros, and their cells were typically next to each other. For security reasons none of them was on the ground floor; rather they were all in the first and second floors, particularly the latter, looking towards José Ellauri street to the north and the beachside *rambla* to the south.

The cells were adequate: Tupas rarely complained about their quality. Each measured approximately 4 x 2.5 x 3.5 meters. There were three men per cell, with bunks built into the side walls. A small window allowed brief glimpses of the outside world. The door was not barred, but rather fully plated with only a slit for communication with the hallway. Finally, each cell had a table, a shelf, a sink, and a toilet.

Lockdown was at 20:30; everyone had to be in by that time, and there could be no communication between cells until the morning. Constant metallic noises accompanied the Tupas' sleep, not to mention the occasional howls and growls of lunatics, prison "bitches", and other characters.

In the Uruguayan justice system, the maximum sentence for a convict, no matter the gravity of the crime, was thirty years of prison plus fifteen of preventive security detention, for a total of forty-five. As such, it was and is one of the most lenient in the world. A reminder of this approach was in place inside the prison, in the form of a large sign repeating an article of the Constitution guaranteeing a dignified treatment to all prisoners.

Punta Carretas housed many criminals who had been handed those toughest of sentences. In one of his books, Eleuterio Fernández Huidobro draws portraits of many of these personages the Tupamaros had to coexist with, from the man who had slaughtered his entire family to Duraznito (Little Peach), "a cheerful young man, harmless, helpful, always attentive to everything, who was in fact serving the maximum time for having killed his girlfriend, then raped her after death, then buried her in his backyard, and later unburied her multiple times for repeated assaults until it was no longer possible".

Life with these characters, who made up the other half of Punta Carretas' inmate population, took getting used to. Some were shadowy but ultimately harmless; they were more interesting in an anthropological sense. From improvised witch doctors to (male) prostitutes and cannabis planters, they provided a clear reminder of an underworld that was poles apart from the Tupamaros'. Other prisoners did mean business. Many liked to carry *cortes*, or shivs, everywhere, including to courtyard football matches. As Fernández Huidobro put it, "It was not (...) unusual for there to be many expulsions from the pitch over stabbings inside the penalty area".

Others liked to "own" younger, sexually abused prisoners – which became a problem with the MLN if that young prisoner drifted towards the Tupamaros' courtyard lectures and organizational meetings. In one of those cases, a criminal who was guilty of two homicides threatened the MLN instructor whose lectures his "bitch" attended. Julio Marenales and another Tupamaro went directly to him and made it clear *no one* could mess with them, no matter how psychopathic they were. Marenales's words, in his own recollection, were "I will slice you up into little pieces myself and then throw you out the window to get eaten by rats".

Life in Punta Carretas was thus about survival, particularly for Tupas who did not have the experience to match up with Uruguay's toughest hoodlums. Every day there were encounters with mentally unbalanced criminals, brusquely transgendered men turned bitches, sadists carrying shivs, toothless fellatio providers, and so forth. Soon enough, however, even hardened criminals realized where their limits lay, because there were new people in charge.

With survival essentially ensured -no Tupamaro was injured or killed while at Punta Carretas-, there were plenty of opportunities to make something of the idle time there. Courtyard breaks in particular turned into discussions of various aspects of the insurgency, and into practical workshops. Some turned sour. Major theoretical disputes emerged between the feisty Sendic and others. One was the debate over Cacao tactics with Adolfo Wasem.

Another was with Andrés Cultelli. To respond to Sendic's positions attacking dialectic materialism, Cultelli circulated among the Punta Carretas Tupas a tract which he entitled, in neoclassical fashion, "El AntiBebe". Sendic also huddled with Fernández Huidobro to work on plans such as Hipotótamo, which was designed to stage a Pando-style attack in the middle of Montevideo.

C1 and C2 were not the only subdivisions of the Punta Carretas MLN. C2 had numerous commissions for dealing with various issues. For instance, Amodio, a pipe always in his mouth, was in charge of communications security, in recognition of his insuperable talent for it. The doctor Bassini was tasked with maintaining an internal pharmacy, with medications available to ill Tupas and other prisoners. Mujica's old criminal friend turned Tupamaro, David Melián, managed relations with the *gambusas*.

There was also a special team called Comisión Aspirina, or simply Commission A. To "Aspirin" oneself ("*aspirinarse*") was, in prison lingo, to escape.

Operation Star

Commission A worked in a compartmented fashion: its members did not discuss its activities, nor its existence, with non-members. Beginning in 1970, the Aspirin worked on several schemes to break out. All sorts of ideas were considered, including improvising bridges from neighboring buildings towards the prison, hijacking a helicopter and landing it in the courtyard, and rocket-propelled nets that would help inmates climb the walls. To the Tupamaros' credit, a direct guerrilla assault on the facility, though militarily feasible, was rejected. The MLN of 1971 arguably could have pulled off such an attack, but some form of carnage was probable. According to Jorge Zabalza, "it could have meant the death of innocents. You looked at the Punta Carretas guards and you felt sorry for them: the ones atop the walls were all over sixty. One of them even had a limp".

The first practicable idea for an escape came in late 1970, from the observant mind of MLN engineer Juan Almiratti. The plan was to dig a tunnel starting from the sewer network -a favorite MLN haunt- and from thence dig up into the prison's laundry room. The codename of the plan was Gallo, or Rooster. It was the third concept the leadership included in its agenda for 1971 after Cacao and Cárcel del Pueblo.

In preparation for Gallo, a specialized squad entered the underground and deployed some of the necessary equipment. Shortly afterwards a major storm washed everything away, and the police got wind that something was going on. Among the objects found on a nearby shore were frogmen suits, sleeping bags, communications equipment, batteries, and more. No one but the MLN could be involved in an act requiring such equipment. The game had been given away before the first shovel struck the ground. Gallo was dead before it had started.

To replace it, a different plan was tried: it was codenamed Mangangá.* The scheme was again based on a tunnel, but this one would connect a home in Joaquín Núñez street, adjacent to the prison, with a service room in the facility. Unfortunately for the Tupas, Mangangá was deemed impracticable, and was scrapped.

The MLN was back where it started, so discussions drifted towards a different idea. The codename was Operación Estrella, or Operation Star. It was also a prison escape, but from a different facility: the women's prison in the Tres Cruces neighborhood. Ever since the famous Operación Paloma, many Tupamaras had been recaptured, and now they were housed in a far more secure facility than the old convent-prison hybrid.

The plan for the Estrella escape came from the "free" MLN. First, Mauricio Rosencof used his contacts to obtain the blueprints for the entire sewer network of Montevideo; combined with the Tupas' own knowledge of the place, navigating it would now be easier. He and Henry Engler then crafted a plan to tunnel their way towards the jailed Tupamaras, who were less in number than their male counterparts, but who were nevertheless a core component of the MLN.

The prisoners, who were organized similarly to their *compañeros*, were required to follow orders carefully and do everything according to the needs of the rescuers. Instructions were simple. On the night of the escape all had to make their way to a specific room inside the prison, where the entrance to the tunnel would open up. They had to ensure the guards noticed nothing odd was taking place.

---

* The mangangá is a local insect with a particularly painful sting.

The Tupamaras would have to be at the chosen tunnel-digging spot twice. The first time was when the digging was completed, during the day. The prisoners were required to make as much noise as possible to disguise the sounds of tunnel-boring in its final stretch. The second time, hours later and deep at night, would be to actually peruse the tunnel and leave the facility.

At 20:30 in the smaller of two inmate dormitories, there were three faint but clear knocks on the ground, coming from below. The MLN had successfully dug all the way to the prison. Three knocks from above told the diggers to proceed. With that, a hydraulic jack struck from below and carefully chipped away at the floor tiles. The Tupamaras began to make a great deal of noise. The main distraction during the "spontaneous" partying was dancer Cristina Cabrera, loudly performing a traditional River Plate dance known as *malambo* on top of a table. Others distracted the guards or requested their presence elsewhere. With the hole opened, the smell of dirt began to fill the room.

The rescuers handed the Tupamaras a few pistols, although they were to be kept hidden and only used to immobilize guards who noticed suspicious moves. Orders were to return to the cells and the usual routines, assemble doll-like figures to place on the beds, and show up at the escape point later at night. In the meantime, the hole was covered again to disguise the penetration of the prison.

At 22:00, all the Tupamaras hurried to the small dormitory. They were still allowed to circulate freely; conditions were lenient compared to the men. Once gathered, they lifted the covering tiles and revealed the mouth of the tunnel, which loomed like a pathway to freedom. Despite the excitement and anxiety of the situation, the procedure was completely silent. Before entering, each escapee gulped a candy the rescue squad gave her –so as to better tolerate the fetid smells from the sewers. One by one, the Tupamaras sat on the edge of the hole and were helped down by their comrades. Upon touching ground, another Tupamaro handed them a flashlight.

Instructions for this phase were clear. The escapees had to wear their best shoes, with the laces tight and the ankles bandaged. A hat or net of some sort had to be worn on the head to keep the hair of each woman in a tight bundle. The required clothing was pants with a skirt on top, so as to effect a quick change and adopt a street appearance in case of having to emerge from a manhole.

Silence had to be kept no matter if rats or other unpleaseantries made an appearance.

After traversing the narrow tunnel and arriving in the sewer, the rescuers took over with a strict procedure. The escapees were clustered in groups and marched with escorts, led by Column 15's Gabriel Schroeder carrying an AR-15, the most powerful combat rifle available in Uruguay at the time. Behind him were ten Tupamaras, two of them carrying handguns. Later came another Tupamaro with an AR-15 and a group of twelve Tupamaras; after them one more *guerrillero* with an AR-15, followed by sixteen more Tupamaras and a final AR-15-carrier to close the ranks.

All marched for a kilometer and a half, in complete silence, in a "parade of flashlights". They pointed the light mostly at the ground, to avoid leaking any of it through the manholes, which had been tied with wire anyway. Outside, Engler had stationed backup vehicles with fire squads ready to provide armed support. The *guerrilleras* emerged directly in a hijacked home; from there they boarded the MLN's vehicles and left without seeing where they were.

The operation yielded a record thirty-eight Tupamaras, three times the amount in the previous escape. The government only found out what happened the next morning, when the guards checked the sleeping quarters and found dummies instead of prisoners.

The success of Estrella involved a single downside for the MLN: the option of escaping from a prison complex through a tunnel that connected to the sewers had disappeared. Both the Mangangá and Gallo plans depended on outside diggers reaching Punta Carretas and opening a hole inside the perimeter. Estrella meant the police would be most attentive to the sewers. It was too risky to invest such a large number of resources in a chess move that was so openly burned, advertised, and telegraphed.

Starting From Scratch

The MLN sent plenty of signals of its intentions with the escapes of the engineer Almiratti (who ran away from a courthouse and was slightly wounded by gunfire in the process), of the trigger-puller Raúl Bidegain, and now of virtually every Tupamara of importance. In Punta Carretas, Mujica and his two cellmates discovered that the materials making up the walls that separated the cells were old and weak. Bricks could be removed with ease. They passed the information along, and thus the groups of three Tupamaros making up each cell began to experiment with digging *boquetes*, or holes, between adjacent cells. Ultimately, gaps big enough for a man to pass through became possible. Posters, sheets, and other objects suddenly began to cover every wall. Regardless, it was best not to dig a *boquete* on every wall: otherwise, inspections or accidents could ruin a promising discovery.

The *boquetes* could connect cells with each other and thus gather dozens of Tupas together, but the problem of escaping the prison and its walls remained. It was here that a third option emerged from the mind of Héctor Amodio: digging a tunnel from the *inside* of the prison. With the right resources and conditions, maybe the Tupas could dig beneath the prison, below its walls, and emerge somewhere else (ideally, a nearby home). In other words: a reverse Mangangá.

The main inconvenient was that any such proposal required the rather loud and invasive act of digging inside a prison. In fact, a massive escape like the one the MLN wanted to pull off required a large area from which to dig – but naturally all spaces were heavily monitored and guarded. The courtyards in particular -the ideal spot from a logistical perspective- were under constant vigilance. The Tupamaros never had a chance to speak to the sentries manning the walls and the towers, and it was thus impossible to bribe them. The police also knew how to compartmentalize operations.

Gifts and bribes for the inside guards were varied, but soon the Tupamaros had nearly the entire prison staff in their pockets: "Monthly payments, doubled salaries, complete furnishing of policemen's homes, bottles of whisky, various kinds of threats and, occasionally, if things got rough, a coercive threat". To Jorge Zabalza, who ran this operation and actually had the keys to many of the cells, Punta Carretas was not a prison but rather "a Tupamaro camp with certain restrictions". The MLN owned much of what was no longer a prison, but rather as inmate Luis Nieto put it, "a carnival".

With the *boquetes* available and the guards in a muffled position, the MLN had to develop a good plan for the escape. The Tupas mostly occupied the first and second floors, while common criminals dominated the ground and top floors. The next task was selecting which spot to dig in to descend from the first floor to the ground floor, determining whose cell that would be, and persuading its "tenant" to cooperate.

In the winter of 1971, prisoners dug the *boquetes* at breakneck pace and finished them successfully. With the holes complete, it was possible to walk continuously from one end of the cell block to the other. The decision was there would be a hole in the ground on the easternmost cell of each of three key floors. One hole led from the second level to the first level; another led from the first level to the ground level. The last hole was at ground level, and was the mouth of the tunnel.

All of this was briefed and coordinated with the free Tupamaros, who prepared their own side of the operation under Engler's command. The outside MLN had a lot of homework. A large number of Tupamaros scouted every square meter surrounding the prison, carefully studying viewing angles from the streets to the prison and vice versa; the topography of the area, the communications infrastructure, the human geography of the neighboring families and businesses, the movements of the security services, and more. MLN nannies began to serve various nearby families to make surveillance easier. Pepe Mujica's old group, Column 10, retained a safe house just a block and a half away from Punta Carretas, on Joaquín Núñez street. The Tupamaros were closer than everyone thought.

The results of these activities arrived in the hands of Commission A: "excellent, ancient blueprints of the Punta Carretas prison; maps of the area; aerial photographs; blueprints of nearby homes, etc."* One home in particular was selected as the best place for the tunnel to emerge. The Tupamaras who prowled the Punta Carretas neighborhood verified every proposal, measurement, map, and angle that required on-the-spot study. Combining all of it, the MLN had a three-dimensional geographical and human map of the area.

The two luckiest people in all of Punta Carretas, and possibly in all of Uruguay, learned their fate from the mouths of Aspirin

---

* The MLN obtained the blueprints for the prison in a circuitous way: they helped three common criminals escape the facility. One of them was secretly the homosexual lover of a Punta Carretas official. In return for this liberation, the official handed the most detailed blueprints in existence of the facility.

"visitors". Their names were Arión and Carlos; they were common criminals, and they inhabited the cell MLN planners had determined would be home to the tunnel mouth. Therefore, Arión and Carlos were added to the roster of escapees. Both did their jobs well; on one occasion Arión discouraged an inspection of the cell by displaying what he was famous for: lunacy. Lying naked on the ground and flailing uncontrollably, he threatened to cut his own throat and uttered numerous profanities, all above the spot where the loose ground covered the incipient tunnel. Below, anxious diggers short of breath and enduring great heat awaited for Arión to disgust the inspectors into leaving.*

The toughest task was digging below ground with rudimentary instruments for a total of thirty-seven meters, as forecast by the engineers. Commission A selected twenty Tupas to become the squad of sappers. The criteria were physical aptitude, size –the shorter the better-, health, and visitation schedules at Punta Carretas. The majority came from the UTAA *cañeros.*[402] The length of the tunnel was kept secret from everyone but them: inside the prison, only the diggers and Commission A knew the truth. That way, any leaks to treasonous prisoners would be diminished in impact. In typical Bebe fashion, Sendic demanded the right to descend and participate in the digging himself. His consolation prize upon being rejected, aside from providing mordant commentary, was to be given kitchen duty - to the chagrin and despair of those who now had to ingest his famously terrible cuisine.

The diggers endured many hardships. Not only did they exert themselves physically with improvised tools. The deeper they went the less oxygen and light they found. Sappers wore shorts, the best shoes available in the prison, wool hats to protect their heads, and pretty much nothing else. The work was grimy and tiresome. For long stretches the digger lay on his back, carving at the earth while his elbows turned to shreds from repeated friction.

On top of this there were lethal risks, including that of a cave-in that left them trapped underground. A rule was decided for that scenario: the Tupas themselves would try to rescue their buried *compañeros* for twenty-four hours. If unable, they would then give up the plan and call the emergency services.

---

* The incident happened on August 26th, more than halfway into the digging operation.

In order to alleviate some of these issues, the diggers were spoiled. Per instructions from the highest echelons, they were provided with the best food and deference from the others. There were medical doctors and cooks dedicated especially to their needs. As Fernández Huidobro noted in his account, "They were our queen bees (...) Soon they began to get cuddly. -I'd like to eat grapes, said one in the middle of August".

The infrastructure of the tunnel required special attention from the MLN's craftsmen. Lighting was a primary issue: the solution was to hang battery-powered flashlights crafted by Manera and placed inside plastic soap containers, along the tunnel. Each digger also strapped one to his forehead. Additionally, a special pump was constructed to funnel air from the cell block down and into the tunnel. It would have to be permanently worked by a member of the digging team, who later rotated positions with the diggers.

The earth was removed by carving it out in chunks, so as to minimize any noise that might be heard in the above world. In any case, the MLN contingent in Punta Carretas provided generous doses of blaring radios, cross-cell shouting and assorted noises to provide cover for the diggers and the blacksmiths. Like all tunnels, the Tupamaros' was as narrow as possible, so as to concentrate efforts on length and speed. That meant the twenty sappers were never there at the same time. In fact, they descended in teams of four: one dug, another bagged the loosened earth, another operated a sled to move the bags to the mouth of the tunnel, and the last one pumped oxygen.

The bagged dirt was distributed throughout the dozens of connected cells the Tupamaros had across two floors of the facility. They were hidden beneath the bunks and sinks, and blocked from prying eyes with various objects. They could not, however, withstand a *real* prison inspection, and neither would the *boquetes* or the tunnel. Once the digging started, the operation had to be completed in precious little time before the next mandatory full search. Thanks to Zabalza's bountiful bribes, the officer in charge of the searches agreed to delay them for one month - but no more than that was possible. Thus, the date for the completion of the *boquetes* and the beginning of the tunnel-digging was August 11.

Digging for long stretches underground required some spatial guidance, so that the tunnel did not point in the wrong direction or overshoot its target. Jorge Manera, "El Inge", was called upon to solve this. Using improvised tools he accurately oriented the tunnel so that it did not miss its mark. While Manera directed the technical and theoretical aspects, his old partner from Column 2, Julio Marenales, supervised the work on a nightly basis. The rest of the time, the MLN founder taught courses on explosives and combat tactics.

Preparing for Breakout

Héctor Amodio Pérez came up with the idea for digging a tunnel from the inside. He also baptized it El Abuso, as the best way to summarize the possibility that it could work: it was simply too excessive and spectacular to seem realistic. Lastly, Amodio served as the general coordinator of the escape operation, in recognition of the above plus his record of accomplishment and experience leading the Paloma escape of the Tupamaras.

There were a great number of tasks to be completed in order for the escape to be successful. Although the outside organization did not have any digging responsibilities, once the mouth of the tunnel opened on the other side of the street, it would be responsible for an enormous number of Tupamaros urgently seeking shelter from an incoming, large-scale police persecution.

Therefore, the outside MLN developed a plan to stealthily take over at least two private residences in the area and manage the arrival of the escapees. Each would need a change of clothes, fake identification papers, weapons, and an evacuation route across various MLN vehicles and safe houses in Montevideo. Whenever the night of the operation happened, hundreds if not thousands of Tupamaros would be moving around the city working for the escape.

With the tunnel underway, a major issue that needed deciding was who would actually get to escape. Not every member had a ticket out, although not for lack of intent. The reason was simple: the tunnel was being dug in a west-to-east direction, on two floors of the northern cell block. The Tupamaros would move across the *boquetes*, all the way to the east, then descend two floors to reach the cell of Arión and Carlos. This left out the entire southern cell block, which was separated by hallways and gaps that were impossible to overcome.

C1, in consultation with Commission A, created the list of who would escape. It was later transmitted to C2, which had to find a way to house all the nominees in a single block. The MLN used its corrupted guards to arrange for the chosen Tupas who were housed in the wrong section to be transferred to the correct one, looking north towards José Ellauri street. Soon all the significant Tupamaros began to magically be concentrated in the same block, to the point where one *gambusa* shouted that the jail would tilt and fall over, given how one side was getting packed with "heavies".

The criteria for determining who would escape were clear. According to Fernández Huidobro, the first one was "those whose escape would imply a political blow for the enemy, be it because they were members of the MLN leadership or because of the importance they had at the time of their capture". Second came the gravity of the charges they faced. Prisoners who had been in jail the longest had priority; later came heads of columns, of column divisions, or particularly talented Tupas like medical doctors or engineers.

Julio Marenales was at the top of the list. He had been behind bars since 1968, shortly after the kidnapping of Ulysses Pereira. In September of 1971 it was close to three years since he had been out of action. Soon after him came a list of names like Sendic, Fernández Huidobro, Manera, Amodio, and many more.

The men chosen to notify the others of their fate were José Mujica and Alberto Candán. Wearing a long black trench coat in the depths of the harsh Montevideo winter, the reputedly strict Mujica approached other Tupamaros in courtyard breaks to deliver the news. Many, upon learning they had to yield their cells to other Tupas, felt disappointed. To a great number, the anxiety of not having yet talked to Mujica and thus not having learned whether they would escape consumed endless hours of concern.

The deeper the diggers reached, the less oxygen they had for their increasingly difficult and darkened task. Some fainted and were taken out of the digging operation; new ones were brought into the squad, and constantly monitored by MLN doctors. A blacksmith was posted permanently in the Arión cell to provide maintenance for the tools; no resources were spared.

While this was happening, the outside MLN finalized the details of its side of the operation. A total of three homes would be taken over. First came a double residence on Solano García street, directly across the street from the east wall of the prison which the Tupas were breaching underground. The house was split into two apartments, so the Tupamaros would take over both. One apartment housed a woman and her daughter; the other a journalist and her son. All became the targets of the MLN's eyes and ears, in order to ensure there were no sudden changes in routine on the day of El Abuso.

The third house was not on Solano García, but rather on Joaquín Núñez street – the parallel one to the east. The target home was the one adjacent, through the back, to the one on Solano García. The Tupamaros decided they would not evacuate from the Solano García house; parking the vehicles there, or simply being in plain sight of the prison walls and its sentries, was too risky. Instead, the exit point would be the front door of the house on Joaquín Núñez, with the vehicles parked outside it. *Boquetes* were to connect the two houses through the back. With that, the plan was complete: the journey of the escaping Tupamaros would lead them through their cells, down a floor or two, into the tunnel, up into one house, then through the walls into the other house, and finally into the vehicles that would evacuate them.

MLN surveillance indicated the takeovers of the homes had to take place at around 18:00, when all residents were expected to be at home. This fit well with the expectation that the escaping Tupas would only be able to complete the tunnel after 20:30, when lockdown and lights out were enforced inside Punta Carretas. Surveillance also indicated that the Curi family, the owners of the house on Joaquín Núñez street, had, in inevitable Montevidean fashion, an MLN connection. The niece of the head of the household, José Curi, was a Tupamara. Her name was Carmen Beretta, and she was asked to participate and guarantee there would be no violence.

The first few days of September were filled with considerable anxiety for all Tupamaros concerned. The tunnel was ahead of schedule: it started on August 11 and by September 2 it reached, according to estimates, a spot directly under the living room of the entry home. Approximately half a meter of earth and floor tiles separated the Tupamaros from freedom, but nevertheless patience and care had to remain top of mind. An incoming cell inspection loomed. To avoid such a scenario, the chosen date for the escape was September 4.

El Abuso

On the night of the 4th, everything was prepared to initiate the escape. The MLN activated its protocols one by one. As Fernández Huidobro's account tells it, at 19:00 he received a slip of paper revealing his contact, code word, and medical emergency evacuation point in case he fell into trouble outside. The group's emergency ambulance network was activated in several points throughout the city. He was also given a new pair of shoes.

At 21:00, the prison locked down for the day, with the prisoners counted and in their cells. Half an hour later, the order was passed down across the cells to crack open the *boquetes* one last time. With all open, the two cell blocks became corridors from one end to the other. While all of this was taking place, an MLN lawyer raced to the prison and urgently asked to speak to Marenales, the chief Tupamaro inside Punta Carretas. His news was disquieting: the Tupamaro tasked with delivering messages and plans concerning the escape, Aurelio Fernández, had just been in a motorcycle accident: he crashed in the suburbs of Montevideo.

Fernández lay unconscious on the road for some time, and was later taken to the hospital.* The Tupamaros could not yet ascertain whether the security of the operation had been compromised. Out of precaution, Engler had the operation of the outside MLN canceled, so the inside Tupas could not effect their escape that night. Many furiously asked for the execution by rifle squad of the idiot who had ruined everything.

The risk had not just been in Punta Carretas, but also with an additional component to El Abuso. It was a subsidiary operation called Tero, after a bird native to Uruguay known for chirping in areas distant from its nest, in order to lure predators away from its eggs (in Eleuterio Fernández Huidobro's book the given name is Teru-Teru, more closely resembling the bird's famous chirping). The MLN's Tero was, similarly, a decoy targeted at Montevideo's police. The centerpiece was the greatest use of the MLN's Tupamaro Support Committees, or CATs, ever attempted.

---

* All of this was surprising considering who Fernández, a trusted and experienced cadre of Engler, was: one of Mitrione's killers and the commander of the great jewel heist.

The CATs were made up of radicals unready or unwilling to become full-time *guerrilleros*, but who still were strong supporters of the MLN. With ample experience in preparing Molotov cocktails, setting up barricades, and causing trouble in the streets, the mission of the CATs in the Tero was to cause a massive riot in the Cerro neighborhood. With the police diverted so far from Punta Carretas, there would be extra breathing room for the MLN's Abuso.

With the abortion of the escape on the night of September 4, the MLN was lucky to stop the Tero plans, as well as the takeovers of the private residences, in time. Upon waking up in his hospital bed, Aurelio Fernández rummaged through his personal objects and discovered the all-important MLN documents were missing. That was when he had telephoned his contacts and sounded the alarm. He later found the papers carefully stuffed inside his shoes. The MLN had inadvertently struck again: silent Tupamaros, so notorious among Uruguay's medical professionals, had noticed the papers and their significance, and thus made their silent contribution to the group's security.

Although the escape operation remained secure and was postponed for twenty-four hours, the Punta Carretas Tupamaros still had to face the issue of permanently opened *boquetes*. The air corridor brought them sounds and smells from their colleagues several meters down the line, and were quite visible for anyone who approached the cells. There was no choice but to hold their ground and push their luck for a full day filled with tension, all without outwardly giving any clues.

Fortunately for the Tupas, the following day passed by without any inspections or outside emergencies. Both the outside and inside MLNs proceeded with their plans. The outside team started earlier. Multiple squads took their positions: the CAT rioters started their disturbances in the afternoon; the ambulance service deployed to the pre-convened areas of the city. Three teams also headed for Punta Carretas, and waited for the order to proceed.

Biding their time in local bars, two assault teams walked the short distance to the target homes on Solano García and Joaquín Núñez streets. A light drizzle accompanied them on the way through parks, residences, schools, and churches, as they approached some of the quietest residential streets in Montevideo. There would be light rain for the rest of the evening.

The groups took over the houses in typical MLN fashion: with minimal violence. No firearms were on display, no shots were fired, and no one was hurt. With Alicia Rey in command, the presence of Beretta made things easy in the Curi homestead. In the other two simple ruses like delivering Frente Amplio propaganda allowed the Tupas, led by Engler in person, to get inside. After a few minutes of small talk, the MLN commando revealed the truth: "Well, actually we are not from the Frente...we are Tupamaros and we are going to need this house for something we got going on. I'm going to have to ask you to lock the dog inside the bedroom".

By then, after years of reading and hearing about MLN operations taking place in their city, Montevideans were not completely shocked upon the sight of Tupamaros claiming they "needed" a vehicle or a home for a few hours. There was an understanding that no harm would come to the owners, and therefore none resisted. One young woman exclaimed "Tupamaros? I have always wanted to see one!" Some asked to leave the premises to avoid being around the operation, but were politely yet firmly "asked" to stay until it ended.

The outside digging operation then started, commencing with the holes to connect one house with the other. While this was taking place, a separate cluster of MLN action teams spread around Montevideo and stole fifteen different vehicles. Unbeknownst to the police, there were two hundred Tupamaros in action throughout the city.

Inside the prison, once lockdown was in place, Amodio gave the keyword for the prisoners to proceed: "Abuso!" A human stream started from the farthest cells to the eastern ends of the block, and then down across two floors to gather as close as possible to the hole in Arión's cell. The suppression of sound was a top concern: each Tupamaro was to wrap his shoes in old socks, and to wear a wool hat. The inhabitants of each cell were responsible for laying down a small pathway made up of pillows and mats between the holes on either wall, so that the entire route was padded.

One concession to necessity was that no souvenirs were to be taken from the cell. To compensate for this, many chose to leave special messages in the MLN tradition of armed propaganda. Some read "For land ownership and with Sendic", "For rent", and, right by the accumulated dirt bags, "We hereby donate this earth to serve as filling in the courtyard pitch".

Eleuterio Fernández Huidobro recounts a surreal trip from his cell, one of the farthest to the west, across his colleagues' and then down two floors. While doing so he was able to see what each group of *guerrilleros* had done with their personal space. In prison since the October 1969 attack on Pando, Fernández was one of the older prisoners in terms of jail time. Despite his young age, proof of the pre-eminence he had as MLN leader came when despite being far away from the exit holes, he was allowed down before others, who waited for their turn. He descended headway through the hole into Arión's cell, held by the arms of a team manning the proceedings.

While Fernández and the other Tupas gathered around the tunnel mouth, the diggers finished their work at its far end. The final opening of the tunnel, on the freedom side, took longer than expected. Inside the house, in the parlor where windows looked directly towards the darkened prison walls, Engler and his men waited and cleared the floor tiles. The delay was due to the room not being at ground level, but rather atop the front stairway of the house. It was a half-meter that had not been accounted for in the calculations, but it seemed manageable.

As Engler listened first with his stethoscope and later with a whisky glass, he guided his own diggers as close as possible to the origin of the voices seeping in from below. The banging on that room, which was directly after the front door of the house, was timed for the moment when a police foot patrol was at the opposite side of the prison perimeter. At one point, the Tupas occupying the adjacent house telephoned to warn about excessive noise - but there was no choice but to continue. Dogs barked; curious neighbors emerged briefly from their homes; cigarettes were lit, in tension, and promptly snatched by Engler. The operation could not be stopped. At one point, music boomed from a nearby church, playing the Spanish version of "Bony Moronie", which the digger tried to synchronize with his hammering. Inside the prison, the Tupamaros huddled in only a few cells close to the tunnel mouth, and waited on their feet for over four hours.

It was Marenales, ever the handyman, who descended and personally directed the last moments of the dig, with the inevitable anxiety that a six-hour delay could cause. Suddenly, the main digger above ground had his measuring bar snatched downwards, and moments later a light emerged from below. A hand rose from the ground, and Engler groped it: at last, the tunnel was completed. The first person to emerge was a sapper, with the flashlight still attached to his head. Immediately afterward Marenales was pulled up through the bent tunnel exit by the arms of Henry Engler and Gabriel Schroeder. There was real glee, but no time to celebrate.

Each Tupa made his way from Arión's cell into the barely lit tunnel to freedom. There were ups and downs in the pathway; the shoes of the Tupamaros ahead of each escapee raised puffs of dirt close to his follower's face; all that could be heard in the darkness was the muted sound of feet moving, clothes brushing against the walls and the ground, and the anxious breathing in the straight line that extended for over a hundred meters. The heat was unbearable.

Four of the strongest arms in the MLN reached down and pulled each escapee up. The arrival was jolting: suddenly men who had lain in a grimy prison for years were standing in a middle-class family's living room. It took just twenty minutes for a total of one hundred and eleven men, of which five were common criminals, to be pulled out from the hole. A few portlier Tupamaros had trouble exiting and suffered scratches or injuries, but insistent pulling did the trick.

Engler and his men had thought of everything. Each Tupamaro was escorted to the back of the house and into the adjoining Curi house, also under MLN control. Once there, they were given new clothes. The dirty prison uniforms were discarded in an increasingly large pile. From there they were directed to a table with small pouches containing weapons, ammunition, and money.

After that, there was but one step left, which Fernández acknowledges was far less orderly than the painstaking operation they had undertaken so far: simply, "to the lorries!" The outside MLN had brought in trucks with large beds to take great numbers of Tupas around the city. As each quickly exited the house, Column 15's Gabriel Schroeder directed them to the corresponding vehicle, from which they would in turn descend at pre-established evacuation points where other vehicles would take them to safe houses. In those instants Joaquín Núñez street concentrated, for the first and only time in history, over one hundred Tupamaros, including all the founders and top commandos. The historical leadership was put in automobiles especially tasked to evacuate them: Sendic, Fernández, Marenales, Manera, Amodio, Martínez, Tabaré Rivero, Lucas Mansilla, Alberto Candán, Mujica, and two more were spirited out with deference.

At the same time, the Cerro neighborhood was burning thanks to the explosion of the Tero operation: "They chopped trees, invaded streets, assembled barricades, burned bus tires, torched vehicles". As Martínez Platero described it, "the city was depleted of patrol cars, free of policemen (...) There were thousands and thousands of people there". There were ten full hours of Tero mayhem, more than enough for helping the Punta Carretas operation.

With the final escapes taking place before dawn, the Tupamaros were in a position to wait for news of their feat while comfortably listening to the radio. Sendic and Fernández Huidobro did so in an MLN shelter directly across from a government facility. With them was the lunatic criminal Arión, who had been so important to the success of the operation. They could rest assured for any contingency: Arión claimed to have "the entire area -please take note, all of it- protected with an impenetrable layer of high psychic potency".

The assault teams completed the operation with military discipline. They gave the owner of the breached apartment a sum of money for her troubles and for the repairs to her destroyed floor and back wall. They liberated their hostages, cleared each residence of all evidence, including clothes, dirt, and other indicators, and slowly began to take off. At one point, two members of separate cells performing these tasks recognized each other. It was a quintessential MLN experience: they knew one another from "legal" life, but had no idea the other was a Tupamaro - until that night.

At four in the morning, with the rain gone from Montevideo on one of the last nights of the winter, all that was left was a single Tupamaro, tasked with closing the door behind him and taking off on foot, whistling. One of the greatest prison escapes in history was complete, and no one outside the MLN and the chosen residences knew about this. Only seventy-four out of a hundred and eighty "subversives" remained inside Punta Carretas.

Red Alert

At dawn, when the authorities noticed the escape, a massive alarm and state of siege was declared. The self-evident complicity of the prison staff led to their being fired and detained. It counted for little then, for the deed was already done.

El Abuso was one of the greatest shocks in Uruguayan history. Overnight, the MLN insurgency was burning with an intensity unseen before. Not since the days of the Dan Mitrione hostage situation was there such a sense of dread, of an incoming onslaught, than immediately after the Punta Carretas prison escape. Everyone knew the country was set for a renewed conflagration with far greater magnitude. The Tupamaros were now able to combine their escaped leadership with the formidable recruits and resources accumulated in the past years.

Once again, the perspective of the American embassy is useful, given the meticulousness of its records, in comprehending how these events were perceived at the time. On the day after the escape, the embassy reported "Our impression remains that escape has shocked public security forces into near catatonic state".[403] Three days later, in a report entitled titled "The Great Escape – A Preliminary Political Assessment", the country team reported El Abuso "has shaken Uruguayan public to degree unknown in recent years. Disgust, anger, bewilderment and fear seem to be most common elements in reaction of general public. Among senior government leaders, there is also outrage that Uruguay's image in international community has been further besmirched and national pride trampled upon. As expected, pro-MLN students are jubilant. Government, police and armed forces are disheartened and disconcerted".[404] Polls that month showed popular justification for the MLN's actions down to 36%.[405]

Given how the careful work of years of counterinsurgency evaporated down a tunnel, the government decided to ask Parliament for an upgrade in emergency laws. More specifically, the request was for the campaign to be transferred to the armed forces. The Parliament agreed, and with a clear majority vote the military was ordered to organize its own campaign to wipe out the MLN. Pacheco signed the decree ordering the military into action on September 9; it was the greatest change in government strategy since the beginning of the fight against subversion, close to a decade before.

In the days and weeks after El Abuso, the MLN re-organized itself to resume the revolutionary struggle in full strength. Some in the leadership ranks were expecting to yield the *dirección* of the group back to the newly freed founders. However, the latter chose to respect the rules of the organization and return to the so-called bases. In other words, they would disperse, join a column, and serve as regular Tupamaros under the command of others.

Sendic almost immediately decided to move away from Montevideo and back to his favorite environment: Uruguay's *campo*, in the north. While there, he served in a cell under the command of the engineer Almiratti, and worked hard to craft a campaign specifically tailored to that part of the country. Fernández Huidobro, his usual partner, deployed to a column tasked with jumpstarting an MLN campaign in the periphery of Montevideo. Amodio returned to his old ways, circulating around Montevideo disguised as a priest, bible in hand, or as a blind man, while coordinating Column 15 cells.[406]

José Mujica returned to Column 10. Years before, he had served under the command of María Elia Topolansky, a more senior Tupamara than he was. After El Abuso and his return to operations, he met María Elia's sister, Lucía. The latter had recently been in a relationship with Armando Blanco, a prominent cadre from Column 15. In Column 10 she started a new one with Mujica.[407] Pepe, in turn, switched his *yuto* from Facundo to Emiliano, and underwent reparative surgery in an MLN safe house. During recovery, Mujica stayed at the Montevideo neighborhood of Punta Gorda performing weapons maintenance and discussing strategy with fellow *guerrilleros* Efraín Martínez and Tabaré Rivero.

While the old Tupas found new places to operate in, the *comité ejecutivo* continued to perform political work to consolidate the influence of the MLN. Both Rosencof and Wasem traveled to Cuba and Chile to solidify relations with the Castro and Allende regimes. Weapons flowed in thanks to these efforts: in 1972 the MLN would finally get a modest shipment of wartime German MP-40s and pistols, shipped from Cuba via Chile.[408] Engler, in turn, was planning a trip to Viet Nam for 1972, to learn advanced guerrilla tactics from that country's increasingly victorious insurgents.[409]

The Most Controversial Election in Uruguayan History

El Abuso happened right in the middle of Uruguay's electoral campaign. As noted before, there were plenty of candidates to go around. Per Uruguayan electoral rules, the votes of all candidates from each party would be combined and counted first by party rather than individual. Once the winning party was determined, its most voted candidate became president. The Colorados fielded President Pacheco, former minister Bordaberry, liberal senator Jorge Batlle, and social-democrat Amílcar Vasconcellos. There was clear hostility between the latter and the first two.

Next came the Nationalists, eager to take back the presidency after losing it to Gestido and Pacheco in 1966. The days of the party's liberal reformists were long gone. Their star candidate was Wilson Ferreira, the best orator in Uruguay and the one with the most populist platform. In addition, the Nationalists fielded Mario Aguerrondo, the former general and Minister of the Interior, as the candidate of the conservative faction. He stood no chance: Wilson was simply too popular and dominant.

The Frente Amplio smartly presented a single candidate: former general Líber Seregni. His caravans around the country often met hostile populations, thanks to the presence within the coalition of totalitarian Communists, apologists of MLN violence, and a number of other unlikeable radicals. All locations outside of Montevideo were anti-Frente. For instance, in the town of Treinta y Tres, residents made a point of thoroughly cleansing the spaces where the Frente's rallies had taken place. In other towns there were stones thrown, glasses shattered, and more. In turn, in Montevideo – where the Marxists were strong- there was constant violence against party bases of the Colorados and, to a lesser degree, of the Nationalists.[410] Conservative-nationalist youth gangs began to grow in size right in time for the election. On one occasion, they clashed with a squad from the Communist youth militia in the middle of the Pocitos neighborhood; over fifty gunshots were fired.[411]

For many years there had been tensions around the possibility of a Brazilian and/or Argentine intervention in Uruguay, particularly if Marxists took power. With the Frente Amplio in action, not to mention the Tupamaros and El Abuso, in 1971 an invasion was once again in the cards. American diplomatic traffic from the embassy in Buenos Aires confirmed from confidential sources at the highest levels of the Argentine regime that no invasion of Uruguay would take place in *any* eventuality. This was a sharp contrast to just a few years before, when dictators in Brasília and Buenos Aires had agreed to a joint invasion contingency plan.[412]

Two months after El Abuso, in November, the national elections took place. The results were controversial. First, there was a crushing defeat for the Frente Amplio, which failed to reach a fifth of the total vote. This was combining all Socialist, Communist, MLN, and other votes. Although the number of total votes was a historical record for Uruguay's *izquierda*, there was no question that the country had completely rejected Marxism and its radical variants.

The other results were not so easy to comprehend. The Partido Colorado had won the election if it combined the votes for all its candidates. However, individually, the Partido Nacional's maverick Wilson Ferreira was the most voted candidate. Lastly, Uruguayans had rejected Pacheco's constitutional reform project.

This meant that in a race with heavyweights like Pacheco, Wilson, and the newly minted Seregni, it was Juan María Bordaberry who became president of Uruguay. Much like Salvador Allende in Chile, he would be a president with a weak mandate. Only 23% of all voters had inserted a ballot with his name as candidate for president. It was the peculiar Uruguayan electoral system which gave him the office: with Pacheco defeated he was the most voted candidate of the most voted party. In retrospective, this was possibly the way in which the Uruguayan electorate announced that it agreed with Pacheco's general political instincts, but not with all of his methods.

The results could be interpreted in other ways, and it is important to consider this because the 1971 election is the best evidence available for how the Uruguayan people decided their fate. The most voted candidate for president was Wilson Ferreira, with 26% of the total. Following him was Juan Bordaberry with 23%, Líber Seregni with 18%, Jorge Batlle with 14%, Mario Aguerrondo with 13% and Amílcar Vasconcellos with 7%. President Pacheco's drive for re-election got 30% of the vote.

Clustering the parties yielded 41% for the Colorados, 40% for the Nationalists, and 18% for the Frente Amplio. This meant Bordaberry the conservative nationalist rode to victory thanks in no small part to votes for the liberal Batlle and the social democrat Vasconcellos. The nationalist socialist Wilson's near-victory owed over a third of his party's votes to the conservative nationalists who picked Aguerrondo.

In contrast, clustering ideologies -across parties- gave socialists of various sorts 51% of the vote (Wilson plus the Frente Amplio plus Vasconcellos), conservative nationalists at least 36% of the vote (all of Bordaberry's and Aguerrondo's votes); and liberals roughly 15% (Batlle's). It was, and remains, quite a puzzle.

Wilson and the nationalists would forevermore protest the election results as fraud. There was, after all, only a 1% difference between the votes tallied for the Colorados and for the Nationalists. Rumors spread like wildfire of stuffed or missing ballot boxes, an issue that was particularly sensitive for a party that had been the minority for almost a full century. The accusation has never been proven, for recounts and commissions that investigated the matter found no signs of fraud. Curiously enough, in a declassified conversation he had in the Oval Office, Richard Nixon told his associates that Brazilian dictator Emilio Garrastazú told him that he "arranged" the Uruguayan election to produce the right result. Despite the lack of proof of both Wilson and Garrastazú's claims, there was sloppiness evident throughout Uruguayan institutions and practices as reported by journalists at the time. According to such reports, the facility where the ballot boxes were gathered for the main count, the Cilindro Municipal indoor arena, had an alarming lack of security. Both journalists and members of the Partido Nacional were caught illegally trespassing there.[413]

Garrastazú and Nixon were not the only ones discussing the Uruguayan election. At the time, Fidel Castro was personally spearheading a major Cuban effort to link up his regime with Salvador Allende's in Chile, and thus secure an expansion of Communism in the Americas. Speaking to the press from Santiago about the results of the nearby Uruguayan election, Castro said "Violence is the only path left in Uruguay for obtaining power".[414] Not coincidentally, almost immediately Cuba increased aid to the MLN-Tupamaros as they prepared for a new campaign against the government.

A New Phase

Juan María Bordaberry came to power with a timid mandate for pro-market economic policies and a clearer one for continuing the campaign to suppress the MLN. He inherited the reins of a government under siege. Labor unrest, more bitter than ever over its political defeat, was as strong as always. The newly strengthened MLN was a formidable threat. The military was slowly starting to make noise while it prepared its formal campaign to take out the Tupamaros.

What lay between the November election and the swearing-in of the new president in March was a typically extended Uruguayan summer, during which everyone –including combatants on all sides of the conflict- slowed the pace of their operations. The Tupamaros also promised that they would not damage Uruguay's growing tourism sector with their operations, as streams of Argentines increasingly packed the country's sandy beaches.

In the meantime, the Tupamaros gave themselves the privilege of freeing British ambassador Geoffrey Jackson in exchange for nothing. As they explained, there was no longer a need to exchange him for captured Tupamaros, since the organization had recovered most of them by itself.

Looking at the coming year the MLN felt strong and capable of withstanding any fight with the military. However, its triumphant position hid one flaw. The Tupamaros still had not come up with a plan to defeat the Uruguayan state. That was an essential precondition for revolutionary victory, particularly after the undoing of all the goodwill generated by armed propaganda in the wave of Satán and Cacao terrorism. With the police and now the military in the way, the revolution would never triumph, no matter how charming the Tupas proved - unless those enemies were suppressed.

In considering these facts, the MLN allowed for an innovation. Given how the identities of all escaped Tupamaros were well known, and how the group's clandestine Montevideo network was bursting with Tupas to hide, the organization decided to launch a rural *foco* for the first time.

This meant 1972 promised to see some of the most sophisticated MLN plans ever. Almost all of them were designed to take escalation as far as possible. One plot was called Plan Magnífico or "Magnificent", and its objective was none other than kidnapping president-elect Bordaberry. "Magnífico" was the codename for Bordaberry himself; the plans for his kidnapping -discovered later by the military- revealed once again how far the MLN's tentacles went.

A complete surveillance program of Bordaberry's homestead and security detail was in effect; incognito Tupamaros had walked right up to the entrance, and gotten to know key employees of the president-elect by name and by habit. The Tupamaros noted the identities, numbers, and equipment of the house's guards and employees. They noted which vehicles were in operation around it, at what times they moved, how they traveled, who was inside, and which traffic stops they respected.

An even more ambitious plan was codenamed Plan Nerón. It was a guerrilla raid that would have demolition teams detonating the "entire fleet of the National Navy" docked in Montevideo harbor, thus permanently obstructing the city's all-important port. The economy would be crippled without its essential infrastructure for exports. However, the MLN never found the resources, time, or willingness to pull off these plans. Years later, the Argentine Montoneros –a far larger organization- went as far as downing aircraft carrying National Guardsmen and sinking a naval vessel, but that was never feasible in Uruguay.[415]

With a new president, an empowered military, and a guerrilla organization swollen with multiple generations of fighters, the period beginning in late 1971 was clearly going to be different, particularly once the summer was over. The conflict had been reset; the pieces were redistributed and none of its participants could possibly know where they would be six months, much less a year, after that moment.

CHAPTER ELEVEN:

RISE OF THE CENTURIONS

THE MILITARY ECHELONS in Uruguay lacked any significant experience in combat, much less in counterterrorism. Their last campaign had taken place in 1904, when the Colorado government of José Batlle & Ordóñez ordered the pacification of areas in the northeast of the country taken over by a Nationalist *caudillo* named Aparicio Saravia. It had been a typically Uruguayan affair in that the scale was minuscule.

Almost seventy years had passed since the days of Saravia. To most Uruguayans in the early 1970s, the most recent memory of the army making an appearance in public life was during the catastrophic floods of 1959. A national emergency was decreed and the military was summoned to help in the rescue efforts. Other than that, despite the occasional alert over the intentions of aggressive dictators like Argentina's Juan Perón, not much was to be said about the armed forces. Unlike other countries in the region, where societies were more stratified, Uruguay never had a military class. Recruits came from all walks of society, and there was nothing glamorous or widely admired about serving in any branch of the armed forces.

With this lack of activity and of interest from society, the military was almost an afterthought in national politics. In the 1960s soldiers were thus employed for anything but soldiering. In fact, the political decadence of the time hurt the force.

First, the pay –as was the case with the police- was modest, if not inadequate. Soldiers are rarely paid generously in any country, but nevertheless in the case of Uruguay it meant that many were living close to poverty. Second, working conditions were precarious. For instance, the historically most important military base in the country, in strategic terms, was the one installed atop the Cerro – the hill that dominates the bay of Montevideo. Yet, the Cerro was, and remains, surrounded by some of Montevideo's worst slums. The hilltop base was in such terrible conditions that it was not all that different from its environs. Officers serving there maintained their dignity as best they could, but there were little to no resources, from paper to write in to food.

This did not impede politicians from ordering the military to perform questionable tasks. For instance, many of the soldiers at the Cerro base were ordered to help with the construction of a nearby stadium for the neighborhood's eponymous football club. Rather decadently, the facility was named after the Colorado lawmaker who shepherded the project through the Parliament, Cerro Football Club president Luis Troccoli.[416]

Political chiefs like Troccoli had taken to bossing the military around to perform all kinds of unbecoming tasks. Specific roads were to be repaired, homes had to be constructed first in certain housing projects, and legislators or ministers were always protected. At one point, General Líber Seregni was ordered to deploy his anti-air support floodlights to the Cantegril Country Club of Punta del Este for a summer weekend. The top-notch venue was hosting the yearly Miss Uruguay contest, and someone had ordered the Army to contribute to the *mise en scène*. The soldiers, doing guard duty outside the venue and manning the floodlights, were not even provided with dinner, but they did have to watch guests waltz in and out of the glamorous event.[417]

All of this was happening in a country that according to a 1969 survey already had a stunning 198,846 state employees - close to 11% of the adult population.[418] Nevertheless, the number was still insufficient for guaranteeing the basic functioning of the government and required adding many of the 27,509 in the military and the police to its tasks.[419] In a society that prided itself on solidarity, those who were not well connected to the redistributionist feast, politically or personally, were often left out.

Petty incidents with the armed forces accumulated throughout the decades, although no one complained formally. Military discipline was high, and the body was by nature conservative in political and especially social terms. Orders were to be followed, although many began to ponder the contrast between the patriotic mission they signed on for and the actual, pointless tasks they were doing. Soldiers, like everyone else, saw the occasional news reports, like some in 1968, of legislators voting to raise their own salaries and later trying to hide it from the public, of special tax breaks for politicians, of generous benefits and job programs for party "militants", and so forth.

None of the non-military tasks was more vexing to the rank and file than the deployment of the armed forces during the great labor strikes that dominated the second half of the 1960s. As discussed before, the Communist Party and the union confederacy it controlled, the CNT, used constant general strikes to speed up the downfall of the political system. Time and again employees from all sectors walked out of their jobs, often combining them with occupations, barricades, riots, and more. This happened in both the private and government sectors, and spared no one: the power utility UTE, the banks, the taxi drivers, the bus drivers, the petroleum refiners, the ports, and many more.

Facing these constant walkouts, the governments of the Nacional and Colorado parties began calling up the military to fill in the gaps. On many occasions, soldiers were tasked with manning the workstations of the strikers: operating telephone exchanges, providing water sanitation, stevedoring at the docks, or picking up and disposing Montevideo's trash. On other occasions, they were ordered to break the strikes by militarizing the workforce, meaning that groups like banking employees were forced into a military regimen. Soldiers supervised as the civilians got buzz-cuts, were transferred to military quarters, and were marched to and from their workplaces every day until the strike was over. Apart from the disagreeable and non-military nature of the task, there was no extra pay for this additional duty in the streets, no compensation for time lost to see their families, and so on. Soldiers had become pawns, a tool the system used to patch up glitches.[420]

In the midst of all of this, men like Colonel Luis Agosto, who served at the Cerro base, had to endure welfare-financed slum dwellers in the surrounding area soliciting him for freebies, despite being penniless and overworked himself. Things were not working out, and the ranks were increasingly -though reservedly- noting it.[421]

Training and Influence

Apart from this growing involvement in internal affairs that had nothing to do with their mission, Uruguay's armed forces maintained a professional level of training and interest in security issues. Their most traditional international links were to the United States and European countries like France. From the first Uruguay got weapons and training. More specifically, between 1950 and 1982 (but mainly during the 1960s), 2,832 Uruguayan soldiers trained in the United States, particularly in counterinsurgency. Most of the training focused on fighting rural, low-intensity wars.[422]

Trips to the United States were far from what conspiracy theorists on the *izquierda* imagined them to be. Rather than bonding over cigars and plots to assemble anti-Communist death squads, there were plenty of misunderstandings, shortages of trust, and other wrangles that meant there was no alliance, much less a symbiosis, between the two forces. For instance, former army colonel José Gavazzo recalls how during his 1970 visit to the United States, he was more impressed by the conveyor belt moving the luggage at Miami International Airport than by anything the Americans taught: "The American officer who taught us had been in Viet Nam, but his experiences were so different from ours that they contributed little to our purposes".[423]

The misunderstandings continued. The hosts were generous: the Uruguayans got to see the Pentagon, Fort Benning, Fort Bragg, and Fort Leavenworth, among a number of top American military facilities. Most were impressive due to the size, the resources, and the all-around strength of the U.S. military. However, all the military hardware in the world was proving unable to grant the United States a victory over the Vietnamese Communists. In other words, when looking for foreign trainers to upgrade their capabilities, both the military and the Tupamaros found, roughly around the same dates, allies whose training was inadequate due to its focus on rural operations. In the words of Gavazzo, "our armed forces lacked specialists in guerrilla and counter-guerrilla warfare (...) This tactical and strategic weakness led to our becoming self-taught in these matters".[424]

With the United States providing equipment and training, from France came not any direct military liaison, but rather the doctrinal influence of the Indochina and Algerian conflicts. As confirmed by Colorado politician Julio Sanguinetti, former general Líber Seregni, and others, many of the young officers serving in the Uruguayan military were closely following the recent record of the French in those two wars, particularly the latter.[425]

Although Uruguay's officer corps did not study directly under French instructors, they did learn from their neighbors in Argentina (who had French veterans as instructors), and particularly through the literature in books like former counterinsurgency officer Roger Trinquier's *La Guerre Moderne* and Jean Lartéguy's novels about the French imperial wars, particularly *Les Céntürions.*[426]

The French had been plenty violent in many of their counterinsurgency operations. As early as 1955, in response to savage terrorist attacks by the ALN -the armed wing of the revolutionary, pro-independence FLN-, the French massacred thousands of Algerians in collective punishments. Frequently they moved into a village suspected of ALN activities and arrested, then "processed", every male of fighting age who lived there; many were never seen again.

French civilian authorities half-heartedly slapped formal bans on inhuman treatment, but the military was in control of all colonial actions, and its mind was set on victory at any cost. In fact, it was often the colonels and the field commanders who made the decisions on when to fire, who to fire at, whom to interrogate, how to do it, and more. The French did everything in order to win: placing electrified fences on the borders of Algeria; clandestinely interdicting weapons shipments for the ALN arriving through the Mediterranean; conducting assassinations in Europe; and even bombing their own headquarters to blame the ALN and thus continue the fight until it was annihilated.[427]

Much of this was kept away, for years, from the eyes and opinions of France's citizens and its Socialist governments. It was a dark affair: the army was essentially told to do a job with little supervision – but when the abuses came out, it was the officers who got blamed more than the civilians. Years into the war, this caused significant rifts between the military and the rest of France. The war tore the country's political system apart and left many officers bitter, jobless, or a combination of both. France was defeated in two wars of insurgency, but its men gained valuable lessons.

Roger Trinquier was a popular French counterinsurgency theoretician of the 1960s, particularly in the Southern Cone. A veteran of both Indochina and Algeria, Trinquier wrote in his book that Western states and their militaries should have no illusions about how to fight insurgents: it was an exhausting affair which went beyond shooting at the revolutionaries. The enemy was to be fought not just in combat, but in the political, economic, and psychological fields. Therefore, the military needed to have a say in all of those governmental matters. Otherwise, the enemy would have a superior, unified strategy comprising all of those categories, while the state fought with one hand behind its back. For both of these reasons -its doctrinal mandates and its influence, not least in Uruguay-, Trinquier's manual deserves special mention.[428]

The Frenchman had learned that the key to winning or losing an insurgency was the population. Whoever had it on their side had the best chances of being victorious. In Algeria, the FLN had not benefited passively from the fact that it was spearheading national liberation against a colonial empire. It also imposed itself on the population, including through intimidation and violence, to strong-arm it into helping the rebels. In Viet Nam, the problem had been that the population secretly helped the rebels in territory the French (and later the Americans) controlled.

To Trinquier, winning over a hostile population meant controlling it. Therefore, in his manual the populace is to be thrown into a regimen of strict military supervision: "Control of the masses through a tight organization, often through several parallel organizations, is the master weapon of modern warfare". With the populace under physical control -in occupied villages and areas with pervasive surveillance-, the counter-insurgent can afford to build his own influence networks to compete with the insurgents'.

The manual "La Guerre Moderne" is not most famous for these population control proposals, but rather for what it says about dealing with the insurgents themselves. According to Trinquier, the key component of the struggle is intelligence, and the best way to gather intelligence is to interrogate captured rebels. Interrogations were not to include "unnecessary violence". The opposite, meaning violence against the detainee that was necessary to achieve victory, *was* allowable in the hands of "specialists". Much was left unsaid.

A more troubling aspect of Trinquier's doctrine was the continued role of counter-insurgents *after* the insurgency was smashed. In fact, psychological operations directed at the population -in other words, propaganda- were optimal if they waited until the enemy was crushed: "propaganda will play an important role in causing the sometimes impatient masses to understand the variety of problems that must be resolved before a return to normal existence is possible".

If Trinquier's doctrine is followed, counterinsurgency must have political components to the point of redesigning the structure of the entire country. The effort is particularly invasive of private life: identifying each citizen individually, determining where they can live, where they can move to, when they can get around their own city, examining and regulating what persons can read, who they can talk to, and so forth. The domestic intelligence components of such a campaign alone are so intrusive that they are practically impossible to implement in any serious liberal democracy. This is the problem Uruguay faced when the military was brought in to take over the fight against the Tupamaros.

Trinquier's doctrines had stuck deeply with militaries in the early 1970s in countries like Chile, Argentina, and Uruguay. Variants of the term "national reorganization process" soon appeared in their strategic documents as the ultimate objective of the more immediate battle against armed subversion.

In contrast to Trinquier there was another French theorist, named David Galula, with his own doctrine for governments seeking to defeat revolutionary subversives. Galula, just like Trinquier, had served in Algeria, although afterwards he moved to Boston to do scholarly work at Harvard. His main work on counterinsurgency was, in distinctly un-French fashion, written in English, and completed in 1963.

The book, called "Counterinsurgency Warfare", brilliantly illustrates the many asymmetries insurgents can exploit to compensate for their weaker military position *vis-à-vis* the government.[429] They can operate clandestinely and undetected; their actions are cheap and cost-effective; raids have enormous multiplier effects and can be combined with propaganda for greater impact. Finally, insurgents have far less responsibilities towards the population than the state. They are the relentless critics; they have little or no record to defend, whereas it is the government that has to address a presumably long record of injustices and inefficiencies.

Galula's understanding of the insurgent led him to propose a plan for countering him that contests, piece by piece, each of the subversive's advantages. It is designed specifically to cancel out the asymmetrical advantages of the insurgent, while taking care to win the population over to the government's side. The difference with Trinquier's approach is that there is not such a strong-arming of the population towards supporting the forces of the state at any cost.

Part of Galula's clarity of thought is revealed in his rejection of state-sponsored terrorism. The reason, presumably in addition to the moral one, is that "It would be self-defeating, since terrorism is a source of disorder, which is precisely what the counterinsurgent aims to stop". Galula's lesson was learned painfully in Algeria, where paramilitary terrorism on the part of pro-French elements was tolerated and led to a spectacular deterioration in the rule of law - and ultimately the collapse of the entire effort to maintain French authority.

Galula matters because he made it essential in his doctrine not to fall to a key temptation that most other counterinsurgency proposals ended falling into: "to let the military direct the entire process (...) is so dangerous that it must be resisted at all costs". In words reminiscent of Mao's own on the process for insurgency, Galula wrote "Essential though it is, the military action is secondary to the political one, its primary purpose being to afford the political power enough freedom to work safely with the population". Galula warned in 1963 that the militarization of *everything* "would mean that the counterinsurgent government had acknowledged a signal defeat: Unable to cope with the insurgency through normal government structures, it would have abdicated in favor of the military".

This outline of contemporary thinking on counterinsurgency matters because during the 1960s there were theoretical study sessions on the subject at the Uruguayan military's in-house strategic think tank, the Instituto Militar de Estudios Superiores or IMES (National Institute of Superior Studies).[430] Students read Trinquier there, and also discussed experiences from various countries around the world. It is unlikely that Galula was in the syllabi, or no evidence could be found that it was.

The manual resulting from the IMES study sessions, entitled "Contributions to a Doctrine of War", became the guiding text for future operations against local subversives.[431] The influence of one French author, and the lack of influence of the other, was about to become visible with the unleashing of the Uruguayan military.

Organizing for War

The military's plan, developed in the weeks and months after September of 1971, was ambitious. The strategic documents that circulated among the brass, and among key civilians in the defense sphere, contained unusual language. One of the objectives the armed forces set out for themselves was "to consolidate and maintain an active support among the population for democratic and republican ideals". Another document called for the "neutralization of (...) an environment that is favorable to the emergence of subversion (administrative disorder, socio-economic crimes, public corruption, etc.)"[432]

This latter point suggested a noble mission - but how exactly could military power be deployed to accomplish it? It remained an open question, one which many civilians began to ask themselves. In fact, these documents, presented as early as September 9, gave ministers who had the opportunity to review them, like Julio Sanguinetti, significant pause. Right around this time, a poll showed a higher approval rating among Uruguayans for the military than for the Parliament.[433]

Naturally, the military was not inheriting a *tabula rasa* from the government. There were years of police work preceding their arrival, and the benefits were clear to both sides. Colonel Gavazzo goes out of his way to credit Alejandro Otero's first successor, Pablo Fontana, as a "genuine brain (...) Clearly no one at the time knew the enemy better (...) It is impossible to forget his file system, which consisted of an excellently organized series of shelves with shoe boxes that went from the floor to the roof across two walls in the room".[434] Thanks to these files and the work of top police officers like Otero, Castiglioni, and Campos, the military was starting with a full radiography of the MLN in its hands. Additionally, by then the American Public Safety Program had trained 113 policemen in the United States, and 700 more in Uruguay itself.[435] All of them would now serve under the military's orders.

The commentary of Colonel José Gavazzo is relevant because it is one of the few accounts of the period showing the military's side of things. Therefore, his autobiography is valuable in understanding the viewpoint of a soldier thrown into the counterinsurgency campaign after El Abuso. After said escape, Gavazzo got a transfer he had specifically requested: from regular service to SID, the military intelligence agency. With the military taking over the counter-MLN effort, SID was going to be at the forefront of the campaign. Combat units would raid and capture as needed, but it was SID that would perform surveillance, interrogation, mapping, infiltration, and all other non-"kinetic" activities involving the MLN and other subversives.

Ramón Trabal, the man behind this key institution, was the one who gave the introductory talk on SID's secrecy and unique operational style. In Gavazzo's recollection, the first and major difference with regular military work was that his uniform would from then on gather dust in the closet. In his fieldwork he would now dress as a civilian, and ride in civilian rather than military vehicles.

Trabal impressed everyone with his intelligence, professionalism, and loyalty to the force. He was also an inscrutable man. Nobody really knew what Trabal thought, particularly in political terms. There were rumors that he had socialist leanings, combined with a "forward-looking" conception of the military as an institution with a role to play in public affairs. Despite being a colonel and not a general, Trabal also controlled the military's liaison activities with foreign intelligence services, particularly the European ones. This, combined with his past at the police academy, his directorship of SID, and all the factors outlined here, gave him a superb position to handle information in Uruguay, possibly better than anyone else's.[436]

While SID got started on the critical information component of the military's efforts, other parts of the force readied as well. To analyze them, it is convenient to describe how the armed forces of Uruguay were set up at the time. The military structure beneath the president and the Minister of National Defense consisted firstly of the commanders of the three branches: Armada (Navy), Ejército (Army) and Fuerza Aérea (Air Force). There was also an entity to connect them, the Estado Mayor Conjunto (Joint Chiefs of Staff), which had its own commander. The EsMaCo, as it was known, was tasked with providing military advisory, planning, and coordination to the operational heads of the military. With a sufficiently talented general on the post, it could serve as the central planning position in the entire military.[437]

The head of the Joint Chiefs was possibly the most important military officer in Uruguay: Gregorio Álvarez. A man of humble means but great ambitions, Álvarez was said in Army circles to harbor "fantasies of monuments". He rose quickly through the ranks, and at age forty-five became one of the youngest generals in Uruguayan history. General Álvarez was widely recognized as a deep but evasive thinker. Unlike other officers, it was unknown if he leaned towards the Colorados, the Nationalists or the *izquierda* in his political views. In 1968-9 he was noted celebrating the arrival of a nationalist-socialist dictatorship in Peru, under General Juan Velasco Alvarado. This government functioned as a beacon, for a period of time, to South American socialists interested in operating outside the Soviet sphere of influence. In that sense, experiments like Peru attracted men both like Álvarez and like the Tupamaros. The role of the generals, furthermore, generated talk of *Peruanismo*, or "Peruvianism": the prospect of revolutionaries within the military.

In September of 1971, with a recent promotion to general in tow, the strategic posting of EsMaCo was ideal for Álvarez. According to historian Alfonso Lessa, "ESMACO became (...) a considerable source of power for General Gregorio Álvarez, who had been lacking an assignment since his days as a colonel (...) he had been left in that status for insisting on the looming risks of subversion from the early 1960s". Now, with a real need for military brains to fight subversion, Álvarez was an obvious fit. In addition to all this, he represented the force to the core. His family alone contributed three of his brothers, all colonels, to the Army, not to mention his father and grandfather had also been generals.

Slightly but not technically beneath Álvarez came the commanders of the three branches. The commander of the army was General Alcides Tamiel, a little-known officer who would soon be replaced by similarly low-profile successors. The Air Force, the weakest of the branches, was also under the command of an uncontroversial chief. The commander of the last force, the Navy, was Contra-Almirante Juan José Zorrilla. Placed in his post by politically-minded Colorados, Zorrilla was known to be a strict republican constitutionalist of the cleanest credentials, and a supporter of mainstream Batllismo.

The next significant subdivision in the military came in regional divisions, especially for the Army. There was one general in command of each of four military regions. The one titled Military Region I, which was based in Montevideo and tasked with protecting the national capital region, was obviously the most important. Therefore, any troops that were to fight the Tupamaros in their preferred urban battleground had to come from this division. The commander of the division was a key general named Esteban Cristi. Another man of unknown partisan affiliations, Cristi was more of a "man of action" than the pensive Álvarez and Trabal, who became the main planners behind Uruguay's military counterinsurgency. Both were interested not just in defeating the subversives, but also in tackling the causes of their uprising. Commanders like Cristi, meanwhile, would lead the operational effort.

SID had the names and addresses of all the Tupamaros who had ever been captured, as well as their contacts, liaisons, reports of their operations and activities, and so forth. It looked at everything carefully, and spared no effort in pursuing every track to recapture the escaped Tupas. That meant the MLN had to maximize the resilience of its clandestine network, for there was little margin for mistakes. Following El Abuso, Uruguay's population began to be bombarded with public broadcasts and government alerts on the many fugitives that were now wanted.*

Hands Dirty

After El Abuso, the police continued to conduct anti-MLN raids under military direction. One task the officers reserved for themselves was interrogation. In fact, the Army had secretly begun using harsh interrogation techniques – which often amounted to torture-, to obtain valuable information. By the admission of both sides, it worked efficiently.

The military approach to counterterrorism, particularly for the coming year of 1972, would be based on a crude cycle: captured Tupamaros were made to talk no matter what; immediately the army would launch raids based on that information to net more safe houses and Tupamaros. The captured data would be cross-checked with documents and other detainees' words, and then used to

* Naturally, intelligence and infiltration went both ways: the military was vulnerable itself to MLN penetrations, although on a small scale. Transcripts of military strategy documents from the Estado Mayor Conjunto and SID were later found circulating among the Tupas.

conduct more raids. The process would be pursued until all Tupamaros were killed or captured.[438]

There were many techniques in use to force detainees to talk. Perhaps the commonest was known as "*picana*", which consisted of an electric cattle prod applied to the body of the victim - particularly the most sensitive parts. Oftentimes, the victim had first been soaked in water so that the pain was maximized. Other techniques were less dependent on technology, but nevertheless excruciating. Accounts of torture repeat the same ones over and over again.

One method was the "*tacho*" (drum) or "submarino", which consisted of repeatedly dunking the head of a bound prisoner into a barrel filled with filthy water, and keeping it there long enough to cause panic or surrender. Another was the "*caballete*", meaning a wooden easel. Naked prisoners of both genders were forced to sit directly on them, with one leg on each side and weights tied to their feet, until the hard wood and its sharp edges started to have their crippling effect.[439] Yet one more technique consisted of hanging prisoners –again, naked- from their arms without the possibility of touching the ground. A sign hanging on every one of the counter-subversion military units partly read "To combat subversion it is necessary to sink one's hands into the mud and get dirty".[440] The Tupamaros, in their slang, called these new military tactics "the beast line".[441]

Once the military started applying these techniques it attained decisive effects. The Tupamaros, at peak strength, had a formidable array of resources and capabilities. Now, upon being captured they would enter an information extraction cycle that could hurt the organization badly. The prisoners *would* speak; there was little question about it.

The MLN had no inkling the military was about to introduce the beast line. With record numbers of *guerrilleros*, CAT collaborators, the old leadership now liberated, important foreign liaisons increasing in intensity, and lastly with multiple campaign plans authorized to take place at the same time, there was a lot going on.

The influence of Sendic and other founders could be seen in the brief return of armed propaganda. MLN cells raided the offices of municipal governments to steal documents; briefly took over small airports to hijack aircraft and use them to release leaflets over Montevideo (once again, on the anniversary of Che Guevara's death), and also hijacked radio stations to broadcast propaganda.[442] Ever unpredictable, near the end of the year Sendic also issued a "proclamation of war" from his new base in Paysandú, in the north of the country. It amounted to a complete renewal of the Tupamaros' vow to stage a revolution.

Sendic was in Paysandú to participate in an old personal project of his: a rural insurgency campaign. After arriving in town he had a rhinoplasty to make clandestine life easier. Furthermore, during their time in Punta Carretas, he and fellow Tupamaro Jorge Zabalza had developed a plan to deploy guerrilla cells in Uruguay's countryside. It was known as Plan Tatú. The MLN's top *caudillo* was not going to be one of its commanders. Instead, he joined the Tatú guerrilla column marching in the area, under the command of one of his UTAA cane workers and of master engineer Almiratti.[443] Carrying his bicycle everywhere with characteristic stubbornness, Sendic was at last in a national liberation insurgency in Uruguay's rural interior. It was supposed to be just like the great campaigns of Mao and the Cubans.

Montevideo and all the main operations were left in the hands of the leadership that executed El Abuso. That was precisely the role, first and foremost, of Column 15, which resumed Plan Cacao in a veritable wave of operations: it torched golf clubs, murdered a prison inspector, assaulted police stations, invaded the homes of policemen and other government officials, and kidnapped several people.

An Unpromising Start

The greatest novelty in Uruguay was, in addition to El Abuso, the arrival of a new president. Juan María Bordaberry seemed like a weak figure. He won one of the least conclusive elections in recent memory, with more attention paid to Pacheco's failed campaign for re-election than to his own. He was not well known to the people of Uruguay, not even to many politicians. As described by Sanguinetti, Bordaberry was a "traditional cattle rancher, a ruralist political leader, a devout Catholic and a good head of his family, with a sizable offspring consisting of nine children".[444] The president did not excel at public speaking nor at expressing major initiatives or ideas. The American embassy, years earlier, had described him in one of its catalogues of prominent Uruguayans as "clearly not brilliant".[445]

Bordaberry's presidency was troubled literally from the first few minutes he held it. The hostility of the MLN was enough to require constant police protection, but the new president also had to face hostility inside the Parliament, when giving his inaugural speech.[446] First, Communist leader Rodney Arismendi loudly heckled the proceeding. His deputy, Jaime Pérez, joined moments later, yelling the outrageous line "No more concentration camps!" (Pérez, it should be noted, was a rabid supporter of the Soviet Union, and the son of escaped European Jews to top it off). More legislators piled on, including the radical Nationalist turned Frente Amplio lawmaker Enrique Erro, who shouted "Violence comes from the regime! You have no right to disrespect the Parliament! What you are saying is an affront to this country!"

Bordaberry continued his speech, which was not particularly hostile to anyone but the Tupamaros, while cross-shouting took place between the hecklers and some of his own supporters in the Colorado ranks. The indignities taking place were an act that any Marxist government, then or now, would have denounced as "destabilizing", "fascist", and indicative of a coup d'état. It was also an incident the hecklers could not expect *not* to have an effect on Bordaberry, whose inauguration was ruined and whose first perspective as president on the merits of parliamentarian democracy could not have been worse.[447]

CHAPTER TWELVE:

THE FINAL ROUND

THE TATÚ IS an armadillo-like animal that roams the Uruguayan countryside. Its burrows are called *tatuceras*; that was also the name the MLN picked to name its new type of rural hideout.

The Second Front

Plan Tatú consisted of networks of *tatuceras* dug in various locations around Uruguay, preferably near small cities, which would allow the Tupamaros to conduct a hide-and-seek guerrilla campaign. In the conception of creators Sendic and Zabalza, Plan Tatú was a rural harassment campaign against minor population centers and vulnerable government positions. It was a second front.

This strategy contradicted the decisions of the Tupamaros as far back as the days of the Coordinador. The MLN's own Document 1, co-authored by Sendic and Fernández in 1967, said "Our countryside cannot be used to install a permanent guerrilla *foco*".[448] Nevertheless, Sendic had long thought that rural workers, like his UTAA cane harvesters, could be recruited as revolutionaries. Others thought it was an insane proposition.

The difficulties of operating in Uruguay's flat and open countryside remained unchanged. Once a guerrilla raid was conducted against a small town, the retreat towards a hideout depended on speed, stealth, and operational secrecy. If the location of the attackers was discovered, the military could easily isolate any patch of forest in the country. Furthermore, the distinctly un-revolutionary populace of inner Uruguay could be helpful to the Army. Strangers were easily noticed.

One indirect use of Plan Tatú was decompressing a swelling in the number of Tupas present in Montevideo following El Abuso. As Tupamaro Marcelo Estefanell explained, following the escape "We were bumping into each other in the street. You would walk around and think 'that guy has to be a Tupa, look at the way he walks, the way he dresses'".[449] The MLN called this *saturation*: the ratios of *guerrilleros* per square kilometer and per inhabitant of the city were too high. The Tupas nicknamed one part of Montevideo "the Mekong Delta", because of the high number of safe houses present in a small area.[450]

In other words, Plan Tatú did not happen because the MLN thought it could win a rural insurgency. Rather, it was born from combining the problem of saturation with the decade-long focus on rural guerrilla of Sendic and others.[451*] Huddling with his cell in remote La Horqueta, wearing disguises, make-up and sporting a modified nose, Sendic retreated and was not heard from for a number of months.

The Main Front

While Tatú was hatched, Montevideo remained the core of the insurgency. The main line of operations remained a combination of Plan Cacao -officially dismantled, but alive in spirit- and Line H. In other words, urban guerrilla attacks against policemen, businessmen (from banking, industry, and so forth), and last but not least the wealthy.

There were numerous hits on patrolling policemen, on the private homes of police inspectors and other members of the security services, on police stations, and on many civilian targets. One particular wave of attacks, the MLN's most ambitious to date, was launched in late January 1972 to support the establishment of Plan Tatú in the north. The Tupamaros kidnapped an editor of the

---

* During the months of the Tatú campaign, in an act uncharacteristic of his MLN leadership but consistent with his unpredictable and stormy personality, Sendic showed up at the front door of Army officer Gustavo Criado, in the city of Mercedes. Sendic shot Criado, whom the MLN accused of torturing and murdering a captured Tupamaro, in the stomach. The officer survived.

Colorado newspaper Acción; assaulted the Soca police station (with Engler personally in command and two policemen killed in action, one of them at the hands of Yessie Macchi); took over a village named Constancia, and also assaulted the airport of Paysandú city and a radio station.[452] It was an ambitious undertaking, which both police and Army were unable to stop. Days later, in an assault on a suburban Montevideo police station, between thirty to fifty Tupamaros attacked. Carrying high-powered AR-15 rifles stolen from the naval academy in 1970, the *guerrilleros* took over a few buildings in the area and rained fire on the police station. One of their own, plus one policeman, died that day.[453]

These actions continued to enrage many in the government. The secret parapolice groups that had murdered radicals beginning in 1971 continued making their presence known in 1972, to the point where they became the focus of the MLN itself. The Tupamaros thought of them as death squads, mainly because they murdered individuals who were at the time unarmed and not engaged in acts of violence.

After killing their confirmed third and an unconfirmed fourth victim the clandestine group fizzled – possibly because the military's effectiveness made them unnecessary.* To this day, the true degree of formalization of these "death squads", and particularly their membership, remains unknown.

The MLN was yielding no clues to the major changes coming to its leadership and to its strategic decisions. Because of this, it is worth stopping to recap who exactly was in charge of what.

After El Abuso, none of the MLN's founders made it back to the *dirección*: there was almost no overlap between the two leaderships. In fact, the 1972 *ejecutivo* evolved from a tetrarchy to a pentarchy. A fifth member, named Mario Píriz, joined the established Henry Engler, Mauricio Rosencof, Donato Marrero and Adolfo Wasem. Each enjoyed equality within the committee, but also had special responsibilities to uphold compartmentalization.

Wasem supervised Column 15, which was now headed by Gabriel Schroeder (after having been led, in the past, by Amodio, Candán, and Engler). Marrero was the supervisor of Column 10,

---

* The four victims were the aforementioned Manuel Ramos and Íbero Gutiérrez, plus the disappeared Abel Ayala in mid-1971 and Héctor Castagnetto in early 1972.

which was then the only one to have a female leader: Alicia Rey. Engler oversaw a column dedicated to the periphery of Montevideo, codenamed Collar or Necklace. Rosencof supervised Column 70, which he himself had founded: it was the almost all-political backbone of the 26 de Marzo legal party. The commander of this column was, oddly enough, noted trigger-puller Alberto Candán.[454] The newcomer Píriz had joined in 1968, aged twenty-one, with a background in the Socialist Party. He was thus the youngest of the leaders.[455] He was given supervision of columns 20 and 30, which would spearhead Plan Tatú and operate in rural Uruguay, far from Montevideo.[456]

One change the leadership permitted was the restoration of Héctor Amodio to a position of special responsibility: the Montevideo General Command. Once again, Amodio was to coordinate the guerrilla operations of every MLN unit operating in the capital, although he would have no say in Plan Tatú. Happy with this change and with the upgrade in his girlfriend Alicia Rey's responsibilities, and with the MLN at peak capacity, 1972 promised to be a fruitful year for the Tupamaros' power couple. Amodio, like Sendic, Lucía Topolansky, and other Tupas, also used this post-Abuso period to undergo plastic surgery.

In addition to all this, Wasem was given an additional responsibility: the "Secretariat" of the MLN. This was a special administrative and external liaison role, which took him to meetings with Fidel Castro, Salvador Allende, and local politicians like Wilson Ferreira and Líber Seregni.

Mauricio Rosencof was the other MLN leader in charge of external liaison. He also visited Fidel Castro and got a Browning pistol as a gift from the Cuban leader. Rosencof, as the "intellectual" of the MLN, also met with Greco-French filmmaker Constantin Costa-Gavras, who was in Uruguay doing research for the movie later known as *État de Siège*. Rosencof's artistic talents worked like a charm on the European, who was hooked on the story of the Tupamaros and of the Mitrione incident.[457] Soon after, the movie starring Yves Montand as the murdered OPS advisor brought the names of the Tupamaros and of Mitrione to wide international renown. The government banned it from Uruguayan theaters.[458*]

---

* Later on, Costa-Gavras and Montand transferred some of the proceeds from the film to the MLN, through Uruguayan exiles in Paris.

The Hour of Restoration

Following El Abuso many of the escapees were recaptured, in some cases before 1971 was over. One by one, famous names began to re-join Punta Carretas, by then the laughing stock of the country.

Efraín Martínez and José Mujica had been together since the escape, particularly because Mujica was undergoing health problems and benefited from having a close friend helping out. However, the *gambusa* Carlos Lapaz, who escaped with them during El Abuso, was recaptured and gave up their hideout. When the police swooped in, both were captured along with MLN founder Tabaré Rivero. Martínez was struck with a rifle butt on the head: with the military in charge, arrest procedures were changing.[459]

Jorge Zabalza headed to the interior of Uruguay immediately after escaping. After committing some pointless robberies in the city of Paysandú, a military patrol managed to intercept him and fellow Tupa Ángel Yoldi. The two were outnumbered, outgunned, and out-sped. Zabalza fought with his .45 pistol, but was shot in the stomach and blacked out. He woke up in a hospital, and was then transferred back to the place he had escaped from: Punta Carretas. Less than two months had passed since El Abuso: the elections had not yet taken place, and there was already an MLN contingent back where it had started.[460]

Shortly afterwards none other than Amodio also showed up and got placed in the same cell as Zabalza.* Something about him was different: he appeared to be unscathed, as if his arrest had been non-violent. In prison discussions, Amodio spoke out against Sendic and against Eleuterio Fernández, but highly of Donato Marrero, Mario Píriz, Henry Engler and, naturally, Alicia Rey.[461] Zabalza and Mujica were sufficiently concerned about these observations to write to Fernández, who was still free although not in the *dirección*.

The context was the emergence of tensions between the old leadership and the new one, both strategically and, in some cases, personally. Some of this was old news: the Amodio-Rey duo had had disputes with Sendic and other leaders since at least 1968.

---

* With Amodio back in prison, the Montevideo General Command became the responsibility of Julio Marenales –back in a command position for the first time since 1968-.

In February, a sitting member of the *ejecutivo* summoned Fernández Huidobro to Parque del Plata. It was Mauricio Rosencof, more often than not the odd man out in the Column 15-heavy post-Almería leadership. Rosencof told Fernández there were strong disagreements inside the MLN: Sendic's most devoted followers were heating things up in hopes of restoring him to the *dirección*, while getting rid of Píriz and Marrero. After tense discussion sessions of what Fernández himself called an internal "coup" at the core of the MLN, important changes were decided. It was March 15.

The changes were mostly in the leadership, while the MLN's strategy remained a question mark. The decision was that Henry Engler and Mauricio Rosencof would remain in the *comité ejecutivo*, but Donato Marrero, Mario Píriz and Adolfo Wasem -all originally from Column 15- would be removed. Their replacements were Eleuterio Fernández and Alberto Candán: one to represent the founders, and the other to represent the generation between the founders and the newest Tupamaros.[462]

According to accounts from the time, Amodio's partner, Alicia Rey, was the only one to make a scene in response to the "coup": she felt the influence of her faction, Column 15, was waning too much. Old enmities were resurfacing: all the removed leaders had faced disputes with, or the disapproval of, Sendic. From far away in the north, El Bebe retained significant influence. He would, however, hear nothing of joining the leadership himself.

Despite the installation of a new leadership, the MLN continued work on an existing plan for a major offensive in Montevideo. Before its launch there was one key *acción* to perform: a second escape from Punta Carretas. Any such caper could not be a repetition of the first one. There could be no digging from inside the perimeter (much less for over a month), no hiding of the dirt, no controlling the prison by "owning" the guards. Furthermore, the scale would have to be reduced: only a fraction of the over one hundred Tupas who had escaped in September had a chance of doing so in April.

Return of the Rooster

There was little eventfulness in Punta Carretas for the *guerrilleros* jailed there. Aside from football and volleyball matches, the most notorious incident is the case of Rodolfo Leoncino. The man in question was a prison sub-inspector who worked the night shift in the Tupamaros' cell block. One January night, while he was on duty, a prisoner slipped and fell to the ground, hitting his forehead against the sink before landing heavily on the floor. According to the Tupamaros, despite his cellmates' cries for help, Leoncino yelled back at them to be quiet, and that the infirmary would be open at six the next morning. When that moment came, hours later, the fallen prisoner was dead.

The death was reported to the prison warden; Leoncino claimed he never heard any cries for help, and the other sentries backed his story. Unfortunately for the guard, the Tupamaros now had him, as the expression goes in Uruguay, *entre ceja y ceja* - right between the eyebrows. A trio made up of Jorge Zabalza, Efraín Martínez and José Mujica requested the outside MLN liquidate Leoncino for his crime. Mujica called the plot Plan Corcho, or Cork, and it was chillingly executed: a Column 15 squad showed up at Leoncino's house and gunned him down. In their public statement claiming responsibility for Leoncino's death, the Tupamaros were clear: "The clandestine power of the MLN will not tolerate injustices".[463]

Leoncino was killed for an additional reason: he had a role in filtering inmates for visits to the dentist.[464] This was important because an old escape plan was re-activated: Plan Gallo, or Rooster. Discarded in the run-up to El Abuso, mainly because the method had been "burned" in Operation Star, the Rooster required digging a tunnel that connected to the sewers. The diggers would work from the outside and emerge at an agreed time and place within the prison perimeter, just as had been the case with the women's prison the previous year. The jailed Tupas simply had to be ready for that moment.

The plot proceeded uneventfully, with Alicia Rey, Heraclio Rodríguez Recalde and the engineer Santiago Cocco in command.[465] The outside Tupas successfully dug a tunnel from the sewers to the infirmary of the main cell block. Communicating via lawyers and visitors, the agreed date was April 12, 1972.

Inside Punta Carretas, Amodio was in charge given his seniority. During the night of April 12, he activated the plan. Amodio used a key ring he had acquired through the MLN's prison-corrupting efforts to get out of his cell and open those of the Tupas chosen to escape. Martínez Platero, Mujica, Zabalza, and others were among them, for a grand total of fourteen. They were few compared to the 106 of September, but compensated for that in importance within the "orga".

The next step was for one of them to be smeared with fake blood – in reality tomato sauce-, and to pretend to be sick and injured. He was carried moaning by this contingent of fellow comrades directly to the door that separated the cell block from the infirmary. Bover, the guard on duty at the time, was known to be intimidated by the sight of blood. He waved the group directly to the hospital facility.[466]

Once inside, the Tupamaros overpowered five members of the staff and waited.[467] Right on schedule, the floor tiles of the infirmary began to leak scratching noises, and then a discrete mechanical rumble began to break through. The outside MLN was using a manual jackhammer to punch the hole. Below, a tunnel would take them through sixty meters of pathway to an entrance into the Montevideo sewer network, from whence they would be evacuated. Jumping inside –along with a number of common criminals who joined the escape-, the group left the prison staff tied up and disappeared into the hole.

The MLN always insisted on protocol. For Operation Rooster, it stated that Mujica would be given the top escape slot (as with Marenales in El Abuso), because his physical condition was the worst. He carried with him several bullet wounds in his stomach, two reparative surgeries that had failed to heal properly, police beatings, the life of a prison inmate, and a chubbier build. Second came Zabalza, for comparable reasons. Then came others, who might be asked to help push the weaker ones in front. According to Zabalza, an anxious Amodio broke protocol and was the first to throw himself in, belly down.

Once inside the tunnel, the escapees were given small carts to move as quickly as possible. Martínez Platero remembers riding one behind Mujica, crashing against his slowed down *compañero.* The police and the military were well aware of the Tupas' exploitation of the sewers for operations, and often descended to hunt them down. For this reason, this time the MLN rigged several manholes with fake battery-powered explosive devices with blinking red lights that discouraged pursuers from descending.[468] A sign or two said the sewer network had been "mined".

Zabalza's account of the escapees' trek, as told by biographer Federico Leicht, is vivid: "In the first portion the pipes are no wider than half a meter; it was a free fall that ended in an enormous channel with walkways on both sides. [The escapees] fell into a pool of excrement and raw sewage almost two meters deep. To Jorge those were the longest 800 meters of his life. He had to navigate them first by swimming and then by grabbing on to ledges full of rats and cockroaches, until reaching a space under Avenida Brasil. Once there they heard police gunfire: they were opening manhole covers and firing machine gun bursts. Desperation made one of the refugees open one of the covers and emerge dripping shit in Chucarro and Avenida Brasil, smack in the middle of Pocitos. The rest of the group continued walking the pipes and emerged behind the Villa Dolores zoo, directly into a truck with a hole on the floor".[469]

Amodio needed help to climb out of one of the refuse pools. He was up to his neck in it and, given his short height, had difficulty making it out. Upon reaching the final landing, he was doing worse than the others: "He was hysterical and all smeared in shit; he had lost control of his nerves". The fresh suit and pistol waiting for him on arrival compensated for this. Amodio's people were dedicated.[470]

Once the evacuation was complete, each of the Tupas got an assignment. Efraín Martínez Platero headed the "sewer commando", tasked with mastering the underground network and deploying across the city to help Tupas in compromised positions. With more safe houses containing openings to the sewers, there were better opportunities to evacuate "burned" bases. This marked the completion of Jorge Manera's Plan Gardiol, a project inspired by the Warsaw resistance fighters of the Second World War, and an MLN trademark.

In the weeks that followed Martínez became the "lord of the sewers", the greatest expert in the entire country in how to move about them. He and his special squads (comprising a total of nine *guerrilleros* and one sewer specialist)[471] were able to move across the city, in nearly direct lines, faster than any vehicle could aboveground. Conditions were rough: oftentimes, they had to move for long stretches with their bodies bent forward. The stench was obviously terrible; rats and noxious fumes continued to be a severe issue. It was *always* hot. The walls, the grates, the rust and the moss were everywhere.

The team adopted an operational uniform: "Shorts. Mid-calf boots. Elbow pads (...) A hat and a backpack. After that there was a t-shirt and nothing else, because you sweat like crazy down there (...) The sewer is one-twenty-five [meters tall], which means you have to move around crouched, pressing against the walls with your elbows (...) We would run! We ran in those sewers".[472]

Martínez Platero spent two and a half months on sewer duty. He and his team became essential to the MLN: navigating the dark, fetid mazes without an experienced guide was no alluring prospect. One of the subterranean bases he established was called La Catedral, given an unexpectedly tall roof that produced a church-like echo. It allowed *guerrilleros* not to just to stand erect, but to actually play football matches. Another base in the sewers was capable of housing up to twenty people in emergency situations, had a sandy floor, and was directly under the Legislative Palace.[473] Some Tupamaros spent up to three full weeks there, waiting until the coast was clear.[474]

Plan Hipólito

With changes in the leadership, a second escape from Punta Carretas, and the sewer network fully primed, the MLN was ready for what turned out to be the last leg of its revolutionary insurgency. It began on April 14 1972, just two days after the Rooster escape. It was the most violent operation in MLN history, and it was codenamed Plan Hipólito. The attack, directed by Alberto Candán, consisted of a series of targeted assassinations across various parts of Montevideo.[475]

The day began with MLN cells hijacking five civilian vehicles, and sending fire teams aboard each one to conduct the hits. The first happened at eight in the morning, at the busy intersection of Avenida Fructuoso Rivera and Ponce de León street. The target was police *comisario* Óscar Delega, one of the two inspectors who had busted the Tupas in Almería. The Tupamaros shot up his patrol vehicle; immediately they dismounted and "finished" both Delega and his driver, Carlos Leites.

Simultaneously, an MLN squad drove by a bus stop where naval officer Ernesto Motto was waiting for his ride to work. He never had a chance: the Tupamaros gunned him down and he became the first military casualty in the conflict.

There were more targets. During the morning, MLN snipers infiltrated a church almost exactly on Montevideo's busiest spot and took positions inside its bell tower. From there, at eleven in the morning they fired their AR-15s and killed a civilian, Armando Acosta y Lara, as he kissed his wife goodbye on the doorstep of his house, directly across the street.

Acosta y Lara was a former high school professor who had served as deputy Minister of the Interior, as well as Pacheco's special appointee to run the troubled secondary school system. He had long been in the Tupamaros' targets: on July 4 1970 he was injured in an MLN attack, and on September of 1971 he escaped a kidnapping attempt.

A man named Miguel Sofía was an additional civilian target that day. An assassination team consisting of Tupamaros Norma Pagliaro and Nicolás Gropp was tasked with killing him. Someone alerted Sofía to the presence of two vehicles near his home with armed people inside. He called top policeman Castiglioni, who deployed his men. The police intercepted the Tupamaros and killed them in the ensuing shootout.[476]

The Tupamaros have always claimed these targets were members of the parapolice *escuadrón de la muerte*, or death squad. In their propaganda they claimed Plan Hipólito was part of a larger campaign seeking to impose a "double power" in Uruguay. An advanced stage of insurgency, exercising *doble poder* meant replacing the government's functions with the MLN's own brand. It was thus developing its own "police", its own jails –at the Cárcel del Pueblo-, and now its own brand of justice.[477] The MLN's "courts" had publicly sentenced the men in the hit list to death just hours before the attacks. The evidence the Tupamaros claimed for their "rulings" came almost exclusively from the interrogation of a man named Nelson Bardesio.

Bardesio was a police photographer at the Intelligence and Liaison section. Weeks before the attacks, the MLN kidnapped him to ask questions about ties between the Ministry of the Interior, the police force, the United States advisory team, and the mysterious gangs that had murdered members and sympathizers of the MLN.

Mauricio Rosencof interrogated Bardesio in search of evidence of these and other connections. The photographer complied and gave his interrogator the names of people tied to the "squads".[478] A majority were high-ranking officials from the Ministry of the Interior. The MLN transcribed Bardesio's interrogation, summarized it, and distributed a brief to the press. It was accompanied by a declaration of war on the "escuadrón", and carried the hostage's fingerprint on the cover as proof of his giving truthful testimony.[479]

The question of who conducted the extrajudicial murders remains murky. The Tupamaros drew a picture of a motley crew of policemen, politicians, and military officers, all supported by the CIA station in Montevideo. In stating this they employed a single source, and nothing in terms of verification mechanisms or due process.

The available evidence shows that the United States embassy repeatedly told the Uruguayan government it was strictly against any extrajudicial methods for fighting the Tupamaros – even after the Mitrione incident. It was also unlikely that the military was involved. First, because it arrived late to the game, at a time when most of the murders had already taken place. Second, it did not fit the profile of how military operations proceeded. A regimented, more disciplined body, the Uruguayan Army was not exactly in need of extrajudicial methods to eliminate its enemies if it wanted to. Third, the selection of the victims required a degree of familiarity with the MLN, one which the military would not acquire for some time.

What is most likely is that vengeful individuals at the Ministry of the Interior, following the methods of previous abusers like Héctor Morán Charquero, were behind the murders. The support of a high-ranking figure is also likely; the Tupamaros fingered former Minister of the Interior Santiago de Brum and, naturally, Acosta y Lara. According to Sergio D'Oliveira, an Army colonel at the time, the illegal group "appears to have had a structure that allowed it to operate with relative impunity and secrecy".

The American embassy suspected both the police and foreign elements of being behind the case: "Brazilians are known to have advised and trained Uruguayan police and military officials involved in counter-terrorist groups who have undertaken bombings, kidnappings, and even murders of suspected members of radical left terrorist groups. It is reported that Brazilians have supported these activities by providing funds, vehicles, arms, ammunition and explosives".[480]

On April 14 1972, as the country learned of the attacks on Delega, Motto, Acosta y Lara, and the others, it became clear that a major MLN offensive was taking place. Reports of violence piled up, all before noon. What nobody foresaw was how on that same day the military decided to show its true strength, after months of mostly monitoring the situation.

Counter-Strike

Unbeknownst to everyone but a few police and military officers, the security services had been closely monitoring many of the MLN's safe houses for weeks. Now, with the Tupamaros in action throughout the city, was a good moment to take them out. For Luis Agosto, a colonel, the war against the MLN began that day.

First came the home on Amazonas street of Luis Martirena, who was both a Tupamaro and a Cuban agent.[481] The police and Army surrounded the property, and after those inside failed to surrender the raid happened quickly. The owners of the house were gunned down, and the police –including top officers Víctor Castiglioni and Hugo Campos- burst in.

According to one account, while searching the house some policemen noticed a hatch on the roof of the main bathroom, but did not disclose it to their superiors or open it. They preferred to later loot it for private gain. However, Campos entered and noticed not just the hatch, but traces of blood oozing down from it.

As it turned out, none other than Eleuterio Fernández Huidobro was hiding in a sizable secret compartment directly above the roof. He had been injured but stayed in the *berretín* hoping to wait out the police inspection. The Tupamaro codenamed Jesús was resisting enormous pain from at least four gunshot wounds, including one to the neck. It was at least his third time being struck by enemy gunfire. Now the security services had themselves a major coup: Fernández represented the hardest core of the MLN, an indisputable leader, and a recently restored member of the *dirección*. The capture of Fernández Huidobro illustrates an important point: orders were to preserve the lives of captives, not just for legal but also for tactical reasons: they could be interrogated and milked for more information.

In addition to him, the police acquired the most important document cache so far in the war against the MLN. Finds included activity reports for all columns, a budget for the entire organization, and papers that were decisive in identifying and locating safe houses and Tupamaros, both legal and clandestine.

The house on Amazonas street was not the only one attacked that morning. At a nearby home located in Pérez Gomar street, also under secret surveillance, Tupamaros were meeting to discuss the day's events. Telephone intercepts depicted them directing and monitoring Plan Hipólito from there; fragments have survived into the present day.

Despite the wiretap, the government failed to prevent Plan Hipólito because MLN communications were compartmentalized and encoded. Third parties could not understand the meaning of names, times, and places. Nevertheless, when the police assaulted the house, it turned into an enormous hit against the "orga": every occupant of the home was killed. This included important leaders such as Alberto Candán, Armando Blanco, and Gabriel Schroeder. The luckiest man that day was Adolfo Wasem, who had left the Amazonas house for the Pérez Gomar one ,moments before the first was raided. He arrived at the second in time to notice and avoid the police siege.

Armando Blanco had risen in the ranks of Column 15 in the aftermath of Almería. Two years earlier he had interrogated Dan Mitrione. At the time of Plan Hipólito he was Lucía Topolansky's love interest. Schroeder, another top Column 15 cadre, was a key operator in two of the MLN's greatest prison escapes: the Star jailbreak from the women's prison, and El Abuso. Both were significant losses.

Alberto Candán was the biggest catch of all: his death was the most damaging fatality in MLN history thus far. Before his death, no member of the Tupamaros who had led a column or belonged to the *dirección* had been killed. A member of the second wave of recruits, Candán climbed the ranks quickly. He was Mitrione's last interrogator, and endured the entire Almería crisis without revealing the location of the People's Prison where the OPS chief was held. Clutching the Browning pistol Fidel Castro had given Mauricio Rosencof, Candán's life ended leaving many strategic and leadership ends loose.

April 14 was the most violent day in Uruguay in many decades. It was a stunning setback for the MLN. In the words of historian Leonardo Haberkorn, "That day the aura of Tupamaro invincibility was definitely buried". Despite the change in leadership a month earlier, the MLN had failed to adopt a strategy that was more political than warlike. While Engler and Candán were known and expected to be action men, the other two members, Rosencof and Fernández, were supposed to have broader mindsets.

Fernández Huidobro has recognized "I did not find the courage to oppose it (...) I have no other explanation". Rosencof has a similarly weak explanation: "I am also responsible for what was done. I did not vote against it in the Executive; I am not washing my hands off of it". In other words, they were either not really opposed to Plan Hipólito or they were and failed to speak up.

It was not just the MLN that came in for a beating. The Communists were involved in violence too - exactly what they had feared would happen as a consequence of *foco* adventurism. The next day, in a climate of severe shock in society, a "strongly armed parapolice commando" raided the headquarters of the party.

Then, on the night from April 16 to the 17 a police unit appeared at the PCU's Club #20 in Montevideo, demanding those inside present themselves outside for an inspection. A confusing stand-off ensued, until suddenly the officer in charge was shot in the head and killed. Immediately, the police shot up the Communist club and destroyed it, in the process killing seven members of the Party. No weapons were found inside.[482]

The response to the massacre could have been violent. However, as the absolute ruler of the Party, Arismendi gave strict orders to his armed apparatus not to retaliate. Even at the bloodiest moment in the PCU's history, it stuck to its strategy and waited until the right moment came.[483]

Combining all the incidents, Uruguay had suddenly experienced an onslaught. On April 14, twelve people died: eight Tupamaros, one civilian, and three policemen and soldiers (a fourth died days later of his injuries). Adding the eight dead from the raid on the Communist club, it was a total of twenty-one in just three days. April 14 became not just a date, but also a reference - like Almería, shorthand for a milestone in the conflict with the Tupamaros.

Plumbing the Depths

Popular clamor was clear: the MLN had to be wiped out, for it was far too much of a menace to society. The Parliament agreed: on

April 15 it voted to establish a state of siege that gave the military plenary powers to conduct operations. Patrols, raids, arrests, and surveillance jumped significantly.

With Fernández Huidobro captured and Candán killed, half of the MLN's leadership was taken out in Plan Hipólito. That meant changes were once again due. The most obvious candidate was Sendic: a majority felt it was time for the return of Rufo. Therefore, Jorge Zabalza tracked him down in the north, and ensured he returned to a besieged, Army-patrolled Montevideo. He did so inside a car trunk.

For the remaining slot, Sendic is said to have vetoed Amodio, and instead suggested Marenales. Upon Amodio's capture in between prison escapes, the Tupa codenamed Zenón had replaced him at the helm of the Montevideo General Command. Now came his return to the *dirección* for the first time since 1968. The reshuffle disappointed Amodio but did leave him with the position of MLN intelligence chief. What interested Amodio more, however, was sharing his reservations about the MLN's strategy with Engler and Marenales. They were receptive to his arguments, so he wrote a full report that concluded it was best to cancel the current wave of violence, and instead withdraw to rethink the group's strategy. Amodio faced opposition to his positions in Sendic, a heavyweight bar none. The Tupamaros were paralyzed.[484]

April 14 was not the only major mistake the MLN made. Only days later, some of its key members learned of one that could not be stopped. At a house in the Unión neighborhood, Sendic, Zabalza, and others met with a militant named Enrique Osano, who revealed the darkest secret in the history of the group.

In late 1971, a guerrilla cell operating as part of Plan Tatú in Maldonado department had been accidentally spotted by a local, a 46 year-old modest ranch hand named Pascasio Báez. The Tupas, under the command of Jorge Manera, had a large, sophisticated *tatucera* in the area, known as Caraguatá. The base sported an underground shooting range, a major explosives workshop, a weapons depot, and a prison. The *estancia* where the *tatucera* was built, known as Spartacus, contributed to the *façade* by showcasing its animals in exhibits and competitions, as is customary in Uruguay. The arrangement was just taking off, but the encounter with Báez changed everything.

In order to protect themselves from potential disclosures, the Tupamaros kidnapped Báez and kept him prisoner. The issue became what to do with him; weeks passed with Báez in captivity. People would increasingly notice he was missing (not least his wife and children), but the group thought it could not afford to free him. A plan to spirit him out of the country proved impracticable.

Lastly, they suggested murdering Báez, and the leadership agreed. Henry Engler arrived at the facility and prepared an injection with a lethal dose of Pentothal. He handed it to Ismael Bassini, the MLN's first and most important medical doctor, who injected Báez and ended his life. The victim was buried, clandestinely, in a spot selected by Néstor Sclavo, the MLN collaborator who owned the property.[485] Pascasio Báez became one of the first *desaparecidos* in recent Uruguayan history.[486]

Enrique Osano revealed all of this to Sendic and the others. There was disbelief and shock. Rather than exploding in rage at this mistake, Sendic asked "Was it necessary to kill a ranch hand?" The answer was obvious. While Henry Engler has publicly recognized his responsibility for the murder, it was the entire *dirección* that decided on it.[487]

It was not just the MLN that was sinking morally. Following April 14 the Army escalated its campaign to destroy the group. It was then that torture became a key instrument for the collection of intelligence.

Torture by the Uruguayan police had been amateurish. There were punitive, vengeful tinges to it. Typically it involved a combination of beatings and electrocution, and was episodic rather than systematic. Parliamentary commissions and numerous public complaints documented examples, but the true extent, even by the admission of Tupamaros and Communists, was never great.

The military's takeover of the fight signified a qualitative and quantitative change. The cases increased exponentially: essentially every captured Tupamaro who refused to talk was subjected to one form of torture or another. It typically began with the *plantón*: forcing the individual to stand on one spot for hours upon hours, with no chance of moving, speaking, or anything else. Next came the easel, the submarine, and others. Mario Teti, contrasting this to police interrogatories in previous years, said that "Compared to what happened in 1972, [those had been] a gathering of ladies".[488]

No one in Uruguay knew much about torture, but its historical universality suggests it does not take much to engage in it. According to colonel Luis Agosto, "Nobody taught us how to interrogate; we learned as we went". Although some officers were aware of the French methods in Algeria, there had never been any courses in what is today called "enhanced interrogation".

As for the Tupamaros, Fernández Huidobro claims they adopted one simple directive from the Colombian FARC, the Spanish ETA, and the Algerian FLN. Captured Tupas were to resist, for twenty-four hours, whatever they were subjected to. This would give the MLN enough time to evacuate people and safe houses the detainee knew about. If given that time, the organization believed it was capable of absorbing the blow.

Many Tupamaros talked during their first interrogation without the need for harsh techniques. Others had to endure psychological "treatment" first. For example, Armando Miraldi was kept hooded as captured *guerrilleros* walked into the room and disclosed everything he had done for the MLN. Carlos Koncke's interrogators played recordings of other Tupamaros giving him up. When possible, questioners preferred these methods for "breaking" prisoners over getting their hands dirty.

Torture methods for the toughest Tupamaros, the ones who rejected all overtures and withstood the "soft" techniques, were severely painful. Some left permanent scars and other forms of physiological damage.

The worst of all were the ones that used electricity. One victim described the ensuing sensation as having one's body explode in a million needles of burning, never-ending pain. Interrogators frequently combined more than one method in a single session. Juan José Domínguez recalls being forced to lie naked on a board as buckets of freezing water were thrown at him – after which he was electrocuted. Jorge Torres was tied to a wooden plank, face up, and lowered to submerge his face in water as long as possible. Immediately after emerging, short of breath, he was electrocuted simultaneously in his testicles and in his eyes, nose, and mouth.

Other accounts speak of torture methods that remain insufficiently verified. MLN journalist Samuel Blixen says the wives or girlfriends of detained Tupamaros were brought before them and raped. The sexual abuse of female Tupamaras, although remarkably unspoken of in MLN accounts of the events, may well have happened. It is certain that Tupamaras were subjected to the same forms of torture as the men, most often naked: forced standing, freezing water, submarines, electroshocks, false executions, beatings, and more.

The relentlessness of the interrogations filled the questioners' notebooks with a torrent of anguished, often desperate bits of information. Everyone dealt with it in a different way: "I know of comrades who resisted torture thinking of Christ, and others who thought of Marx", recalls the Tupa Hugo Wilkins. Few held.

Only a few men directed this vast program combining intelligence and counter-terrorist operations. The overall commander was Esteban Cristi, who ran the Montevideo military region and thus controlled every base in the area. Most interrogations of captured Tupamaros, particularly the well-known ones, were taking place in the capital region, and thus in bases under his control.

Second, though more directly involved than Cristi, was Ramón Trabal. As the director of SID, he was specifically in charge of the military's intelligence collection. Interrogation was, along with the acquisition of captured documents, the most important method for gathering information. SID's interrogators reported to Trabal.

As the rest of April and May went by, dozens of Tupamaros fell in this dragnet. All of them were useful, but clearly some names were more important than others. The military's counter-terrorist machine began to hone its efforts in pursuing them: Sendic, Marenales, Rosencof, Engler, Amodio, Mujica, Martínez Platero and many others. It was only a matter of time until the pursuers caught up with them, as they did first with Mario Píriz. Formerly in the leadership but demoted in March to a lower rank, the young leader nicknamed "Tino" fell some time around May 10.[489]

The Day of the Soldier

Barely a month passed since Plan Hipólito and the parliamentary authorization for emergency military operations when the Tupamaros further provoked the Army. It was the group's first major operation since the bloody days of April. Instructions were to respond to the military's advances against the Tupamaros with a strong retaliatory attack. Therefore, a Column 15 fire team was tasked with attacking the home of the commander of the Army, General Florencio Gravina.[490]

The attack happened late on the night of May 18, with the general inside his home. As the team approached riding a Volkswagen Kombi, a sentry standing on the roof of the house spotted them. The MLN immediately moved to neutralize the main guard unit, which consisted of four soldiers sitting inside a jeep parked directly in front of the property.[491]

Using automatic weapons especially prepared by former soldier turned Tupamaro Carlos Liscano, the *guerrilleros* led by Esteban Pereira sprayed the vehicle multiple times and then fled. They killed all four soldiers inside, who did not have time to budge. The AR-15 bursts struck neighboring homes multiple times, and shattered the peace not just in that street, but in all military ranks.

This was the final straw for the Army, which now truly unleashed its strength against the Tupamaros. The attack happened on the national day of celebration of the soldier, one that passed unnoticed every year for the general population but that was significant to the rank and file. For years afterwards, on that date jailed MLN leaders were "reminded" of the crime they committed by being subjected to various torments. The "four soldiers" became a universally recognized incident for everyone in Uruguay: it was the MLN's most direct attack against the military.

Tupamaros with military experience, like Liscano and Carlos Koncke, knew the military would react like an enraged animal. A code had been broken. The Army had never murdered a Tupamaro; it was involved in the fight because it was ordered to do so by civilians. When attacking, it did so frontally and wearing a uniform. This had been a cowardly execution, one for which the MLN would pay dearly. As Koncke put it, "If the MLN killed a single soldier, the entire Army would fan out to kill anyone who had anything to do with it. And the MLN did not kill one soldier. It killed four! It was an absolutely mad operation". In Colonel Agosto's words, "It was the worst thing the Tupas could have done". Liscano recalls thinking the military would take out the MLN in only a year.

The MLN in Crisis

The military's first act of vengeance took place the following day, when a Tupamaro held in its custody died in a so-called accident. The message was unmistakable, and marked yet another step in the degradation of both sides' rules of engagement. Additionally, that same night of May 19 an event with enormous reverberations took place.[492]

An MLN cell that included José Mujica, Alicia Rey, Héctor Amodio and Rodolfo Wolf was meeting at a safe house belonging to Tupamara Gracia Dri in the neighborhood of Pocitos. Intelligence obtained through interrogation led a military patrol there; the squad insistently knocking on the door were members of the Naval Fusiliers, the Navy's recent contribution to the Uruguayan military's infantry forces.*

For the Tupamaros there was no chance of fighting back against such a well-trained unit. That meant the only way out was evacuation through the sewers. The safe house had a Plan Gardiol tunnel that connected to the underground, so the team fled through it, in the direction of the far-away neighborhood of La Comercial.

The military noticed all of this and started a pursuit above ground, fanning out across the area to check manholes for Tupas lurking below. The situation for the group underground was complicated, so a decision was made to split up. Amodio and Wolf would emerge to the street, steal a vehicle and find help from another MLN squad. The rest would continue on foot, through the sewers, trying to lose the pursuers.

The leader of this second team was Amodio's partner Alicia Rey, at the time in charge of Column 10. Rey was in a cast since suffering a motorcycle accident earlier that year. She was thus slower than the rest, particularly when it was necessary to crawl on all fours. Outside it was pouring rain, which made navigating the sewer network extremely complicated.

Amodio and Wolf emerged from a manhole right by Pocitos' *rambla*. The latter recalls: "When I emerged -barefoot, soaked, stinking, with a grenade in one hand and a pistol in the other- I could fully understand the exclamation of the person waiting for the bus at the nearby stop: 'Oooohhh no, no, no, no no!'"

Ignoring the panicking civilian, the duo hijacked a taxicab, which Amodio drove himself. They made it to a meeting of the MLN leadership and notified them of what happened to Rey, Mujica, and the others. Amodio, who characteristically cleaned his

---

* Henry Engler was supposed to arrive moments later.

sewage-contaminated gun with great care, had to face his worst fear: that his partner Alicia, codenamed Mercedes, might fall to her pursuers.

The *dirección* tasked Efraín Martínez and his sewer expertise to lead the rescue effort, so they returned to the tunnels to aid Rey and the others. While racing back with the relief team, Amodio had to halt. His leg muscles gave painful cramps, so Martínez sent the rest of the team ahead while he massaged and assisted Amodio. Deep in the underground, the latter despaired. He showed himself at his most vulnerable to Martínez, whom he knew from their days as Socialist delegates to the Coordinador. The situation was despairing, and Amodio said he was emotionally spent and unable to go on with the struggle. It was overwhelming.

In the meantime, the police had descended to pursue the Tupamaros. As they approached -the Tupas could tell from a distance if someone approaching was MLN or not by whether they complained about the smell- the fleeing group found itself increasingly out of options. Contact was made and shots exchanged; the Tupamara Dri was struck. Rey decided to make a judgment call. The contingent, now led by Mujica, would continue and escape. She stayed behind, alone.

The cops arrived and opened fire, but Rey yelled for them not to shoot. Identifying herself, she surrendered and was duly arrested. The rest of the team spent the night in the underground and barely escaped, also by emerging from distant manholes and hijacking cars. Mujica, leading them, thus spent his thirty-seventh birthday in the depths of Montevideo, gripping a pipe and hoping it would rain no more.

The security services had captured the most important of all Tupamaras, but the day was not yet over. In separate operations, Mauricio Rosencof –a member of the *ejecutivo* since 1970- also fell to the police. He was captured with another member of Column 70, a biochemist named Ricardo Ehrlich.[493*]

The following day, May 20, Héctor Amodio Pérez was devastated. There was a long list of setbacks in the past few months, but the events of the previous night had been the worst of all. In light of this, he held a major meeting with the MLN's top leadership. He learned then, from an emotive José Mujica, what Rey had done

---

* Ehrlich served as mayor of Montevideo decades later.

in the sewers to save Pepe and the others. This only deepened the feeling that he and Rey were giving the organization more than it was giving back to them. Privately, he later confessed, he was feeling "The detention of La Negra [Rey's nickname] severed what little was left to connect me to the MLN, particularly the leaders who drove us to the debacle".

A bitter discussion took place, with recriminations and insults flying back and forth between the leaders of the Tupamaros. The MLN's 1972 crisis added fuel to a pre-existing dispute (harking back to 1968 and even earlier) over strategy and leadership. Shouts and insults were exchanged and tempers flared like never before. Referring to Sendic by his codename, he said "incorporating comrade Rufo to the Executive Secretariat even before thoroughly discussing the issue [of the failing Plan Tatú] was a mistake". Amodio, calling his interlocutors "*hijos de puta*", added that he assigned responsibility for the disasters to leaders like Sendic, Fernández, and Marenales ("wishful thinkers lacking any kind of organizational capability"), rather than to the younger radicals others chose to blame.

Amodio's analysis not coincidentally placed his leadership style in the best light, but he was correct in criticizing the rural Plan Tatú as a voluntarist, possibly selfish deviation from the MLN's original mission. His words were harsh: "I opposed the Second Front and its tatuceras at every turn, especially when I knew that what little weapons the MLN had were being sent there almost in their entirety". Others agreed with him: Engler has said "To me Plan Tatú was a disaster. I was against Plan Tatú. Wasem was totally against it. Rosencof was against Plan Tatú. It was a very stubborn thing". The rural plan, which was failing spectacularly, was giving the military significant victories over the MLN, not least in the form of capturing guerrilleros, acquiring intelligence, and removing numerous weapons from the Tupamaros' arsenal.

Following the arguments, there was no conclusion or agreement, except that Amodio would leave the organization (some say he quit, others that he was expelled; Amodio himself claimed he was not dropped at all). It was allegedly Sendic, of all people, who told Amodio he was no longer a member of the MLN. None of them knew it, but it was the last time they saw each other.

Taken to a safe house to prepare his full disconnection from the MLN, Amodio insisted he wanted to organize a rescue for Alicia

Rey, who had twice participated in spectacular operations to free him from Punta Carretas. It also bothered Amodio that others had a problem with his positions. In his mind, he had already given more than enough to the organization, and proven his mettle as a clandestine Tupamaro and operational commander endless times.

Before the day was over, the MLN suffered one more in the bitter series of blows: Adolfo Wasem, an influential member of the leadership in recent years, was also captured. In a matter of hours Rey, Rosencof, and Wasem, plus the disengaged Amodio, were all out of action.

Just days later, on May 23, while staying in an MLN apartment with his minder Rodolfo Wolf, Amodio heard knocks on the door. Shaken, he opened it and saw a soldier staring him in the face. The founder of Column 15 posed no resistance, and simply asked how they had found him. The response was that the police received a tip. Apparently, this made him angrier than he already was. Amodio raised his hand with the palm open and said his would not be a confrontational arrest. He had some things to discuss with the officers.

The Hunt

Life in Montevideo beginning in mid-April of 1972 was pure chaos. There were prompt security measures, curfews, checkpoints, military patrols, house searches, identity checks, shootouts, and other forms of violence every single day. Being present during bank robberies had for years been a common occurrence. Now, most if not all Montevideans experienced life in a city with an urban guerrilla and a military force fighting to vanquish each other, everywhere.

The *guerrilleros* hijacked vehicles constantly -now adding buses to their targets- and took over homes, factories, and all sorts of places. The military and the police raided relentlessly, and searched thousands of people and their homes for suspected links to the MLN. As usual, there were no religious, ethnic, visual or otherwise evident traits for identifying the Tupas: anyone and everyone could belong to the organization.

Numbers can help illustrate how much the conflict had grown in size. In Hebert Gatto's estimation, there were then about fifty thousand members of the combined security forces (now officially using the name "Fuerzas Conjuntas" or Joint Forces) involved in the fight against subversion. The Tupamaros are often estimated to have peaked at about two thousand *guerrilleros*, with as many more in supporting positions at the 26 de Marzo and the CATs. That meant an approximate total of between three and five thousand.[494] In a small country like Uruguay it was easy to know someone, or see something, involved with the conflict.

Many soldiers were eager to come face to face with these famed but cowardly warriors and smash them to pieces. Rules of engagement imposed care. Soldiers were ordered to focus on captures and on collecting valuable information for intelligence analysis, and not simply shooting up houses or physically annihilating the enemy. Despite MLN protestations and inevitable deviations from this norm, evidence indicates the military followed said protocols.[495*]

Successes came unexpectedly and triumphantly. On April 15 the military announced it took out the MLN's main intelligence base, in Brito del Pino street. Later on SID announced it broke the encryption the Tupas used in written communications, which helped unlock additional information from captured documents.[496] Thanks to these coups the joint forces were able to dismantle looming MLN plots. Upon being publicized, many outraged the population – the more prominent being a plan to bomb the main power station in Montevideo.[497]

While these clashes continued in the capital, the rural Plan Tatú unraveled at an even faster pace. Reports on what happened there are sketchy, but the fate of Jorge Zabalza's campaign in Paysandú is illustrative of what happened.

Zabalza arrived on April 22. At the time there were two hundred *guerrilleros* in the area. They were too many: Paysandú's saturated MLN was easy to detect to the security services. To preserve the group, Zabalza disobeyed an order from Sendic to attack a military outpost, despite his "quasi-religious respect" for El Bebe's opinions.[498] Days later he and other Tupamaros like María Elia Topolansky got advance warning that a raid was coming.

Fleeing the town, the group launched the much-awaited period of true rural guerrilla. Now they could really play the roles of

---

* Not least in the fact that the overwhelming majority of the Tupamaros, including all of its leaders, survived arrest.

Fidel Castro, Che Guevara, and Vo Nguyen Giap. The hunt would take place in the roads, woods, and creek beds of northwestern Uruguay.

The first order of business was reaching a *tatucera*, but it proved too small for the group. Instead, they moved to the wooded shores of the main river in the area, the Queguay. Another group of Tupas, also fleeing a pursuing patrol, arrived around the same time, and thus the two merged.

It was June, deep in the southern hemisphere's winter. The squad of nineteen had few supplies to go by, and nothing in the way of heating or winter clothing. Fires could only be lit exceptionally: the group was under pursuit by military squads with lethal authority. Long walks by the shore were silent, accompanied only by the sound of the water and the bone-chilling winds that give the Uruguayan winter its bleak appearance.

During a rest stop, Tupamaro Carlos Varela sat down in a relieved rush and accidentally shot himself with his Winchester rifle. There was nothing the rest could do. He died there, isolated from the outside world, and was buried on the shores of the Queguay. Later that day it rained. Temperatures were freezing; many were falling ill, particularly because few were accustomed to living outside the city for prolonged periods of time.

New characters appeared and disappeared. One was a fourteen year-old nicknamed "Bonete", lost to the history books but apparently serving as some sort of voluntary MLN child soldier. Other times the marching Tupas came upon small groups of hunters, who held their stare until both groups continued their paths without saying a word.

Despite the unsustainable conditions, Zabalza insisted on holding out for the duration of the winter. There was no radio contact with the outer world, but his instincts rightly told him that elsewhere the MLN was getting wiped out. Survival depended on each team. The march continued; there were near-fatal river crossings, and times when the Tupas climbed trees to watch pursuing helicopters and jeeps searching for them.

Weeks passed, until the group reached a small ranch house from which it could "procure" supplies. The fields were muddy; it rained incessantly, and the men were tired and underfed after so much marching. As the eighteen-strong MLN squad approached the house, the ranch workers put their hands up and held still. The

Tupas got close and said they were only passing by, looking for supplies to move on. However, the foreman emerged with a gun and ordered the Tupamaros to leave.

The Tupa Aníbal De Lucía moved towards the strong-built man and tried to subdue him, but he resisted and struggled. After getting rid of De Lucía, he opened fire on the Tupas. Zabalza did the same thing, and shot both the man and his wife. The leader of the eighteen Tupas was also shot, and was soon on the ground bleeding from a punctured lung. After that, all there was to do was race towards the road to try and save his life. Zabalza woke up chained to a hospital bed in Paysandú, only a few meters from the bed where the man he shot also lay wounded. It was June 17, 1972. Days later he got a visit from Francisco Silveira, the deputy director of SID.[499]

Just as the Tupamaros themselves had concluded a decade earlier, the Uruguayan *campo* was unfeasible for a Marxist insurgent organization. Despite Uruguay's homogeneity, they failed the test of being sufficiently "of the people", and paid dearly for it. People had paid attention and knew what the MLN stood for. The Tupamaros' government program, published a year earlier, called for a massive Khmer Rouge-style campaign of forced displacement and re-settlement of the interior of Uruguay, both for social engineering and for Soviet-style industrialization campaigns. In other words, every single aspect of the MLN's rural guerrilla campaign was mistaken.

Urban Guerrilla Undone

Urban guerrilla was faring barely better.[500] Pursuers like D'Oliveira noticed the army captured Tupas roaming the streets, shelterless, seeking contacts at liaison points to which no one showed up. Upon being detained and questioned, some confessed they did not know what column they were supposed to be operating in, or who their commander was.

In such a depressing and confusing situation, many found arrest a godsend compared to living clandestinely, risking a shootout at any moment. In one case, the driver of the van used in the attack on the four soldiers drove himself to the La Paloma military base atop the Cerro, mattress in tow, to surrender.

The MLN's problems were not just in the streets. The political consensus after April 14 was almost completely in favor of terminating the Tupamaros. After that day, there was no question that they were a minority within a minority, for not even the Frente Amplio and left were fully supportive. Top figures like Líber Seregni and Rodney Arismendi distanced themselves from their shocking actions. Wilson Ferreira, the wild card of Uruguayan politics, openly denounced them and voted to declare the state of emergency.

This was a curious turn of events, for Wilson had thought, in the depths of the Pacheco years, that he would ride a wave of MLN fueled social discontent into a presidential position. In the aftermath of April 14 he *had* to condemn the MLN, but his personal hatred for Pacheco, Bordaberry, and the Colorados was greater. As early as April 17 the nationalist *caudillo* returned to his populist, morally relativist brand of politics: "violence is not just a shootout. Violence is also (...) hunger, penury. Violence is illiteracy (...) Violence is the inescapable fact that thousands of children in this country have never drank a glass of milk in their lives. Violence is malnourishment, unsanitary conditions, and the delinquency to which thousands upon thousands of Uruguayans are pushed every day". Wilson was for years secretly engaged in illegal contacts with the MLN. In 1972 he received clandestine leaders like Marenales in his own home, to discuss potential alliances and focus on bringing down their common enemy, the Colorado government.

Bordaberry's government started in a weak position on March 1, but the MLN strategically shot itself in the foot on April 14 and laid the groundwork for its own defeat. Now the president had more popular support than he had generated in the ballot box. Wilson knew that any strengthening of the president and his party only distanced him further from his ambition of remaining the central figure of national politics. He was running out of options: the middle ground was on the way to extinction, and between the government and the Tupamaros he had little choice but the former.

Witnessing all of this, the Communists made the decision to permanently disengage from the MLN. The Tupas had proven too disorderly, too haphazard for the studious Marxist-Leninist strategists of the PCU. Accused in the Parliament of connivance with the Tupamaros, Arismendi darkly replied "If we thought [guerrilla] action was useful, we would have engaged in it already". In other words, the Communist refusal to employ violence was neither moralistic nor republican. It was simply a matter of strategy.

One thing that united all members of the political opposition, as well as disparate actors like the Catholic Church and the medical doctors' association, was the issue of torture. Public condemnations of such practices emerged insistently in 1972, and they quickly got on the nerves of the officers in command.

In fact, many of the latter began to wonder what exactly was the purpose of such complaints, when after all everyone had agreed the military was necessary for smashing the MLN. Might it be complicity with the Tupamaros? The officer corps, the mess halls, and the military academies all started to discuss these criticisms with skepticism and disgust.

A strong response to the criticism arrived shortly after. Backed by the April authorization to operate widely to suppress the MLN, the military published decrees regulating the speech of legislators and of anyone else who criticized "the decisions of public authorities concerning anti-subversive action". The association was clear: complications, including criticism, of the military's campaign against subversion were equivalent to subversion itself, and could potentially be dealt with in similar terms.

Few realized this at the time, but beginning in April of 1972 the decision-making center for the fate of Uruguay as a country migrated to military bases. It was also there that high-ranking officers had at their disposal the results of the interrogations of the Tupamaros. Perhaps the greatest of all coups the joint forces could extract from the weakened MLN was one that had never been tracked before: the People's Prison.

Critical Damage

The MLN had more than one Cárcel del Pueblo.[501] In mid-1972 all were empty except one, housing civilian hostages Ulysses Pereira Reverbel and Carlos Frick. As before, the issue was whether the government had in its hands the right Tupamaro or Tupamara, meaning one who actually knew the location of the facility. This time it did have such individuals.

While undergoing interrogation, former MLN leader Adolfo Wasem learned from his captors that they were close to finding the house where the hostages were held. SID knew the general area where it was, and was in the process of refining telephone intercepts to pinpoint the address. Wasem became convinced that it was only a matter of time before the house was identified.

Meanwhile, in a separate base, Amodio and Rodolfo Wolf were also undergoing interrogation. While neither Wasem nor Amodio knew the location of the prison, Wolf did. He held, after all, the typically grandiloquent title of MLN General Prisons Inspector. Wasem was brought to the base where Amodio and Wolf were held, and presented his arguments to the two men. If they volunteered the location of the prison, the military would agree to a managed surrender instead of a shootout that might kill the Tupas inside, the hostages, and possibly the family occupying the house as cover.

Amodio and Wolf listened to Wasem's arguments and agreed: it was true that there could easily be a bloodbath if the military arrived on its own. It was not an easy conclusion to reach. The facility was the MLN's ultimate secret. Unlike its leaders, the Cárcel del Pueblo had *never* been captured. Its location had never been revealed in any interrogation, and it had been searched for with a degree of celerity not seen anywhere else in Uruguay.

With high-ranking diplomats and businessmen subjected to the MLN's will, the prison was an embarrassment for the government, and at the same time a great source of pride for the Tupamaros. It had also evolved since the first one in 1968. According to a secret report by an MLN prison overseer, by 1972 the facilities were supposed to have improved infrastructure in the form of medical services, clinical analyses, psychological support services, recreational resources and the possibility for prisoners to work on their "defense" for trials.

The fateful day was May 27, 1972. Under Wolf's guidance, the military set out well into the evening for what turned out to be a simple, inconspicuous house, surrounded by equally unremarkable homes, in a neighborhood smack in the middle of Montevideo's busiest areas. Outside the house, at almost all times during the day, four young girls played on the sidewalk. They were the daughters of the couple who lived there, one of hundreds of thousands of Montevidean middle-class families.

The military knew it was about to deal a devastating blow to the MLN: therefore, the commander of Military Region I, Esteban Cristi, was there in person to lead the operation. Also at the scene were Wasem and Amodio, brought especially per Cristi's orders. It was they who had to negotiate the surrender of the Tupas inside, who in turn had instructions to murder the hostages if the prison fell.

The military convoy arrived without fanfare so as to avoid alerting the occupants of the house. Unlike many MLN *berretines*, this People's Prison did not yet have an exit tunnel towards the sewer network, which meant the only way out for all its inhabitants was through the front door, dead or alive.

With military-grade floodlights illuminating the house, the officers' orders were for Wasem and Amodio to approach, knock on the door, and negotiate the surrender of the prison. Wasem had recently been a member of the *dirección*, and Amodio was one of the five historical leaders of the Tupamaros. They were extremely important individuals with, hopefully, sufficient authority to impose themselves on the people inside. While many Tupamaros claimed it was Wasem who approached the house, Amodio has claimed Wasem broke into uncontrollable sobbing and a fit similar to an epileptic attack. This meant it was Amodio who had to walk up to the door and demand the surrender. If anything went wrong, Cristi's orders were for the MLN leader to be gunned down along with the resisting guards.

The owners of the house were named David Porras and Zulema Arena. The secret compartment in their home housed the hostages Pereira and Frick, as well as four MLN guards: Margarita Dupont, Adriana Castera, Óscar Bernatti and Eduardo Cavia; Bernatti was a criminal who had escaped with the Tupas during El Abuso and had joined the organization.

The hostages were able to hear as the scene unfolded: knocks on the door, muffled conversations in the distance (Amodio claims he started a "monologue" to the windows of the house, not knowing if he was being heard), the realization by the guards of what was happening, and then the raised voices and shuffling here and there. During the negotiations, Dupont told Amodio/Wasem to go to hell. Her preference was for murdering the hostages rather than giving them up; Castera felt the same way. Only after long and tense negotiations did the guards agree to surrender.

Ulysses Pereira Reverbel, in his second MLN kidnapping, had been held hostage for over a year. The news of his liberation exploded in the front pages of all newspapers and in the airwaves. It was clear to all involved: the Tupamaros had been dealt a terrible blow. They lost a key component of their "mirrored power" doctrine, as well as important bargaining cards in their struggle with the government.

It was the first and only time that MLN hostages were rescued. In every other occasion, it was the "orga" that decided their fate: liberation, ransom, or murder. In cases like those of Gaetano Pellegrini, Aloysio Dias Gomide, Ricardo Ferrés[502] and Jorge Berenbau, the Tupamaros benefited greatly in financial terms. This time, they got nothing. Operationally they were breached to their deepest core: if the People's Prison was no longer safe, nothing was.

The press was thrilled with the downfall of the Cárcel del Pueblo: the Tupamaros were now in full retreat. Granted access to the narrow spaces of the *berretín*, a journalist for the newspaper El País wrote: "any person descending there begins to feel a sensation of enclosure that is demolishing and hard to bear. Breathing becomes difficult, and the air is invariably foul with impurities and various stenches. The guards lived in the first room. They had a small kitchen, a rudimentary bathroom, and a bookshelf. The cells were in the back, with two tiny bunks and a precarious sanitary system. To the right of the guards' living quarters there is a large number of piled-up dirt bags: they were digging an escape tunnel towards the sewer network, and it was only meters from completion. There was also a lighting system connected to the one in the house above". Color video images of the "prison" survive to this day.

The Path of Commander Gustavo

Amodio's name made it to the newspapers as a defector, which meant his situation changed dramatically. Returned to military barracks, he learned from sporadic contacts with Wasem and others that the MLN leadership decided to pin the blame for the entire incident exclusively on him. It is then that he made one of the most consequential decisions made by a member of the leadership since the foundation of the organization.

It happened when his captors appeared in his cell and showed him something extraordinary. Previously captured MLN leader Mario Píriz, a much younger and inexperienced man, had spent the better part of a month spilling his guts to them. Personally interrogated by SID chief Ramón Trabal, Píriz gave away "the complete organizational chart of the MLN; he had given away the safe houses and militants he knew, made reports about the personalities of the most prominent Tupamaros, and reported on contacts with politicians, both Uruguayan and foreign. He also wrote a list of the names and/or pseudonyms and divisions of those responsible for the most relevant operations: Morán Charquero, Mitrione, and the more recent Plan Hipólito".[503]

It was a boatload of information.* Some had already been used in smashing Plan Tatú. Píriz, despite his young age, had perforated the principle of compartmentalization and had inside knowledge of all the most important columns.† However, the military was proving incapable of decoding many of the pseudonyms and passwords contained in "Tino"'s confessions.[504]

The officers presented the founder of Column 15 with a proposal: if he sat down with the Píriz papers and "made sense" of them, essentially working as a temporary counter-intelligence analyst, he would continue to be treated well. All he had to do was turn raw information into a useful written product. Despite his privileged position in *la orga*, Amodio felt that given the MLN's compartmentalization and his lack of experience with rural operations he would be of limited use. Nevertheless, he recognized an opportunity when he saw one.

"Gustavo" consulted with his partner Rey -also held captive there-, and both decided on a counter-offer. Amodio would indeed give the army what it wanted, but in exchange he and Rey had to be given safe passage out of the country, forever. They had to be given new, false identities, and a way past Uruguay's borders. It was all or nothing: Amodio and Rey would escape the collapsing edifice of Uruguay and the MLN, or they would surely perish in it now that they had enemies on all sides.

The Wheels Come Off

The situation was reaching rock bottom for the MLN. An analysis of the months of June and July 1972 provides clear evidence

---

* Amodio also saw transcripts of the interrogations of fellow leaders like Fernández Huidobro and Rosencof.

† Píriz emerged from Column 15, was temporarily put in charge of Column 70, and had operated as supervisor of Column 7 and Plan Tatú. He had also served in the leadership for many months.

of how bad things turned for it. Army raids proliferated and had incredible yields: twenty, thirty-four, forty Tupamaros captured at a time, multiple times.

Detainees were harshly interrogated if not tortured, which in turn netted more MLN safe houses – all at a time when the organization had lost its kidnapped bargaining chips and was more exposed than ever. In June alone the Tupas lost 492 members to arrests, five who were killed in combat, and also two dozen safe houses. The organization persisted, though: in that single month they killed four hostiles, attacked government vehicles at least twenty times, and assaulted homes, political clubs, or other buildings over sixty times.[505] On June 21, MLN founder Jorge Manera fell in a police arrest, and joined the growing number of "viejos" in military custody.[506]

The police and the military were surprised by how unimpressive many of the captured Tupamaros were. There clearly was a curve of decreasing returns: the newer, younger, and fresher the captured *guerrilleros* were, the less formidable they proved to be. Crucially, they posed far less resistance to interrogation or torture than the "old" ones like Manera. In the words of high-ranking officer Daniel García, "the first Tupamaros had iron backbones. Later, when they recruited more men, the ones who came in were made of tin. The last ones were made of butter".[507]

The many downfalls exposed, in an almost archaeological fashion, just how sophisticated the MLN was as an insurgent organization. One captured safe house had an underground space with "a complete medical installation: X-ray equipment, instruments to conduct cardiothoracic, abdominal, and trauma surgery; three beds for patient recovery; and alarm systems".

It was not the only one. The facility was part of the MLN's medical service, whose head was Elbia Toledo, the chief nurse at one of the country's top medical facilities. Thanks to this *servicio sanitario* the Tupamaros had some of the best health care in Uruguay. According to Henry Engler, the MLN's doctors told guerrilla cells preparing for an operation "try not to get shot in the head, because then we'll have trouble. If it's in the rest of the body we can fix it".[508]

According to top policeman Víctor Castiglioni, the best facility of the MLN health service was the "Hospital de Pueblo", or People's Hospital. It had six emergency surgery units, each led by one of Uruguay's most distinguished surgeons. Only the surgeons and their nurses knew its location. When a Tupamaro was injured in combat, his squad had to telephone a certain number and bring the patient to a pre-arranged site. From there, a disguised MLN ambulance driven by the only non-doctor who knew the location would take the patient to surgery. In other words, the MLN's hospital was completely compartmentalized.[509]

With the People's Hospital fell an avalanche of Tupas. The fate of the MLN did not differentiate men from women: the Tupamaras met the same one as their male counterparts. On July 8 Cristina Cabrera fled through the back door as a military patrol burst into the house where she and other Tupas were hiding. The shootout was violent: two soldiers and an officer were wounded, while a Tupamaro was killed. Cabrera was shot twice from behind. She lay bleeding in the backyard for hours, after barely managing to swallow a piece of paper with MLN intelligence, discarding her small handgun, and grabbing on to a picture of her family. The military evacuated her in an ambulance; Cabrera underwent several surgeries to repair her liver, a lung, and the rest of her badly damaged torso.[510]

One Tupamara who fell during this period was the famous Yessie Macchi. The former front-page star and hardline guerrilla fighter was hiding, three months pregnant, with her partner Leonel Martínez Platero, brother of Efraín. They were staying at an MLN safe house in the beachside town of Parque del Plata, not far from Montevideo. It was June 13 of 1972.

Once again, the *caída* followed a pattern: someone had given away the location of the house, and now the police were knocking on the door. Martínez Platero chose to resist and engaged in a shootout with the pursuers, while telling Macchi to escape. She fled through the back to neighboring areas, knocking on as many doors as possible in search of shelter. Unable to do so, the police tracked her down in the streets and opened fire. Leonel Martínez Platero's encounter with the police ended in defeat and death. Macchi struck many policemen with her pistol fire until she emptied three magazines. She then threw her gun at the soldiers, shouted abuse at them, and fought back as they trapped her. She had been shot once in the leg. To subdue her, the arresting officers beat her up, and as a result she suffered a miscarriage.

The convalescent Macchi became an attraction for interrogators like José Gavazzo, for high-ranking officers like Trabal, Álvarez, and Cristi, for psychiatrists, and many others. She was tortured for information, although she felt uncomfortable about detailing what she endured. In her strange interactions with her tormentors, she witnessed their admiration for her resistance efforts and for not "singing".[511]

The MLN was reaching its end having failed its women: none of the Tupamaras was ever given a position in the *dirección*. Worst of all, some of the most committed female members had to tolerate misogynist skepticism at the very core of the organization: "Julio Marenales said he would not be going around saving women (...) Raúl Sendic said women were the repose of the warrior".[512]

Out With a Bang

There was no respite for the Tupamaros. Another blow struck where it hurt the most: in public perceptions. As it turned out, the defector Píriz had not only given SID information on the organizational aspects of the MLN. He also revealed the Pascasio Báez incident.

With that information in hand, the military sent a detachment to the Spartacus *estancia*, and on June 19 duly dug up the body of the murdered ranch hand. The news broke out immediately, and there was no way to spin it. In previous murder cases, the Tupas had managed to get away with certain explanations: Dan Mitrione was an imperialist torturer; policemen or soldiers shot in the back were "repressors".

The death of Báez, however, could never be explained even by the MLN's talented propagandists. The organization of the Robin Hoods and witty romantic *guerrilleros* had mutated into one that bound, tormented, and later cruelly "disappeared" an innocent man. Any remaining sympathies the MLN had in society were completely demolished. The Tupamaros were not dying honorably, but rather by betraying the best of their ideals before doing so. They were not yet done.

Incidents in this final period were some of the most violent of all. During one in Montevideo, Antonio Mas Mas, the same man who executed Dan Mitrione, murdered a civilian bus driver during a hijacking-shootout with the police. Another bus driver died in a similar incident days later. A failed kidnapping of civilian medical doctor Julio Marató ended in his cold-blooded murder, inside his own home. Shocked bystanders witnessed an MLN hit squad walk into the store of retired policeman Luis Barbizón and gun him down without saying a word. Private homes of the so-called "oligarchy" were bombed, at a rate of up to ten in a single day. Tupamaros were killed resisting arrest and trying to escape pursuing patrols. Multiple guerrilla attacks on these patrols took place around Montevideo every single day.[513]

Between April 15 and November 15, a full 2,873 Tupamaros were captured, as were hundreds of weapons. A total of 62 Tupamaros were killed, and approximately 844 escaped to foreign countries before the insurgency was liquidated. Before they knew it, the joint forces had victory in their grasp.[514]

The military was bent on making its victory decisive by taking out the remaining leaders of the MLN. With Eleuterio Fernández Huidobro, Jorge Manera, Héctor Amodio, Mauricio Rosencof, Alberto Candán, Mario Píriz, and others already out of the picture, there were not many left. One of them, Henry Engler -who had never been captured before-, remembers it as "a truly rough period. Sleeping wherever it was possible, with one eye open, in the tall grasses, inside a movie theater. Every day was spent on the verge of a firefight. Shootouts and dead or captured comrades were a daily thing. There was but a single political idea: to take as many people as possible out of the country, and then stay and die fighting". Jumping through roofs, fighting dogs off and evading Naval Fusiliers, Engler at one point fell into a deep, exhausted sleep while sitting on the toilet.[515]

Raúl Sendic remained the most wanted man in Uruguay. He roamed the streets disguised as an old pensioner, switching safe houses every day, and providing much-needed leadership to the ranks.[516]

One of the last "viejos" or "históricos" at liberty was Julio Marenales, the fourth member of the *ejecutivo*. The hardened sculptor decided with Sendic and Engler to stay in Montevideo and fight until the end. Just as before, he was the most realistic of the leaders: he knew the group had "an arsenal that was ridiculously inadequate for starting a war against the Army".[517]

Marenales knew the MLN had ample resources to spirit him, Sendic, and everyone else in the leadership out of the country, to continue the war in exile. Chile and Argentina were filled with friendly terrorist organizations, which in fact had been inspired in no small part by the Tupamaros themselves. Surrender, however, was never an option for him: "if the organization surrenders I will kill myself. You may surrender my body, but I will never give up".

Julio Marenales's final moment as an insurgent happened on July 27, when he came across a military patrol in Montevideo. Riding onboard the jeep was none other than Héctor Amodio Pérez, sporting an Army uniform.* The two men recognized each other instantly, with everything that it meant. Marenales primed himself for combat, ready to fulfill his vow: "I grabbed my Walther P-38 and threw a grenade we had previously expropriated from the Navy. It didn't explode (...) They shot at me without any concern or consideration for nearby civilians. A burst hit me in the leg and in my shoulder area. Incredibly, one of the bullets struck my gun and destroyed it". Marenales survived, and was typically stoic about what happened.[518]

These incidents became matters of considerable, explosive anger within the MLN. The story became that the Tupamaros were being defeated because they were grievously betrayed from the inside, especially by Amodio. The word spread among the ranks, and turned for most Tupas into the single explanatory factor of the defeat. In reality, others like Colonel D'Oliveira have said the acts of the "traitors" Amodio and Píriz were not decisive in the downfall of the MLN. Top SID interrogator Gavazzo agrees, saying Amodio was most helpful in tactical rather than strategic counterinsurgency operations. Some Tupas have acknowledged that Amodio was selective in his betrayals: there were individuals and safe houses which he could have given away, but that the security services never attacked.[519] Nevertheless, at the time what mattered was that he was going into the streets with the military (by his own admission), quite possibly hunting Tupamaros (which he denied).

By the middle point of 1972, the only free members of the MLN leadership were Engler, Sendic, and Marenales' replacement, Martínez Platero. José Mujica was also free, now in an enhanced position of responsibility as the Montevideo General Commander. The MLN worried: Amodio was out patrolling with the military,

---

* The two sides strongly disagree on the meaning of this incident. While Marenales claimed Amodio was accompanying his new friends in the Army in the hunt for clandestine Tupas, Amodio claims he was forced to wear the uniform while being transported to see his ailing mother. Both accounts agree the encounter was pure chance.

hunting Tupamaros – and he was capable of recognizing Sendic, the number one target left.

Unfortunately for French revolutionary theoretician Régis Debray, 1972 was the year when he supplied a preface to the MLN's official history of its most legendary operations, entitled "Los Tupamaros en Acción". In it the French writer sought to "greet the fistful of founders of what later became the Tupamaros, a military organization that today is literally indestructible and a decisive political actor".[520]

Debray could not know how different things were on the ground. The military described events as follows: "hundreds upon hundreds of the seditious are captured (...) the entire infrastructure built by the organization (bases, hospitals, workshops, laboratories, arsenals, craftworks for fake documents, weapons, propaganda, shelters, subterranean excavations, 'tatuceras' and 'people's prisons') is destroyed". At the same time the MLN internally recognized "We are receiving one of the hardest blows in our entire history, if not the hardest (...) the succession of captures, strikes against us, and casualties is becoming, considering its quantity, an enormous political blow".[521]

The fate of the revolutionary Tupamaros was sealed: they were about to become extinct. However, before meeting their end they experienced one more twist to their story.

Chapter Thirteen:

The Napoleonic Twist

WHEN THE TUPAMAROS emerged, they did not do so in a vacuum. Rather, the group was a new actor -clearly the most attention-catching one- in the political game to determine who governed Uruguay. The MLN engaged in contacts and alliances with some of the country's major political actors, often flirting with the idea of benefiting each other in the pursuit of power.

This was the case with politicians like Enrique Erro, Héctor Gutiérrez, and Wilson Ferreira of the Partido Nacional, and Zelmar Michelini and Líber Seregni of the Frente Amplio. Seregni was his party's presidential candidate; Michelini and Gutiérrez were elected legislators who not only met with the MLN, but also helped it spirit some of the stolen Mailhos gold out of the country. Gutiérrez even collaborated with the Tupamaros in a fake kidnapping of himself to make contacts simpler.

Late 1971 introduced a new actor to this game: the military. Naturally, there were no politicians in active duty in the armed forces, but ever since Pacheco summoned them following El Abuso they increasingly developed a political identity. The military's alerts to the population; the speeches of its generals; the published texts of its objectives and diagnoses of society; all exceeded the realm of military planning and elbowed their way into politics. In other words, now the military had an opinion.

The most important political aspect of the military was a pillar of its counterinsurgency doctrine: that the Tupamaros and their armed *sedition* was simply the tip of the iceberg of the far larger, submerged portion of political and social *subversion*. The military was going to tackle both, and stated so openly. On June 19 1972, a national holiday celebrating the birth of Uruguayan founding father José Artigas, the main military speaker said "The struggle is not yet over and it will not be over until we not only remove the cancer, but also deploy the same energies towards the patriotic task of removing the causes of violence (...) The efforts of economic oppressors or of false ideologies shall fail".[522]

The figure of the talented military officer who becomes popular during a period of crisis, and thus enters politics as the rescuer of the nation, is timeworn. Populism -the politics of theatrical symbiosis between the leader and the "people"-, after all, had existed since ancient Rome. Its champion was the father of all savior-generals in history: Gaius Julius Caesar. Ever since, triumphant generals becoming their nation's emergency rulers appeared everywhere, including figures as disparate as Napoléon Bonaparte and Gamal Abdel Nasser.*

In the 1970s, complaints about the shortcomings of the republican-democratic political system in the Americas were already old. Generals like Mexico's Porfirio Díaz or Argentina's Juan Perón long served as models of the Latin American *caudillo* dictator, complete with balcony salutes and crowds chanting the name of the general, only to years later suffer from the consequences of those bad choices – and decades later, repeat the mistake.

It was thus not new at all for military officers to see themselves as having a mission to "save" the nation. As explored in the first chapter, Uruguay was not a typical Latin American country, and thus this tradition was weaker there than in any country in the Americas south of the United States. Nevertheless, the seed was there.

In early 1972 Uruguay's army burst into the scene flying the standard of order and stabilization. The reaction of the political establishment to this novelty was similar to what happened with the rise of the Tupamaros. Some ruled out any possibility of the generals

---

* Further military "saviors" include Porfirio Díaz, Lázaro Cárdenas, Fulgencio Batista, Rafael Trujillo, Hugo Chávez, Juan Perón and Augusto Pinochet -and that is only in the Americas. Outside of them, examples continue to abound: Charles de Gaulle, Francisco Franco, Mustafa Kemal, Muammar Gaddafi, Idi Amin, Pervez Musharraf, and countless others.

having a place in the political system; others embraced them, and others waited to see how things evolved.

Combining all of the above, in 1972 a game of attraction and co-optation developed. On one hand, there were contacts to weave an alliance between certain politicians -named above- and the Tupamaros. On the other, there were politicians trying to link up with the rising military leadership, in every major party.

There was a third possibility. What if the Tupamaros found allies in the military? Surely it sounded too strange to be true - and yet, it happened.

The Florida Talks

The story is known as the Batallón Florida plot, because it was at the Florida Battallion's headquarters in Montevideo that it took place.*

In mid-1972, some of the most important Tupamaros were being held there. First and foremost was Eleuterio Fernández, who fell on April 14. By June-July others joined him, including Marenales, Manera, Amodio, Rey, Wasem, Zabalza, and many more. After interrogation, each was kept in custody and thus in interaction with his jailers.

The Florida base was the premier center of activity for the military's efforts against the MLN. The officer in charge was Colonel Carlos Legnani. He could count on a key supporter nearby: his brother, Minister of National Defense Augusto Legnani. The minister was living there out of precaution over potential MLN assassination attempts. Another frequent presence was intelligence master Ramón Trabal.[523]

During the interrogations of Tupamaros, some army officers engaged in discussions with the prisoners over the purpose of the MLN. Topics included national liberation, socio-economic equality, and concern for the fate of the poor. At the time, the Tupamaros had bottomed out in public opinion at a respectable 20% - slightly above the votes the Frente Amplio got in September.[524]

Some young officers at the Florida base were interested if not intrigued by this new but apparently reasonable set of ideas. What exactly was so problematic about bettering the lot of society? Some

---

* Florida is a small *departamento*, an administrative subdivision of Uruguay.

guerrilleros managed to convince the officers of the merits of their cause, and of how capitalist society was bankrupt.

It was a typically Uruguayan thing: in such a homogenous and small country, it is common for bitter rivals to be lenient on each other, and to casually converse about any given topic. The Florida base was not the exception. In the words of the MLN's Miraldi, the Army officers "began to realize we did not have horns and tails".[525]

The main instigator of these conversations was Mauricio Rosencof, one of the MLN's best orators and writers. At one point, Rosencof managed to talk to generals Esteban Cristi and Gregorio Álvarez, the top overseers of the military's campaign. An agreement was reached for the generals to have a more formal discussion with the Tupamaros and consider what they had to say.

The first negotiation took place on the early hours of June 26. On that occasion, Eleuterio Fernández, the engineer Jorge Manera, and Rosencof spoke with their counterparts in the military. Each brought something different to the table: Manera focused on stopping the military's employment of torture against Tupamaros. Rosencof and Fernández glimpsed something broader: an unprecedented opportunity to flip the entire defeat around.[526] After all, Álvarez and Trabal in particular seemed personally and ideologically receptive to much of the Tupamaros' language.

For the MLN this was the final opportunity to impose its ideological program on the country through the most powerful vector possible, one they could not even dream of in the early days of the Coordinador and armed propaganda.

The Punishers

What was now a peace negotiation between the military and the MLN proceeded on one track. Another track of interaction between the two sides was created for a separate purpose: working together to effect changes in Uruguay. In this latter case, the Tupamaros and young officers led by Trabal formed joint task forces to pursue corrupt businessmen. At last, the filthy capitalists would pay.[527]

The Tupamaros and those who thought like them (from the publishers of Marcha and the leadership of the PCU to some in the military) had been speaking of "corruption" in Uruguay for over a decade. Judging by their words, Uruguay was in the grip of a veritable kleptocracy, comparable only to the most decrepit banana republics, mafia-held provinces or Asian satrapies in the world. Businessmen and politicians were said to be running wild, looting here and there, making off with the country's resources, spiriting the money overseas, and spending it in mansions and luxurious vehicles. This picture of Uruguay portrayed masses of wretched, hungry proletarians sadly looking on as magnates wearing top hats sped by in their fancy automobiles, guarded by sadistic policemen and CIA bodyguards.

Once joint MLN-military cells initiated operations against "illicit economic activities", concrete examples of rampant corruption were needed to actually conduct arrests and raids. There were plenty of dossiers: the Tupamaros and their informers had the names of numerous people and firms to pursue. Some were smugglers, illegally importing products (usually liquor) from Brazil or Argentina for sale in Uruguay. Others sold wool at differential prices, in a form of illegal arbitrage. One case involved the contents of hot dogs that foreign-owned (but Uruguayan-ran) meatpackers and slaughterhouses were selling in the market.

It remained unsaid among the hunters, both in the MLN and in the military, but the emerging trend was of a vague constellation of petty and simplistic scams. There was even a name for that already, typical in the River Plate region: *ventajismo*. Put simply, it consists of the exploitation of small "advantages", loopholes, absences of state supervision, or inadvertent legal vacuums, which allow someone to break the law and make off with some extra pesos, possibly a few thousand dollars - rarely more.

Interrogations of civilians under this program began on August 18 1972. With drums full of filthy water nearby, accountants, managers, and other businessmen were tied to chairs and jointly interrogated by hardened military officers and Tupamaros on issues like accounting gimmicks, the ownership of "ghost" firms, transfers of money within companies, exchange rates, checks, and more. Some of these men -it is unknown if women were targeted- were subjected to the dreaded "submarine".

The old dream of directly attacking Uruguay's "oligarchic" bourgeoisie, expressed all the way from the Coordinador to Plan Cacao, was finally becoming true. The joint military-MLN cells experienced surreal scenes. Tupamaros accompanied military patrols, in full uniform, joining in on arrests and carrying rifles. One of the Tupas' main operators for the economic crimes program, Ettore Pierri, recalls being delighted in imparting Marxism to a poorly educated military audience.

There were two economic crimes task forces operating in Montevideo in mid-1972. The first one was at the Florida base, and the second at another called La Paloma, atop Montevideo's iconic Cerro.

What happened in La Paloma was at least as strange, or more so, than the activities at the Florida base. One day during that winter a Tupamaro who had risen in the ranks, David Cámpora, walked in and announced to his imprisoned partners in arms that as of that day, there would be "collaboration" between the military and the MLN. The new mission was to "collaborate in the investigation of economic crimes, based on documents the Army had captured and that we would process".

Suddenly, there were no more abuses. The detained *guerrilleros* got better treatment; the hoods and blindfolds were gone. They could read, write, and later, do the accounting for their jailers. Analytical task forces were set up, all within the base, by economic activity: on beef exports, on the construction of a port in eastern Uruguay, on potential petroleum infrastructure, and more. At one point Henry Engler, one of the most wanted men in the country, freely visited to supervise efforts. Trabal, chief of SID and a main proponent of the "economic crimes" campaign, also stopped by to coordinate.

On July 12, a captured MLN collaborator named Fernando Secco was brought in, shivering and shaking in fear. He was none other than the owner of the country's most important beef-exporting concern, Frigorífico Tacuarembó. His crime had been lending his private airplane to the Tupamaros; Sendic and Wasem used it earlier in the year for various purposes, including international travel. The new prisoner arrived just in time for the twist in MLN-Army relations.

Odd things began to happen. Secco flipped from tormented prisoner to happy camper. He ordered his firm to deliver delicious *milanesas* and all kinds of meals, in great quantities, for all –soldier and Tupamaro- who were quartered in La Paloma. Everyone shared in the bribes and, soon enough, in the loot from the campaign against corrupt businessmen. One day, a black Mercedes Benz town car arrived in the base, and stayed there. It had been "expropriated" from someone who ended up in an economic crimes list, and now its comfortable leather seats belonged to the justice-givers of La Paloma.

Task force member Carlos Koncke, a Tupamaro, was allowed to sleep in his own home, wear an Army uniform, teach Marxism to junior soldiers, and hatch plans for a spectacular looting of every safety deposit box in Montevideo's financial district. Furthermore, he "participated in multiple operations designed to capture the accounting documents of several companies. With no judicial warrant (...) we would burst into those places in typical military fashion: violently, stomping about, and subduing everybody. I did that at two or three places".

Someone who could easily imagine himself in the targets of the economic crimes task forces was old MLN acquaintance Ulysses Pereira Reverbel. As the only man the Tupamaros kidnapped twice, Pereira knew they might try to hit him again. This led to a bitter winter night. On August 2, Pereira arrived with armed bodyguards to a dinner party at a friend's house, only to find the hosts and guests tied up in captivity under three armed intruders. There was a shootout and the criminals were subdued (one was killed). It turned out they were common thieves rather than Tupamaros: it was not a third kidnapping attempt.[528] Pereira was finally lucky, but many others were not.

The unspeakable crimes committed by the "crooks" taken to La Paloma were just as underwhelming as those pursued by the Florida task force. One of these monstrous offenders was apparently guilty of taking bribes for speeding up applications at the Banco de Previsión Social, Uruguay's equivalent of the U.S. Social Security Administration – hardly a capitalist institution. Others had undeclared assets inside the country, much like the Mailhos family of the 1970 MLN heist.

Unmentioned, and by extension unanalyzed, was that typically people broke these laws in order to avoid the relentless persecution of Uruguay's overburdened socialist state. Everyone tried to avoid taxes; those who had more power and resources simply did it on a larger, wealthier scale.

The fact that the MLN was complaining about violations of the law when its entire revolution was predicated on the illegitimacy of said laws was also conveniently unmentioned. Another missing observation was that the cases of corruption being uncovered did not reflect the nightmarish vision of Uruguay the Tupamaros had. In fact, it could be argued that at the time the republic's institutions were still working. In early June, during Parliamentary hearings, an alleged former member of the parapolice murder squad testified as part of an investigation into the murders of 1971-2. Alleged government tolerance of these activities had been the MLN's pretext for Plan Hipólito, from which all subsequent defeats for the group had flowed.

The greatest deviations of the "economic crimes" task force took place here, as revealed exclusively in a book by Uruguayan journalist Leonardo Haberkorn. Three Jewish men, the Wegbrait brothers and their accountant León Buka, were brutally tortured. The latter allegedly ended up making *aliya* to Israel and never returned to Uruguay.* Everything in the arsenal was deployed against them: some Tupas acted as prisoners undergoing torture in order to intimidate these latest arrivals into "confessing".

That was not all: the Tupamaros themselves tortured people to further their goals. Indeed, as the MLN's Koncke has admitted, he personally saw a fellow Tupamaro join an interrogation and later boast about it: "'I dunked his head in the drum, yes I did!'" Others confirmed this to Haberkorn, directly stating "MLN people tortured Buka". No Tupamaro has ever paid for this, despite it having been verified independently by multiple sources.[529]

The end of the La Paloma carnival came with the arrival of SID's José Gavazzo, with instructions to restore order. Gavazzo relieved Luis Agosto of his command and purged the entire regiment; it was permanently barred from the counterinsurgency campaign. The climate, particularly for the Tupamaros, immediately changed: they went back to their true status as prisoners. Gavazzo would soon become known as Uruguay's top practitioner of torture against captured "subversives"; one named Roberto Gomensoro is said to have died while undergoing the "submarine" at La Paloma under his supervision.

* Buka strangely told Haberkorn that "it may be said that in general I was treated respectfully", and that he did emigrate but only years after these events.

Striving for a Deal

While in July and August the economic crimes hunt took place, the deal emerging in negotiations between the two leaderships involved the military accepting the surrender of the MLN, in a public and dramatic way, in exchange for the announcement of a nationalistic and socialist program of government.[530] The Tupamaros would provide the military with a formal, Second World War-style capitulation, ideally through a press conference. The script was drafted in advance. It was stiff and inadequately thought out: the Tupamaros were supposed to use the language of the military, including terms like "*sediciosos*" or "*subversivos*", to refer to themselves.

After capitulation, the Tupas would be transferred to a model agricultural commune in northern Uruguay, amnestied to the last man and woman. This would include those held in civilian prisons, serving sentences handed out by an independent judiciary. Meanwhile, the military would take it upon itself to cleanse the country of malign political and economic elements.

Not only was such a deal unprecedented. As Sanguinetti points out, none other than the president of Uruguay, Juan Bordaberry, was not a part of it. He had no say in the negotiation nor, more importantly, in the new Uruguay the plot sought to bring to fruition. There was thus an alarming demonstration of military independence taking place.

In reality, the military was divided. The three most instrumental men in organizing the talks were Álvarez of EsMaCo (Joint Chiefs of Staff), Trabal of SID, and Cristi of Military Region I. Álvarez and Trabal knew full well what they were doing: engaging in politics had been in their minds for some time. Trabal had personally seen the Peruvian "experiment" with collectivist nationalism. He also spoke openly of reinstating relations with Cuba, and made his liking of the Frenchman Jean Lartéguy's army-idolizing novels known.

Álvarez had, as early as 1971, pseudonymously crafted a proposal introducing the participation of the military in governmental affairs, from economic development to internal security. Flipping around French wartime leader Georges Clemenceau's famous quip, Álvarez suggested that the economy was too important a matter to be left to the civilians. In the last election he was said to have voted for nationalist-socialist candidate Wilson Ferreira.

The third man spearheading the negotiations, Cristi, acted from a less thought-out position. It would be difficult to tell where he stood at multiple points of the following twelve months. Cristi was nominally a conservative nationalist, and was in favor of an unconditional surrender of the MLN. He did not object to continuing discussions with the Tupamaros to obtain said surrender. There were others, like Navy chief Rear Admiral Juan Zorrilla, who were resolutely against any excursion outside the bounds of republican legality.

At a meeting in the wee hours of a winter morning in Bordaberry's private home –he allowed Jorge Pacheco to continue benefiting from the safety of the presidential residence until he left the country for an ambassadorship in Madrid-, the president discussed the negotiations with his top advisers. On the political-civilian side he included Julio Sanguinetti and Luis Barrios Tassano; both were openly hostile to the military's participation in politics or straying in any way from its constitutional mission.

The officers reporting to Bordaberry were Álvarez and Cristi. As the two generals explained, the Tupamaros were proposing a conditional surrender involving a series of economic concessions from the government. Bordaberry sided with his civilian advisors and his own instincts: the MLN had to surrender unconditionally. There would be no quid pro quo.

The president complained then and multiple other times to his generals about any collusion with the dreaded MLN. To prevent this he ordered the presence of anti-negotiation officers in the talks, in order for them to clearly state there would be no outcome other than an unconditional surrender. Since men like the Navy's Zorrilla, as well as army chief Florencio Gravina, would hear nothing of a friendly interaction with the Tupamaros, Álvarez and Trabal would be isolated in their efforts.

With those orders, the entire military leadership of Uruguay showed up at the Florida base for the next meeting. Thanks to Eleuterio Fernández's memoirs, many of the details –including the names of the participants- can be known. The military brought Florencio Gravina, José Pérez of the Air Force, Juan Zorrilla, Ramón Trabal, Gregorio Álvarez, Esteban Cristi, Rodolfo Zubía, Carlos Legnani, and Pedro Aranco. That meant, respectively, that the commanders of the three branches of the military, plus the commanders of military intelligence and of the Estado Mayor Conjunto (EsMaCo), and the field commanders in charge of operations against the Tupamaros, were all present. The MLN's ranks included Fernández himself plus Mauricio Rosencof, Jorge Manera, and Adolfo Wasem.

All sorts of topics were discussed, including specific issues like amethyst exports. Rosencof recalls briefing hardline generals like Cristi on the power of the so-called oligarchy and the tools that allowed it to dominate the country. Smokes and drinks were shared, and attendees spent hours upon hours debating these topics. The meeting was inconclusive, but it allowed each side to measure the other up. The Tupamaros did most of the talking, trying to persuade the generals of how rotten the situation in Uruguay was. The officers mostly listened. Later, on July 31, Frente Amplio Senator Zelmar Michelini publicly revealed the talks had taken place, injecting a heavy dose of confusion and uncertainty into the political and social life of a country that was already on edge.

Michelini's revelation generated a tense situation. Taking to the floor of the Parliament, many lawmakers openly questioned whether the military was stepping out of bounds in its counterinsurgency activities. The president and his ministers came in for criticism, even from their own party. Unlike the police in previous years, this time the military publicly responded to the criticism of legislators, journalists, and others who questioned its strategy or its methods. This in itself concerned and outraged the critics more.

The Political Geography of the Armed Forces

The military had many political clusters within it. The most vocal one was made up of socially conservative, culturally nationalist anti-Communists. In partisan terms they were closest to old Partido Nacional figures like Benito Nardone and Luis Alberto de Herrera. They were not at all aligned with the socialist Wilson Ferreira, then the dominant *caudillo* of that party.

In 1972 periodicals with names like "El Rebenque" ("The Horsewhip") and "Azul y Blanco" ("Blue and White"), began to publish attacks on the Constitution, on liberalism, on Jews, and more.[531] Heavily influenced by the decaying remnants of Spain's conservative nationalism under Francisco Franco, the articles spoke of an impossibly complex "Judeo-Freemason-Batlli-Bolshevik-Tupamaro conspiracy".* Behind this propaganda was a loose group of like-minded military officers and civilians started a decade earlier by top general and recent presidential candidate Mario Aguerrondo. At the time of the downfall of the Tupamaros generals Esteban Cristi and Hugo Chiappe were known to belong to it.

In addition to this conservative faction there was a traditional republican one, mostly incarnated in the head of the Navy, Zorrilla. Numerous soldiers and officers belonged to it, for it was the default mindset for the Uruguayan military after seven decades of modest activity: defend the republic under civilian leadership.

In the late 1960s there was a third current emerging. Despite being the newest, it was remarkably powerful. Known as "Peruvianists" after their attraction to the 1968 nationalist-socialist coup in Peru, they had powerful leaders in General Álvarez and Colonel Trabal. These were the officers most receptive to the MLN's "economic crimes" message.

When negotiations reached an impasse, both sides decided to re-energize the effort. On the MLN side, Eleuterio Fernández Huidobro convinced his custodians to allow him to travel to the city accompanied by officer Carlos Calcagno. The objective was to meet with clandestine Tupas and discuss a broader arrangement. Calcagno would keep silent the entire time and never disclose the locations of the meetings he attended, a promise he honored.

The leaders of the remaining Tupamaros whom Fernández sought were mainly Marenales, Martínez Platero, Sendic, and Engler. The joint forces were hunting all of them; there was little possibility of offensive operations. Instead, their daily routine consisted of survival: disguises, shelters, and running from one place to the other. Contacts, safe houses and other resources fell to the military day after day. They never knew where they would find a *ratonera*, a patrol, or an act of treason next. That is exactly what happened to Marenales, in the incident where he spotted Amodio inside a military vehicle, threw a dud grenade, and was gunned down.

One figure who helped the Tupamaros considerably at the time was Frente Amplio lawmaker Enrique Erro.[532] The old Partido

---

* "Batlli-" is a reference to Batllismo, the Colorado Party's dominant social-democratic faction.

Nacional populist had been their acquaintance since the early 1960s. After all, José Mujica worked for him in the late 1950s. Erro had parliamentary immunity and ample resources, so in this moment of greatest need he allowed many Tupas to stay in his house.

Mujica, his old assistant, lived there for some time, as did the latter's new girlfriend, Lucía Topolansky. At different points in time, major cadres like Candán, Martínez Platero, and Manera were hosted there. María Herminia, the lawmaker's wife, washed the filthy clothes of *guerrilleros* arriving from the sewers.

Nevertheless, by mid-winter Erro's house was no longer safe. Military intelligence noticed the prodigious amounts of bread being eaten at the always-suspicious Erro home. Upon inheriting the MLN's Montevideo General Command from the successively fallen Amodio and Marenales, Mujica left the property and settled in a wooded suburban area, near a series of semi-abandoned warehouses and former factories. Using the codename Ulpiano following his last escape from Punta Carretas, Pepe carried an Uzi sub-machine gun everywhere. At night he slept in a makeshift camp among the trees and the grass. With enough discretion, he could pass for one of many vagrants.

Mujica spent the days sharing meager meals with fellow transients Manera, Topolansky, Marcelo Estefanell, and others. The latter reported a disturbing sight: Eleuterio Fernández sharing a table at a bar with two military officers. It was a rough winter and there was hardship everywhere. Consensus concerning discussions with the military was against rejecting any notion of surrender, but for the negotiated exit involving the collective farm.

Manera, Estefanell, and others fell one by one to the *fuerzas conjuntas*. For a few days following Marenales's fall, Mujica became a member of the leadership for the first time. In early August Ulpiano saw a military patrol emerge from a eucalyptus grove. Carlos Calcagno pointed a rifle at him and shouted "Mujica! Freeze, don't move an inch!" Mujica had a fully loaded Uzi and a grenade, but the trap was well sprung: unable to move, all he was able to mutter was a series of expletives.

His girlfriend, Lucía Topolansky, also roaming the city to avoid capture, carried a .38 pistol and a grenade. She also fell to the police. Like many other Tupas she was beaten, subjected to a combination of the submarine with the *picana*, and made to walk blindfolded on a high ledge. Mujica was tortured brutally, with an electric prod applied to his naked body. The torment permanently damaged him, and left the fallen Tupamaro with an incontinence problem. After squeezing him of all the information they could get, Mujica's captors sent him to the Florida base, to join his friends in the negotiations.

The military now had a considerable number of high-ranking Tupamaros, not seen since before El Abuso. Still free remained Henry Engler, Efraín Martínez Platero -back in the *dirección* following the fall of Mujica-, and others. Naturally, there was one name missing in particular. Perhaps the presence of one man could provide much-needed leverage and decisiveness for the surrender.

Into the Lion's Den

What Trabal obviously wanted was for Raúl Sendic to be present at the negotiations. His weight as an indisputable MLN leader could perhaps provide the closure the SID chief wanted so badly.[533]

Sendic had refused to escape the country; his decision was to fight to the end. A meeting was finally arranged in a Pocitos apartment where Fernández Huidobro conveyed the opinion of the jailed Tupas in favor of negotiations. As the Army escort Calcagno watched in strict silence, and Engler in turn monitored him (armed to the teeth beneath his clothes and blankets),* Fernández Huidobro informed Sendic of the progress reached in the talks with the military, and offered him a murky path: to enter the base and speak directly to the commanding officers and the jailed Tupamaros.

It was a considerable wager. Sendic had been the most wanted man in Uruguay for almost a full decade. Despite his recent rhinoplasty, he was a well-known man actively hunted by the security services. Lately, these services were benefitting from the collaboration of turncoats like Píriz, Amodio, and others. It was virtually unheard of for a wanted insurgent leader to engage in peace talks not just in territory that he did not control, but also directly in the lion's den. If the military betrayed Sendic's trust, there was

* According to Amodio, Engler told Fernández in private that they should kill Calcagno and free Fernández right then and there. In turn, Fernández revealed this to his military captors, which only made them more anxious to take Engler out.

nothing he or other Tupamaros could do. It would all be over in an instant.

Sendic agreed to the proposal, and ended up entering the headquarters of his enemy at least three times, accompanied by Martínez Platero. Each time, they successfully left without being harmed. Martínez was loyal to Sendic despite his disagreement with the whole enterprise.

Exchanges with the generals, as usual, went into great detail. Sendic and Mujica crafted one of the main MLN proposals: "expropriating" the top five hundred rural estates in the country and placing them in a collectivist colonization program. It was symbolic, drastic, and an old wish of men like El Bebe. It was also a recipe for a bloodbath, as it would inevitably face resistance from the looted owners and cause the displacement of entire populations (first the uprooted, and then up to 300,000 settlers from Montevideo to the *campo*). This without mentioning the obvious risk of foreign intervention from Brazil, Argentina, or both.

Unfortunately for the Tupamaros, the talks failed. There could be no negotiated surrender because the president forbid it, and the government was the stronger side anyway. In turn, the Tupamaros rejected an unconditional surrender. Both sides had non-negotiable conditions the other rejected. A key military demand, which was that Sendic formally turn himself in and surrender, was completely out of the question for the MLN leader.

During one meeting at a military facility between the captured Fernández and Marenales on one side, and the clandestine Sendic and Martínez on the other, an incredible idea was tabled. Fernández had with him a piece of paper from which he read the military's proposal: Sendic would be captured after resisting arrest in a fake firefight. There would be plenty of high-caliber blanks fired, smoke grenades, and noise, after which the MLN's founder would be able to surrender with his honor intact. According to Martínez, "Eleuterio had warmed to this proposal far more than you can imagine". Upon dismissing the idea, Sendic said of Fernández, while addressing Martínez: "This piece of shit is a greater traitor than Amodio Pérez".*

---

* Fernández had to apologize. It was the lowest point the MLN's two core founders ever reached.

The military's Sendic file was the work of the turncoat Mario Píriz. It said Sendic was a hothead, an expert navigator of the woods of Uruguay, and "is always armed, lately with a .45 pistol. He always dresses like a poor person, with the appearance of a humble working man". Once Sendic left the base following each failed negotiation, he successfully re-entered anonymous clandestinity in Montevideo.

The talks failed for more reasons than just the disagreements or Sendic's refusal to surrender. There was an additional, far more concrete cause. On July 25 1972 the Tupamaros José Luis Rodríguez and Roberto Luzardo assassinated none other than Colonel Artigas Álvarez, the brother of Estado Mayor Conjunto chief General Gregorio Álvarez. Artigas was at the time the commander of the Servicio de Defensa Civil, a national disaster response agency. The victim's brother was a key participant in the negotiations, and one of the most amenable to the ideology of the Tupamaros. It remains unclear how such disconnection emerged within the MLN, to the point where one side of the organization was violently sabotaging the careful efforts of another.

After the assassination of Artigas Álvarez there could be no negotiated surrender. The military would never consent to relations with an enemy it considered treacherous, subversive, and honorless. The talks at the Florida base were suspended and the jailed Tupamaros returned to prison life. With the truce in tatters, the military resumed its persecution of the MLN. Álvarez's assassins were captured and sent to the La Paloma base. One of their interrogators was none other than Álvarez's son. Despite the obvious possibility of exacting revenge, the young man never proposed abusing or murdering the prisoners.

There were only a few leaders of the MLN left in the wilderness, and the next one to fall was Henry Engler. The master *guerrillero* alternately known as Octavio had never been in police custody. In fact, he managed to maintain his "legal" status throughout the insurgency, from his first days in the MLN in 1968 to his sudden ascension to the leadership after the Almería debacle. The government only identified him as a member of the MLN in 1972.

On August 17 Engler risked his luck and showed up for a contact at a bar in the working-class neighborhood of Unión. Shortly afterward, a military patrol raided it. When the squad arrived, Engler failed to raise his hands and was shot; his only and failed attempt at resistance lay in his pocket, in the form of a grenade. It all happened too fast.

Targeting Politics

A second spike in the military's activities attacking "corruption" happened in October, months after the suppression of the MLN. It was a grave series of incidents that revealed the military was aiming directly at politicians and not just businessmen.[534]

There was reason for the Army's leaders to be confident. A poll conducted by Gallup in September of 1972 showed overwhelming support for their counter-insurgent activities. Naturally, this was likely due to the losses caused to the Tupamaros, but some officers interpreted such reports as evidence of *general* support for the military.

The American embassy noted the same phenomenon: public reaction to a parliamentary report on harsh interrogations and torture met a disinterested response. According to the U.S. analysts, "We think there are two reasons for this: first, as terrorists continue waves of machine gunnings and murders, we sense public feels 'Tupamaros' deserve whatever they get at hands of security forces. Second, thus far, armed forces and police generally considered by public to be limiting any harsh treatment to suspected subversives".[535] The military could afford to expand its horizons.

The most important victim of the renewed effort was Jorge Batlle. The scion of Colorado politics, and one of the more liberal politicians in Uruguay, Batlle carried the most seasoned name in national politics. In the early 1960s he inherited from his father a large faction of the party apparatus, plus a radio station and a newspaper to disseminate his opinions. Although Batlle was the product of Uruguay's nepotistic political tradition, he also happened to be a man of superior intelligence and tireless political capabilities.

In 1968 a Parliamentary commission investigated Batlle and other individuals over an alleged exploitation of classified financial information. The Colorado senator had been present at a dinner in which an upcoming devaluation of the Uruguayan Peso was apparently leaked. Rumors that Batlle made currency transactions to take advantage of said insider knowledge became *vox populi*. A formal parliamentary investigation -which included among its participants plenty of Batlle's political foes, like Wilson Ferreira- had cleared him of wrongdoing. However, in Uruguay's heated politics hostile propaganda continued to insist he was guilty.

In late 1972 something extraordinary happened. Batlle learned through friendly judicial sources that a military squad, apparently accompanied by none other than the MLN's Héctor Amodio Pérez, raided the court where his case's dossier was archived. Forcing judicial employees to surrender it, the military's "economic crimes" unit took off with the Batlle file. It was clearly an attack on the political establishment: military courts would re-open the case against Batlle, now apparently fueled by "national libcration" ideology that saw itself above republican institutions.

Batlle was outraged, so he made one of the most dramatic media appearances in Uruguayan history. On the night of October 27 he took to the airwaves and publicly revealed and condemned what had taken place. Batlle mentioned the illegality of the proceedings and demanded answers from the military for this clear invasion of the Judiciary's autonomy. He also honed in on the Amodio fact: the senator demanded the military corroborate it was conducting operations hand-in-hand with a delinquent charged with some of the highest crimes in the land - which is what they were really supposed to be fighting.

Batlle's speech left no room for misunderstandings: the military attacked and he responded. Whatever happened next would be a clear indicator of the direction the country was taking. It did not take long: minutes later, the military's own public communications announced an arrest warrant in effect for citizen Jorge Batlle, who was accused of morally impugning the armed forces.

Roger Trinquier, the French theorist of counterinsurgency, had demanded precisely this of his students. In his view, a successful campaign required that "The nation attacked must fall in behind the government and its army. An army can throw itself into a campaign only when it has the moral support of the nation (...) Its unquestioned actions should be praised by the nation (...) Any propaganda tending to undermine its morale, causing it to doubt the necessity of its sacrifices, should be unmercifully repressed". In Uruguay, the military took Trinquier's message to heart: there could be no victory without the nation standing, come what may, behind its soldiers.

By demanding the arrest of a sitting, elected senator who had not broken any laws, the military was gambling more than ever before. Batlle summoned his closest associates to prepare at least a symbolic resistance. Armed with a pistol and a flashlight, he escaped his home through the rooftops, went through the windows of neighbors' homes, used their telephones to speak to key allies, and continued to move to spend the night in freedom.

Given his untenable situation, Batlle later notified the army he would be found, in the morning, at the main office of his newspaper Acción. Colonel Luis Queirolo, one of the hardest-line officers in the conservative-nationalist bloc, personally led the operation to "arrest" him. In reality, as the invisible barrier between legality and illegality began to crack, lawful arrests were becoming little more than kidnappings. The hints were already there: Batlle was hooded once inside the military vehicle that transported him.

The Colorado leader was taken to the headquarters of Military Region I, under the command of General Cristi. All sides agree he was treated well, although conversations with his captors were tense. During his internment, Batlle understood some of the dynamics taking place inside the secretive world of the armed forces: General Gregorio Álvarez and especially Colonel Ramón Trabal were behind these "Peruvianist" moves, but Cristi was unconvinced.

Julio Sanguinetti, Batlle's right hand and a minister in the Bordaberry government, was one of his two lawyers. Naturally, he and all other members of their faction resigned from their posts in the executive branch immediately upon the explosion of the Batlle crisis. The Colorados were thus decisively splintered.

Mere hours after the Batlle case, on October 31, another famous name that just so happened to be an old MLN obsession emerged again: Peirano. That day, brothers Jorge and Juan Carlos, of Uruguay's most famous banking family, were "arrested". They were unable, however, to avoid the fate Batlle shirked: "They were forced to stand for hours and subjected to other forms of torture. They were interrogated in various military facilities. Trabal signed invoices documenting his receipt of dollars, pesetas and Swiss Francs belonging to the Peiranos which he deposited in SID's safe deposit box". The staff of the Peirano brothers, just like Batlle's, was also taken into custody and tortured. Despite this in-depth investigation, the military found no grounds on which to jail Jorge Peirano, who had in any case not been formally involved in banking since 1968. A former Minister of Foreign Affairs had just been tormented.

In the closing weeks of 1972, more military interventions crippled the judicial branch of the Uruguayan state. In one instance, a judge ordered the liberation of four medical doctors in military custody. The Army simply ignored it. The Minister of National Defense, Augusto Legnani, dismissed SID chief Ramón Trabal for insubordination, but somber conversations with top generals made it clear Colonel Trabal was going nowhere.

Later on, the military intervened in the Junta Departamental, or Legislative Council, of Montevideo. It felt compelled to do so after scandalous revelations of corruption emerged in the press. The details included audacious expenditures on vehicles, fuel, newspapers, relatives hired as government employees, phantom invitations to justify trips overseas, nocturnal outings, bribes for journalists, prostitutes, pets, and a total of six thousand meals -in a single year- at Montevideo's finest restaurants. The council was purged.

One desperate reaction to this wave of incidents came from the Parliament. In mid-November of that most eventful year, the legislative branch passed a law that criminalized certain economic practices. It was its way of responding to the avalanche of social discussion and outrage over corruption, and of trying to stay one step ahead of the military. The country's republican and democratic institutions had to demonstrate they were better at addressing pressing issues than Trinquier and Lartéguy's "centurions". Passage of the law signaled the system still worked, although it was clear there was now an extortive dynamic in place.

There was more happening behind the scenes. Unbeknownst to all but a few men, a cell of military officers was preparing a broad vision for a new Uruguay, and putting it in writing. The chief composer was Trabal; other officers like Álvarez chipped in as well. Concepts arising from the counterinsurgency campaign, from the clash with the Tupamaros, from the economic crises, and from the pervasive political decadence of the time all flowed into Trabal's typewriter.

CHAPTER FOURTEEN:

THE LAST DAYS

BEFORE 1972 WAS over, the MLN was completely destroyed. Between the clumsiness of Plan Tatú, the lack of popular and political support, and the military's relentless pursuit, the edifice of the organization failed to hold.

The Escape Hatch

Having an escape route out of the country was particularly important in such a scenario. Approximately 844 men and women left Uruguay before the year was over, and thus evaded the onslaught.[536] Most of them went to Cuba, Chile and Argentina, hosted by friendly governments and organizations.

The evacuation of the MLN from Uruguay became a veritable migration system. Tupas who wanted out were first given false documents and money with which they escaped to Buenos Aires. In 1972, Argentina was undergoing its own upsurge in guerrilla and terrorist activity. Two groups in particular were waging bold campaigns to bring down the military dictatorship in place since 1966. The larger of these, the Montoneros, sought the return of the exiled dictator Juan Perón from Madrid and the restoration of his nationalist-socialist regime. The more ideological Ejército Revolucionario del Pueblo, or ERP, was a Communist organization dedicated to waging a full insurgent campaign that included rural, urban, political, and terrorist fronts.

The MLN had been an inspiration to both the Montoneros and the ERP. Thus, both organizations were generous in offering shelter to the Uruguayans seeking refuge. However, with both Montoneros and ERP hunted by the Argentine security services, the Tupamaros arrive to find a risky situation. Some stayed in Argentina and helped their allies perform spectacular operations, particularly kidnappings. Many more left for the next stop: Santiago.

In Chile, the Tupamaros found a welcoming sponsor in the regime of Salvador Allende. The president's minority government had aspirations of radically altering and collectivizing Chile's society and economy. By 1972 it was aligned with Cuba and had excellent relations with the KGB.[537] On top of that, Allende had paramilitary groups ready to spearhead initiatives like the collectivization of private companies or rural establishments. Numerous Chileans strongly resented these developments.

Allende provided housing and subsidies to arriving Tupamaros. Many were lodged at Santiago's San Borja towers, where other foreign insurgents also found a home. For the moment, Chile was safe - but the instability was palpable.

There were two more stops for the exiles. The main one was Cuba, by then a consolidated Communist regime with a formidable police state apparatus. Cuban intelligence provided the Tupamaros with sustenance to live indefinitely in the island, as many do to this day. In exchange the majority had to work, while a few joined the ranks of Cuban foreign intelligence. The alternative to Cuba was fleeing to Europe.

Destinations in the Old Continent were quite narrow. The obvious cultural choices, Spain and Portugal, were still ruled by the rancid nightmares of the ultra-conservative Francisco Franco and António de Oliveira Salazar regimes. It was everything the Tupas stood against. Similarly, although on the opposite extreme, no Tupa who prided himself as such would seek refuge in Communist Europe or the Soviet Union, where totalitarian society without a friendly Cuban *sherpa* was simply out of the question. Thus, it was countries like Sweden, France, and Italy that began to take in a trickle of Uruguayan radicals.

The man in charge of organizing this preservation of the MLN's human assets was one of its two remaining leaders, Efraín Martínez Platero. His task was essentially to shut down operations in Uruguay. Money had to be distributed, safe houses abandoned, archives destroyed, and most critically people needed to be spirited out of the country while they still could. Many did so, although a few –by no means a majority- chose to stay. Of these, the most notorious was Raúl Sendic, a man accustomed to insurmountable odds.

The Legend of Sendic

In the winter of 1972 Sendic was roaming the city of Montevideo and its suburban areas clandestinely, as he progressively lost contact with a collapsing organization.[538] Sometimes he slept in safe houses; other times on the freezing beaches. He moved on foot and constantly wore disguises. Operationally he was not doing anything at all, since survival consumed each day. The hunt for him was fully on, following the brief cease-fire during the talks with the military.

Still, El Bebe found himself in unique situations that are possible perhaps only in an urban guerrilla. The most wanted man in Uruguay sat on a bench, dressed as an old man, in Independence Square– thirty meters from the office of President Juan Bordaberry. This boldness was not for show, but rather an old Sendic belief that hiding in plain sight often worked better than the opposite.

Sendic's antics made his friends and allies nervous. Many Tupas, including those closest to him, "foresaw that if he were to die in combat, or taken prisoner, all hope would be lost" and advised him to escape from Uruguay. Rufo never considered the proposal.

Unfortunately for the MLN leader, the situation could not last. The end came on the first day of September 1972, less than a year after the spectacular escape from Punta Carretas prison showed the Tupamaros at the peak of their might. On that rainy night, there were only two MLN leaders still at large: Martínez Platero and Sendic. At 1 AM, intelligence led a military patrol to a safe house -a shop- in a centric but quiet section of Montevideo, a short distance from the naval academy the Tupamaros looted in 1970.

The patrol followed procedure, knocked on the metallic shutters, and called for the surrender of those inside, which unbeknownst to them included Sendic. It was the first time the founder of UTAA and the MLN was in direct contact with the security services -apart from the Florida talks- since his 1970 arrest in the Almería safe house. With him were his girlfriend Xenia Itté, and a Tupamaro named Jorge Ramada.

Sendic's orders to his two fellow *guerrilleros* were clear: grab your pistols -there was one for each of them- and fight. With that, a shootout ensued against what turned out to be a group of Fusileros Navales -Naval Fusiliers-, the elite naval infantry unit created following the embarrassment of the CIM raid which Sendic himself led.

As the results of the firefight became inevitable, Sendic ordered Ramada and Itté to surrender and evacuate. Shouting to the raiders to hold their fire, but without identifying himself, Sendic explained that two individuals would leave the premises unarmed. The soldiers agreed and let them leave, immediately demanding the surrender of the mysterious third one who stayed inside.

Now Sendic identified himself by name, announced he would not give himself up (he still had "a few caps left" left), and the shootout continued. During this final firefight Sendic was shot directly in the face, an event followed by silence coming from inside the house. The fusiliers breached the door and dragged him out into the rain, bleeding profusely from his face while his arrested *compañeros* watched, aghast.

The first man to become a clandestine Tupamaro was thus the last to fall. As Mauricio Rosencof said, "The downfall of Sendic meant it was all over". A legend emerged in the press the following day, claiming Sendic screamed "I am Rufo and I will never surrender" before the final shootout, but his biographers have acknowledged it is unlikely to be true.

The only remaining founder and leader of the MLN was Efraín Martínez Platero, a man whose entire family participated in the uprising of the Tupamaros. Sendic and Martínez had agreed that neither of them would surrender nor escape the country, but the situation proved too asphyxiating. At least some of the original MLN had to survive to tell the story. In October, Martínez escaped to Argentina: for the first time in close to a decade, there were no active Tupamaros in Uruguay. From Buenos Aires he tried to organize the disjointed embers of the MLN, while at the same time rebuffing Tupas who wanted to re-launch guerrilla operations inside Uruguay.

All participants and analysts agree that the insurgency of the MLN-Tupamaros ended then and there. During those long early hours of September 1, inside the military prison where they were being held, top Tupamaros Fernández, Marenales and Mujica were summoned to see Carlos Legnani, the commanding officer. Legnani reproached the Tupamaros for having failed to surrender previously; clearly Sendic's fall, as he put it, was their fault. His words were "Everything ends now. You have no idea of what is coming".

With the Tupamaros liquidated, a new process could begin. Their defeat was rather anticlimactic, for there was no moment of celebration or victory. By September 20 the military estimated it had captured at least 2,552 Tupas; there were only about three hundred more captured when November arrived. Rather than stopping to celebrate, the armed forces escalated their investigations into non-Tupamaro "subversive elements". The attacks on Jorge Batlle and other prominent Uruguayans came only weeks later.

Moving On From the Tupamaros

In order to make the pursuit of non-MLN "subversives" easier, a new project codenamed Operación Ceibo 302 began.[539] Under the supervision of colonel José Gavazzo, leading Tupamaros were transported to a new facility in Puente, Tacuarembó, where each was carefully interrogated.

Gavazzo had earned the assignment. He had helped out in the preceding months by operating as a hands-on commander for SID, personally apprehending Tupas in the streets, leading assaults on safe houses, getting shot at by *guerrilleros* sporting assault rifles, and more. At one point, he detained a leader of the MLN's medical services unit that, once again in classic Uruguayan fashion, had provided free care to his daughters and wife as part of his day job.

The purpose of Ceibo 302 was to get out of the Tupamaros all the actionable intelligence the military had not yet acquired. Copious reports began to circulate inside SID of MLN leaders' relations with various members of the Uruguayan political system. The information covered the Tupas' contacts with politicians, liaisons with foreign entities through the International Affairs Committee, and helped clarify unsolved killings.

Gavazzo thus got to interrogate, one by one, a who's-who of the MLN's most prominent names: Wasem, Engler, Rosencof, Mas Mas, Marrero, Esteban Pereira, and many others. The first generation of MLN leaders was kept apart: Fernández Huidobro was carefully kept isolated from everyone else; Marenales and Manera were in the hands of a separate SID cell. The latter two were subjected to some of the most grievous interrogations, which included torture that left severe injuries and involved brutal sexual abuses.

With the liquidation of the MLN and its increasing focus on other matters, the military decided it needed to retain in its custody only the most important members of the organization. Therefore, it released a large number of "processed" Tupamaros. One contingent was freed in November, and a far larger one of 1,500 was set free in February of 1973. The rest -numbering in the hundreds- was to remain in prison indefinitely.

Apart from the interrogations of Tupamaros, much information to pursue "subversion" came thanks to the turncoat Héctor Amodio. The founder of Column 15 had long stopped looking back at his life as a *guerrillero*. His last meeting with fellow Tupas took place in the barracks he was living in; his interlocutors were fellow captives Mujica and Marenales. According to the latter, "I told him he was a traitor, that he had been sentenced to death, and that I had nothing to discuss with him".

The MLN was destroyed but the Army did not yet give Amodio and his partner Alicia Rey their promised way out of Uruguay. Given this delay, the Tupamaro concluded he needed to help his own luck, and to do this he decided to pen his memoirs. Amodio's plan was to get the top Marxist media entrepreneur in Uruguay, a man named Federico Fasano, to visit him at the base. Commander Gustavo would pitch the memoirs right there. If everything turned out well, the public would get a salacious book with an inside look at the Tupamaros, while Amodio would get much-needed money to fund his escape from Uruguay.

SID chief Trabal learned of the meeting and kidnapped Fasano. Once in custody he was forced to give up the names of the officers who facilitated his illegal entry into the base. All four captains were purged, and SID kept the manuscript Fasano had typewritten. There could be no book.

When weeks later the military attacked the judicial system, Senator Wilson Ferreira and others publicly focused their condemnations on the subversive Amodio and his alleged influence on the Army to destroy democracy. In reality, Wilson and others knew -thanks to Fasano- that Amodio had "burned" them as MLN contacts in his disclosures. In other words, it might only be a matter of time before the Army got to them.

The months between September of 1972 and June of the following year were packed with public scandals, all of which followed a pattern. Someone in Uruguay's political system found out about military operations or investigations they did not approve of (likely because they were the target), and protested publicly about such intrusions. The military, in turn, publicly demanded apologies and prosecutions of those who criticized them, and leaked more information about the accused's ties to subversion.

The SID investigations were legally unreliable for many reasons, not least that they were conducted by a force summoned to suppress an armed insurgency - not political vices. Many of the military's summons, investigations, raids and statements were based on information collected from captured Tupamaros, which lent them even less credence.

Nevertheless, the military leadership was in an irreversible process of national hegemony. Trabal's SID was enormously powerful: he had a dossier on everyone in politics, business, and other spheres of public life. Furthermore, with an open season on "the corrupt" and other vague contributors to Uruguay's decay, anyone could be targeted by an informant with an ax to grind. Concordantly, Trabal had a busy schedule. Everyone sought meetings with him, including the top leaders of the Communist Party, the Frente Amplio, the CNT, and more. In the meantime, his men tortured people savagely, and General Gregorio Álvarez continued to work on strategic plans to solve Uruguay's problems beyond the immediate one of the Tupamaros.

After the late 1972 incidents with Jorge Batlle, the Peirano family, the captive medical doctors, Fasano, and the Montevideo legislative council, it was clear that the Army was bent on political intrusion. The armed forces' plan for 1973 was to pursue that agenda deeper. Sedition, meaning guerrilla fighters engaged in violent action, was over. Now came the fight to suppress the wider phenomenon of subversion, defined as anything that threatened the "natural lifestyle and basic scale of moral values [of Uruguay], or that deteriorate the nation's social, moral, and economic arrangements".

With that, the last days of the Tupamaros segued into the final days of Uruguayan liberal democracy. This was the MLN's original objective, although it was happening in a way none of its members could have predicted in the mid-1960s.

1973: Death in Two Blows

In February of 1973 the most important institutional crisis since the 1930s, possibly in the century, shook Montevideo to its core.[540] It began when Juan Bordaberry, still less than a full year into his term in office, decided to switch defense ministers. Armando Malet was out; the new minister would be former general Antonio Francese. General Francese was a respected man with more than enough rank in military circles. He also had considerable experience: he had served for three years as Pacheco's Minister of National Defense, and later as his Minister of the Interior.

However, a majority of Army commanders rejected the idea of serving under him. The motive was Francese's strictly republican way of conceiving politics. As a historical member of the Colorados and a moderate, arguably inefficient, pursuer of the Tupamaros, the general's performance record was less than stellar. In that sense, his appointment could be interpreted as a way for the civilian executive branch to contain the power of the military, which was growing exponentially at the time. In fact, according to Bordaberry himself, Francese's appointment was targeted at keeping Gregorio Álvarez, the most ascendant of all the officers, in check.

The military did not mince its words and publicly showed its truest colors for the first time. The opening salvo on February 8, shortly after Francese was sworn in, came in a statement saying the general was "unacceptable" as minister. It was a sheer act of insubordination, one that curiously was lost on many people –not least the general populace- at the time. By then, it was common for the military to comment on affairs of state, or public and even moral issues. Even in a staunchly republican country like Uruguay, the erosion in the norms of political discourse was too deep. The act of not just commenting on, but actually resisting a presidential nomination, was quite audacious.

With the military in the airwaves expressing a political position, Bordaberry was obliged to respond. A man of nebulous convictions, just days earlier he had written the following to Senator Amílcar Vasconcellos: "It shall not be with my consent that the country will stray from its democratic traditions. I reaffirm once more my intent to fulfill my mandate and transfer power only to those the people's sovereign will chooses".

That night the president's decision was to make a call for the population and the political establishment to demonstrate their support for democratic institutions. Bordaberry appeared on the balcony of the presidential office almost at midnight, supposedly to lead a rally at Independence Square. The showing was paltry. Gavazzo of SID was one of the few attendants, dressed as a civilian to report on the gathering back to his boss, Trabal. Representative Julio Sanguinetti, despite having resigned as one of Bordaberry's ministers and criticized him for the excesses of recent months, supported the gesture of institutional continuity by showing up at the presidential office. He recalls only five or six hundred people at the square: "There was no true popular showing. It was all quite eroded by then".

Sanguinetti was mostly alone. Parliament was not in session, and did not bother to reconvene during the crisis. Even politicians who made a few telephone calls to oppose the insurrection, like Jorge Batlle, took the following day off for a birthday party in Punta del Este. Almost everyone else who surrounded Bordaberry in those difficult hours was a member of his old clique from before he became a Colorado: the conservative nationalists of the Benito Nardone ruralist faction.

Early the next day, February 9, the military unleashed what had been brewing in the minds of its leadership for a long time. In a document simply titled "Document N° 4" it enumerated a series of opinion points to the population. The rejection of Francese was only one; the text advanced a specific vision for Uruguay. It conceived a country in development and national harmony, which required the respect of the political establishment for the leadership of the military, which would now participate in *all* aspects of public and political affairs. The language was mostly reflective of the "Peruavianist" brand of socialism.

The roster of men who signed the document was worryingly long. There were eleven colonels, plus a total of five heavyweight generals, on board. The colonels included Trabal, Luis Queirolo -the kidnapper of Jorge Batlle and second in command of Military Region I-, and Rodolfo Zubía -head of the Montevideo police. The generals included Hugo Chiappe -the senior member of the group, in charge of Region III-, Esteban Cristi -in charge of Region I-, Eduardo Zubía -in charge of Region II, and Julio Vadora -in charge of Region IV. Gregorio Álvarez, heading the Estado Mayor Conjunto, completed the picture.

The Army, the most important branch of the military, was thus almost entirely behind the move. The Air Force, historically the least important of the military branches, made no noise, and its commander José Pérez signed Document 4 as well.

That left the Navy and its notoriously republican commander, Juan Zorrilla, who refused to sign. Not only that: Zorrilla staked everything in opposing the insurrection, more than anyone else in Uruguay. The *contra-almirante* activated an operational plan called Efestos, which was originally created as a countermeasure against an MLN assault on Montevideo.

Zorrilla's orders were for his men to cordon off the small peninsula comprising the Ciudad Vieja, where a significant part of Montevideo's businesses and government facilities were located. The Navy commandeered civilian vehicles, dumpsters and other objects and thus barricaded the entire area. At the same time, its ships assumed positions all around the Old City, with orders to provide fire support in case the Army launched an assault. The peninsula is so narrow and small that the vessels placed on the shore would easily hit any invading vehicle. The oldest part of Montevideo was about to be turned into a fortress of resistance. From the American embassy, looking directly at the usually calm waters of the River Plate, the entire affair became visible to the naked eye: "There are naval vessels visible offshore, one about 1000 yards away from embassy chancery. We understand their guns trained on army targets".[541]

Zorrilla sought out Bordaberry, whose office was only a few meters on the wrong side of the barricade, to offer shelter in the Navy-controlled area. Given the president's public position, and the military's insubordination, it was quite possible they would go after him. Zorrilla's expectations were two. First, that Bordaberry publicly challenge and purge the insurrection, for which he needed the hard power the Navy was providing. Second, that through his actions he would "alert the Uruguayan people, which had its attention focused on the beach and on football [of the gravity of what was taking place]".

While Zorrilla organized resistance and the protection of the president, the rebel commanders -now by definition engaged in a *coup d'état-* prepared more actions. Trabal ordered his favorite operator, Gavazzo, to kidnap Francese and forcefully remove him from his new post. At the same time, Francese had his own plans: he would enter the headquarters of Battalion 13 and personally command it during the crisis. The former general was too late: waiting at the gates as he arrived were Cristi, Álvarez, and Trabal. The government had no Minister of National Defense.

The insurrectional leaders were planning, if necessary, to violently wipe out resistance to the *golpe*. For this they had the support of a few naval captains who supported Document N°4. An officer named Jorge Nader and some of his men commandeered the naval vessel *Huracán*, effectively removing it from Zorrilla's inventory. The Navy chief's response was to order Julio Franzini, his main operational commander on board the ship Campbell, to open fire on the *Huracán*.

It was an act without precedent in recent times: the Campbell took to the water and adopted a firing position. At least two of its crewmembers mutinied and had to be subdued.

While the jousting for positions took place and the tension increased -who would open fire first?-, Zorrilla got more bad news. The La Paloma Army base atop the Cerro, which had a superior firing position to everyone else, had learned of his intentions and trained its weapons on the ships. There was no way to fire back.

Running out of options, particularly because Bordaberry failed to seize on all he was doing to resist the coup, Zorrilla thought it prudent to cancel his order to open fire on the *Huracán*. At dusk he ordered the Campbell to return to port. At the *Huracán*'s docking area there were scuffles and shots fired between republican and pro-coup officers. The naval battle never took place.

Everything had happened in a matter of hours during February 9: the Navy took over the Ciudad Vieja in the morning, and by 21:30 it was dismantling the barricades. At lunchtime, the commander of the Air Force, José Pérez Caldas, told Zorrilla he would support the republic along with the Navy. Before dinnertime, a public statement from the insubordinates carried his signature. Bordaberry's last gesture was reading a statement on television alongside Francese. Shortly after the duo left, the military assaulted the television broadcasters and barred further transmissions of the speech; thus was degraded the impact of the televised appeal.

It was more than enough to tear Uruguay at the seams. American diplomat James Tull, watching the naval deployments, their later withdrawal, and the relaxed attitude of Montevideo's population, packing the beaches, recalled that "As the afternoon wore on, the reality of nearly a century of Uruguayan democracy slowly faded- poof!- to a dream. It was all very sad".[542] The fact that nothing else happened meant that for the moment the authors of Document N° 4 had won. They openly resisted a presidential nomination, unlawfully detained the nominee, took over the airwaves, and deployed active military assets against military, civilian, and government positions. Yet no one paid for it.

Zorrilla's position became unsustainable, particularly because he realized he was defending the republic more than Bordaberry was. Two days later, he resigned and was replaced by a man named Conrado Olazábal. Zorrilla thus ended his military career as the most honorable man in Uruguay. At the same time, the president made plans to meet with the leaders of the revolt and reach some kind of agreement with them.

The fateful meeting took place on February 13 at a military base called Boiso Lanza, which gives its name to the deal that formalized the new state of affairs. Bordaberry flipped from a shy defense of democratic institutions to an enthusiastic embrace of the military's role in politics. He agreed to govern jointly with the armed forces, which would now be allowed -and expected- to express themselves in ways similar to the Francese incident. A National Security Council was created to institutionalize the deal.

Boiso Lanza meant the executive branch of the government would be simultaneously run by an elected institution –the presidency- and an unelected one, the military. No one could fail to recognize the underlying truth: it was the military that had the true power. At the meeting a decision was made to name Walter Ravenna, a man more malleable to the interests of the armed forces, as Minister of National Defense. Francese thus only served for a few hours. Additionally, Bordaberry surprised his interlocutors by proposing the abolition of political parties. General Álvarez found himself in the position of being slightly more republican than the president: all that was needed to heal Uruguay's politics was to decapitate their corrupt heads rather than dismantle them. The moment would come in due course.

A Long-Awaited Moment

The tone of Document N°4, authored mainly by Trabal, was profoundly collectivist and imbued with Marxist economic concepts. This was the case to such a degree that the entire Frente Amplio came out in favor of it. This included its presidential candidate, former general Líber Seregni, as well as member entities like the Communist Party and the CNT.

For the Communists, the February 1973 crisis was the closest they got to the moment they had been waiting for two decades. The uprising of the Tupamaros had failed to destroy the system and ease the way into communism, as had parliamentary politics. Perhaps it was the military that would be the vehicle towards success after all.*

The military's public statements explicitly rejected Marxism-Leninism, but other than that they had many socialist elements. They discussed the corruption and moral evils of the "oligarchy", the state's role in the means of production and national economic development, and so forth. Who would have imagined, only months earlier, that there would be a military uprising against a conservative Colorado president, and that its leaders would spread collectivist, populist, and even socialist language all over their discourse? This was no opportunity to be wasted.

With this in mind, the Frente Amplio, the Communists, and the latter's newspaper, El Popular, went out of their way to support the February coup. In an event on the day of greatest tension, February 9, Seregni headlined with an enthusiastically supportive speech. Speaking before him, Senator Zelmar Michelini said institutions mattered less than other things. Days later, in the reconvened Parliament, Socialist leader Vivián Trías glowingly described military putschists like Peru's Juan Velasco and Egypt's Gamal Abdel Nasser, and openly defended the insurrectionist path to socialism. El Popular blasted Colorado Social Democrat Amílcar Vasconcellos for condemning the military's advances. Ramón Trabal of SID joined in, ordering military intelligence to disseminate black propaganda against Vasconcellos. It was another sign of the descent into illegality: military intelligence was now publicly defaming an elected politician.

---

* The mother of all communist revolutions, the Russian one of 1917, had benefited from army mutinies and defections to the revolutionary camp.

There was a lot more going on. In secret, the Party began to finance a pro-Gregorio Álvarez newspaper that popped out of nowhere almost immediately. It was named precisely after the date of the summer coup: 9 de febrero. The paper was a national embarrassment: it engaged in a Soviet-style cult of personality of Álvarez and his family, claiming there was nationwide glee over his two-year anniversary as commander of EsMaCo.

This collusion with the military extended to meetings, previously unimaginable, between *golpista* generals like Álvarez and Chiappe with Communist leaders. The message from the generals was for the PCU-controlled unions to continue "working", because important reforms were coming. Years later, the Communists would lump Bordaberry and generals like Álvarez or Cristi together as members of an American-controlled neoliberal-fascist conspiracy. Their own support for the coup and their meetings with the perpetrators were almost completely erased from history.

In aiming for the highest prize, the Communists failed to understand a crucial truth. Despite all the power socialists like Álvarez and Trabal had, there were others in the brass who still belonged to more nationalist or conservative branches of thought. It was here that the old military cells founded by Mario Aguerrondo and other generals, a decade earlier, began to make themselves heard. Witnessing the flirtations of the Frente Amplio, the Communists, and others, with their Army, generals like Esteban Cristi decided Document N°4 leaned too much towards Marxism.

To mend things, they pushed for a new document to "clarify" the military's ideology. Creatively titled Document N° 7, this new manifesto was just as confusing as the previous document. It reflected heterodox thinking on every political and economic issue, and a multiplicity of authoritarian influences. Notably, it more strongly rejected socialist concepts and distanced itself from the anti-capitalist rhetoric of Document N° 4.

Líber Seregni was not the only presidential candidate from the previous election to disgrace himself. Wilson Ferreira, the single most voted candidate in 1971, failed to properly oppose the coup. His boldest move was to cross the barricades, meet with Zorrilla behind the president's back and discuss a plan to "save" the republic. Under Wilson's offer, Bordaberry had to resign, but his vice president Jorge Sapelli would not become president. Instead, a new election would be held before the year was over, with a custom-made binary ballot between himself and another candidate.[543]

Wilson ensured the proposal reached top generals Álvarez and Cristi, both of whom had nationalist rather than Colorado credentials. Clearly seduced by the allure of power and revenge, the *caudillo* was flirting with disaster. There was nothing in Uruguay's electoral laws contemplating his scenario, particularly with an elected vice president in place. In the hours and days that followed the February crisis, Wilson confidently patted his closest advisors on the back and told them to gear up for elections in September. Those signs never arrived, and Wilson lost out.

Everybody Loses

With the successive defeats, electoral or otherwise, of the Batllista Social-Democrats, of Wilson's nationalists, of the Frente Amplio, of the Tupamaros, and now an apparent taming of the socialist wing of the military through Document 7, there was only one cohesive group left. It was also the most unlikely: the conservative-nationalists.

After the events of February, generals Álvarez, Chiappe, and Cristi had all the initiative. With the independence of the judiciary undone in October of 1972, and the executive branch hijacked in February, there was only portion of the state left: the Parliament.[544]

In terms of power, the most important job towards taking over Uruguay was already done. With no police or army under its command, the Parliament did not have any means of defending itself. All real powers of resistance belonged, as in every country, to the executive branch. In fact, the military unit tasked with protecting the Parliament was none other than the Florida Battalion, the same one starring in the 1972 intrigues with the Tupamaros.

The leadership of the armed forces was bent on liquidating all subversion before year's end, with an emphasis on politicians who had collaborated with the MLN. Not a few of these were elected senators and representatives at the Parliament. The main name to appear in the military's sights after Boiso Lanza as a suspected subversive was Enrique Erro. The Frente Amplio lawmaker had radical, pro-violence beliefs and was known to harbor sympathies for the Tupamaros. The question was whether he had crossed the red line of collaborating with the MLN.

The truth was clearly that he had, as described in previous chapters. In fact, during interrogation more than one Tupamaro gave up Erro's role in sheltering them in his own home. The military thus started an investigation, and on April 25 the president formally requested the Parliament lift his immunity from prosecution. That was still the procedure required by the Constitution for sitting lawmakers accused of illegal acts.

The pressure was sufficient for the Parliament to open the inquest. The investigative commission requested access to Erro's alleged main accuser: the Tupamaro Héctor Amodio, who was still in custody. It was May 8 of 1973. The Army reluctantly complied.

In his conversation with the parliamentarians, Amodio "verified Erro's collaboration with the Tupamaros beginning in 1969, and said it had started through the conduit of José Mujica, who had previously been his secretary and had remained his friend". The investigators were skeptical. They knew, thanks to the journalist Federico Fasano, that Amodio was in the process of smearing more than just Erro. In other words, they themselves could be in for a similar treatment soon. Why should they trust anything he said?

Immediately after his meeting with the legislators -and after having been a protagonist of politicians' public statements for more than six months-, Héctor Amodio Pérez gave an unprecedented press conference at a military academy. It was the first time ever that a Tupamaro spoke to the media openly, unmasked, and using his real name. His role as a military collaborator was thus fully public.

Amodio's escort, by his own insistence, was SID's José Gavazzo. As it turned out, Amodio and Gavazzo knew each other from childhood: they had been in the same group of children playing street football in the Brazo Oriental neighborhood. Amodio confided in Gavazzo that he feared he would be assassinated; once more, the personal lives and career choices of two Uruguayans intersected in a remarkable way.

The appearance at the press conference of the master *guerrillero*, whose name and face Uruguayans had come to know in previous years through countless arrest notices, was legendary. Every news medium in the country was present: television, radio, and print. Although he looked calm, he flinched from the relentless flashing of the cameras, amid scuffles to get shots of the near-mythical figure of the MLN chief. The man who had commanded guerrilla assaults on so many banks and on the city of Pando was at last before them.

Amodio's conference was brief and to the point. He displayed awareness of how notorious he had become with his opening statement: "I am Héctor Amodio Pérez; enough said". Immediately he acknowledged having met with a commission of senators, and later noted he had been condemned to death by the MLN. Becoming such a public figure was a way for Amodio to enhance protections for himself and for his partner, Rey. Watching on the television, politicians like Wilson, Seregni, and Michelini watched anxiously: if their names came out of Amodio's lips, their fate would be sealed and the knocks on their doors would follow. Fortunately for them, those words were never said at the conference.

It would still be some months before Amodio and Rey finally got their wish. In the end, the Army leadership gave them a way out. In October 1973, Esteban Cristi, who had both in his custody, granted them new identification documents. Colonel Luis Queirolo then drove the couple to the border with Brazil and left them to their own devices. The couple traveled by land to São Paulo, and from there flew to Madrid. Then, they disappeared from history and were seen no more.

Whatever remained of the MLN in Uruguay in 1973 was caught in the final Army raids. Gavazzo still had some action ahead of him. In one case a Tupamaro resisted arrest through the creative means of fainting every time someone yelled at him. In another, he successfully tracked down a Tupamara nicknamed La Fedayina. The target was hiding alone in a rural safe house. One night, Gavazzo surrounded the house with a full military unit and used a bullhorn to call for her surrender. He got a bullet storm in response. Later, La Fedayina emerged from the darkness of the house, carrying a sub-machine gun and walking directly towards the soldiers. She opened fire wildly and relentlessly until she ran out of ammunition, failing to hit any of her targets. Upon being tackled she resisted detention like a feral animal, kicking and screaming until she was subdued by several men. In her "legal" life, La Fedayina was a middle-class resident of the Punta Carretas neighborhood, with no background other than that of a student. It was typical for a member of the MLN.

The investigation into Enrique Erro continued while the Army completed these operations. The military's request for the removal of the senator's parliamentary immunity was still standing, and in June the Parliament had yet to vote on it. Only a few people realized this was the last showdown. Erro was guilty of many illegal acts of support for an armed insurgency; interrogated Tupas had said so themselves. However, the Parliament was the only institution constitutionally allowed to remove the immunity of one of its own.

Debates on the Erro case were long and tiresome. The military, accustomed to doing things at its own speed, grew increasingly frustrated both with the process and with the content of what was being said. Lawmakers took every chance they had to denounce the armed forces' bullying of elected politicians, and to remind its officers they could not arrest any of them without parliamentary approval. With a clear climate of hostility towards Bordaberry and the military, on June 21 the House of Representatives at last voted. The result, by a single vote, was that Erro kept his immunity from prosecution or arrest.

The responses from the executive branch in the days following the vote made it clear that something major was going to take place. The Parliament's failure to give up Erro would cost it dearly. The wanted senator had already fled to Buenos Aires anyway, as a measure of precaution. The military pressured Bordaberry to issue a decree sentencing Erro to prison, in the manner of the French kings of yore's *lettres de cachet.* The air in Montevideo was thick with tension. The Colorado Party, Bordaberry's own, publicly stated that since the Parliament had exonerated Erro, there could be no decree as that proposed by the military. As if to underline this point, they threatened to impeach Bordaberry if he ignored the warning.

In the end, the decision came not from the generals, but rather from Bordaberry himself. The president had changed considerably since February. Not only did he agree with the military that there were subversive elements in Uruguayan politics that needed to be purged. He went farther and decided that *all* Uruguayan politics were poisoned, to their very core. The entire system of government had to change from liberal democracy towards something else.

Meeting with the military leadership and the cabinet to decide how to proceed, Bordaberry saw no way out other than shutting down the Parliament. Four of his ministers immediately disagreed and resigned.[545] The rest was with the president.

In the Legislative Palace, few lawmakers were in attendance in the last few days of June 1973. All its members felt a climate of impending doom, and leaks to the press from the executive branch were clear: the national security apparatus was going to respond furiously to the Parliament's intransigence. In the final session, on the night from June 26 to the 27th, the last political speeches in a generation boomed in the Chamber of Senators.

That night, Wilson Ferreira gave the most famous speech of his career. The *caudillo* was given precedence over the rest of the few attendants: only sixteen senators were present. Fiery and combative, the opposition leader swore revenge in the name of the Partido Nacional. Just moments after saying his party bore no hatred -unlike Bordaberry's-, Wilson mocked the president for "continuing to believe he will die of old age, or that his family and people will forever be safe (...) Maybe he fails to understand that he is condemning himself to fear, eternal fear; that he condemns himself to die far from his homeland; that he condemns himself to endure for as long as he lives -which I doubt will be for long-, the hatred, the legitimate hatred, of the Uruguayan people". Wilson also condemned the military, the Tupamaros, and the entire tragedy that befell country.

Unfortunately, the senator failed to recognize his own role in degrading Uruguay's political culture. He was the most important Uruguayan politician outside of presidents Pacheco and Bordaberry, but his populist speeches, his legitimation of violence, his undermining of private property, and his conspiracies with the Tupamaros and the military, contributed nothing at all to the country's well-being.

Wilson fled the premises of the Parliament immediately after his speech and escaped, hidden inside a boat and later a small airplane, to Buenos Aires. This act clued everyone else in on what to do: nothing. There was no shootout with Bordaberry's forces. Other senators also spoke that night: Amílcar Vasconcellos went slightly further than Wilson and in Hellenistic fashion promised ruin for those responsible for the coup, as well as their descendants. After the last speeches, shortly before two in the morning the premises were emptied and the Legislative Palace became a tomblike void. It would remain in that state for over a decade.

Hours later, on the cold winter morning of June 27, an unprecedented act took place in the center of Montevideo. Columns of armored vehicles swarmed in, and Army soldiers took over the building. Generals Esteban Cristi and Gregorio Álvarez personally led the breach of the empty site, in full view of the cameras that immortalized the event. Colonel Luis Queirolo personally directed his men in searching the facility for evidence of subversion and corruption.

It was an appalling moment for a country with strong liberal traditions. In less than a decade Uruguay went from a Swiss-inspired rotational executive branch and a society hostile towards any entity or person with too much authority, to a day in which the undefended house of the Legislative branch was taken over by men wearing military uniforms and carrying firearms.

The inevitable trappings of a coup d'état were fully on display. The armed forces took over all news media and forced them to broadcast only certain contents. In the weeks that followed, the military shut down every institution that constituted a problem to its goals, including the unions and political parties. The joint forces released arrest warrants for a long list of people tied to political "subversion".

For many who had not left the country it was now too late. Bordaberry told the international press that his hand did not tremble when signing the decree shutting down the Parliament. Uruguay's ambassador in Spain since 1972, former president Jorge Pacheco, sent his best wishes to his *golpista* successor - thus endorsing the coup.

At the headquarters of the Colorados' Acción newspaper, Jorge Batlle and Julio Sanguinetti awaited their fate. The newspaper immediately condemned the coup in the strongest terms possible, so they knew a reaction was coming. Fate arrived in the person of Ramón Trabal, who informed them that their newspaper would now close. With that, Uruguay's main liberal voice went silent. One of the solitary Marxist voices with democratic convictions, that of Carlos Quijano, was also shut down. Neither Acción nor Quijano's magazine Marcha would ever be published again. From then on, all political discourse in Uruguay, if there was to be any at all, would be controlled by the military.

At SID headquarters, right around the time of the closure of Acción, there were celebrations taking place. Trabal, codenamed

Ceibo 1, dutifully informed Sable 1 -Gregorio Álvarez- of the progress in the raids and kidnappings taking place to checkmate any attempts at resistance. There was in fact no need for such efforts, for there was almost no opposition. External observers, such as the U.S. Embassy, noticed this as well: "Most indications that we have are that the population at large is either supporting the actions of the military (...) or is apathetic to them".[546]

After the rush of excitement of February, the June coup was perhaps hardest on the Communists. They had survived, almost unscathed, while around them the Tupamaros were annihilated, the Colorados fragmented, and the Nationalists defeated. Party chief Rodney Arismendi's plan for taking power had been hatched almost two decades before, in 1955, and he was never closer to his objective than in the first half of 1973. His hope was to sit out all the confrontations and deploy his many assets at the critical moment. Alas, it was not to be. The Communists were furiously persecuted, and Arismendi was reduced to living a clandestine life until the inevitable moment of his capture.

Everything happened so fast that, outside of the politicians, few knew what sense to make of it all. The unique mindset of the military is perhaps revealed in its official chronology of the period. The entry for June 27 1973 reads "neutralization of the political front [of subversion], prohibition of its activities and dissolution of the Parliament on grounds of its degree of infiltration". That was all: the Parliament was one more target in the counterinsurgency campaign to rescue Uruguay from itself.

Epilogue: A Fatherland for None

"In war the result is never final" - Carl von Clausewitz[547]

The Aftermath

THE DICTATORSHIP THAT began in Uruguay in June of 1973 lasted until March of 1985. It was one in a number of military regimes in the region.

Less than three months after the Uruguayan coup, Chile had its own. It was far more dramatic and violent. It involved the use of aerial bombings and a complete military assault on the country's political institutions, which included the siege of the elected president, Salvador Allende, and his desperate death by suicide.

The Chilean coup and the military dictatorship that followed have always been tied to a single man, and for good reason: Augusto Pinochet. As the commander of the military, Pinochet was the decisive figure behind the coup, and remained the undisputed dictator of the country for nearly two decades. The general took total control of the country, and used it to wipe out the old Chile and replace it with his own. In total, Pinochet's dictatorship is estimated to have killed close to 3,200 people.

In 1976 the commanders of the Argentine armed forces staged a coup d'état; the dictatorship of their *junta* lasted until 1983. The regime of Jorge Videla, Emilio Massera, and others was even more violent than Chile's. Its "death flights" over the Atlantic became particularly infamous; a few Uruguayans living in exile in Buenos Aires were caught up in them and met grisly deaths. Although most estimates of the number of killed between 1976 and 1983 are politically manipulated, the more solid ones suggest close to 9,000 people "disappeared" in the killing machine of the Argentine military and police.

The Southern Cone thus touched rock bottom in the 1970s. It was not alone; violence there paled in comparison with other parts of the Americas where true strife took place: 200,000 dead in Guatemala, 70,000 in El Salvador; 30,000 in Nicaragua, and an unknown number in Colombia. Guatemala's dictator, Efraín Ríos Montt, in the words of historian Hal Brands, "made even Pinochet and Videla seem like dilettantes".[548] What this context serves to show is that, in the greater picture, *golpistas* like Bordaberry, Álvarez, Cristi, or Trabal were minor fare.

Uruguay was the opposite of Chile in that no single man ever led its dictatorship.[549] President Juan María Bordaberry was the nominal figurehead, although he and everyone else knew real power lay in the hands of the generals. The president had by 1973 developed a full-blown ideological construct for a new Uruguay, heavily inspired by turgid, ultra-conservative Hispanic politics. With obvious deference to the dying regime of Francisco Franco, Bordaberry argued for the dismantlement of Uruguayan liberal democracy. This was to include the abolition of political parties and of the Parliament, and their replacement by a system led by unelected, conservative civilians working with the military.

Bordaberry did not stop there. He also defended the view that the real ill that had befallen Uruguay was a conspiracy on the part of Freemasons, Communists, international capitalists, and others. Only the Jews were missing, although they would never be too far. These ignorant ramblings later led Bordaberry to conclude that Uruguay's whole decade of chaos was simply an internal conflict between Marxist-leaning freemasons and capitalist-leaning freemasons.

This ideology placed the once timid and mysterious Bordaberry as one of the most radical and authoritarian political figures in Uruguayan history. Not a single one of the top generals or admirals serving in the *junta* agreed with his ideas. In fact, most of them –particularly General Gregorio Álvarez- saw the military's intervention as an interregnum after which liberal democracy, cleansed of malign influences, should be restored.

Tensions flourished in 1976, when the time for constitutionally-mandated elections came up. The military ran out of patience with Bordaberry's bizarre proposals to throw the entire system out the window, and in a curt message let him know that he had been fired and replaced by the vice president. A civilian named Aparicio Méndez was placed as figurehead president in what was now a mostly ceremonial position. Once Méndez's term was up, it was Gregrio Álvarez himself who took the long-sought mantle of president. Fearful for his life, Álvarez rode in the presidential limousine with an Uzi sub-machine gun next to him. The phantom of the Tupamaros lurked.

During the long years of dictatorship Uruguayan civil society essentially lay dormant. They were years of quietness on the security front and modest economic growth, although most of the latter evaporated in a financial crash in 1982. Top politicians from the past, like Jorge Batlle, Julio Sanguinetti, Wilson Ferreira or Líber Seregni were either in exile, in prison, or silenced. Seregni was forced to endure the humiliation of torture and incarceration, at the hands of his former subordinates, well into the 1970s.

Wilson Ferreira evaded the persecution of the Uruguayan regime from his exile in Buenos Aires. When in 1976 the Argentine military staged its coup d'état, he fled once again. His new choice of home in exile was curious: London. Senator Ferreira thus joined a long list of individuals who benefited from Britain's generous liberal traditions, irrespective of his politics. Wilson remained in London until 1984, when he returned to Montevideo.

Other politicians were not as lucky in surviving persecution. On May 21 1976, a car was found in Buenos Aires with four Uruguayans dead inside. They were William Whitelaw and Rosario Barredo -leaders of the MLN's exiled Argentine cell-, plus former lawmakers Héctor Gutiérrez and Zelmar Michelini. The former had served as Speaker of the House of Representatives. Michelini was a key founder of the Frente Amplio. Both men had collaborated extensively with the Tupamaros during the final years of the insurgency, and benefitted from money the MLN stole in its various robberies. Responsibility for the deaths of the four Uruguayans remains unknown.

The Communist Party tried, as was the norm per Soviet instructions, to continue operating clandestinely in order to attempt a return to power. However, in May 1974 a police investigation conducted by Víctor Castiglioni penetrated the Party's security. Once again, police intelligence and SID combined their efforts and executed a plan codenamed Operation Morgan. Castiglioni personally arrested Arismendi in an apartment. He was sitting on a bed, unarmed, wearing a wig and a fake beard.

Arismendi only spent seven months in custody; he was then cleared to leave Uruguay for exile. His chosen destination was once again a statement in itself. Latin America's most influential chief of a Communist Party chose Moscow, not Havana. The reason Arismendi was treated leniently, according to Gregorio Álvarez, is that he betrayed all of his comrades by giving up the Party's secret files, detailing all its activities, facilities, and codenames.* This was the true purpose of Operation Morgan. With the new information, the police dismantled the Communists' secret guerrilla force. It was a stunning find, one that was only forgotten in the historical record because it took place entirely under an authoritarian military regime.

The Communist militia had more firepower than the MLN ever did. While the Tupamaros had barely acquired a small number of AR-15 assault rifles after assaulting the naval academy, the force commanded by Aurelio Pérez and Iván Altesor had six hundred of them, fresh off a Soviet-brokered Vietnamese shipment of captured American arms, dropped off the coast of Maldonado. In addition to this they had a small ship, an airplane, and improvised weapons factories producing mortars and other combat systems. The quality of the Communists' training, their clandestine medical and logistical facilities, and so forth, were similarly remarkable thanks to direct Cuban and Soviet aid.

Thus, Arismendi's private army was dismantled before it fired a shot. In pursuing the remnants of the Communists and other Marxist organizations the military regime committed some of its greatest abuses, and "disappeared" a number of individuals that reaches close to one hundred. According to former officers now on trial for those crimes, 80% of those who "disappeared" were Communists.

The MLN was never re-activated. It was simply too fragmented, too depleted of resources, and in general defeated. A secret treasury continued to exist in exile. The money stash or stashes of the Tupamaros remained a mythical issue for years: the military estimated that between 1966 and 1973 the group stole approximately $60 million in 2014 dollars. During the years of exile,

* Later on, in 2008, President Tabaré Vázquez returned those files to the party.

Tupas added to this with proceeds from kidnappings in Argentina and Europe.

On December 19 1974, Ramón Trabal was shot six times while pulling into the garage of his apartment building in Paris. He died immediately, and his was the most prominent assassination of any figure tied to Uruguay's military dictatorship.

As the former chief of SID and a top architect of the dictatorship imposed in 1973, Trabal was a singularly important person. Soon after the coup he fell out of favor and was skipped for promotion from colonel to general. In the internal power disputes that were taking place, the socialist-leaning wing he championed lost to the conservative-nationalist one that Aguerrondo, Chiappe, and now generals Esteban Cristi and Luis Queirolo helmed. With Bordaberry fully on board with the latter, the hardcore nationalists won. Gregorio Álvarez, however, remained as the country's top military officer, alone in his nationalist-socialist beliefs.

Trabal's consolation prize, after this political defeat, was getting sent to Europe as military attaché. Although he specifically asked for London, he was instead sent to Paris - a destination he feared because in 1974 it was a hotbed of terrorist activity. Shot through the open window of the driver's seat, Trabal was unable to react at all, despite his being armed and having repeatedly expressed a fear of being killed. Days later, an organization never heard of before or since, the *Brigada Internacional Raúl Sendic*, called Agence France Presse and claimed responsibility for the hit. The group said it was French, and that it was acting out of solidarity with Uruguay's people and its iconic *guerrilleros*, victims of a regime Trabal obviously incarnated.

The night of Trabal's death, in Soca, Uruguay, the military murdered five Tupamaros in its custody in cold blood, as retaliation for what it imagined was a "hit" by the MLN in exile. Although multiple theories have been thrown about, particularly by conspiracy-minded members and sympathizers of the MLN, the only serious investigation of the attack has concluded that it was indeed European *guerrilleros* who killed Trabal.

The Hostages

The fate of the MLN in Uruguay deserves special mention. For the duration of the dictatorship, the military chose nine

Tupamaros for differential treatment from the hundreds who languished in prisons. The nine were split equally into three groups, and always placed in solitary cells close to each other. For over a decade, the three trios cycled throughout various military facilities, in secret, as the armed forces' warranty against new uprisings.

The first group was made up of the MLN's main "star", Raúl Sendic, along with fellow founder Julio Marenales and young gunman Jorge Zabalza.[550]

Sendic was slowly recovering from the damage to his mouth caused by the bullets that pierced it in September of 1972. Immediately following his bloody brush with death, which left considerable amounts of blood and skin in the shot-up safe house, the Tupamaro was subjected to four hours of surgery. For one portion of the procedure, he had to stand up while undergoing a tracheotomy, in order to avoid asphyxiation, and benefitted only from localized anesthetics. Sendic lost every tooth and the tonsils on one side of his face, as well as seven centimeters of jawbone - reconstructed with grafts from his ribs. His tongue and gums in particular sustained serious damage, ravaged yet preserved. The first person to see him after learning of his survival, his girlfriend Xenia Itté, could only see his eyes, welling up in tears, through the many bandages covering his head.

Between the wounds and the imprisonment, Sendic was probably the prisoner who suffered the most. This was no coincidence: the most iconic, the most unpredictable of Tupamaros, the one that most resembled an impetuous wild horse, was bound to be the most oppressed by his new dwelling. Sendic, Marenales, and Zabalza were kept prisoner in terrible conditions, and their location was changed every couple of years from one military base to another. This "tour" included five winters at the most dreadful location of all: the underground cells of Paso de los Toros.

Built inside an emptied horse-watering pool, the cells were makeshift constructions covered by an enormous steel plate (in fact, an old American wartime Bailey bridge). All the prisoners could see was the concrete stairwell the guards used to descend to check on them. The three Tupamaros spent up to forty days without bathing or fifteen days bound with ropes on a row, and had paltry rations of food and water. Information was scant, if there was any at all: many knew that Salvador Allende had been toppled in 1973, but did not learn he died on the day of the coup until 1984. One night, a guard had the deference of informing Zabalza that "he" had won in Viet Nam.

Sendic and Marenales were men of forceful character, and Zabalza was not intimidated despite his younger age. The three fought with each other often. To vent their anger and spend their time, the three Tupamaros held debates in tiny letters they left for each other in the shared bathroom. Topics ranged from whether Uruguay's indigenous Charrúas were Melanesian or Polynesian in origin to various aspects of the Skylab space station, complete with drawings. Furious arguments ensued on the Skylab issue, to the point where the three did not speak to each other for weeks. Reality and sanity became malleable concepts.

Each prisoner experienced his own version of suffering. Marenales defied his captors again and again: "I would shower without a care in the world - I looked at them as I rinsed my testicles". Zabalza's father, the former senator, had to go through humiliating situations to see his son.

Sendic had frequent temper tantrums that went from kicking the doors of the cells -he broke several- to punching dentists in the face. Sessions with the latter were excruciating, given the delicate condition of his mouth: he would often be returned to his cell kicking and screaming, howling in anger at one or another slight, and immediately resuming his furious protests upon being dumped back in his hole. The guards provoked him by waking him up, removing any privacy barriers when he was showering, forcing him to bend over naked to pick up a pair of handcuffs with which to bind himself, forcing him to defecate in a bucket, inside his cell, for a full week, and more.

Marenales and Zabalza did all they could to calm Sendic down and help him preserve his energies. Later in his incarceration, fearful of going insane, Sendic used more permissive conditions to read books on mental illnesses and to practice handcrafting with the sculptor Marenales ("El Bebe would make horrendous pendants out of bone, and then he'd give them away to the soldiers and they'd be happy as clams").

The next triad of Tupamaros especially held by the military was made up of Eleuterio Fernández, José Mujica and Mauricio Rosencof.[551] Perhaps the three most famous Tupamaros in contemporary Uruguay, all have since documented their experiences there. Although in isolation from each other, the three were treated equally: frequent beatings, underfed, cramped, unable to see the sunlight, and more.

Rosencof has extensively discussed his hallucinations resulting from extended hours of solitary confinement. He and Fernández Huidobro have also written about their secret communications across cells, mainly through the development of a Morse code of sorts. The two men attempted all sorts of things to try to gain control over their own fate. Rosencof acted as if he were physically and psychologically ill - in other words, like he was sick and crazy, wetting himself in the process. Later on, the Tupamaro formerly known as Lionel performed small services for his guards in the form of ghostwriting poems and love letters to their girlfriends. Each successful letter got Rosencof slightly better treatment, although he claims he was treated worse than the others for being Jewish.

Eleuterio Fernández Huidobro tried faking an ulcer. His letters to his partner Nelly Jorge (who was in prison herself) revealed some of the small torments he had to endure. On one occasion, he was given a rare, single glass of water to drink. At the time he had been going two months without a shower, so Fernández chose to save half of the glass to bathe. To do this he soaked a handkerchief in the water and slowly slid it across his body. Once he was finished, Fernández's guards summoned him for a shower; it was the kind of thing that drove a man crazy. To this most loquacious of Tupamaros, the worst of all punishments was isolation.

José Mujica also had it rough: he claims he spent two years without bathing. Pepe never participated in the coded exchanges across the cells. The reason was that he lost his mind. Just like Fernández and Rosencof, Pepe began to talk to himself in the cell, in order to hear the sound of his own voice. He also developed hallucinations about military microphones and recorders secretly kept somewhere in his cell. The Tupamaro fell into a state of paranoia, "hearing" the static of the recording devices and yelling for the guards to turn them off so he could sleep.

Mujica was also in pain from the bullet wounds and beatings sustained in recent years, not to mention the torture that left him with permanent physical impediments. According to Rosencof, "Pepe had long lost track of the frontier between reality and imagination (...) It was a horrible thing to witness". Whenever the cells were shuffled and Mujica was placed in the one between Fernández and Rosencof, the two healthier Tupas decried their bad luck, for they were effectively cut off from each other. With the passage of the years -a decade of physical and psychological abuse-, he was left practically toothless. Later on in their imprisonment, when conditions improved, Mujica was allowed to read and to plant small patches of vegetables. He chose books on the natural sciences and on agronomy.

The final triad of captives was made up of latter-day MLN leader Henry Engler, along with Adolfo Wasem and founder Jorge Manera.[552] Engler suffered greatly in prison, both as a result of his own pathologies and of the "special" treatment he received as a militaristic and action-prone Tupamaro. The *guerrillero* known as Octavio became convinced that the military doctors who removed bullets from his body also inserted mind-reading CIA implants. Later, in his own words, he began to believe that "Extraterrestrial beings were sending me messages and taking over my brain". Additionally, he became fully convinced that he was the new Messiah, and that he was in a deathly struggle to control his own thoughts, which he relayed out loud from time to time to his guards. Occasionally ingesting his own refuse, Engler was in deep trauma.

Adolfo Wasem fared worst of all the nine special prisoners: in 1974 he slit his wrists in a failed suicide attempt. A decade later, while still a prisoner, Wasem developed a cancerous tumor that killed him. His letters describe ghastly conditions and foresaw a death in solitude and darkness.[*] Nothing is known of Jorge Manera's experiences in prison.

All three trios spent over a decade rotating among various military bases rather than regular prisons, where all the other Tupas were held. They did have the right to receive visitors, but many desisted due to the shame they felt over their physical condition. The pictures taken upon their liberation leave no question about it: the nine chosen Tupas were held in harsh conditions and with a restricted food supply. All who talked about their experiences described tiny, makeshift cells constructed in ditches in the courtyards of military bases. They rarely saw the sky or had an understanding of their surroundings. When transported, they had a noose hanging around their necks. Other times they were covered

---

* Wasem was transferred to a military hospital shortly before his death. He was allowed one visit from his wife, Sonia Mosquera, who was herself in prison.

from head to toe in large bags, and bound tightly. On occasion they were thrown from helicopters and kicked out of truck beds.

The Followers

Internationally, during the period when the Tupamaros were in prison, a large number of Western terrorist organizations clearly inspired by them emerged. The MLN's masterful use of the media and of armed propaganda did not go unnoticed. In their heyday, in the words of the American government, the MLN was considered "one of the best organized and, until recently, the most successful urban terrorist groups in the world".[553] Despite their many imitators, the urban *guerrilleros* of the 1970s displayed far less creativity and more murderous sadism than those of the 1960s.

In the United States, an organization known as the Weather Underground became famous for a series of terrorist attacks. The group's post-1968 -and therefore more radical- inspiration was in evidence in that revolution was not the only reason people joined: "Young couples living in 'Weather collectives' were required to 'smash monogamy' and to reject natural parenthood. The 'Weather Bureau' ordered that all female revolutionaries sleep with all male revolutionaries, and vice versa".[554]

In California, the separate Symbionese Liberation Army announced, upon kidnapping media heiress Patricia Hearst in 1974, that she would be returned to her family if "'quality food' worth $70 per package [was] distributed by Hearst to all people in need in California".[555] It was a "Robin Hood" move, an almost exclusive province of the Uruguayan MLN. Just like the Weathermen, the SLA fizzled and was never heard from again.

Europe saw a greater number of urban guerrillas. The German Rote Armee Fraktion and the Italian Brigate Rosse openly expressed admiration for the MLN and interest in emulating its actions. There was even an organization called Tupamaros-West Berlin. Most of these groups' operations turned out to be crude terrorist acts. Instead of emulating armed propaganda and exposing corruption or other social ills, the excited Europeans simply murdered and bombed.

None of these organizations gained real traction. As noted by terrorism expert Brian Jenkins, "Certainly the Tupamaros have been the most daring of all urban guerrillas, operating with imagination and panache unequalled elsewhere".[556]

It was the Palestinian *fedayeen* who dominated global headlines from the 1970s onward, in a way the Tupamaros or other groups never did. The spectacular airplane hijackings and other terrorist attacks of these groups caught the attention of the world, and considerable sympathy. However, decades have passed without any real solution to the sovereignty problem of the Palestinian people.

The Restoration

During the early 1980s, new generations of politicians slowly emerged in the quieter sections of the banned political parties. The leadership of these clandestine entities made a point of meeting semi-publicly at Montevideo's top restaurants, to ensure people could see the old flame of party politics was alive, somewhere.[557]

In 1984, the Uruguayan dictatorship knew its time was up. This was, after all, a country that did not coexist easily with military rule. Negotiations between the armed forces and the resuscitated political parties converged towards presidential and legislative elections set for late that year. Politicians who had been found guilty of being involved in "subversion" were banned from running for president. This included Wilson Ferreira, Líber Seregni and Jorge Batlle. Therefore, the decisive figure became the Colorado Julio Sanguinetti, a smart and articulate man unstained by the slimy politics of the pre-dictatorship era.

After winning the election, Sanguinetti was inaugurated as president in March of 1985. Days later, all "political" prisoners were freed, including all Tupamaros. The new president signed a blanket amnesty that applied indistinctly of the crimes committed by each individual.

The most prominent people to be freed were the *rehenes* or hostages. On the day of their liberation, the MLN organized a press conference. All were present except for Adolfo Wasem, who had died the previous year, and Raúl Sendic. Eleuterio Fernández read a declaration in name of the eight, one which reflected the thinking that Sendic had transmitted to them in the preceding months: the age of insurgency was over. The Tupamaros would not seek violent revenge over the events of the past. Instead, they would turn the page and join in the normal exercise of democratic politics. There would be, as he put it, no aces up their sleeves.[558]

Only a leader like Sendic could have decided on such a radical and clear-cut change of identity.* Every single one of the other top Tupamaros except for Henry Engler disagreed, at times strongly, with this idea. Once again consolidated as the true leader of the Tupamaros, El Bebe remained a withdrawn, reserved man. This was far more the case after leaving prison, for the injuries to his face never truly healed. Outside of his family and his partner Xenia Itté, Sendic only granted access to one Tupamaro: Eleuterio Fernández Huidobro.[559]

The MLN leader was unable to speak adequately or make himself understood, and sought corrective surgery to fix the problem. He got what he needed in Cuba, along with a warm reception from Fidel Castro. Sendic then spent an entire year in the island and traveling in the free countries of Europe, finally returning to Uruguay in 1987.

In December of that year the icon of the Tupamaros gave the first and only public speech of his life. The recorded images -the only ones on video in existence of Sendic- show a man with a quiet confidence and inscrutable expression, with a voice that was famously timid before and was now crippled by pain. Outwardly, none of the injuries show: Sendic's appearance is that of a gentle-spoken artist or grandfather, with white hair and a white beard. Around the time of this speech Sendic also granted a rare and brief interview to the New York Times, in which he made it clear that originally there was no intention of murdering Dan Mitrione. El Bebe also refrained from calling Mitrione a torturer.[560]

The Fate of the Tupamaros

Soon after the restoration of liberty a few divisions emerged in the MLN, and four types of Tupamaros emerged. The first was the exiles. Many never returned to Uruguay. Others, like Henry Engler, left the country immediately after their liberation. Once the epitome

---

* At the time, Sanguinetti told his security team that the safety of two individuals was paramount in the new Uruguay. One was Gregorio Álvarez; the other was Sendic. If either was harmed by avengers for his enemy's side, there was no telling how conflagrations would explode again.

of MLN militarism, Engler experienced dramatic changes, not least his acknowledgment and contrition over his role in some of the Tupamaros' gravest actions, including the murders of Roque Arteche and Pascasio Báez.

After losing his mind in prison, Octavio had trouble adjusting to life in freedom. One of his difficulties was his inability to "process" colors -in people's clothes, in nightclubs, in the stars above his head- adequately. The former medicine student thus chose immediate exile to Sweden, where he still lives. While there Engler got married and resumed his medicine studies, naturally as the oldest of the students in his class. Decades later he is a repentant, religious, soft-spoken, and accomplished medical researcher. He does not, however, renege from his choice to be a Tupamaro.[561]

Reflecting upon the "militarist" career that gave him his reputation for violence, Engler admits "in the toughest periods I increasingly hardened myself as a person, and lost much of that humane tenderness that had once been the most important thing, and which drove me to the MLN. It is very, very difficult to harden oneself without losing one's tenderness". On the specific case of the ranch hand Pascasio Báez, Engler's confession is straightforward: "It was an enormously grave mistake on the part of the organization's leadership (...) I have great responsibility in it".[562]

The second category of Tupamaro is made up of those who never again sought anything to do with the MLN, revolution, or politics in general. This includes the engineer Jorge Manera, by far the most reclusive of the surviving founders of the group.

Of all the men who founded the MLN and made up its historical leadership, El Inge has been the most silent of all. He has given few interviews since 1985; no pictures of him after that date are publicly known. He was the first of the prominent Tupamaros to resign from the MLN -doing so in 1988-, and his actions suggest he has at least in part reneged from his past as a violent insurgent.[563] Countless other Tupamaros of varying degrees of importance in the organization have made the same choice as Manera, and quietly blended in Uruguay's democratic society. They live quasi-anonymous, normal middle-class lives.

The two remaining categories are both made up of men and women who maintained an interest in political activism or agitation after they left prison. One of them is made up of hardline Tupamaros who believe the MLN and its original objectives and methods are as valid as before. They have expressed little regret over major acts of their insurgency, and remain defiant on issues like the bloodiest terrorist attacks of the MLN, or the desirability of preserving individual rights and democracy in Uruguay and other countries. Julio Marenales and Jorge Zabalza are notoriously in this category.

The last group is that of those who did heed Sendic's leadership, and formed a new political grouping inside the restored Frente Amplio. Called Movimiento de Participación Popular (MPP), or Popular Participation Movement, the grouping coalesced around a few key figures. One of them was Eleuterio Fernández Huidobro. However, although Fernández is the most representative Tupamaro of the organization as it was, a different Tupa became the most popular nationwide as a politician. This, unlikely as it may be, is the case of José Mujica. It started when Pepe was asked to front public speaking engagements for the group in the early days after leaving prison. The reason was that he had previous experience speaking in public, unlike many MLN leaders who lacked either the skill or the background in politicking. Sendic, for instance, said "I do not see myself acting in front of a television camera".[564] Other than Mujica, only Fernández Huidobro and Mauricio Rosencof had those skills. At MPP, the man known simply as "Pepe" grew into a successful campaigner and populist brand. His partner, Lucía Topolansky, also joined.

Mujica, Fernández Huidobro, and Topolansky found growing success as members of Parliament in the second half of the 1990s. The old Tupamaros slowly gained popularity in a different Uruguay. Although clearly socialist in their ideology, moderation was there for everyone to see, expressed with the peculiarity that characterized the Tupamaros since their foundation. One video of a Mujica rally shows him saying "One's life is not only offered when holding a rifle in some street corner, in some heroic gesture. Life is also offered in the service, minute after minute, to the cause of the people. That's what a revolutionary attitude is today".[565]

Before this was to happen, the group had to go through what may have been its toughest trial of all: the death of Sendic. Ridden with Charcot disease, which he began to detect in early 1989, Sendic's condition deteriorated quickly. Only four months transpired between his diagnosis and his death in Paris, while pursuing medical treatment. Upon dying on April 28 1989, Sendic had barely had time to organize the Tupamaros' new identity. His 1987 speech remained the only one he gave in public.

The funeral of Raúl Sendic was a moment of deep grief for the Tupamaros. Despite everything that happened, the country unquestionably lost an iconoclast anti-hero with completely original, albeit flawed, ideas. Decades after the event, few if any of the surviving Tupamaros have displayed the same sense of adaptability or austerity that Sendic had.

His last contribution to the MLN-Tupamaros was his decisive moderation of its political strategy, from one that included violent guerrilla warfare to one that did not. Before dying, he capably analyzed the performance of his urban guerrilla force: "we tried to act in consideration of the Uruguayan mentality, keeping violence to a minimum. It was then that we conducted those actions that were so celebrated internationally due to the imagination we applied to avoid violence: the massive prison escape, the takeover of the naval base (...) at a later moment we escalated our violence. We called it the Guatemalization of the guerrilla, and it was exactly what he had originally tried to avoid".[566]

This was not to say the man was perfect. The economic ideas he defended in the restored Uruguayan democracy were illiterate and violently authoritarian: all debt would be canceled, there would be an unlimited printing and distribution of currency, the money and valuables people had deposited in banks would be "expropriated", rural land would be collectivized, and so forth. Although Sendic died on one of humanity's finest years, he did so wrongly convinced that "The world has never seen hunger like the one we see today".[567]

Other icons disappeared from the scene during that time. Wilson Ferreira returned to Montevideo in 1984; he was imprisoned and barred from participating in that year's elections. He died a few years later, still a popular politician in the Partido Nacional, but having never been president of the country. Líber Seregni died in 2004. His leadership waned earlier than that, as all parties including the Frente Amplio gave way to new leaders and policy platforms.

The Partido Colorado has had three governments since 1985: two by Julio Sanguinetti and one by Jorge Batlle. Combining all three terms, they enacted a mix of liberalizing economic policies and free trade but clearly failed to modernize the gargantuan Uruguayan state bureaucracy, or to stop crime and informal, marginal economies from blooming. For many Tupamaros, Batlle and

Sanguinetti remain the *bêtes noires* of an allegedly "oligarchic" Uruguay, most likely because they are some of the few politicians who were active in the 1960s and 1970s and who are clean of any association with both the dictatorship and the MLN.

While the Colorados governed, the other parties evolved. The Partido Nacional changed the greatest, with Luis Lacalle and his liberal wing taking over instead of Wilson's socialist wing. There was one Lacalle presidency in between the two Sanguinetti administrations. The Frente Amplio witnessed the emergence of socialist oncologist and former mayor of Montevideo Tabaré Vázquez as top leader. After many attempts, Vázquez finally changed history when he became the first candidate from the *izquierda* to become president of Uruguay. His term in office began in March of 2005.

The surge of popularity in the Frente Amplio was not limited to Vázquez. To the contrary: the coalition's most voted sub-group in 2005 was the MPP, whose main figure was and is the folksy Mujica. The MPP leader was not the only Tupamaro who made a name for himself during the 1990s and 2000s. Many others, particularly among the other "hostages" became public figures. All of them have benefited from one of Tabaré Vázquez's more unfortunate measures: a law he signed granting pensions for life to members of the MLN, which means men like Ismael Bassini get a lifelong subsidy, while the family of his 1971 victim by lethal injection - Pascasio Báez- remains unrecognized by the national government.[568]

Jorge Zabalza remains the most radical of the well-known Tupamaros. He is the go-to figure for Uruguayan media in search of incendiary, extremist commentary. The son of a former prime minister, Zabalza has been true to his "class suicide", and lives to this day in a modest dwelling close to the slums of Montevideo. His only political position has been in the Montevideo legislative body, where he agreed to name a street after Pascasio Báez.[569]

Mauricio Rosencof became a notorious public figure in Uruguay. He is one of the go-to figures not just of the Tupamaros, but also of the Uruguayan *izquierda.* The man known as El Ruso is also a writer of both prose and poetry, including many books referring to, or conceived in, his long years in prison.

Both of Rosencof's parents, who patiently waited for his liberation, died less than a year after recovering their son in March of 1985. Their story was a sad one: they endured uprooting in

Europe, the annihilation of the extended family in a European genocide, the premature death of the oldest son Lionel, and the near-death experiences of the only son that remained, Mauricio. The Rosencof-Silberman couple ended up living in penury, but did see their son free before dying.[570]

Efraín Martínez Platero spent a long time moving between different countries -Argentina, Chile, Cuba- before finally settling down in Sweden. For a few years he was the MLN's top representative to foreign entities. This allowed him to meet with Salvador Allende (with whom he practiced shooting from the same AK-47 the Chilean later used to commit suicide), Argentina's top terrorist leaders, Fidel Castro, European politicians, representatives of the Algerian and Libyan regimes (the former offered only moral support, while "the Libyans were eager to join anything that involved mayhem and guerrilla warfare") and more. Allende in particular wanted the MLN to share its best security protocols with him and his entourage.[571]

In the end, after decades in Sweden, Martínez's outlook became far more moderate. He did not return to Uruguay in 1985, but rather in 1995, a full decade after the restoration of democracy. Upon his return, he was a virtual unknown: he had not written as much as Fernández and Rosencof; he did not have Mujica's galloping political career, nor the legends that had been built around characters like Sendic. Nevertheless, Efraín Martínez Platero became perhaps the most reliable former MLN source in providing information to journalists and investigators. In the present days, he relays the purpose of the MLN thus: "We were fighting for a very abstract objective, which was the possibility that Uruguay could achieve happiness. We fought for happiness for this country, for development, for the poorest people".[572]

Julio Marenales did not have the remarkable post-prison career of Fernández Huidobro, Mujica, and others. He nevertheless remains a point of reference when it comes to the Tupamaros, mainly by sheer force of will and consistency. He acquired the nickname "the Taliban", for his hardline statements supporting dictatorial regimes in the Americas, and has repeatedly called for abolitions of property and liberties.

Additionally, Marenales complains about the excessive attention given by the MLN's veterans and historians to the issue of torture. As one of the strongest and most inclined to resist, not to mention the first one to be tormented by the police as early as 1964, his shot directed at the other *guerrilleros* is clear: "I find the cult of martyrdom that is being practiced to be obnoxious (...) I would say torture in Uruguay was not that harsh".[573]

Eleuterio Fernández Huidobro is the most difficult of all Tupamaros to pin down. The MLN founder retains brilliant rhetoric, a flair for writing, and an irresistible sense of humor. However, his statements display constant alternations between introspective honesty and deceitful propaganda.

Fernández ended up being a representative, a senator, and lastly a minister in the same democratic, republican system he set out to destroy. The man who confesses to thinking he would be young forever, the very embodiment of 1960s radicalism, now tells his interviewers that his latest thoughts are simply "Holy shit, I'm a minister".[574] One of the most stirring political advertisements ever shown on Uruguayan television shows Mujica presiding over the Senate, summoning an emotional Senator Fernández Huidobro to take his oath of office: "Life has these tumbles. This is the game we play now. Not even the greatest novelist could have imagined these things. *Compañero del alma de todas las horas*, come take my oath".[575]

Fernández's criticisms of practical Communism ("socialism cannot consist of transforming the country into a large public office"), as well as of the Soviet Union ("22 million dead: a genocide") and even the sacred cow of Cuba ("That's not socialism; that's nothing"), are revealing. As part of these reflections, he has given perhaps the best summary of the Tupamaros' journey from insurgents to democratic politicians: "Power does not lie where we thought it did in the 1960s: in the barracks, in guns. It lies in the heart and the conscience of the people".[576]

The story of the defector Héctor Amodio continued to slowly evolve with the passing of the years. After 1985, he failed to return to newly free Uruguay or to make his name or location known. Interviewers asked, journalists investigated, and military officers remained mum. No one knew where he was. In the 1990s and 2000s, books and articles began to be published about the legend of Amodio Pérez. Leading Tupamaros acknowledged having sentenced him to death in absentia, and to having sent assassination squads to find and eliminate him in Europe. Solitary testimonies emerged of people who claimed to have seen Amodio walking the streets of

Madrid, and in turn of the pursued *guerrillero*'s detection of the surveillance and escape, possibly to France.[577]

Everything that was said about Amodio came, however, from only one shore of the Atlantic. In 1982, the former Tupamaro's mother died. Her oldest son was not there to say goodbye - but his handwriting was noticeable in the floral wreath laid at the house's doorstep. Something similar happened when his name appeared first in the list of grievers who paid for an obituary upon the death of the family patriarch in 2009. Héctor Amodio Pérez was alive, somewhere.[578]

Other Tupamaros never reached the prominence of the leaders or the "historicals", but nevertheless deserve mention. Antonio Mas Mas, who was never an MLN leader, became well known for his much-publicized role in murdering Dan Mitrione. The military also pinned on him the assassinations of policemen Héctor Morán Charquero (in the road ambush of 1970) and Germán Garay, as well as of numerous other victims. In prison, the guards gave Mas Mas one of the worst treatments of all prisoners. According to Samuel Blixen, every single night his guards knocked loudly on his door, interrupting his sleep with taunts.[579]

He in turn liked being provocative: from aiming an imaginary weapon at his guards and "firing" it to shouting about how he had killed Mitrione and was ready to do it again, Mas Mas's descent into bitter madness was not a pretty sight. Out of prison in 1985 he sounded defiant, saying what the MLN ordered were "executions" rather than murders. However, inside he was a broken man, tormented by guilt and the intensity of everything that happened. Mas Mas left for Spain and died a street sweeper in 2002.[580]

Yessie Macchi was an iconic Tupamara given her physical attractiveness and her status as a strong female *guerrillera.* She was wounded in her 1972 arrest, a time in which she also lost her life partner, Leonel Martínez, and the baby she was carrying in her womb. Later on, she was tortured. During her custody, "In the rotation across the bases, officers harassed me, because I was the best-known female member of the MLN, and because I had several charges of murder in the books. Nevertheless, there was something worse: a kind of lasciviousness, which led to them constantly hitting on me (...) This relationship between a torturer and a woman, which was fed by a sort of legend that emerged around my femininity, led to a series of gropings and very raw attempts [at sexual abuse]". In fact, Macchi is the only Tupamara to have openly revealed she was raped while in military custody.[581]

After leaving jail she stayed mostly off the radar in comparison with other Tupamaros, although she remained one of the better-known female ones. In interviews she never relented in the opinions she held since the 1960s, and like Jorge Zabalza confessed to having killed as part of her operations. She died in 2009.[582] A daughter she conceived while in captivity was named Paloma.

Column 15 Tupamaro Samuel Blixen became an important journalist in Uruguay's radical Marxist media. His excellent work as the author of the best biography of Raúl Sendic is stained by his ideological, fact-free journalism. Blixen also believes political violence is more justified in the twenty-first century than it was in the 1960s.[583]

Raúl Bidegain, once the most famous of the MLN's guerrilla fighters, was never heard from again, and died in 1989. His brother, who had such a curious and creative role in Raúl's escape from Punta Carretas in 1971, is a demographer at the United Nations.

Carlos Koncke ended up in Mozambique, fighting on the Communist side of that country's civil war. Fernando Garín, the cadet who was essential in Sendic's assault of the naval academy, left the country in 1972 and never returned. He died in Leuven, Belgium, in August of 2012.[584] Jorge Torres, a founding member of the MLN and a top developer of its urban guerrilla doctrine, died in 2008. Before his death he penned a scathing critique of the MLN's strategic failure.

Fernando Secco, the friendliest businessman in Uruguay to the Tupamaros, fully recovered from his detention and continued to run the country's main meatpacking company. In more recent times, the family sold the company to a larger Brazilian conglomerate - one more example of the "foreign-ization" of the Uruguayan economy that the Tupamaros so opposed.

The Rise of Pepe

On the day of his liberation, José Mujica left prison with one object in hand: the pink chamber pot he had carried from one hole to the other, which in his final months had turned into an improvised marigold flower pot.[585] Beginning then, he became the most important Tupamaro post-1985. This was despite having achieved leadership positions only in the final months of the insurgency. In the Uruguayan democratic spring he displayed more talent than everyone else at organizing the new identity of the group.

While Marenales, Zabalza, and Fernández Huidobro often looked like crackpot cold warriors filled with resentment over the past, Mujica traveled the country and developed a politicking style that was down to earth, attentive to what people had to say, and plain. A photograph of him attending a meeting presided by Sendic, at UTAA headquarters of all places, best captures what happened: Mujica became the spiritual successor to El Bebe. Many of the traits that once made the latter an iconic leader emerged in the former. As described by Samuel Blixen, in "exchanges over what is quotidian and trivial, he gained an often inexplicable unconditional support, all without setting out to do so". This is a description of Raúl Sendic, not of José Mujica - but it clearly defines the instinctive, singular form of charisma they shared and led with in their own time.

Upon the death of Sendic, Mujica embodied the redeemed Tupamaro: the fighter for social justice who had dreamed of national liberation in the 1960s, failed in his honest attempt, and paid for it with terrible prison conditions. Now back in society, he was the ultimate man of the people: poor, humble, simple. All Mujica talked about was how to improve the lot of the poor, plank by plank, cinder block by cinder block.

Leaving prison also allowed Mujica to reunite with Lucía Topolansky, who spent the entire dictatorship behind bars with the rest of a sizable contingent of Tupamaras. Once the couple accumulated some savings -combining their work, international donations and, most likely, MLN funds-, they acquired a small, fourteen-hectare *chacra*, or farm, in an area in the outskirts of Montevideo known as Rincón del Cerro. The property, which is registered to Topolansky and is called Puebla, is mostly dedicated to growing flowers for sale in the markets of Montevideo - just as Mujica did in his childhood and teenage years with his mother. It is also a shared space: other families live on the premises. Beyond Puebla lie the fields of other properties and a dirt road that passes through poor areas before reaching the city.

Meetings with the politician Pepe Mujica were not speeches, but rather shared *mateadas*, -an early insistence of Raúl Sendic for his own meetings since the days of the Bella Unión labor movement. Every attendant -and virtually anyone *could* attend- saw how Mujica dressed and lived in modest conditions. The MPP *caudillo* worked for a living, and gave most of his lawmaker's salary back to the MPP, the MLN, and the Frente Amplio treasuries. His aphorisms and statements to the media, in particular, became legendary. Mujica picked up on Sendic's style, his silences, his musings on consumption-driven society, his plans to end *latifundismo* in Uruguay and invest in regions far from Montevideo, and plenty more.

The first collective memories of Mujica as a national political figure hail from 1996, when he campaigned against the privatization of state power company UTE. He did so by boarding the city's public buses and appealing to the passengers for their support in a public referendum. Soon enough, he gained coverage in the media, and his unique manner of speaking made him an appealing radio and television personality. In a 2001 interview he confessed he still carried a gun with him on the streets.

Mujica's lack of a formal education mattered little in his becoming a firebrand politician, and in fact became an advantage. A master populist with a slurred, streetwise speech that remains incomprehensible to most foreigners and to many Uruguayans, Mujica seeks to represent the most common and modest-salaried of all citizens in the country. Unlike other populists in the continent, he puts his money where his mouth is. During the 1990s he became famous for riding to Parliament, as an elected representative, in a motorcycle, or in a battered Volkswagen Beetle, or by bus. He often sported a denim jacket.

Mujica has been the Tupamaro most publicly forgiving of the military and its many abuses, be they directed at himself or at others. In fact, he has confessed to feeling proud of his country's military, even while he was in their custody. In one occasion in 1982, during the Falklands War, an Argentine military officer visited the cells where Mujica and other Tupamaros were held. The visitor remarked how in his country these prisoners would have long been underwater rather than kept alive in prisons. The Uruguayan officer's proud rejection of such criminal possibilities made Mujica feel proud himself.

The Tupamaro formerly known as Facundo and Ulpiano has colorfully illustrated many aspects of the MLN's insurgency and what happened around it. On fighting as a *guerrillero* he recognized "A revolutionary feels fear, just like everybody else". Like Marenales, Mujica prefers to skip over the details and the seriousness of the torture he suffered: "I'm not fond of talking about torture and about how bad I had it. I am even annoyed by it, because on occasion I have witnessed a sort of race measured with a 'torture-o-meter'".

The MPP was born as a minor subdivision of the Frente Amplio, but Mujica and his faction rose symbiotically in share of the vote with every election after 1995. The Frente leadership had normally been the dominion of a certain type of "*izquierdista*". Uruguay's intellectual and well-educated middle classes dominated the Socialist and Communist Parties that made up the core of the coalition. Its presidential candidates had first been Líber Seregni -a general- and later Tabaré Vázquez, also an accomplished medical doctor (and an oncologist at that). A third pillar in the Frente's history was and is Danilo Astori, a Social Democrat with impeccable non-violent credentials who in 2005 became Vázquez's quasi-prime minister and director of the Frente Amplio's moderate economic policies.

In March of 2010, after winning a national election the previous November, Mujica was inaugurated as Vázquez's successor. He was the first populist president for many decades in Uruguay, as well as by far the least educated in almost all of its history. Still, his margin of victory in the election was essentially as large as that of Vázquez: a full half of electors voted for him. Flanking Mujica were the new "first lady" Lucía Topolansky, who was also the country's most voted senator, and his future Minister of National Defense, Eleuterio Fernández Huidobro. The Tupamaros had come full circle, in a turn of events that has rarely been seen in the history of insurgencies or revolutions. In Mujica's view, "We did not make it to the presidency because of what we did in the past. That would be false. We made it because of what we are doing now, and maybe because our past has been forgiven. Maybe it has not been given much importance".

As president, Mujica has starred in inevitable disappointments and contradictions. At the same time, he has also let loose on his best, and healthiest, libertarian instincts. Under his presidency Uruguay has legalized egalitarian marriage -meaning homosexuals now have the same civil rights as heterosexuals- and has signed the most important drug legalization law in modern history -an Eleuterio Fernández idea, according to the president himself. He has also signed a law allowing the abortion of unwanted pregnancies in the first trimester, although naturally that is a separate, more controversial issue.

This program is based on the MPP's brand of socialism, which has been described as follows: "There is a certain mentality in this country. We do not live in a society that has a Tsarist past, as was the case with the Soviet Union, nor one presided by Mandarins as China had been. We have a strong-rooted democratic tradition in the mentality of the people, a tradition of liberties, and we need to adapt socialism to Uruguay's reality. A form of socialism that is compatible with that tradition, which we may call libertarian, of the Uruguayan people". These words came out of Raúl Sendic's mouth in 1987, but Mujica could have uttered them at any time during his presidency.

Mujica, Global Star

During the second half of his administration Mujica unexpectedly became a global pop icon of sorts. His speeches at various international fora and his television interviews with media from all over the world went "viral" numerous times.[586] It is easy to see why: whatever his flaws, Mujica's brand of austere, philosophical and meditative leadership is remarkably unusual. While presidents, prime ministers, monarchs and despots around the world parade in expensive clothes, abusive security details and decadent, self-important customs, Mujica continues to live in the Puebla farmhouse. His bed is unmade: he serves journalists water in old liquid cheese glasses, as Uruguayans love to do, and shares his secret tomato sauce with them. As he himself said at the United Nations, "Republican governments should increasingly resemble their peoples in the way they live".

This newly discovered charm has led him to meetings with Barack Obama, Jorge Bergoglio -the Argentine turned Pope Francis-, George Soros, David Rockefeller, Ricky Martin, Sean Penn, the rock band Aerosmith, and numerous others.

Mujica's opinions on everything have become highly quotable, on many topics. His meditations on the 1960s and the long road of the *guerrillero* are particularly notable. In 2013, in Havana of all places, he said the true revolutionary, violent or non-violent, must "Start all over a thousand times (...) Social change is not just around the corner". His generation, he said, "Filled itself with Quixote. We dreamed that in fifteen or twenty years it was possible to create an entirely different society - and we crashed into history". One time he put it this way: "I belong to a generation that sought to change the world. I was defeated, crushed, pulverized". However, "If there were no dreamers in this world we would still be walking around the jungle wearing a loincloth". Thus, he continues to define himself as a "fighter. Feverish with dreams" and "I am still a Tupamaro. I never stopped being one. A Tupamaro is someone who rebels against injustice". Being a *guerrillero* is not so much about killing others, he has said, but rather about having the courage to die. Even at the podium of the United Nations General Assembly, Mujica raised the oldest flag of the MLN: "I carry with me the duty of fighting for a fatherland for all".

On topics beyond revolution, Mujica has also surprised many with his romantic musings. During the same Havana speech he said "Mankind will emerge from pre-history the day military barracks become schools and universities". He has openly called himself an atheist, and in one interview slipped in another historical MLN banner: "Republics came to this world to show that no one is more than anybody else".* On relations with Brazil and other countries, he said with a smirk "No one is going to fear Uruguayan imperialism". On the vicissitudes of life: "In life we must learn to carry a backpack full of pain - but also not to live looking at the backpack". On modern life: "There is a form of solitude in the middle of our great cities that bites, that hurts".

Even as president, Mujica continues to have lunch at modest eateries, chat with historians at his favorite bars, walk the streets of Montevideo to hand out leaflets on violence against women, work in his farm and, quite famously, donate over 80% of his salary to a housing program for the poor. To those paying attention, Mujica has acknowledged much of this does have its origins in his days as a Tupamaro. As he told a CNN interviewer: "It is very likely that I would not think this way if I had not been through what I endured".

Outside of the Tupamaros, the tables have turned for many of the individuals involved in the revolutionary conflict of the 1960s and 1970s. Almost everyone who was their enemy has since met a neutral or a negative fate. Jorge Pacheco, for example, died in the

---

* Mujica repeated the "Naides es más que naides" line, in its slang original, in a major interview with Spanish public television, TVE.

late 1990s, full of pride over his administration and accompanied by a few hardcore followers. His name remains severely stained due to the excesses of the 1960s and 1970s. According to Sanguinetti, who both served as a minister in his government and has criticized him, "Pacheco is a very unknown person. I think this continues to be the case. He is a very little-known character".

Former general and president Gregorio Álvarez has been pursued for his crimes in the press, in public opinion, and in the courts. Most recently he has been forced into home arrest and prison.

So was former president-dictator Juan Bordaberry, who insisted for decades on the rightfulness of the coup, on the malign influence of freemasonry, and on the corrupt nature of liberal democracy. He died in 2011, hounded and demonized partly by honest public opinions and partly by Communist propaganda. Indeed, the PCU has made an effort to turn many of these individuals into pariahs, claiming they are guilty of "genocide" and all sorts of exaggerations that do a disservice to what really happened. Not coincidentally, these messages hide the role the Communists themselves had in the events of the 1970s.

Alejandro Otero, the police commissioner with the formidable MLN-hunting skills, quietly retired after a lifetime of service to his country. He was never violently pursued by vengeful Tupamaros (nor were Álvarez, Bordaberry, or anyone else). In fact, he remained a considerably admired and respected figure among his erstwhile enemies, and went as far as sharing interviews and various meetings with Eleuterio Fernández.

His name remains little-known to those who did not live at the time of the conflict. Otero sadly remarked to the author "I gave my life doing this. I believe my country has not recognized this adequately. I hope some day they do (...) I think [what I did] will become more important the day that I die (...) I have received more recognition from my enemies, my pseudo-enemies, than from the people I fought with". Comisario Otero died on August 13 2013.

A Circle Not Quite Closed

Fifty years have passed since the days when armed subversion began in Uruguay, with the robbery of the rifles at the Nueva Helvecia shooting range. A surprising number of things have not changed since then. A glaring one is political nepotism. The names keep on repeating themselves, in an unfortunate trend that guarantees inheritances and dynastic successions -and by extension, corruption- but not quality among politicians.

The Batlle family appears, for the moment, to have had its last major representative in Jorge (who was president, son of a president, grandson of a president and great-grandson of a president).[587] Luis Alberto Lacalle, the young representative from the 1970s who was president in the early 1990s, was the grandson of Nationalist *caudillo* Luis Alberto de Herrera. Lacalle's son is named Luis Alberto Lacalle as well, and has already been precociously designated as the next presidential candidate for his father's faction. The children of many politicians of the 1960s and 1970s, carrying names like Bordaberry, Abdala, Hierro, Ferreira, Gallinal, Pacheco, Heber, and many others have held political appointments and fast-tracked elected careers in the 1990s and beyond.

Not even the Frente Amplio has escaped this fate. The Marxist coalition that was going to end such practices has proven that nepotism is not a partisan, but rather a national cultural vice. Two cases of Frente Amplio nepotism are so stunning given their hypocrisy that they merit special mentions. The first concerns the name Arismendi. In 1955, a main pillar of the Communist Party's internal "coup" against Secretary General Eugenio Gómez was that he had been grooming his eponymous son to succeed him dynastically, handing him key party offices well before he was ready to absorb them. The man who took over the party then was Rodney Arismendi.

The new chief presided over the PCU in Uruguay, later in exile, and then again upon returning, from that day until close to his 1989 death. His successor in 1992 was his daughter, Marina Arismendi, who lived with him in exile in Communist Europe and studied in Cottbus during the 1970s.[588] It was a clear example of that most bizarre of hybrids, inherited Communist monarchies (as seen, for instance, in North Korea).

The other example refers to the name Sendic. The oldest son of the MLN founder, who is also named Raúl and bears a strong physical resemblance to his father, was raised and educated in Cuba. Far more committed to Marxism-Leninism in his youth than his father ever was, Sendic's son has also been fast-tracked to the top ranks of the Frente Amplio, and was elected vice president in the

2014 election after being promoted by Mujica towards a national candidacy.[589] In fact, that election had as candidates for various offices individuals named Sendic, Lacalle, and Bordaberry - all repetitions, in some cases by more than one instance. Such a degree of decadence, in a different time, would doubtlessly have inspired outraged youths to rebel and shake things up.

With Mujica well into his presidency, as this book was being written, there was one more twist to the story of the Tupamaros. It is the spectacular return of Héctor Amodio Pérez, forty years to the date when Uruguay had last learned of him. He lived through the entire period, in a secret exile, closely watching everything that happened in Uruguay - including what was said about him. In response to multiple historical accounts that placed him as the ultimate MLN traitor -death sentence included-, and in particular to statements Jorge Zabalza made in early 2013, Amodio reappeared in April of that year in a series of letters he mailed to various newspapers. After a few weeks of back-and-forth over their authenticity, Amodio dispelled all doubts by sending the newspapers pictures of himself in the present day. It was indubitably him.

The Uruguayan journalist who broke the story, Gabriel Pereyra of El Observador, visited Amodio in Madrid shortly afterwards.[590] The result was a video interview with the legendary Tupamaro. Among the revelations -many of which, when reliable, were incorporated into this book- is that he has already been in Uruguayan territory, returning for the first time in 1998 to see his family. He also claimed he has no plans to permanently return to Uruguay. Amodio revealed nothing about erstwhile partner Alicia Rey except that they divorced in 1990, although he did confirm that much of what he did in 1972 was for her ("I would have done anything to pull La Negra out of the can"). Curiously, the Tupamaro most known for spectacular MLN actions claims to have fired his weapon only eight or nine times. Lastly, in a conciliatory statement, Amodio expressed happiness at Mujica's election as president.

The return of the mythical figure of Amodio left present-day Tupamaros dumbfounded. Lucía Topolansky said it meant nothing to her, for he was "a dead man". Zabalza complained bitterly about Amodio's treason and alleged complicity in human rights violations, while grudgingly recognizing that the MLN was guilty of gross crimes like the murders of Roque Arteche and Pascasio Báez. Clara Aldrighi, the most serious of the Tupamaros' professional historians, even said "No turncoat or impostor can become a source for historians". Eleuterio Fernández, who in the opening pages of his history of the Tupamaros recognized "We are not (...) by virtue of having lived through it, the ideal providers of cold objectivity to the historical account we are supplying here" and also said "No reader should look here for the most minuscule mention of traitors", was predictably dismissive. In general, the surprise to the dominant Tupamaros of facing a man they had turned into a ghost clearly pushed them into embarrassing positions at the peak of their power and prestige.

Of Dreams and Their Price

In the end, the case of Uruguay and the Tupamaros serves to illustrate just how varied and unpredictable the courses of history can be. Men and women in the 1960s and 1970s, both among the Tupamaros and their opponents, respectively sought to turn utopian dreams into reality, or to thwart those ideas because they viewed them as sinister. The quest that promised a fatherland for all or a fatherland for none ended in the latter, when everybody lost and darkness prevailed for over a decade.

The remarkable return of Mujica and other Tupamaros, with their apotheosis in an elected government, shows that in Uruguay their sins have been forgiven and their original intentions recognized or at least acknowledged. Their actions as urban *guerrilleros* and armed propagandists, decades ago, continue to grant them a place as some of the most innovative insurgents on record. Their remarkable pursuit of high ideals and principles became a tragic story as they progressively violated all of them. There is rarely a sadder bookend to the spirit of the late 1960s.

Today, their definitions of what being a Tupamaro is retain the romance of the original. In the words of the transformed Henry Engler, "A Tupamaro is any person, anywhere in the world, who is outraged by injustices committed against any human being anywhere in the world, and reacts concordantly".

As the time of the Tupamaros leading a government comes to a close, it remains an open question what aspects of their long ride will have *value*, rather than simple historical significance.

If achieving victory, a politically united South America, and state-driven socialism was all possible through the ballot box, then perhaps the insurgency -and all the violence it involved- was pointless. However, this is not a costless realization, and it should not have taken decades to materialize. In the process, many individuals were left behind in shootings, executions, and torture chambers: civilians, insurgents, policemen, and soldiers. For them there really was no more fatherland.

ACKNOWLEDGMENTS

The person who came up with the idea of my doing research on the Tupamaros was my esteemed Georgetown mentor, Bruce Hoffman. As if that were not enough, he continued to offer his support and advice throughout the project. Everyone else at Georgetown's Center for Security Studies, including David Maxwell, Lauren Covert, Elizabeth Robbins, Michael Walker, Ellen McHugh, and my other guide, Philip Mudd, also gets my thanks.

I must also thank John Allen Gay for his early editorial support. I am indebted to Hal Brands, who provided advice, encouragement, and most generously a review of the manuscript. Rodolfo Reyes also has my thanks for his superb work on the cover artwork.

In Uruguay I must first thank Javier Bonilla Saus, my mentor at Universidad ORT. Thank you for teaching me how to think critically. My sources Alejandro Otero, Efraín Martínez Platero, Henry Engler, and Julio María Sanguinetti were generous with their time and willingness to share history as they lived it. The authors of the many books I consulted, particularly Gerardo Tagliaferro, as well as the staffers at Archivo CEIU, also have my thanks for their work. María Chiacchio also has my recognition for the excellent maps she crafted.

Last but not least I will thank my friends Germán Brea and Guzmán Castro for their continued support and interest; my extended family; my parents Diego and Laura; my brother Juan Manuel; my other parents Joselo and Mirta, and especially my wife Mari. She has shaped my life in so many ways I cannot even begin to thank her.

ABOUT THE AUTHOR

Pablo Brum is an international security analyst based out of Washington DC. He has a graduate degree in Security Studies from Georgetown University. This is his first book.

ENDNOTES

[1] According to British historian Angus Maddison's Historical Statistics of the World Economy, the average income of Uruguayans was above those of the French in the years 1910, 1918 and 1919. In every other year France's was higher, at times by only a few modern dollars. For detailed information see http://www.ggdc.net/maddison/Historical_Statistics/horizontal-file_02-2010.xls

[2] Díaz, Ramón P. Historia económica de Uruguay. [Montevideo, Uruguay]: Taurus, 2003. Page 260

[3] Gatto, Hebert. El cielo por asalto: el Movimiento de Liberación Nacional (Tupamaros) y la izquierda uruguaya (1963-1972). Montevideo: Taurus, 2004. Page 150

[4] Hunt, E. Howard, and Greg Aunapu. American Spy: My Secret History in the CIA, Watergate, and Beyond. Hoboken, N.J.: John Wiley & Sons, 2007. Page 95

[5] Leibner, Gerardo. Camaradas y Compañeros: Una Historia Política y Social de los Comunistas del Uruguay. [Montevideo, Uruguay]: Trilce, 2011. Pages 196-9

[6] Leibner, op. cit. Page 286

[7] Markarian, Vania. El 68 Uruguayo: El Movimiento Estudiantil Entre Molotovs y Música Beat. [Quilmes, Argentina]: Universidad Nacional de Quilmes Editorial, 2012. Page 71

[8] Mao, Zedong. On Guerrilla Warfare. BN Publishing, 2007. Pages 42-3

[9] The quotes in this paragraph come from Guevara, Che. La guerra de guerrillas. La Habana, Cuba: Ocean, 2006. Pages 13, 46, and 51

[10] Audio of the speech is available online. See http://youtu.be/4OnQwlZmkg4

[11] Killing noncombatants to advance political and strategic purposes is a timeworn tactic. There are many documented cases in ancient and medieval times. For more see Hoffman, Bruce. Inside Terrorism. New York: Columbia University Press, 2006

[12] Hoffman, op. cit. Page 35

[13] It should be noted that just paragraphs later in the text Guevara did endorse the execution of specific individuals, following certain conditions. Guevara, op. cit. Page 29.

[14] Marighella, Carlos. Mini-Manual do Guerrilheiro Urbano. São Paulo, 1969. http://www.marxists.org/portugues/marighella/1969/manual/

[15] Agee, Philip. Inside the Company: CIA Diary. Toronto: Bantam Books, 1976. Pages 402-6

---

[16] Aldrighi, Clara. La izquierda armada: ideología, ética e identidad en el MLN-Tupamaros. Montevideo, Uruguay: Ediciones Trilce, 2001. Page 16

[17] Department of State, United States Embassy in Montevideo. Airgram, April 20 1963. Declassified by the Universidad de la República's GEIPAR program. http://www.geipar.udelar.edu.uy/wp-content/uploads/2012/07/Descla%20Duffau%20nov11-renombrado2/RG%2059%20Files%201963-1969/RG59.SNF.1963.PD.BOX4083/RG59.SNF.1963.PD.BOX4083_0049.jpg

[18] Department of State, United States Embassy in Montevideo. Airgram, August 19 1966. Declassified by the Universidad de la República's GEIPAR program. http://www.geipar.udelar.edu.uy/wp-content/uploads/2012/07/Descla%20Duffau%20nov11-renombrado2/RG%2059%20Files%201963-1969/RG59.SNF.1964-1966.E.BOX919/RG59.SNF.1964-1966.E.BOX919_0032.jpg

[19] Department of State, United States Embassy in Montevideo. Airgram, November 4 1966. Declassified by the Universidad de la República's GEIPAR program. http://www.geipar.udelar.edu.uy/wp-content/uploads/2012/07/Descla%20Duffau%20nov11-renombrado2/RG%2059%20Files%201963-1969/RG59.SNF.1964-1966.E.BOX919/RG59.SNF.1964-1966.E.BOX919_0028.jpg

[20] Agee, op. cit. Page 449

[21] Leibner, op. cit. Page 493

[22] D'Oliveira, Sergio. El Uruguay y los Tupamaros. Montevideo: Centro Militar, 1996. Pages 50-1

[23] In the present day the OPS no longer exists. Assistance in police matters has been left to other agencies.

[24] Langguth, A.J. Hidden Terrors. New York: Pantheon Books, 1978 Page 234

[25] Aldrighi, Clara. El Caso Mitrione: La intervención de Estados Unidos en Uruguay (1965-1973). Montevideo: Trilce, 2007. Pages 387-8

[26] Rusk, Dean. Telegram from the Department of State to the Embassy in Uruguay. June 12 1964. http://history.state.gov/historicaldocuments/frus1964-68v31/d459

[27] Tagliaferro, Gerardo. Fernández Huidobro: De las armas a las urnas. Montevideo: Fin de Siglo, 2010. Page 53

[28] Sasso, Rolando. Tupamaros: Los comienzos. Montevideo: Fin de Siglo, 2010. Pages 52-60

[29] Fernández Huidobro, Eleuterio. Historia de los Tupamaros. Montevideo: Ediciones Tupac Amaru, 1986. Page 46

[30] The original Basque Sendic was pronounced "Séndic", just like the correct form of "Mujica" is "Mújica".

[31] Blixen, Samuel. Sendic. Montevideo: Trilce, 2000. Pages 20-2

[32] Blixen, op. cit. Pages 11 and 44. See also page 31 for Sendic's reasons for remaining a solicitor and not becoming a full lawyer.

[33] For more on the foundation of UTAA see Blixen, op. cit. Pages 61-4. Also see Sasso, Rolando. Tupamaros: Los comienzos, op. cit. Pages 71-2

[34] Naturally, non-Communists agreed with this assessment, which was backed up by the paltry numbers of the cane workers and the fact that many spoke more Portuguese than Spanish. According to Julio Sanguinetti, "They were in search of a peasantry that did not exist in Uruguay". Author's interview with Julio Sanguinetti.

[35] Author's interview with Efraín Martínez Platero.

[36] Technically the group rode in trucks for the vast majority of the 535 kilometer-long trek to Montevideo.

[37] Sasso, Rolando. Tupamaros: Los Comienzos, op. cit. Page 113

[38] Aldrighi, La Izquierda Armada, op. cit. Page 212

[39] Aldrighi, Clara. Memorias de insurgencia: historias de vida y militancia en el MLN-Tupamaros 1965-1975. Montevideo, Uruguay: Ediciones de la Banda Oriental, 2009. Page 76

[40] Fernández Huidobro, Historia de los Tupamaros, op. cit. Pages 19-23

[41] Sasso, Rolando. Tupamaros: Los Comienzos, op. cit. Page 125

[42] Sendic and virtually all other UTAA participants claimed the shots were fired from the CSU. They failed to understand those shots would never have been fired if they had not assaulted the place, which makes them responsible for the woman's death in all cases. For more on the incident see Sasso, Rolando. Tupamaros: Los Comienzos, op. cit. Pages 17-8 and 85-6. See also Blixen, op. cit. Page 67

[43] Vallarino, Raúl. ¡Llamen al Comisario Otero! (Memorias de un policía). Montevideo: Planeta, 2008. Pages 34-7

[44] Author's interview with Alejandro Otero

[45] Sasso, Rolando. Tupamaros: Los Comienzos, op. cit. Pages 52 and 181-2

[46] Blixen, op. cit. Page 73

[47] Tupamaros: La Fuga de Punta Carretas. Montevideo: Anima Films, 2009. https://www.youtube.com/watch?v=WlpSmPIeHOQ

[48] Most of the weapons were 1935 Czechoslovak-made Mauser rifles lacking the necessary bolts for their operation. Sasso, Rolando. Tupamaros: Los Comienzos, op. cit. Page 128

[49] See Sasso, Rolando. Tupamaros: Los Comienzos, op. cit. Page 106 and Blixen, op. cit. Pages 78-9

[50] For details of the police investigation see Sasso, Rolando. Tupamaros: Los Comienzos, op. cit. Pages 130-1 and Blixen, op. cit. Pages 81-3

[51] Blixen, op. cit. Pages 83-7

[52] Héctor Amodio claims Jorge Manera recruited him, and that in turn he recruited Julio Marenales. Amodio attributes fundamental teachings on security and compartmentalization to Manera. El Observador special on Héctor Amodio Pérez. May 23 2013.

[53] "We read Régis Debray up and down, from the side, vertically, horizontally, every which way. We read him totally and absolutely". Author's interview with Efraín Martínez Platero

[54] Sasso, Rolando. Tupamaros: Los Comienzos, op. cit. Page 54

[55] Torres, Jorge. Tupamaros: la derrota en la mira. Montevideo, Uruguay: Editorial Fin de Siglo, 2002. Page 114

[56] Blixen, op. cit. Pages 116
[57] Junta de Comandantes en Jefe, op. cit. Page 459
[58] Junta de Comandantes en Jefe, op. cit. Page 465
[59] The Tupamaro who said this is Luis Nieto. Haberkorn, Leonardo. Historias Tupamaras. [Montevideo, Uruguay]: Fin de Siglo, 2008. Page 31
[60] Blixen, op. cit. Page 97
[61] Campodónico, Miguel Ángel. Mujica. Montevideo: Fin de Siglo, 1998. Pages 107-8
[62] Fernández Huidobro, Historia de los Tupamaros, op. cit. Page 102
[63] Sasso, Rolando. Tupamaros: Los Comienzos, op. cit. Page 151
[64] Márquez Zacchino, Sergio. Marenales: Diálogos con el Dirigente Histórico Tupamaro. Montevideo: Argumento, 202010. Pages 36-9
[65] Amodio Pérez, Héctor. Memorias Completas. Montevideo, unpublished, 1973. Disseminated in the website of retired military officer José Gavazzo: http://www.envozalta.org/LIBRO_DE_HECTOR_AMODIO_PEREZ_1_Fundaci_n_del_Coordinador___G_nesis_del_M.L.N.pdf
[66] Fernández's group was called Movimiento de Apoyo al Campesino (MAC), or Movement to Support Peasants.
[67] Only reluctantly does Fernández Huidobro admit that ordinary citizens voluntarily use the banking system to protect their savings. Tagliaferro, Gerardo. Fernández Huidobro, op. cit. Page 51
[68] Fernández Huidobro, Historia de los Tupamaros, op. cit. Page 109
[69] The word "piratas" was often used in radical propaganda to portray Americans and others as looters or pillagers. Department of State, United States Embassy in Uruguay. Telegram. December 8, 1964. Declassified by the Universidad de la República's GEIPAR program. http://www.geipar.udelar.edu.uy/wp-content/uploads/2012/07/Descla%20Duffau%20nov11-renombrado2/RG%2059%20Files%201963-1969/RG59.SNF.1964-1966.PD.BOX2793/RG59.SNF.1964-1966.PD.BOX2793_0600.jpg
[70] Fernández Huidobro, op. cit. Page 241
[71] Amodio Pérez, op. cit. Page 12
[72] Campodónico, Miguel Ángel. Las Vidas de Rosencof, op. cit. Pages 180-1
[73] It was Mario Rivero, brother of Tabaré, who came up with the star-shaped logo. Márquez Zacchino, op. cit. Pages 45-6
[74] Tagliaferro, Gerardo. Fernández Huidobro, op. cit. Page 76
[75] Campodónico, Miguel Ángel. Las Vidas de Rosencof, op. cit. Page 181
[76] Tagliaferro, Gerardo. Fernández Huidobro, op. cit. Pages 28-32
[77] Tagliaferro, Gerardo. Fernández Huidobro, op. cit. Page 59
[78] Blixen, op. cit. Pages 132 and 144
[79] Tagliaferro, Gerardo. Fernández Huidobro, op. cit. Pages 45 and 60
[80] Márquez Zacchino, op. cit. Pages 17-9
[81] Author's interview with Efraín Martínez Platero
[82] Fontana, Hugo. La Piel del Otro: La Novela de Héctor Amodio Pérez. Montevideo: Punta Obscura, 2001. Page 46
[83] This account of Mujica's life is based on Campodónico, Miguel Ángel. Mujica, op. cit. Pages 31-3, 51-2 and 90-2; Pernas, Walter. Comandante Facundo: El

Revolucionario Pepe Mujica. Montevideo: Prisa, 2013. Pages 24-8, 104, 152, and 247; Israel, Sergio. Mujica: El Florista Presidente, op. cit. Pages 38-43 and 64-5; and Márquez Zacchino, op. cit. Page 46

[84] Biographical notes on Mauricio Rosencof are based on Campodónico, Miguel Ángel. Las Vidas de Rosencof, op. cit. Pages 50-1, 60-3, 104, 131-2, and 137

[85] Lessa, Alfonso. La revolución imposible: los Tupamaros y el fracaso de la vía armada en el Uruguay del siglo XX. [Montevideo, Uruguay]: Editorial Fin de Siglo, 2002. Page 330

[86] Susana Carli in Cavallo Quintana, Mauricio. Guerrilleras: La Participación Femenina en el MLN-T. Montevideo: Arca, 2011. Page 132

[87] Ana Casamayou in Cavallo Quintana, op. cit. Page 132

[88] Kohl, James and Litt, John. Urban Guerrilla Warfare in Latin America. Cambridge: MIT University Press. 1974. Page 290

[89] Junta de Comandantes en Jefe. Las Fuerzas Armadas al Pueblo Oriental: La Subversión. Montevideo, 1977. Page 106

[90] Ruiz, Marisa and Sanseviero, Rafael. Las Rehenas: Historia Oculta de Once Presas de la Dictadura. Montevideo: Fin de Siglo, 2012. Pages 35-9

[91] Yessie Maccchi in Aldrighi, Clara. La Izquierda Armada, op. cit. Page 132

[92] Sendic, Raúl (anonymously). 30 Preguntas a un Tupamaro. Santiago, Chile: Punto Final magazine, n° 58, July 2nd 1968. http://www.cedema.org/ver.php?id=1722

[93] Haberkorn, Leonardo. Historias Tupamaras, op. cit. Pages 70-2

[94] These are the words of Carlos Quijano in 1964. The Communists' Rodney Arismendi spoke along the same lines. Fernández Huidobro, Historia de los Tupamaros, op. cit. Page 82

[95] Aldrighi, Clara. La Izquierda Armada, op. cit. Page 155

[96] Specogna, Heidi & Hoffmann, Rainier. Tupamaros. Berlin: Specogna-Film/ZDF, 1996. https://www.youtube.com/watch?v=O1GaWgBG1FY

[97] Guevara, op. cit. Page 55

[98] The source is article 37 of the rule book. Junta de Comandantes en Jefe, La Subversión, op. cit. Pages 402-3.

[99] Junta de Comandantes en Jefe, La Subversión, op. cit. Page 412

[100] Internal MLN document entitled "Instrucciones Reservadas 1969". Courtesy of Archivo CEIU - "Colección David Cámpora" at Facultad de Humanidades & Ciencias de la Educación. Universidad de la República. Montevideo, Uruguay.

[101] Fernández Huidobro, op. cit. Page 263

[102] Márquez Zacchino, op. cit. Page 54

[103] Later, this became a formal instruction for all Tupamaros. See "Circular 5" of 1968. Available at Archivo CEIU - "Colección David Cámpora" at Facultad de Humanidades & Ciencias de la Educación. Universidad de la República. Montevideo, Uruguay.

[104] Tagliaferro, Gerardo. Fernández Huidobro, op. cit. Pages 57 and 87

[105] Blixen, op. cit. Page 135

[106] Fernández Huidobro, op. cit. Pages 259-60

[107] Saenz, op. cit. Page 138

108 According to the Tupamaros, and most importantly to Otero, "The bullet that killed my colleague was not fired from the weapons of the Tupamaros. I have my opinion about who is responsible for the shots, but I cannot prove it". Vallarino, Raúl. ¡Llamen al Comisario Otero!, op. cit. Page 90.
109 Tagliaferro, Gerardo. Fernández Huidobro, op. cit. Page 88
110 Sanguinetti, Julio María. La agonía de una democracia: proceso de la caída de las instituciones en el Uruguay (1963-1973). [Montevideo, Uruguay]: Taurus, 2008, Page 63
111 Tagliaferro, Gerardo. Fernández Huidobro, op. cit. Pages 90-2
112 Blixen, op. cit. Page 139
113 Márquez Zacchino, op. cit. Page 59
114 Fernández Huidobro, op. cit. Page 266
115 "He would grab a log and use it both to leave the door open and as firewood in the stove - the log stretched across the whole place, it was crazy!" Author's interview with Efraín Martínez Platero.
116 Fernández Huidobro, op. cit. Page 316-26
117 Author's interview with Efraín Martínez Platero
118 Tagliaferro, Gerardo. Adiós Robin Hood: 7 tupamaros, 40 años después. [Montevideo]: Fin de Siglo, 2008, Page 169
119 Fontana, op. cit. Page 53
120 Curiously, the slang term for "kill" used on this occasion, and in Uruguay at the time, was "quemar" or "burn". The translation reads "ice" for easiness of understanding among English readers. Fontana, op. cit. Page 54
121 Author's interview with Efraín Martínez Platero
122 Fernández Huidobro, op. cit. Pages 387-8
123 MLN-Tupamaros. Carta Abierta a la Policía. Montevideo: December 7 1967. http://www.cedema.org/ver.php?id=4213
124 Blixen, op. cit. Pages 141 and 150-1
125 See Agee, op. cit. Page 429 and Saenz, op. cit. Page 123
126 Author's interview with Alejandro Otero
127 Vallarino, Raúl. ¡Llamen al Comisario Otero!, op. cit. Pages 10 and 32
128 Department of State, United States Embassy in Uruguay. Airgram: Revision of Potential Leaders Biographic Reporting List. April 23 1969. Declassified in the Universidad de la República's GEIPAR program. http://www.geipar.udelar.edu.uy/documentos/estados-unidos/national-archives-and-record-administration-nara/national-archives-and-record-administration_parte-1/descla-duffau-nov11-renombrado2-7/rg-59-files-1963-1969/rg59-snf-1967-1969-pd-box2576/. Pages 205, 225, 229-33
129 Quotes of Galeano's work come from Galeano, Eduardo. Las Venas Abiertas de América Latina. Montevideo: Universidad de la República, 1971. Pages 21 and 27
130 Author's interview with Julio Sanguinetti
131 Even Sanguinetti says that Fernández "is somewhat right, in that the government's hard line also radicalized leftist youths who moved towards violent action". More interestingly, he also notes that "what is not often recognized is the inverse half truth: that the Tupamaros were, in turn, the greatest creators of

Pachequistas." Sanguinetti, op. cit., page 237. See also the statements of Tupamaro Kimal Amir in Haberkorn, Leonardo. Historias Tupamaras, op. cit. Page 37

[132] Department of State. United States Embassy in Uruguay. Telegram: Equipment for Presidential Guard. September 6 1968. Declassified in the Universidad de la República's GEIPAR program. http://www.geipar.udelar.edu.uy/wp-content/uploads/2012/07/Descla%20Duffau%20nov11-renombrado2/RG%2059%20Files%201963-1969/RG59.SNF.1967-1969.PD.BOX2581/RG59.SNF.1967-1969.PD.BOX2581_0424.jpg

[133] Memoria. Volume 4. César di Candia. El País. 2006. Page 83

[134] Markarian, op. cit. Page 139. Romero Píriz, Antonio. Los Hombres Grises. Self-published online. 2007. http://www.scribd.com/doc/56302670/Los-Hombres-Grises-Antonio-Romero-Piriz

[135] According to the KGB's Nikolai Leonov, Guevara's ill-advised plan to launch the insurgency in Bolivia may in fact have been designed to move on to northern Argentina, with the ultimate purpose of joining with other revolutionaries and taking over that far more important country. Leonov, Nikolai. La Inteligencia Soviética en América Latina durante la Guerra Fría. Santiago, Chile: conference at Centro de Estudios Públicos, 1998. http://www.cepchile.cl/dms/archivo_1140_320/rev73_leonov.pdf

[136] The phrase belongs to Tupamaro Marcelo Estefanell. Lessa, Alfonso. La Revolución Imposible, op. cit. Page 183

[137] Brands, Hal. Latin America's Cold War. Cambridge, Mass: Harvard University Press, 2010. Page 51

[138] Fernández Huidobro, op. cit. Page 356

[139] Markarian, op. cit. Pages 37-8, 73-4 and 93

[140] Fernández Huidobro, op. cit. Page 206

[141] Fernández Huidobro, op. cit. Page 182

[142] This, plus the usual thirty days annual vacation amounted to two months off. Keely, Charles. Uruguay Report: Workers Will Fight to the Last Holiday. Copley News Service, March 18 1966. Declassified in the Universidad de la República's GEIPAR program. http://www.geipar.udelar.edu.uy/wp-content/uploads/2013/06/PPB-SPECIAL-FOLDERS-New-Clippings.-U-1967.pdf

[143] This account of the operation is based on: Pernas, op. cit. Pages 348-9; Fontana, op. cit. Pages 60-4; Márquez Zacchino, op. cit. Page 72, and MLN-Tupamaros. Los Tupamaros en Acción, 1972. Edition the author consulted: Los Tupamaros en Acción: Relatos Testimoniales de los Guerrilleros. Santiago, Chile: Ediciones Prensa Latinoamericana, 1972. Pages 150-62

[144] Markarian, op. cit. Page 43

[145] Saenz, op. cit. Page 127

[146] Leibner, op. cit. Page 557

[147] Markarian, op. cit. Pages 57-61 and 92

[148] Department of State. United States Embassy in Uruguay. Airgram: Student Unrest. October 19 1968. Declassified in the Universidad de la República's GEIPAR program. http://www.geipar.udelar.edu.uy/wp-

content/uploads/2012/07/Descla%20Duffau%20nov11-renombrado2/RG%2059%20Files%201963-1969/RG59.SNF.1967-1969.PD.BOX2580/RG59.SNF.1967-1969.PD.BOX2580_0644.jpg

[149] Holmes, Jennifer. Terrorism and Democratic Stability. Manchester: University of Manchester Press, 2009. Page 136

[150] Tagliaferro, Gerardo. Fernández Huidobro, op. cit. Page 96

[151] Pernas, op. cit. Pages 339-40

[152] Author's interview with Efraín Martínez Platero

[153] Author's interview with Efraín Martínez Platero

[154] MLN-Tupamaros. Los Tupamaros en Acción, op. cit. Page 310. See also Circular 5 of 1968, op. cit.

[155] James L. Tull, Political Officer, 1969-73. In: Association for Diplomatic Studies and Training. Uruguay Country Reader. http://www.adst.org/Readers/Uruguay.pdf

[156] Saenz, op. cit. Page 229

[157] Saenz, op. cit. Pages 237-8

[158] Fontana, op. cit. Pages 66-8; Amodio Pérez, Héctor. Carta 5 Dirigida a Estefanell. Montevideo: El Observador, May 23 2013. http://www.elobservador.com.uy/noticia/imprimir/251335/carta-5-dirigida-a-estefanell/

[159] Márquez Zacchino, op. cit. Pages 67-9

[160] Junta de Comandantes en Jefe, La Subversión, op. cit. Pages 107-8. The quote comes from Blixen, op. cit. Page 150

[161] At one point, one of those devices injured a bystander: "unidentified individuals threw a bomb that fell below a hot dog stand (...) The explosion caused deep slicing wounds to those manning the stand." For this reason, Sendic canceled the program. See El País, January 4 1969 and Blixen, op. cit. Page 165

[162] Caula, Nelson & Silva, Alberto. Ana La Guerrillera: Una Historia de Lucía Topolansky. Montevideo: Ediciones B, 2011. Pages 60 and 75

[163] Fontana, op. cit. Page 72

[164] Sanguinetti, op. cit. Page 111

[165] Author's interview with Efraín Martínez Platero

[166] The attempted use of grenades during the firefight with the police in December of 1966 was thus incongruent. Junta de Comandantes en Jefe, La Subversión, op. cit. Page 475.

[167] Haberkorn, Leonardo. Historias Tupamaras, op. cit. Page 120

[168] Author's interview with Henry Engler

[169] These biographical notes on Zabalza are based on Leicht, Federico. Cero a la Izquierda: Una Biografía de Jorge Zabalza. Montevideo: Letra Ñ, 2007. Pages 16-7, 28-9, 35-48, and 53-65.

[170] This account of the Punta del Este heist and the Mujica incident is based on the following: Leicht, Federico. Cero a la Izquierda, op. cit. Pages 69-71; Israel, Sergio. Mujica: El Florista Presidente. Pages 66-7; Pernas, op. cit. Pages 381 and 387; and MLN-Tupamaros. Los Tupamaros en Acción, op. cit. Pages 189-204

[171] El País, February 19 1969

---

[172] Department of State. United States Embassy in Uruguay. Airgram: Tupamaros - A Break in the Casino Robbery. March 19 1969. Declassified in the Universidad de la República's GEIPAR program. http://www.geipar.udelar.edu.uy/wp-content/uploads/2012/07/Descla%20Duffau%20nov11-renombrado2/RG%2059%20Files%201963-1969/RG59.SNF.1967-1969.PD.BOX2580/RG59.SNF.1967-1969.PD.BOX2580_0722.jpg

[173] For the full text of MLN offer see El País, March 5 1969.

[174] Israel, Sergio. El Enigma Trabal. Montevideo: Fin de Siglo, 2002. Page 90

[175] Author's interviews with Alejandro Otero and Efraín Martínez Platero

[176] Blixen, op. cit. Page 167

[177] Lessa, Alfonso. La Revolución Imposible, op. cit. Page 183

[178] Aldrighi, Clara. La Izquierda Armada, op. cit. Pages 155-6

[179] Guevara, op. cit. Page 127

[180] This account of the Sarandí raid is based on Blixen, op. cit. Pages 165-6; MLN-Tupamaros. Los Tupamaros en Acción, op. cit. Pages 177-81; and Sanguinetti, op. cit. Page 115.

[181] El País. March 22 1969

[182] Department of State. United States Embassy in Uruguay. Airgram: Tupamaros Take to Airwaves. May 30 1969. Declassified in the Universidad de la República's GEIPAR program. http://www.geipar.udelar.edu.uy/wp-content/uploads/2012/07/Descla%20Duffau%20nov11-renombrado2/RG%2059%20Files%201963-1969/RG59.SNF.1967-1969.PD.BOX2582/RG59.SNF.1967-1969.PD.BOX2582_0391.jpg

[183] Author's interview with Efraín Martínez Platero

[184] Leicht, Federico. Cero a la Izquierda, op. cit. Page 80

[185] Department of State. United States Embassy in Uruguay. Telegram: Police Raid Major Tupamaro Hideout. July 29 1969. Declassified in the Universidad de la República's GEIPAR program. http://www.geipar.udelar.edu.uy/wp-content/uploads/2012/07/Descla%20Duffau%20nov11-renombrado2/RG%2059%20Files%201963-1969/RG59.SNF.1967-1969.PD.BOX2582/RG59.SNF.1967-1969.PD.BOX2582_0358.jpg

[186] Sanguinetti, op. cit. Page 133

[187] Sanguinetti, op. cit. Page 120.

[188] This account of the Gaetano Pellegrini kidnapping is based on the following sources: Tagliaferro, Gerardo. Fernández Huidobro, op. cit. Page 104; Leicht, Federico. Cero a la Izquierda, op. cit. Page 76; Aldrighi, Clara. La Izquierda Armada, op. cit. Page 196; Di Candia, op. cit. Volume 4, Page 64, and Eduardo Rey interview with Gaetano Pellegrini, courtesy of Archivo CEIU - "Colección David Cámpora" at Facultad de Humanidades & Ciencias de la Educación. Universidad de la República. Montevideo, Uruguay

[189] Pellegrini did emigrate from Uruguay shortly after being freed. However, in an interview during the 1990s he claimed it had been the greatest mistake in his life. Pellegrini resettled in Uruguay that decade.

[190] They were right to do so. At the time, the government was secretly considering outright banning the Communist Party. This was what its leadership dreaded most. Department of State. United States Embassy in Montevideo. Banning of the

Communist Party of Uruguay (PCU) - Probable Results and Alternatives. July 25 1969. Declassified in the Universidad de la República's GEIPAR program. http://www.geipar.udelar.edu.uy/wp-content/uploads/2013/06/CSM-COMMUNISM-General-1969-Uruguay.pdf

191 Specifically, School N° 157 at Villa García and the Policlínica de Obreros del Frigorífico Nacional. Later on, the school rejected its donation, so both went to the union. El País, November 13 1969

192 This account of the Pando raid is based on the following sources: Blixen, op. cit. Pages 172-7; Pernas, op. cit. Pages 412-4 and 419-22; MLN-Tupamaros. Los Tupamaros en Acción, op. cit. Pages 204-5, 214-5 and 220-39; Sasso, Rolando. La Toma de Pando. Montevideo: Fin de Siglo, 2005; Fontana, op. cit. Pages 87-8; Tagliaferro, Gerardo. , Fernández Huidobro, op. cit. Pages 108-10; Junta de Comandantes en Jefe, La Subversión, op. cit. Pages 589-93; Campodónico, Miguel Ángel. Mujica, op. cit. Pages 148-9, Leicht, Federico. Cero a la Izquierda, op. cit. Pages 86-7, Interview with female Tupamara (names of interviewer and interviewee withheld), courtesy of Archivo CEIU - "Colección David Cámpora" at Facultad de Humanidades & Ciencias de la Educación. Universidad de la República. Montevideo, Uruguay.

193 Department of State. United States Embassy in Uruguay. Telegram: Tupamaros Raid Town of Pando. October 9 1969. http://www.geipar.udelar.edu.uy/wp-content/uploads/2012/07/Descla%20Duffau%20nov11-renombrado2/RG%2059%20Files%201963-1969/RG59.SNF.1967-1969.PD.BOX2582/RG59.SNF.1967-1969.PD.BOX2582_0352.jpg

194 Vallarino, Raúl. ¡Llamen al Comisario Otero!, op. cit. Page 116

195 More specifically, it was firm head Diego Etcheverrigaray who was sentenced to serve time in prison. See El País, October 22 and December 6 1969

196 Original MLN document available at Archivo CEIU - "Colección David Cámpora" at Facultad de Humanidades & Ciencias de la Educación. Universidad de la República. Montevideo, Uruguay.

197 Haberkorn, Leonardo. Historias Tupamaras, op. cit. Pages 48-50

198 Pernas, op. cit. Page 399

199 Aldrighi, Clara. El Caso Mitrione, op. cit. Page 30

200 Sanguinetti, op. cit. Pages 138-40

201 Sanguinetti, op. cit. Page 106

202 The account of this operation is based on the following sources: MLN-Tupamaros. Los Tupamaros en Acción, op. cit. Pages 246-51; El País, December 27-9 1969; Fontana, op. cit. Pages 91-2, and Chavarría, Daniel. Don Sendic de Chamangá. Montevideo: Aguilar, 2013. Page 239

203 Holmes, op. cit. Page 116

204 Blixen, op. cit. Page 167

205 All references to the MLN's year-end report come from Junta de Comandantes en Jefe, La Subversión, op. cit. Pages 562-3 and 566-9

206 In his case, hijacking São Paulo's Radio Nacional. El Día, August 15 1969

[207] Original MLN propaganda of 1969 entitled "Tupamaros Declara". Available at Archivo CEIU - "Colección David Cámpora" at Facultad de Humanidades & Ciencias de la Educación. Universidad de la República. Montevideo, Uruguay.
[208] Gatto, op. cit. Page 187
[209] Leicht, Federico. Cero a la Izquierda, op. cit. Page 91
[210] Sanguinetti, op. cit. Page 143
[211] Department of State. United States Embassy in Uruguay. Telegram: Police Intelligence Head Suspended. January 20 1970. Declassified in the Universidad de la República's GEIPAR program. http://www.geipar.udelar.edu.uy/wp-content/uploads/2012/07/Descla%20Duffau%20nov11-renombrado2/RG%2059%20Files%201970-1973/RG59.SNF.1970-1973.SO.BOX3102/RG59.SNF.1970-1973.SO.BOX3102_0033.jpg
[212] Junta de Comandantes en Jefe, La Subversión, op. cit. Page 655
[213] Haberkorn, Leonardo. Historias Tupamaras, op. cit. Page 49
[214] Aldrighi, Clara. La Izquierda Armada, op. cit. Page 41
[215] El País, March 31 1970
[216] Junta de Comandantes en Jefe, La Subversión, op. cit. Pages 655 and 696
[217] This account of the operation is based on the following sources: Chavarría, op. cit. Page 249; MLN-Tupamaros. Los Tupamaros en Acción, op. cit. Page 255 and Fontana, op. cit. Pages 98-100
[218] Fontana, op. cit. Page 104
[219] "Amodio was in a completely frenzied position. He had absolutely nothing to do with the rest of the leadership". Author's interview with Efraín Martínez Platero.
[220] Fontana, op. cit. Page 69
[221] Fontana, op. cit. Page 70
[222] Ruiz and Sanseviero, op. cit. Page 60
[223] Fontana, op. cit. Page 82
[224] Israel, Sergio. Mujica: El Florista Presidente, op. cit. Page 72
[225] Department of State. United States Embassy in Uruguay. Telegram: Senior Police Official Murdered. April 13 1970. Declassified in the Universidad de la República's GEIPAR program. http://www.geipar.udelar.edu.uy/wp-content/uploads/2012/07/Descla%20Duffau%20nov11-renombrado2/RG%2059%20Files%201970-1973/RG59.SNF.1970-1973.PD.BOX2661/RG59.SNF.1970-1973.PD.BOX2661_01376.jpg
[226] This account of the operation is based on the following sources: MLN-Tupamaros. Los Tupamaros en Acción, op. cit. Pages 261-8; Saenz, op. cit. Page 157; and El País, April 14-5 1970
[227] The story of what happened to José Mujica is based on the following sources: Israel, Sergio. Mujica: El Florista Presidente, op. cit. Pages 70 and 74-5; Pernas, op. cit. Pages 447-9, 458 and 480-1; and Campodónico, Miguel Ángel. Mujica, op. cit. Pages 150-1
[228] This account of the Mailhos operation is based on the following sources: Fontana, op. cit. Pages 106-7; Junta de Comandantes en Jefe, La Subversión, op. cit. Page 657; MLN-Tupamaros. Los Tupamaros en Acción, op. cit. Pages 269-80; Blixen, op. cit., Página 180; Aldrighi, El Caso Mitrione, op. cit. Page 78; Chavarría,

op. cit. Page 272; Campodónico, Miguel Ángel. Las Vidas de Rosencof, op. cit. Page 17; the author's interview with Efraín Martínez Platero, and Tagliaferro, Gerardo. Interview with Juan Almiratti. July 24 2006. http://www.cronicas.com.uy/HNImprimir.cgi?11426,0

[229] It had followed on the heels of an almost identical heist by a Brazilian insurgent organization in July of the previous year. The group responsible for the Brazilian robbery, which targeted a safe box belonging to top politician Adhemar de Barros, was the Vanguarda Armada Revolucionária Palmares. The loot far exceeded the Mailhos take: $16 million. See Kohl and Litt, op. cit. Pages 47-8

[230] Department of State. United States Embassy in Uruguay. Telegram: Tupamaros Stage Largest Robbery in Uruguayan History. April 6 1970. Declassified in the Universidad de la República's GEIPAR program. http://www.geipar.udelar.edu.uy/wp-content/uploads/2012/07/Descla%20Duffau%20nov11-renombrado2/RG%2059%20Files%201970-1973/RG59.SNF.1970-1973.SO.BOX3102/RG59.SNF.1970-1973.SO.BOX3102_0012.jpg

[231] Aldrighi, El Caso Mitrione, op. cit. Page 78

[232] Alfonso, Álvaro. Jugando a las Escondidas. Montevideo: Altamira, 2011. Page 71

[233] As expressed by aspiring MLN member Fernando González Guyer, "The Tupamaros were the pop stars of the time." Haberkorn, Leonardo. Historias Tupamaras, op. cit. Page 53

[234] The account of this raid is based on the following sources: MLN-Tupamaros. Los Tupamaros en Acción, op. cit. Pages 282-93; D'Oliveira, op. cit. Pages 84-5; Chavarría, op. cit. Page 286; Blixen, op. cit. Pages 183-4; Figueroa, Alejandro. Raúl Sendic: Tupamaro. Montevideo: Buen Cine Producciones, 2004. http://www.dailymotion.com/video/x11dw3_raul-sendic-tupamaro_news;

[235] Mao, op. cit. Page 22

[236] Author's interview with Henry Engler

[237] Department of State. United States Embassy in Uruguay. Telegram: Violent Aftermath of Tupamaro Arms Robbery. June 1 1970. Declassified in the Universidad de la República's GEIPAR program. http://www.geipar.udelar.edu.uy/wp-content/uploads/2012/07/Descla%20Duffau%20nov11-renombrado2/RG%2059%20Files%201970-1973/RG59.SNF.1970-1973.PD.BOX2661/RG59.SNF.1970-1973.PD.BOX2661_01417.jpg

[238] Department of State. United States Embassy in Montevideo. Tupamaros Raid Uruguayan Naval Installation. June 4 1970. Declassified in the Universidad de la República's GEIPAR program. http://www.geipar.udelar.edu.uy/wp-content/uploads/2013/07/POL-1-RICHARDSON-WEEKLY-REPORTS-URUGUAY-1970.pdf

[239] The account of this operation is based on the following: MLN-Tupamaros. Los Tupamaros en Acción, op. cit. Pages 295-305; Department of State. United States Embassy in Uruguay. Airgram: Uruguay's "Great Pawn Shop Robbery" Diminishes in Size and Importance. December 3 1970. Declassified in the Universidad de la República's GEIPAR program.

http://www.geipar.udelar.edu.uy/wp-content/uploads/2012/07/Descla%20Duffau%20nov11-renombrado2/RG%2059%20Files%201970-1973/RG59.SNF.1970-1973.PD.BOX2661/RG59.SNF.1970-1973.PD.BOX2661_01507.jpg; the author's interview with Henry Engler; El País, November 13 1970, and Department of State. United States Embassy in Uruguay. Telegram: Further Details on Great Pawn Shop Robbery. November 16 1970. Declassified in the Universidad de la República's GEIPAR program. http://www.geipar.udelar.edu.uy/wp-content/uploads/2012/07/Descla%20Duffau%20nov11-renombrado2/RG%2059%20Files%201970-1973/RG59.SNF.1970-1973.PD.BOX2661/RG59.SNF.1970-1973.PD.BOX2661_01617.jpg

240 The original is available at Archivo CEIU - "Colección David Cámpora" at Facultad de Humanidades & Ciencias de la Educación. Universidad de la República. Montevideo, Uruguay.

241 This estimate comes from top policeman Alejandro Otero. Lessa, Alfonso. La Revolución Imposible, op. cit. Pages 25-6

242 Junta de Comandantes en Jefe, La Subversión, op. cit. Page 360

243 Aldrighi, Clara. La Izquierda Armada, op. cit. Page 238

244 Haberkorn, Leonardo. Historias Tupamaras, op. cit. Page 49

245 MLN-Tupamaros. Los Tupamaros en Acción, op. cit. Page 306

246 Blixen, op. cit. Page 182

247 Fontana, op. cit. Page 81

248 Haberkorn, Leonardo. Historias Tupamaras, op. cit. Pages 39-40

249 D'Oliveira, op. cit. Pages 85-6

250 Junta de Comandantes en Jefe, La Subversión, op. cit. Page 476

251 El Pais, June 27 1970

252 Vallarino, Raúl. ¡Llamen al Comisario Otero!, op. cit. Page 109

253 Author's interview with Efraín Martínez Platero

254 Ronfeldt, David. The Mitrione Kidnapping. RAND Corporation. August 1987. http://www.gwu.edu/~nsarchiv/NSAEBB/NSAEBB324/19870800_0000_The%20Mitrione%20Kidnapping%20in%20Uruguay.pdf

255 Central Intelligence Agency, Directorate of Intelligence. Intelligence Memorandum: Kidnapping as Terrorist Tactic in Latin America. April 7 1970. http://www.foia.cia.gov/sites/default/files/document_conversions/89801/DOC_0000639434.pdf

256 "While Mitrione had been warned to take security precautions, he did not adopt stringent measures". Ronfeldt, op. cit.

257 Department of State. Bureau of Intelligence and Research. Intelligence Note: Uruguay - Kidnapping Possibilities. April 20 1970. Declassified in the Universidad de la República's GEIPAR program. http://www.geipar.udelar.edu.uy/wp-content/uploads/2012/07/Descla%20Duffau%20nov11-renombrado2/RG%2059%20Files%201970-1973/RG59.SNF.1970-1973.PD.BOX2661/RG59.SNF.1970-1973.PD.BOX2661_01384.jpg

258 El Abogado della Valle Fue Quien Negoció y Pagó por la Liberación del Cónsul Brasileño, Secuestrado por los Tupamaros en 1970. Búsqueda, October 11 2012. Page 14

---

259 Department of State. United States Embassy in Uruguay. Telegram: Situation Report - Mitrione Kidnapping. July 31 1970. Declassified in the Universidad de la República's GEIPAR program. http://www.geipar.udelar.edu.uy/wp-content/uploads/2012/07/Descla%20Duffau%20nov11-renombrado2/RG%2059%20Files%201970-1973/RG59.SNF.1970-1973.PD.BOX2661/RG59.SNF.1970-1973.PD.BOX2661_01426.jpg

260 Langguth, op. cit. Pages 255-8

261 Aldrighi, Clara. El Caso Mitrione, op. cit. Pages 37-40 and 47

262 See Aldrighi, Clara. El Caso Mitrione, op. cit. Page 19 and Langguth, op. cit. Pages 17-8 and 27-8

263 "When Dan Mitrione asked Byron Engle to give him another overseas assignment, Engle knew that the reason once again was money". Langguth, op. cit. Page 223

264 Saenz, op. cit. Pages 153-4

265 Aldrighi, Clara. El Caso Mitrione, op. cit. Page 29

266 Hevia, Manuel. Pasaporte 11333. Montevideo: Liberación Nacional, 1985. Page 63

267 Aldrighi, Clara. El Caso Mitrione, op. cit. Pages 37 and 141

268 Hevia's memoir seems reliable, and more than once verifiable through independent sources, until the last chapter. It is only in five pages, out of over 290, that the Cuban makes his allegation against Mitrione. Per his own admission, by mid-1970 he had been living in Maldonado, not Montevideo, for two years. He managed a *parrillada* and did translation work for the CIA, not for OPS (for which he never worked). Suddenly, the freshly arrived Mitrione invites Hevia to meet, and moments later the Cuban is witnessing brutal interrogations. Hevia says he witnessed not just "trial run" interrogations but also real ones - although no one has ever come forward to claim he was interrogated in that basement by those people. Hevia, op. cit. Pages 287-93

269 Some go the extra mile and build on the idea. For instance, in the book "El Enigma Trabal", author Sergio Israel says the "proof" that Mitrione was a CIA officer lies at the Agency's Langley, Virginia headquarters. According to Israel, Mitrione's name is engraved there along with those of others who fell in the line of duty while working for the CIA.

270 See Hevia, op. cit. Page 121 and Aldrighi, Clara. El Caso Mitrione, op. cit. Pages 367-8

271 According to Langguth, the movie included as fact "every undocumented rumor about Dan Mitrione from Santo Domingo or Belo Horizonte because [its] aim was a composite indictment of U.S. policy throughout Latin America". The director also slandered Mitrione in public statements as a religious fanatic who was against "everything that is liberal or Communistic (...) He thinks that ordinary liberalism can plunge society into chaos". Langguth, op. cit. Pages 305-6.

272 Baumgartner, José Luis. Escuadrón de la Muerte. Montevideo: Fin de Siglo, 2011. Page 147

273 Sanguinetti, op. cit. Pages 170-1.

274 Langguth, op. cit. Pages 250-2

275 Aldrighi, Clara. El Caso Mitrione, op. cit. Page 30

[276] Aldrighi, Clara. El Caso Mitrione, op. cit. Pages 89 and 123
[277] Blixen, Samuel. La Comisión Aspirina. Montevideo: Trilce, 2007. Pages 14-5
[278] Tagliaferro, Gerardo. Fernández Huidobro, op. cit. Page 116
[279] Ronfeldt, op. cit.
[280] Aldrighi, Clara. El Caso Mitrione, op. cit. Page 68
[281] Aldrighi, Clara. El Caso Mitrione, op. cit. Page 90
[282] Sanguinetti, op. cit. Page 161 and author's interview with Julio Sanguinetti
[283] Aldrighi, Clara. El Caso Mitrione, op. cit. Page 120
[284] Aldrighi, Clara. El Caso Mitrione, op. cit. Pages 119 and 122
[285] Aldrighi, Clara. El Caso Mitrione, op. cit. Page 315
[286] This account of Mitrione's interactions with his captors is based on the following: Aldrighi, Clara. El Caso Mitrione, op. cit. Pages 47, 77, 91-8, 116, 140-3 and 258; and Langguth, op. cit. Pages 241, 273 and 280-2
[287] Aldrighi, Clara. El Caso Mitrione, op. cit. Pages 163-4 and 187
[288] This account of the Almería incident is based on the following: Aldrighi, Clara. El Caso Mitrione, op. cit. Pages 188-94, 204-14 and 255; El Diario, August 8 1970; Blixen, op. cit. Pages 192-3 and the author's interview with Efraín Martínez Platero
[289] The account of Claude Fly's kidnapping is based on the following sources: Fly, Claude. No Hope But God. New York: Hawthorn Books, 1973. Pages vii, 14, 16-21: Aldrighi, Clara. El Caso Mitrione, op. cit. Pages 188-9 and 229-34
[290] Aldrighi, Clara. El Caso Mitrione, op. cit. Page 244
[291] Department of State. Telegram from Secretary Rogers to Ambassador Adair. August 9 1970. Declassified by the National Security Archive at George Washington University. http://www.gwu.edu/~nsarchiv/NSAEBB/NSAEBB324/19700809_1435_Cable_From_Secretary_of_State_%20to_Ambassador.pdf
[292] The source is a Pacheco family member. The person being discussed was Richard Milhous Nixon. Búsqueda. El Abogado Della Valle (...), op. cit.
[293] Department of State. Telegram from Ambassador Adair to Secretary Rogers. August 9 1970. Declassified by the National Security Archive at George Washington University. http://www.gwu.edu/~nsarchiv/NSAEBB/NSAEBB324/19700809_1503_Reply_From_Ambassador_to_Secretary_of_State.pdf
[294] The account beginning here of the unfolding of the Mitrione crisis is based on the following sources: Aldrighi, Clara. El Caso Mitrione, op. cit. Pages 9, 28, 230-7, 252-67, 361-2 and 372; Ronfeldt, op. cit., the author's interview with Henry Engler, and Aldrighi, Clara. Memorias de Insurgencia, op. cit. Page 173
[295] Lessa, op. cit. La Revolución Imposible, op. cit. Page 188
[296] Aldrighi, Clara. El Caso Mitrione, op. cit. Pages 239, 290 and 295
[297] Tagliaferro, Gerardo. Fernández Huidobro, op. cit. Page 114
[298] Aldrighi, Clara. El Caso Mitrione, op. cit. Pages 194-5
[299] Department of State. United States Embassy in Uruguay. Telegram: Kidnapping - Call by Foreign Minister. August 12 1970. Declassified in the Universidad de la República's GEIPAR program. http://www.geipar.udelar.edu.uy/wp-

content/uploads/2012/07/Descla%20Duffau%20nov11-renombrado2/RG%2059%20Files%201970-1973/RG59.SNF.1970-1973.PD.BOX2661/RG59.SNF.1970-1973.PD.BOX2661_00759.jpg

300 Department of State. Memorandum of Conversation. August 10 1970. Declassified in the Universidad de la República's GEIPAR program. http://www.geipar.udelar.edu.uy/wp-content/uploads/2012/07/Descla%20Duffau%20nov11-renombrado2/RG%2059%20Files%201970-1973/RG59.SNF.1970-1973.PD.BOX2661/RG59.SNF.1970-1973.PD.BOX2661_00984.jpg

301 Department of State. United States Embassy in Brazil. August 7 1970. Declassified in the Universidad de la República's GEIPAR program. http://www.geipar.udelar.edu.uy/wp-content/uploads/2012/07/Descla%20Duffau%20nov11-renombrado2/RG%2059%20Files%201970-1973/RG59.SNF.1970-1973.PD.BOX2661/RG59.SNF.1970-1973.PD.BOX2661_01150.jpg

302 Aldrighi, Clara. El Caso Mitrione, op. cit. Page 98

303 Vallarino, Raúl. ¡Llamen al Comisario Otero!, op. cit. Page 139. According to recently declassified American diplomatic cable traffic out of Rio de Janeiro, "Aymore is politically reliable and has assured [a source] that Otero did indeed make statements attributed to him (...) Otero talked on background basis not for attribution to him, but (...) Aymore felt story too hot to send without giving Otero's name as source. As result Otero considered his confidence was betrayed and therefore denied everything". Aymoré did not respond to the author's queries on this subject. It remains impossible to determine the truth of this case. Department of State. United States Embassy in Brazil. Telegram: Kidnappings - Jornal do Brasil Story Re Mitrione. August 21 1970. Declassified in the Universidad de la República's GEIPAR program. http://www.geipar.udelar.edu.uy/wp-content/uploads/2012/07/Descla%20Duffau%20nov11-renombrado2/RG%2059%20Files%201970-1973/RG59.SNF.1970-1973.PD.BOX2661/RG59.SNF.1970-1973.PD.BOX2661_00597.jpg

304 Aldrighi, Clara. El Caso Mitrione, op. cit. Pages 297-300

305 D'Oliveira, op. cit. Page 163

306 Guillén, Abraham. Philosophy of the Urban Guerrilla; The Revolutionary Writings of Abraham Guillén. New York: Morrow, 1973. Page 270

307 In his 1979 book "Le Temps des Otages", French writer Fabien Gruhier credited the Tupamaros with bequeathing to beleaguered 1970s Europe the "gift" of hostage-taking extortion.

308 Ronfeldt, op. cit.

309 Aldrighi, Clara. El Caso Mitrione, op. cit. Page 114. Department of State. United States Embassy in Uruguay. Memorandum of Conversation. June 1 1970. Declassified in the Universidad de la República's GEIPAR program. http://www.geipar.udelar.edu.uy/wp-content/uploads/2013/07/POL-15-1b-VICE-PRESIDENT-URUGUAY-1970.pdf. Department of State. United States Embassy in Uruguay. Memo of Conversation. December 14 1971. Declassified in the Universidad de la República's GEIPAR program.

http://www.geipar.udelar.edu.uy/wp-content/uploads/2013/07/POL-15-1a-VICE-PRESIDENT-URUGUAY-1971.pdf

310 Department of State. United States Embassy in Uruguay. Memorandum of Conversation: Fly Kidnapping. December 4 1970. Declassified in the Universidad de la República's GEIPAR program. http://www.geipar.udelar.edu.uy/wp-content/uploads/2012/07/Descla%20Duffau%20nov11-renombrado2/RG%2059%20Files%201970-1973/RG59.SNF.1970-1973.PD.BOX2661/RG59.SNF.1970-1973.PD.BOX2661_00206.jpg

311 Department of State. United States Embassy in Uruguay. Memorandum of Conversation: Fly Kidnapping. December 5 1970. Declassified in the Universidad de la República's GEIPAR program. http://www.geipar.udelar.edu.uy/wp-content/uploads/2012/07/Descla%20Duffau%20nov11-renombrado2/RG%2059%20Files%201970-1973/RG59.SNF.1970-1973.PD.BOX2661/RG59.SNF.1970-1973.PD.BOX2661_00210.jpg

312 On previous occasions, the American ambassador had attended meetings with Francese only to find that he was better informed about various aspects of the security situation than the Minister of the Interior himself. Department of State. United States Embassy in Uruguay. Telegram: Kidnapping - Meeting with Acting Foreign Minister and Interior Minister. September 18 1970. Declassified in the Universidad de la República's GEIPAR program. http://www.geipar.udelar.edu.uy/wp-content/uploads/2012/07/Descla%20Duffau%20nov11-renombrado2/RG%2059%20Files%201970-1973/RG59.SNF.1970-1973.PD.BOX2661/RG59.SNF.1970-1973.PD.BOX2661_00458.jpg

313 Lessa, Alfonso. La Revolución Imposible, op. cit. Pages 163-4

314 This portion of Fly's kidnapping is based on Fly, op. cit. Pages 25-31, 74, 84 and 110

315 Aldrighi, Clara. El Caso Mitrione, op. cit. Page 324

316 Department of State. United States Embassy in Uruguay. Telegram: Kidnapping - Brazilian Diplomat Departs. February 22 1971. Declassified in the Universidad de la República's GEIPAR program. http://www.geipar.udelar.edu.uy/wp-content/uploads/2012/07/Descla%20Duffau%20nov11-renombrado2/RG%2059%20Files%201970-1973/RG59.SNF.1970-1973.PD.BOX2661/RG59.SNF.1970-1973.PD.BOX2661_00139.jpg

317 Department of State. United States Embassy in Brazil. Telegram. February 27 1971. Declassified in the Universidad de la República's GEIPAR program. http://www.geipar.udelar.edu.uy/wp-content/uploads/2012/07/Descla%20Duffau%20nov11-renombrado2/RG%2059%20Files%201970-1973/RG59.SNF.1970-1973.PD.BOX2661/RG59.SNF.1970-1973.PD.BOX2661_00074.jpg. Department of State. United States Embassy in Uruguay. Telegram: Kidnappings - GOU Position in Special OAS Council Meeting. August 18 1970. Declassified in the Universidad de la República's GEIPAR program. http://www.geipar.udelar.edu.uy/wp-content/uploads/2012/07/Descla%20Duffau%20nov11-

renombrado2/RG%2059%20Files%201970-1973/RG59.SNF.1970-1973.PD.BOX2661/RG59.SNF.1970-1973.PD.BOX2661_00686.jpg

318 This last portion of Fly's kidnapping is based on Fly, op. cit. Pages 117-40; Aldrighi, Clara. El Caso Mitrione, op. cit. Page 325, Langguth, op. cit. Page 291, Department of State. United States Embassy in Uruguay. Telegram: Kidnapping - Possible Initiative by Fly Family. February 27 1971. Declassified in the Universidad de la República's GEIPAR program. http://www.geipar.udelar.edu.uy/wp-content/uploads/2012/07/Descla%20Duffau%20nov11-renombrado2/RG%2059%20Files%201970-1973/RG59.SNF.1970-1973.PD.BOX2661/RG59.SNF.1970-1973.PD.BOX2661_00068.jpg, Department of State. United States Embassy in Uruguay. Telegram: Kidnapping - Foreign Ministry Reaction to GOU's Refusal to Publish MLN Manifesto. September 22 1970. Declassified in the Universidad de la República's GEIPAR program. http://www.geipar.udelar.edu.uy/wp-content/uploads/2012/07/Descla%20Duffau%20nov11-renombrado2/RG%2059%20Files%201970-1973/RG59.SNF.1970-1973.PD.BOX2661/RG59.SNF.1970-1973.PD.BOX2661_00436.jpg, Department of State. United States Embassy in Montevideo. Debriefing of Ambassador Jackson. November 19 1971. Declassified in the Universidad de la República's GEIPAR program. http://www.geipar.udelar.edu.uy/wp-content/uploads/2013/08/POL-23-2-Reports-Incidents-URUGUAY-1972.pdf

319 This account of Geoffrey Jackson's kidnapping is based on Jackson, Geoffrey. People's Prison. London: Faber, 1973. Pages 17-33, 40-1, 49, 55-7, 64, 74-5, 164, 179, 188 and 207; Foreign & Commonwealth Office. Report by HM Ambassador, Montevideo, on His Capture and Imprisonment by the Tupamaros. London. March 23 1972. Declassified in the Universidad de la República's GEIPAR program. http://www.geipar.udelar.edu.uy/wp-content/uploads/2013/07/POL-23-3a-Forces-Organizations-MLN-Tupamaros-URUGUAY-1973.pdf

320 Department of State. United States Embassy in Uruguay. Telegram: Kidnapping - Views of British Chargé. February 26 1971. Declassified in the Universidad de la República's GEIPAR program. http://www.geipar.udelar.edu.uy/wp-content/uploads/2012/07/Descla%20Duffau%20nov11-renombrado2/RG%2059%20Files%201970-1973/RG59.SNF.1970-1973.PD.BOX2661/RG59.SNF.1970-1973.PD.BOX2661_00083.jpg

321 Department of State. United States Embassy in Uruguay. Telegram: Release of British Ambassador. September 13 1971. Declassified in the Universidad de la República's GEIPAR program. http://www.geipar.udelar.edu.uy/wp-content/uploads/2012/07/Descla%20Duffau%20nov11-renombrado2/RG%2059%20Files%201970-1973/RG59.SNF.1970-1973.PD.BOX2662/RG59.SNF.1970-1973.PD.BOX2662_00992.jpg

322 Department of State. Letter from Deputy Chief of Mission in Uruguay Frank V. Ortiz to Country Director for Argentina and Uruguay Irving G. Tragen. August 31 1970. Declassified in the Universidad de la República's GEIPAR program. http://www.geipar.udelar.edu.uy/wp-

content/uploads/2012/07/Descla%20Duffau%20nov11-renombrado2/RG%2059%20Files%201970-1973/RG59.SNF.1970-1973.PD.BOX2661/RG59.SNF.1970-1973.PD.BOX2661_00557.jpg

[323] Lessa, Alfonso. La Revolución Imposible, op. cit. Page 170

[324] Junta de Comandantes en Jefe, La Subversión, op. cit. Page 176

[325] Aldrighi, Clara. Memorias de Insurgencia, op. cit. Page 307

[326] This was an after-action report bitterly complaining of an operation in which the Tupamaros failed to properly disarm a policeman, who killed the Tupa Pedro Báez. The cop, Walter Custodio, was in turn killed. Original MLN "Informe Sobre un Comando del Hambre", available at Archivo CEIU - "Colección David Cámpora" at Facultad de Humanidades & Ciencias de la Educación. Universidad de la República. Montevideo, Uruguay.

[327] Hoffman, op. cit. Page 64

[328] Kohl and Litt, op. cit. Pages 150-1

[329] El País, May 20 1971

[330] Junta de Comandantes en Jefe, op. cit., p. 676

[331] Original MLN document available at Archivo CEIU - "Colección David Cámpora" at at Facultad de Humanidades & Ciencias de la Educación. Universidad de la República. Montevideo, Uruguay

[332] Department of State. United States Embassy in Uruguay. Airgram: 1973 Country Analysis and Strategy Paper (CASP) Uruguay. January 22 1971. Declassified in the Universidad de la República's GEIPAR program. http://www.geipar.udelar.edu.uy/wp-content/uploads/2012/07/Descla%20Duffau%20nov11-renombrado2/RG%2059%20Files%201970-1973/RG59.SNF.1970-1973.PD.BOX2662/RG59.SNF.1970-1973.PD.BOX2662_00410.jpg

[333] Haberkorn, Leonardo. Historias Tupamaras, op. cit. Page 127

[334] Zerbino was destined for major achievements later in life. Quirino had life-changing injuries. Haberkorn, Leonardo. Historias Tupamaras, op. cit. Page 123

[335] El País, September 30 1970

[336] Junta de Comandantes en Jefe, La Subversión, op. cit. Page 676

[337] Department of State. United States Embassy in Uruguay. Telegram: Outbreak of Terrorist Assaults. September 15 1970. Declassified in the Universidad de la República's GEIPAR program. http://www.geipar.udelar.edu.uy/wp-content/uploads/2012/07/Descla%20Duffau%20nov11-renombrado2/RG%2059%20Files%201970-1973/RG59.SNF.1970-1973.PD.BOX2661/RG59.SNF.1970-1973.PD.BOX2661_00476.jpg

[338] Department of State. United States Embassy in Montevideo. Recommendations for GOU Rapprochement with Hostile Elements. May 4 1971. Declassified in the Universidad de la República's GEIPAR program. http://www.geipar.udelar.edu.uy/wp-content/uploads/2013/07/POL-1-GENERAL-POLICY_BACKGROUND-URUGUAY-71_-Segunda-mitad.pdf

[339] Junta de Comandantes en Jefe, La Subversión, op. cit. Pages 682-3: Langguth, op. cit. Page 289; and El País, September 20 1970

[340] Jackson, op. cit. Page 57

[341] Aldrighi, Clara. Memorias de Insurgencia, op. cit. Page 38

[342] The journalist was the Uruguayan Ernesto González Bermejo, but the publication was Cuban. Kohl and Litt, op. cit. Pages 273-83.
[343] Junta de Comandantes en Jefe, La Subversión, op. cit. Pages 575-6
[344] El País, January 8 1971
[345] Guerrero Palermo, Gustavo. Los Tupas de Tacuarembó: La Izquierda, el MLN y la Represión en el Departamento. Montevideo: Fin de Siglo, 2012. Pages 126-9
[346] Junta de Comandantes en Jefe, La Subversión, op. cit. Page 697
[347] Author's interview with Efraín Martínez Platero
[348] The source for Liscano is Aldrighi, Clara. Memorias de Insurgencia, op. cit. Pages 133 and 145-6
[349] Sanguinetti, op. cit. Page 196
[350] The date was February 13 1972; the incident will be described in greater detail further ahead. Junta de Comandantes en Jefe, La Subversión, op. cit. Pages 709-10
[351] Junta de Comandantes en Jefe, La Subversión, op. cit. Page 701 and 709; Lessa, Alfonso. La Revolución Imposible, op. cit. Page 186
[352] See Department of State. United States Embassy in Uruguay. Telegram: Policeman and Terrorist Executed. August 22 1971. Declassified in the Universidad de la República's GEIPAR program. http://www.geipar.udelar.edu.uy/wp-content/uploads/2012/07/Descla%20Duffau%20nov11-renombrado2/RG%2059%20Files%201970-1973/RG59.SNF.1970-1973.PD.BOX2662/RG59.SNF.1970-1973.PD.BOX2662_00959.jpg and Junta de Comandantes en Jefe, La Subversión, op. cit. Pages 696 and 700
[353] Di Candia, op. cit. Page 43 of Volume 5 and Junta de Comandantes en Jefe, La Subversión, op. cit. Page 681
[354] Junta de Comandantes en Jefe, La Subversión, op. cit. Pages 485-7
[355] Sanguinetti, op. cit. Page 240-3
[356] Author's interview with Efraín Martínez Platero
[357] Junta de Comandantes en Jefe, La Subversión, op. cit. Page 691. See also El País, March 7 and April 5 1971
[358] Campodónico, Miguel Ángel. Las Vidas de Rosencof, op. cit. Page 74
[359] Department of State. United States Embassy in Uruguay. Airgram: Senate Accepts Commission Report on Tortures. October 9 1970. Declassified in the Universidad de la República's GEIPAR program. http://www.geipar.udelar.edu.uy/wp-content/uploads/2012/07/Descla%20Duffau%20nov11-renombrado2/RG%2059%20Files%201970-1973/RG59.SNF.1970-1973.PD.BOX2662/RG59.SNF.1970-1973.PD.BOX2662_00082.jpg
[360] Junta de Comandantes en Jefe, La Subversión, op. cit. Page 696 and Department of State. United States Embassy in Uruguay. Telegram: Policeman and Terrorist Executed, op. cit.
[361] Haberkorn, Leonardo. Historias Tupamaras, op. cit. Page 58
[362] Department of State. United States Embassy in Uruguay. Telegram: Policeman and Terrorist Executed, op. cit.
[363] Department of State. United States Embassy in Uruguay. Telegram: Discussion with MinInterior Sena Re Counter Terrorism. September 29 1971. Declassified in

the Universidad de la República's GEIPAR program. http://www.geipar.udelar.edu.uy/wp-content/uploads/2012/07/Descla%20Duffau%20nov11-renombrado2/RG%2059%20Files%201970-1973/RG59.SNF.1970-1973.PD.BOX2662/RG59.SNF.1970-1973.PD.BOX2662_01010.jpg

364 Department of State. United States Embassy in Montevideo. Letter from Ambassador Charles Adair to Country Director William Stedman. July 20 1971. Declassified in the Universidad de la República's GEIPAR program. http://www.geipar.udelar.edu.uy/wp-content/uploads/2013/07/POL-1-GENERAL-POLICY_BACKGROUND-URUGUAY-71_-Primera-parte.pdf

365 These biographical notes on Trabal are based on Israel, Sergio. El Enigma Trabal, op. cit. Pages 16-9 and 79-87

366 D'Oliveira, op. cit. Page 108

367 The one Benítez attended, an infamous course at Los Fresnos in Texas that was later scrapped, was decisive in the dismissal of United States security cooperation as inadequate, both in the United States and in recipient countries. Furthermore, Benítez contributed half-heartedly to the legend of Dan Mitrione as a dark figure. Baumgartner, op. cit. Pages 98-101

368 Circular 5, op. cit.

369 D'Oliveira, op. cit. Pages 108-11

370 Israel, Sergio. Mujica: El Florista Presidente, op. cit. Page 87

371 This account is based on Blixen, op. cit. Pages 77-80 and Fernández Huidobro, Eleuterio. La Fuga de Punta Carretas. Montevideo: Ediciones de la Banda Oriental, 2012. Pages 129-31

372 D'Oliveira, op. cit. Page 31

373 Central Intelligence Agency, Directorate of Intelligence. Intelligence Memorandum: Urban Terrorism in Latin America. November 6 1969. http://www.foia.cia.gov/sites/default/files/document_conversions/89801/DOC_0000637154.pdf

374 Alfonso, Álvaro. Jugando a las Escondidas, op. cit. Page 75

375 Sanguinetti, op. cit. Page 194

376 Vallarino, Raúl. ¡Llamen al Comisario Otero!, op. cit. Page 129

377 Author's interview with Julio Sanguinetti.

378 Di Candia, op. cit. Pages 39-40 of Volume 5

379 Alfonso, Álvaro. Los Dos Demonios. Montevideo: Planeta, 2012. Page 136

380 Doudchitzky, Pablo. Tupamaros: La Fuga del Siglo. Undated. https://www.youtube.com/watch?v=-r_2bU3K66c

381 El País, May 15 1971

382 See Sanguinetti, op. cit. Pages 204-5 and Junta de Comandantes en Jefe, La Subversión, op. cit. Page 696

383 Tagliaferro, Gerardo. Adiós Robin Hood, op. cit. Page 353

384 Aldrighi, Clara. El Caso Mitrione, op. cit. Pages 34-5 and 231; Haberkorn, Leonardo. Milicos y Tupas, op. cit. Page 43

385 Author's interviews with Efraín Martínez Platero and Javier Bonilla.

386 Aldrighi, Clara. Memorias de Insurgencia, op. cit. Page 175

387 Aldrighi, Clara. La Izquierda Armada, op. cit. Page 190

---

[388] Junta de Comandantes en Jefe, La Subversión, op. cit. Pages 677 and 693

[389] Aldrighi, Clara. Memorias de Insurgencia, op. cit. Pages 107, 247 and 323; Author's interviews with Efraín Martínez Platero and Henry Engler

[390] Haberkorn, Leonardo. Historias Tupamaras, op. cit. Pages 142-4 and Haberkorn, Leonardo. Milicos y Tupas, op. cit. Pages 47-51

[391] Junta de Comandantes en Jefe, La Subversión, op. cit. Pages 576-7

[392] Sanguinetti, op. cit. Page 191

[393] As the U.S. Embassy put it, the Frente's spectrum "runs from liberal democrat to pro-terrorist". Department of State. United States Embassy in Montevideo. Proposed Short Term Courses of Action in Uruguay. August 25 1971. Declassified in the Universidad de la República's GEIPAR program. http://www.geipar.udelar.edu.uy/wp-content/uploads/2013/07/POL-1-GENERAL-POLICY_BACKGROUND-URUGUAY-71_-Primera-parte.pdf

[394] Gatto, op. cit. Pages 312-3

[395] Department of State. United States Embassy in Montevideo. Organization of 'Impact' Task Force. May 24 1971; Letter from Frank Ortiz to Edward Marasciulo; Impact Projects for Uruguay to Counteract the 'Frente Amplio' - 'Brainstorming' Ideas. May 25 1971. Declassified in the Universidad de la República's GEIPAR program. http://www.geipar.udelar.edu.uy/wp-content/uploads/2013/07/POL-1-GENERAL-POLICY_BACKGROUND-URUGUAY-71_-Segunda-mitad.pdf

[396] Dirección Nacional de Información e Inteligencia. Transcripción de los Apuntes de una Libreta Incautada a Nora Malnero Inquintanelli de Mansilla. February 28 1971. Declassified in the Universidad de la República's GEIPAR program. http://www.geipar.udelar.edu.uy/wp-content/uploads/2013/07/POL-23-INTERNAL-SECURITY-GENERAL-URUGUAY-1971.pdf

[397] El País, July 24 1971

[398] Blixen, op. cit. Page 54

[399] Junta de Comandantes en Jefe, La Subversión, op. cit. Page 583

[400] Aldrighi, Clara. Memorias de Insurgencia, op. cit. Page 205

[401] This account of operations Estrella and Abuso is based on the following: Israel, Sergio. Mujica: El Florista Presidente, op. cit. Page 77; Fernández Huidobro, Eleuterio. La Fuga de Punta Carretas, op. cit. Pages 16, 24-7, 32-9, 51, 57, 75, 85, 100-4, 133-4, 145-83, 200-17, 223-31, 236; Márquez Zacchino, op. cit. Pages 78-80, 129, 144-5; Blixen, La Comisión Aspirina, op. cit. Pages 14-9, 28-9, 34, 44, 53-62, 71-89, 94-6, 117, 123, 198; Aldrighi, Clara. La Izquierda Armada, op. cit. Page 190; Leicht, Federico. Cero a la Izquierda, op. cit. Pages 97-100, 122; Cavallo Quintana, op. cit. Pages 70, 79, 102, 13; Fontana, op. cit. Page 157; Haberkorn, Leonardo. Historias Tupamaras, op. cit. Page 52; Chavarría, op. cit. Page 355; Aldrighi, Clara. Memorias de Insurgencia, op. cit. Pages 181-4; Author's interview with Henry Engler; Interview with Henry Engler in Archivo CEIU - "Colección David Cámpora", op. cit.; Author's interview with Efraín Martínez Platero; Tupamaros: La Fuga de Punta Carretas, op. cit.; Teledoce TV network. Código País: Fuga de 38 Mujeres Presas. November 3 2011. https://www.youtube.com/watch?v=61HbRhDtPHw

[402] Samuel Blixen provides the names of the main diggers: Nicolás Estévez -one of Raúl Sendic's closest assistants-, the UTAA cane worker Antonio Bandera, Mujica's long-term associate David Melián, the Russian-Uruguayan Wladimir Sawchuk, and a few others.

[403] Department of State. United States Embassy in Uruguay. Telegram: Reactions to Mass Terrorist Escape. September 7 1971. Declassified in the Universidad de la República's GEIPAR program. http://www.geipar.udelar.edu.uy/wp-content/uploads/2012/07/Descla%20Duffau%20nov11-renombrado2/RG%2059%20Files%201970-1973/RG59.SNF.1970-1973.PD.BOX2662/RG59.SNF.1970-1973.PD.BOX2662_00046.jpg

[404] Department of State. United States Embassy in Uruguay. Telegram: The Great Escape - A Preliminary Political Assessment. September 10 1971. Declassified in the Universidad de la República's GEIPAR program. http://www.geipar.udelar.edu.uy/wp-content/uploads/2012/07/Descla%20Duffau%20nov11-renombrado2/RG%2059%20Files%201970-1973/RG59.SNF.1970-1973.PD.BOX2662/RG59.SNF.1970-1973.PD.BOX2662_00039.jpg

[405] Holmes, op. cit. Page 150

[406] El Observador special on Héctor Amodio Pérez, op. cit.

[407] Caula and Silva, op. cit. Page 96

[408] Junta de Comandantes en Jefe, La Subversión, op. cit. Page 115

[409] However, it was later discarded. Aldrighi, Clara. Memorias de Insurgencia, op. cit. Page 178.

[410] Di Candia, op. cit. Page 54 of Volume 5

[411] Department of State. United States Embassy in Uruguay. Telegram: Four Wounded in Clash Between Rightist and Communist Youths. November 11 1971. Declassified in the Universidad de la República's GEIPAR program. http://www.geipar.udelar.edu.uy/wp-content/uploads/2012/07/Descla%20Duffau%20nov11-renombrado2/RG%2059%20Files%201970-1973/RG59.SNF.1970-1973.PD.BOX2662/RG59.SNF.1970-1973.PD.BOX2662_01037.jpg

[412] Department of State. United States Embassy in Argentina. Telegram: Uruguayan Situation. August 27 1971. Declassified by the National Security Archive at George Washington University. http://www.gwu.edu/~nsarchiv/NSAEBB/NSAEBB71/doc4.pdf

[413] Di Candia, op. cit. Page 65 of Volume 5

[414] Sanguinetti, op. cit. Page 233

[415] Junta de Comandantes en Jefe, La Subversión, op. cit. Page 491

[416] Haberkorn, Leonardo. Milicos y Tupas, op. cit. Pages 21-3

[417] Haberkorn, Leonardo. Milicos y Tupas, op. cit. Page 26

[418] The statistic is calculated based on the number of eligible voters for the 1971 elections: 1,878,132 citizens.

[419] Department of State, United States Embassy in Uruguay. Airgram: Census of Government Employees. September 3 1969. Declassified in the Universidad de la República's GEIPAR program. http://www.geipar.udelar.edu.uy/wp-content/uploads/2012/07/Descla%20Duffau%20nov11-

---

renombrado2/RG%2059%20Files%201963-1969/RG59.SNF.1967-1969.PD.BOX2581/RG59.SNF.1967-1969.PD.BOX2581_0808.jpg

420 Haberkorn, Leonardo. Milicos y Tupas, op. cit. Pages 25-6

421 Haberkorn, Leonardo. Milicos y Tupas, op. cit. Page 69

422 Lessa, Alfonso. La Revolución Imposible, op. cit. Pages 145 and 264

423 Gavazzo, José Nino. Mi Testimonio. Montevideo: Artemisa, 2012. Page 190

424 Gavazzo, op. cit. Page 189, 198-9

425 Caula, Nelson and Silva, Alberto. Alto el Fuego. Montevideo: Ediciones B. 2009. Page 394

426 Sanguinetti, op. cit. Page 227

427 To top this off, the last remaining ALN leader in the capital city of Algiers, after numerous combat operations, was secretly an agent of the French: Safy-le-Pur. See Horne, Alistair. A Savage War of Peace: Algeria, 1954-1962. New York: New York Review Books, 2006. Pages 260-3

428 This discussion of Trinquier's work is based on Trinquier, Roger. Modern Warfare: A French View of Counterinsurgency. Westport, Connecticut: Praeger Security International, 2006. Pages 5-13 and 41-2.

429 This discussion of Galula's work is based on Galula, David. Counterinsurgency Warfare: Theory and Practice. Westport, CT: Praeger Security International, 2006. Pages 6-9, 52, 62-3

430 Alfonso, Álvaro. Jugando a las Escondidas, op. cit. Page 43

431 Alfonso, Álvaro. Jugando a las Escondidas, op. cit. Page 175

432 Lessa, Alfonso. Estado de Guerra, op. cit. Page 70 and Junta de Comandantes en Jefe, La Subversión, op. cit. Pages 364-5

433 Alfonso, Álvaro. Jugando a las Escondidas, op. cit. Pages 158-9 and Holmes, op. cit. Page 138

434 Gavazzo, op. cit. Pages 189-90

435 Holmes, op. cit. Page 183

436 Gavazzo, op. cit. Pages 225-7

437 This discussion of General Gregorio Álvarez is based on Lessa, Alfonso. La Primera Orden. Montevideo: Sudamericana, 2009. Pages 18-21 and 66; Lessa, Alfonso. El Pecado Original: La Izquierda y el Golpe Militar de Febrero de 1973. Montevideo: Debate, 2012. Pages 282-3; Lessa, Alfonso. La Revolución Imposible, op. cit. Page 100; and Sanguinetti, op. cit. Pages 225-6

438 Analysts of urban guerrilla James Kohl and John Litt reached a similar conclusion: "The cycle of arrest and torture is the foundation of counter guerrilla operations". See Kohl and Litt, op. cit. Page 21

439 Catalan television report. Tupamaros: Del Penal a la Llibertat. 1985. http://youtu.be/Sh1LGuLRE-o

440 Tagliaferro, Gerardo. Fernández Huidobro, op. cit. Page 164

441 Torres, op. cit. Page 121

442 Sanguinetti, op. cit. Page 221

443 Tagliaferro, Gerardo. Interview with Juan Almiratti, op. cit.

444 Sanguinetti, op. cit. Pages 245-51

445 Department of State. United States Embassy in Uruguay. Airgram: Conversation with Senator Bordaberry. September 4 1963. Declassified in the

Universidad de la República's GEIPAR program. http://www.geipar.udelar.edu.uy/wp-content/uploads/2012/07/Descla%20Duffau%20nov11-renombrado2/RG%2059%20Files%201963-1969/RG59.SNF.1963.PD.BOX4083/RG59.SNF.1963.PD.BOX4083_0245.jpg

[446] A British documentary of the time shows inauguration day and its security precautions. The untitled and undated documentary may be seen here: https://www.youtube.com/watch?v=uXIuoKtHGYw

[447] Di Candia, op. cit. Pages 81-2 of Volume 5

[448] Junta de Comandantes en Jefe, op. cit. Page 495.

[449] Lessa, Alfonso. La Revolución Imposible, op. cit. Page 225

[450] Sasso, La Toma de Pando, op. cit.

[451] Blixen, Sendic, op. cit. Pages 216-7

[452] Junta de Comandantes en Jefe, op. cit. Pages 709-10. See also Fontana, op. cit. Pages 168-9.

[453] Department of State. United States Embassy in Uruguay. Telegram: Terrorists Stage Unsuccessful Raid on Police Station, Two Killed in Resulting Gunfight. January 31 1972. Declassified in the Universidad de la República's GEIPAR program. http://www.geipar.udelar.edu.uy/wp-content/uploads/2012/07/Descla%20Duffau%20nov11-renombrado2/RG%2059%20Files%201970-1973/RG59.SNF.1970-1973.PD.BOX2662/RG59.SNF.1970-1973.PD.BOX2662_01353.jpg

[454] It was a curious posting: Candán had been the top man at Column 15 and its signature "militarist" style; when people referred to that "deviation" in the MLN, they were often talking about Candán. Now he was leading the least militaristic of all the MLN's subdivisions. Fontana, op. cit. Page 165

[455] Pereyra, Leonardo. El otro "traidor" tupamaro del que casi nadie se acuerda. El Observador, May 26 2013. http://www.elobservador.com.uy/noticia/imprimir/251561/el-otro-traidor-tupamaro--del-que-casi-nadie-se-acuerda/

[456] Lastly, Henry Engler supervised Column 7, which was under the command of MLN founder Julio Marenales

[457] Campodónico, Miguel Ángel. Las Vidas de Rosencof, op. cit. Pages 94-8

[458] Author's interview with Javier Bonilla

[459] Pernas, op. cit. Pages 509-10 and Tagliaferro, Gerardo. Adiós Robin Hood, op. cit. Page 195

[460] Leicht, Federico. Cero a la Izquierda, op. cit. Pages 104-5

[461] Fontana, op. cit. Pages 176-80

[462] Here there is a major disagreement among sources. Mauricio Rosencof and others claim the leadership was made up of Rosencof, Engler, Fernández and Candán. Engler excludes Rosencof and has only himself, Fernández, and Candán. It has proven impossible to reconcile both versions of the story. Author's interview with Henry Engler

[463] Lessa, Alfonso. La Revolución Imposible, op. cit. Page 277

[464] Blixen, La Comisión Aspirina, op. cit. Page 135

[465] Author's interview with Efraín Martínez Platero

---

[466] El País. Cuando Era Árbitro No Toleraba Nada, op. cit. and Vallarino, Raúl. ¡Llamen al Comisario Otero!, op. cit. Pages 153-4
[467] Leicht, Federico. Cero a la Izquierda, op. cit. Page 109
[468] Pernas, op. cit. Page 518 and author's interview with Efraín Martínez Platero
[469] Leicht, Federico. Cero a la Izquierda, op. cit. Page 109
[470] Fontana, op. cit. Page 181
[471] Fontana, op. cit. Page 169
[472] Author's interview with Efraín Martínez Platero
[473] Tagliaferro, Gerardo. Adiós Robin Hood, op. cit. Pages 195-7
[474] Haberkorn, Leonardo. Historias Tupamaras, op. cit. Page 22
[475] This account of Plan Hipólito is based on the following sources: Author's interview with Henry Engler; Junta de Comandantes en Jefe, op. cit., p. 701 and 717; Sanguinetti, op. cit. Pages 152-4; César Di Candia interview with Víctor Castiglioni, available at Archivo CEIU - "Colección David Cámpora", op. cit.; Leicht, Federico. Cero a la Izquierda, op. cit. Page 112; D'Oliveira, op. cit. Page 106; Haberkorn, Leonardo. Milicos y Tupas, op. cit. Page 79; Tagliaferro, Gerardo. Fernández Huidobro, op. cit. Pages 143 and 154-9; Alfonso, Álvaro. Los Dos Demonios, op. cit. Page 156; Caula and Silva, op. cit. Page 116; Campodónico, Miguel Ángel. Las Vidas de Rosencof, op. cit. Pages 57-8 and 196; Haberkorn, Historias Tupamaras, op. cit., p. 98
[476] Almost nothing is known of Miguel Sofía. At the time he was suspected of being a conservative-nationalist extremist with ties to the police, and who thus somehow participated in the murders. He disappears from the historical record in the late 1970s, after a stint as a Uruguayan diplomat in Washington.
[477] Before the insurgency was over Abraham Guillén, the old Spanish acquaintance and plagiarist of the Tupas, correctly warned that the MLN's dual power only imitated the repressive aspects of state authority: prisons and death sentences. Where was the rest? Kohl and Litt, op. cit. Page 191
[478] According to Castiglioni, Bardesio was bound to a chair, had a powerful light shining on his face, and was thus sleepless for several days. Castiglioni adds that what Bardesio confessed was true.
[479] It is worth nothing though, that later in the year military intelligence chief Ramón Trabal interrogated Bardesio, who supposedly confirmed everything he confessed to the Tupamaros was true. Israel, Sergio. El Enigma Trabal, op. cit. Page 22
[480] Department of State. United States Embassy in Uruguay. The Internal Security Situation in Uruguay. December 1 1972. Declassified in the Universidad de la República's GEIPAR program. http://www.geipar.udelar.edu.uy/wp-content/uploads/2012/07/Descla%20Duffau%20nov11-renombrado2/RG%2059%20Files%201970-1973/RG59.SNF.1970-1973.PD.BOX2662/RG59.SNF.1970-1973.PD.BOX2662_00565.jpg
[481] In the MLN, Martirena worked for the Committee of International Affairs (CAI), tasked with liaising with the outside world. Cuba was, along with Chile, the MLN's top foreign connection at the time. As a known Cuban intelligence asset, Martirena's home was thus a foolish choice for an MLN safe house. The head of CAI at the time was Adolfo Wasem.

[482] The incident remains unexplained. Sanguinetti, op. cit. Page 260

[483] Alfonso, Álvaro. Juicio al PCU, op. cit. Page 155. Junta de Comandantes en Jefe, op. cit. Pages 720-1

[484] Engler confirmed to the author his reservations about a battle front in the interior of the country. Author's interview with Henry Engler

[485] Interview with a Tupamaro present at the scene; names withheld. Courtesy of Archivo CEIU - "Colección David Cámpora" at Facultad de Humanidades & Ciencias de la Educación. Universidad de la República. Montevideo, Uruguay.

[486] Chronologically he was the third, following the disappearances of MLN collaborators Abel Ayala and Manuel Ramos in mid-1971. These two disappearances were the work of the parapolice teams known as "escuadrón de la muerte".

[487] Leicht, Federico. Cero a la Izquierda, op. cit. Page 114; Haberkorn, Leonardo. Historias Tupamaras, op. cit. Page 134; David Cámpora interview with Ismael Bassini, op. cit.

[488] This section on torture methods is based on the following: Aldrighi, Clara. Memorias de Insurgencia, op. cit. Pages 86, 113, 157-8, 212 and 254; Haberkorn, Leonardo. Milicos y Tupas, op. cit. Page 100; Israel, Sergio. El Enigma Trabal, op. cit. Page 130 and Ruiz and Sanseviero, op. cit. Pages 97-8

[489] Amodio Pérez, Héctor. Carta 1: Aclarando Algunas Cosas...a Propósito de Cómo se Escribió la Historia.Montevideo: El Observador, May 22 2013. http://www.elobservador.com.uy/noticia/imprimir/251214/carta-1-aclarando-algunas-cosas-a-proposito-de-como-se-escribio-la-historia/

[490] The account of this attack is based on Gerardo Tagliaferro's interview with Henry Engler, op. cit.; Haberkorn, Leonardo. Milicos y Tupas, op. cit. Pages 84-9; Haberkorn, Leonardo. Milicos y Tupas, op. cit. Pages 92-3 and Aldrighi, Clara. Memorias de Insurgencia, op. cit. Page 135

[491] To this day it is unclear whether the target was Gravina himself or his guard detail. According to Henry Engler, "The objective was to attack the Army. We had decided to attack the Army, to engage in frontal combat with it".

[492] This section is based on the following sources: Amodio Pérez, Héctor. Carta 1, op. cit.; Ruiz and Sanseviero, op. cit. Pages 81-2; Author's interviews with Henry Engler and Efraín Martínez Platero; Campodónico, Miguel Ángel. Mujica, op. cit. Page 154; Fontana, op. cit. Pages 187-202; Lessa, Alfonso. La Revolución Imposible, op. cit. Page 283; Amodio Pérez, Héctor. Carta 4 (anexo), op. cit. and Alfonso, Álvaro. Jugando a las Escondidas, op. cit. Pages 113-4

[493] A low-ranking Tupamara also captured that week was María Clara Aldrighi, today the semi-official academic historian of the movement. Junta de Comandantes en Jefe, op. cit. Page 726

[494] D'Oliveira, op. cit. Pages 127 and 169

[495] Haberkorn, Leonardo. Milicos y Tupas, op. cit. Page 99

[496] According to Engler, at least one top MLN cryptogram required the reader to possess a pre-agreed book. He would read a code that pointed to a specific page, paragraph, and letter. With those letters he or she would build the message. Código País: Fuga de 38 Mujeres, op. cit.

[497] Junta de Comandantes en Jefe, op. cit. Pages 719-23

---

498 Zabalza, Jorge. Raúl Sendic, el Tupamaro: Su Pensamiento Revolucionario. Montevideo: Letra Ñ. 2009. Pages 17-8

499 The full, more detailed account may be found in Leicht, Federico. Cero a la Izquierda, op. cit. Pages 114-9. See also Haberkorn, Leonardo. Milicos y Tupas, op. cit. Page 91

500 This section is based on the following sources: D'Oliveira, op. cit. Page 134; Haberkorn, Leonardo. Milicos y Tupas, op. cit. Pages 100-17; Caula, Nelson and Silva, Alberto. Alto el Fuego, op. cit. Pages 72 and 107; Alfonso, Álvaro. Los Dos Demonios, op. cit. Page 178; Leibner, op. cit. Page 605; Junta de Comandantes en Jefe, op. cit. Pages 721-2

501 The account of the People's Prison is based on the following: Pereyra, Gabriel. Contacto con Héctor Amodio Pérez. El Observador, May 21 2013. http://www.elobservador.com.uy/noticia/imprimir/251176/contacto-con-hector-amodio-perez/; Amodio Pérez, Héctor. Carta 1, op. cit.; Lessa, Alfonso. La Revolución Imposible, op. cit. Pages 153-6; Alfonso, Álvaro. Jugando a las Escondidas, op. cit. Page 42; El Observador special on Héctor Amodio Pérez, op. cit.; Junta de Comandantes en Jefe, op. cit. Page 730; Fontana, op. cit. Pages 206-9 and El País, May 27 1972. http://historico.elpais.com.uy/Suple/EntrevistasDeDicandia/05/07/16/

502 If Ferrés was a member of an "oligarchy", he was no longer so after his kidnapping. According to the American embassy, "Although Ferrés at one time headed one of Uruguay's largest investment/business groups, we understand that series of financial reverses he suffered in past eighteen months has left him virtually penniless". Department of State. United States Embassy in Uruguay. Telegram: Terrorists Release Kidnap Victim; Assassinate Prison Official. January 28 1972. Declassified in the Universidad de la República's GEIPAR program. http://www.geipar.udelar.edu.uy/wp-content/uploads/2012/07/Descla%20Duffau%20nov11-renombrado2/RG%2059%20Files%201970-1973/RG59.SNF.1970-1973.PD.BOX2662/RG59.SNF.1970-1973.PD.BOX2662_01356.jpg

503 Amodio Pérez, Héctor. Carta 1, op. cit.

504 David Cámpora interview with Mauricio Rosencof, op. cit.

505 Sanguinetti, op. cit. Page 272

506 Fontana, op. cit. Page 214

507 Alfonso, Álvaro. Jugando a las Escondidas, op. cit. Page 59

508 Junta de Comandantes en Jefe, op. cit. Pages 730 and 741 and author's interview with Henry Engler

509 César Di Candia interview with Víctor Castiglioni, op. cit.

510 Cavallo Quintana, op. cit. Pages 114-5

511 Macchi's fate is based on the following: Ruiz and Sanseviero, op. cit. Page 163; Israel, Sergio. El Enigma Trabal, op. cit. Page 159, and Aldrighi, Clara. La Izquierda Armada, op. cit. Pages 216-221

512 Cavallo Quintana, op. cit. Page 118

513 Junta de Comandantes en Jefe, op. cit. Pages 724 and 741-2

514 Despite a clear record of success, the military rated its own efficiency in 1972 raids at around 15%. Junta de Comandantes en Jefe, op. cit. Pages 365 and 369

[515] Author's interview with Henry Engler and Aldrighi, Clara. La Izquierda Armada, op. cit. Page 136
[516] Blixen, op. cit. Page 236
[517] The account of Marenales' fate is based on: Márquez Zacchino, op. cit. Pages 90-7 and 148 and Alfonso, Álvaro. Juicio al PCU, op. cit. Page 154
[518] "There was a sergeant who fired fourteen rounds at me from six meters away; he failed to kill me by pure chance. I later sent a message to him through the captains: 'you will have no problems from me; you did what you had to do'. If I threw a grenade at him, what was he supposed to do? Combat is combat".
[519] Lessa, Alfonso. La Revolución Imposible, op. cit. Page 279; Alfonso, Álvaro. Los Dos Demonios, op. cit. Pages 152-3
[520] MLN-Tupamaros. Los Tupamaros en Acción, op. cit. Page 13
[521] Junta de Comandantes en Jefe, op. cit. Page 584
[522] Sanguinetti, op. cit. Page 272
[523] Alfonso, Álvaro. Jugando a las Escondidas, op. cit. Pages 114-5 and Lessa, Alfonso. El Pecado Original, op. cit. Pages 166-8
[524] Holmes, op. cit. Page 150
[525] Haberkorn, Leonardo. Milicos y Tupas, op. cit. Page 129
[526] Blixen, op. cit. Pages 245-6
[527] This section is based on the following sources: Caula, Nelson and Silva, Alberto. Alto el Fuego, op. cit. Pages 189-92 and 204-8; Sanguinetti op. cit. Page 303; Alfonso, Álvaro. Jugando a las Escondidas, op. cit. Page 51; Haberkorn, Leonardo. Milicos y Tupas, op. cit. Pages 137-64 and 177-83; Pernas, op. cit. Page 544; Aldrighi, Clara. Memorias de Insurgencia, op. cit. Page 210, and Blixen, Sendic, op. cit. Page 256
[528] Department of State. United States Embassy in Uruguay. Telegram: Pereira Reverbel Incident. August 2 1972. Declassified in the Universidad de la República's GEIPAR program. http://www.geipar.udelar.edu.uy/wp-content/uploads/2012/07/Descla%20Duffau%20nov11-renombrado2/RG%2059%20Files%201970-1973/RG59.SNF.1970-1973.PD.BOX2662/RG59.SNF.1970-1973.PD.BOX2662_01190.jpg
[529] For instance, Tupamaro Mario Teti told Clara Aldrighi that he saw prisoners of the joint task forces taken to torture chambers. Samuel Blixen also recognized this in his biography of Sendic.
[530] This section is based on the following sources: Lessa, Alfonso. Estado de Guerra, op. cit. Pages 48-9, 59-60 and 78-80; Sanguinetti, op. cit. Page 275; Aldrighi, Clara. Memorias de Insurgencia, op. cit. Pages 46-50; Israel, Sergio. El Enigma Trabal, op. cit. Pages 120-1, and Caula, Nelson and Silva, Alberto. Alto el Fuego, op. cit. Page 194
[531] Lessa, Alfonso. El Pecado Original, op. cit. Pages 160-8; Sanguinetti, op. cit. Page 280; and Israel, Sergio. El Enigma Trabal, op. cit. Page 96
[532] The rest of this section is based on the following: Caula and Silva. Ana la Guerrillera, op. cit. Pages 98 and 177; Pernas, op. cit. Pages 544-9 and 562-74; Israel, Sergio. Mujica: El Florista Presidente, op. cit. Pages 89-90; Aldrighi, Clara. Memorias de Insurgencia, op. cit. Page 48; author's interview with Henry Engler; Haberkorn, Leonardo. Milicos y Tupas, op. cit. Pages 92-3, and Specogna, Heidi

& Hoffmann, Rainier. Tupamaros. Berlin: Specogna-Film/ZDF, 1996. https://www.youtube.com/watch?v=O1GaWgBG1FY

533 This last portion of the negotiations is based on: El Observador special on Héctor Amodio Pérez, op. cit.; Blixen, op. cit. Pages 247-9 and 256; Caula, Nelson and Silva, Alberto. Alto el Fuego, op. cit. Pages 143 and 200; Lessa, Alfonso. Estado de Guerra, op. cit. Pages 57-8; the author's interview with Efraín Martínez Platero; Alfonso, Álvaro. Jugando a las Escondidas, op. cit. Pages 131-4: Israel, Sergio. El Enigma Trabal, op. cit. Page 125; Lessa, La Primera Orden, op. cit. Pages 26-9; Haberkorn, Leonardo. Milicos y Tupas, op. cit. Pages 137-8 and 163; Television report on the death of Artigas Álvarez. June 21 2011. https://www.youtube.com/watch?v=b23SH42g39k and Charlo, José Pedro & Garay, Aldo. El Círculo. Memoria y Sociedad and Sur Films. 2008. https://www.youtube.com/watch?v=C1laNbiB68Y

534 The following account of the military's targeting of politicians is based on these sources: Alfonso, Álvaro. Jugando a las Escondidas, op. cit. Page 48; Sanguinetti, op. cit. Pages 287-91; Trinquier, op. cit. Page 24; Israel, Sergio. El Enigma Trabal, op. cit. Pages 131-5; Haberkorn, Leonardo. Milicos y Tupas, op. cit. Page 158; Caula, Nelson and Silva, Alberto. Alto el Fuego, op. cit. Page 184; Lessa, Alfonso. El Pecado Original, op. cit. Pages 148-9 and 216; Di Candia, op. cit. Page 63 of Volume 6, and Gramajo, Yuri and Israel, Sergio. El Golpe de Febrero. Montevideo: Planeta, 2013. Pages 49-52

535 Department of State. United States Embassy in Uruguay. Telegram: "Frente Amplio" Presses Torture Charges as Censure of Minister of Interior Fails. June 27 1972. Declassified in the Universidad de la República's GEIPAR program. http://www.geipar.udelar.edu.uy/wp-content/uploads/2012/07/Descla%20Duffau%20nov11-renombrado2/RG%2059%20Files%201970-1973/RG59.SNF.1970-1973.PD.BOX2662/RG59.SNF.1970-1973.PD.BOX2662_01233.jpg

536 Junta de Comandantes en Jefe, op. cit. Page 370

537 For more on relations between Chile under Allende and the KGB see Andrew, Christopher and Mitrokhin, Vasili. The World Was Going Our Way. New York: Basic Books, 2006

538 This account of Raúl Sendic's fate is based on the following sources: Blixen, op. cit. Pages 240–63; Chavarría, op. cit. Page 271; Raúl Sendic interview conducted in 1987 available at Archivo CEIU - "Colección David Cámpora", at Facultad de Humanidades & Ciencias de la Educación, Universidad de la República; Aldrighi, Clara. Memorias de Insurgencia, op. cit. Page 49; Lessa, Alfonso. El Pecado Original, op. cit. Page 170, and D'Oliveira, op. cit. Page 144

539 This section is based on the following sources: Gavazzo, op. cit. Pages 231-40; Alfonso, Álvaro. Jugando a las Escondidas, op. cit. Pages 52-5 and 116-7; Author's interview with Efraín Martínez Platero; Haberkorn, Leonardo. Historias Tupamaras, op. cit. Pages 52-3; Caula, Nelson and Silva, Alberto. Alto el Fuego, op. cit. Page 235; Amodio Pérez, Hector. Carta 1, op. cit.; Gramajo and Israel, op. cit. Pages 178-9, and Lessa, Alfonso. Estado de Guerra, op. cit. Page 93

540 This account of the February crisis is based on the following sources: Alfonso, Álvaro. Los Dos Demonios, op. cit. Pages 200-2; Lessa, Alfonso. El Pecado

Original, op. cit. Pages 34-51, 65, 130, 155, 202-6, 242-3 and 277-8; Di Candia, op. cit. Page 69 of Volume 6; the author's interview with Julio Sanguinetti; Gramajo and Israel, op. cit. Pages 33, 134-5, 147, 165-70 and 177; Israel, Sergio. El Enigma Trabal, op. cit. Pages 142 and 156; Lessa, Alfonso. Estado de Guerra, op. cit. Pages 89-102; Gavazzo, op. cit. Pages 248-9; Sanguinetti, op. cit. Page 302; Caula, Nelson and Silva, Alberto. Alto el Fuego, op. cit. Pages 319-22 and 329-37; Lessa, Alfonso. La Primera Orden, op. cit. Pages 212-3

[541] Department of State. United States Embassy in Uruguay. Telegram. February 9 1973. http://www.geipar.udelar.edu.uy/wp-content/uploads/2012/07/Descla%20Duffau%20nov11-renombrado2/RG%2059%20Files%201970-1973/RG59.SNF.1970-1973.PD.BOX2662/RG59.SNF.1970-1973.PD.BOX2662_00776.jpg

[542] James L. Tull, Political Officer, 1969-73. In: Association for Diplomatic Studies and Training, op. cit.

[543] It should be noted that later Wilson Ferreira partly denied this happened, and to this day his supporters argue Senator Ferreira was not a *golpista*. Nevertheless, the evidence that Wilson discussed the removal of the president with an active-duty military officer is significant.

[544] This account of the May-June crisis is based on the following: Lessa, Alfonso. El Pecado Original, op. cit. Pages 31-3; Israel, Sergio. El Enigma Trabal, op. cit. Page 123; Gavazzo, op. cit. Pages 35, 262 and 273-8; Fontana, op. cit. Pages 287-8; Alfonso, Álvaro. Jugando a las Escondidas, op. cit. Pages 60, 115 and 148; Sanguinetti, op. cit. Pages 344 and 355-61; Lessa, Alfonso. La Primera Orden, op. cit. Page 83; Alonso, Eduardo. Clandestinos: Blancos y Colorados Frente a la Dictadura 1973-1985. Montevideo: Banda Oriental, 2012. Pages 93-5; Junta de Comandantes en Jefe, op. cit. Pages 364-5, and Blixen, Samuel. Un Sicario de los Militares. Brecha, May 31 2013. http://brecha.com.uy/index.php/politica-uruguaya/1930-un-sicario-de-los-militares

[545] The ministers were José María Robaina, Ángel Servetti, Pablo Purriel, and Jorge Presno. In addition to them, individuals like Ricardo Zerbino, Alberto Bensión and Didier Opertti -all senior officials decades later in Uruguay- also resigned.

[546] Department of State. United States Embassy in Uruguay. Telegram: The United States and Events in Uruguay. July 2 1973. Declassified by the National Security Archive at George Washington University. http://www2.gwu.edu/~nsarchiv/NSAEBB/NSAEBB309/19730702.pdf

[547] Clausewitz, Carl von, Michael Howard, Peter Paret, and Bernard Brodie. On War. Princeton, N.J.: Princeton University Press, 1984. Page 80

[548] Brands, op. cit. Pages 121, 189 and 206-7

[549] This description of the Uruguayan dictatorship is based on the following sources: Lewis, Paul H. Guerrillas and Generals The "Dirty War" in Argentina. Westport, Conn: Praeger, 2002; Lessa, Alfonso. La Primera Orden, op. cit. Page 29; Blixen, op. cit. Page 272; Israel, Sergio. El Enigma Trabal, op. cit. Pages 38, 111 and 257-8; Alfonso, Álvaro. Los Dos Demonios, op. cit. Pages 215-6 and 251; Gavazzo, op. cit. Pages 390-3; Junta de Comandantes en Jefe, op. cit. Pages 128 and 396; Campodónico, Miguel Ángel. Las Vidas de Rosencof, op. cit. Pages 139-

40; Alfonso, Álvaro. Juicio al PCU. Montevideo, Uruguay: Caesare, 2009. Page 106; Gramajo and Israel, op. cit. Pages 194-200; Haberkorn, Leonardo. Historias Tupamaras, op. cit. Page 158

550 The account of these three prisoners' experiences is based on: Blixen, op. cit. Pages 264-80; Figueroa, op. cit.; Márquez Zacchino, op. cit. Pages 107-15 and 274, and Leicht, Federico. Cero a la Izquierda, op. cit. Pages 135-9, 147

551 The account of these three prisoners' experiences is based on: Campodónico, Miguel Ángel. Las Vidas de Rosencof, op. cit. Pages 21-2, 38, 154-5, 291; Caula and Silva. Ana la Guerrillera, op. cit. Page 184; Aldrighi, Clara. Memorias de Insurgencia, op. cit. Page 82; Israel, Sergio. Mujica: El Florista Presidente, op. cit. Pages 104-5; Pernas, op. cit. Page 610; Mallorca television documentary. Cròniques: Estat d'Exili. November 6 2009. https://www.youtube.com/watch?v=zLssf92Kdz4

552 The account for these three prisoners is based on: Charlo & Garay, op. cit.; Aldrighi, Clara. Memorias de Insurgencia, op. cit. Pages 185-92; Alfonso, Álvaro. Preguntas a Líderes Tupamaros. Available at Archivo CEIU - "Colección David Cámpora", op. cit.; Guerrero Palermo, Gustavo. Los Tupas de Tacuarembó: La Izquierda, el MLN y la Represión en el Departamento. Montevideo: Fin de Siglo, 2012. Page 202; Blixen, op. cit. Page 292, Chavarría, op. cit. Page 390, and Adolfo Wasem. Montevideo: Liberación Nacional, 1985. Pages 6-7 and 19

553 Department of State. United States Embassy in Uruguay. The Internal Security Situation in Uruguay, op. cit.

554 Sprinzak, Ehud. The Psychopolitical Formation of Extreme Left Terrorism in a Democracy: The Case of the Weathermen. In: Reich, Walter. Origins of Terrorism: Psychologies, Ideologies, Theologies, States of Mind. Washington, DC: Woodrow Wilson Center Press, 1998. Page 69

555 Schmid, Alex Peter, and Janny de Graaf. Violence As Communication: Insurgent Terrorism and the Western News Media. London: Sage, 1982. Pages 38-40

556 Jenkins, Brian. Soldiers Versus Gunmen: The Challenge of Urban Guerrilla Warfare. RAND, March 1974

557 Alonso, op. cit. Page 101

558 Campodónico, Miguel Ángel. Las Vidas de Rosencof, op. cit. Pages 184-5

559 Author's interview with Julio Sanguinetti; Chavarría, op. cit. Page 401, and Blixen, op. cit. Pages 297-8

560 Christian, Shirley. Uruguayan Clears Up State of Siege Killing. The New York Times, June 21 1987. http://www.nytimes.com/1987/06/21/world/uruguayan-clears-up-state-of-siege-killing.html

561 Tagliaferro, Gerardo. Adiós Robin Hood, op. cit. Pages 345-57

562 Aldrighi, Clara. Memorias de Insurgencia, op. cit. Pages 184-7

563 Leicht, Federico. Cero a la Izquierda, op. cit. Page 167

564 Raúl Sendic interview, op. cit.

565 Cròniques: Estat d'Exili, op. cit.

566 Raúl Sendic interview, op. cit.

567 Blixen, op. cit. Pages 320-3 and 335

568 Alfonso, Álvaro. Los Dos Demonios, op. cit. Pages 274-5

[569] In 2013 Jorge Zabalza gave on television his clearest condemnation and admission of collective guilt over the war crime of murdering Pascasio Báez. Pereyra, Gabriel. En la Mira. May 23 2013. https://www.youtube.com/watch?v=qYK-IvFeciA. See also Tagliaferro, Gerardo. Adiós Robin Hood, op. cit. Pages 16 and 42.
[570] Campodónico, Miguel Ángel. Las Vidas de Rosencof, op. cit. Pages 302-11
[571] Aldrighi, Clara. Memorias de Insurgencia, op. cit. Pages 366-72
[572] Author's interview with Efraín Martínez Platero
[573] Aldrighi, Clara. La Izquierda Armada, op. cit. Pages 233-4
[574] Tagliaferro, Gerardo. Fernández Huidobro, op. cit. Pages 253 and 257
[575] Frente Amplio MPP CAP-L 7373. https://www.youtube.com/watch?v=wZbm7Wk50Yw
[576] Tagliaferro, Gerardo. Adiós Robin Hood, op. cit. Pages 290-316
[577] Caula, Nelson and Silva, Alberto. Alto el Fuego, op. cit. Page 244
[578] Fontana, op. cit. Pages 32 and 320
[579] Aldrighi, Clara. Memorias de Insurgencia, op. cit. Page 124
[580] Haberkorn, Leonardo. Historias Tupamaras, op. cit. Pages 158-61; Aldrighi, Clara. El Caso Mitrione, op. cit. Page 371
[581] Ruiz and Sanseviero, op. cit. Page 94
[582] Aldrighi, Clara. La Izquierda Armada, op. cit. Pages 219-22
[583] Aldrighi, Clara. Memorias de Insurgencia, op. cit. Page 98
[584] See respectively Haberkorn, Leonardo. Milicos y Tupas, op. cit. Pages 33 and 207; Guerrero Palermo, op. cit. Page 132; and Alternativas, August 17 2012. http://www.semanario-alternativas.info/archivos/2012/8%20agosto/230/PORTADA/paginas%20portada/Articulos/fernando.html
[585] This account of José Mujica's life after prison is based on the following: Campodónico, Miguel Ángel. Las Vidas de Rosencof, op. cit. Page 321; Blixen, Samuel. La Comisión Aspirina, op. cit. Pages 96 and 310; Israel, Sergio. Mujica: El Florista Presidente, op. cit. Page 14; Gerardo Tagliaferro interview with José Mujica, available at Archivo CEIU - "Colección David Cámpora", op. cit.; Alfonso, Álvaro. Los Dos Demonios, op. cit. Page 43; Campodónico, Miguel Ángel. Mujica, op. cit. Pages 160-74 and 223; Caula and Silva. Ana la Guerrillera, op. cit. Page 191; Raúl Sendic interview, op. cit.; Emir Sader interview with José Mujica, July 31 2013, https://www.youtube.com/watch?v=wUDJxX8xtO8, and José Mujica interview in Más Info. December 19 2013. https://www.youtube.com/watch?v=4u3vfjaf2JQ
[586] This account of José Mujica's international popularity uses the following sources: De Armste President Ter Wereld. NOS, February 15 2014. http://nos.nl/artikel/611348-de-armste-president-ter-wereld.html; José Mujica Speech at the 68th United Nations General Assembly, September 24 2013. http://webtv.un.org/meetings-events/watch/uruguay-the-eastern-republic-of-general-debate-68th-session/2688845016001; Entrevista a José Mujica, Presidente de Uruguay, en Los Desayunos. TVE, May 31 2013. http://www.rtve.es/alacarta/videos/los-desayunos-de-tve/entrevista-jose-mujica-presidente-uruguay-desayunos/1847647/; Speech in Havana on July 26 2013,

https://www.youtube.com/watch?v=nppesPSz-j4; Jorge Ramos interview on Univisión, December 17 2013. https://www.youtube.com/watch?v=Qiuyo-wXBng; Interview with Zero Hora, December 2 2013. https://www.youtube.com/watch?v=BI_S3aGkaT4; Talk to Al Jazeera, October 29, 2013. https://www.youtube.com/watch?v=152q4Fwe9zc; Interview with Folha, December 2 2013. http://www1.folha.uol.com.br/multimidia/videocasts/2013/12/1379276-tv-folha-traz-entrevista-com-mujica-e-pesquisa-datafolha-sobre-o-governo-de-sp.shtml; Interview with Russia Today, February 1 2014, http://actualidad.rt.com/actualidad/view/118628-version-completa-entrevista-rt-jose-mujica; Interview with Ismael Cala on CNÑ, December 12 2013. http://cnnespanol.cnn.com/2013/12/12/mujica-peor-que-la-droga-es-el-narcotrafico-porque-rebaja-la-etica-de-la-delincuencia/, and the author's interviews with Julio Sanguinetti and Alejandro Otero

587 Technically Luis Batlle, Jorge's father, was the nephew and not the son of President José Batlle & Ordóñez. However, José raised Luis from an early age, and in practice thus lived his life almost like a son of José. In turn, José Batlle & Ordóñez was the son of President Lorenzo Batlle.

588 Alfonso, Álvaro. Juicio al PCU, op. cit. Page 112

589 It is also worth nothing that two of murdered Senator Zelmar Michelini's sons, Rafael and Felipe, are also prominent Frente Amplio politicians. Rafael in particular has based part of his career around the fate of his father. It is fair to note that given that the murder occurred in 1976 and democracy was restored in 1984-5, they obviously never benefitted from their father's help in advancing their political careers.

590 The sources for the return of Héctor Amodio are: El Observador special on Héctor Amodio Pérez, op. cit.; Amodio Pérez, Héctor. Carta 1, Carta 2, and Carta a Marcelo Estefanell, op. cit.; Topolansky Sobre Amodio: "Para Mí es un Hombre Muerto". El Observador, May 22 2013. http://www.elobservador.com.uy/noticia/imprimir/251252/topolansky-sobre-amodio-para-mi-es-un-hombre-muerto/; Pereyra, Gabriel. En la Mira, op. cit.; Álvaro Alfonso interview with Henry Engler, op. cit., and La Previa. Brecha, May 31 2013. http://brecha.com.uy/index.php/politica-uruguaya/1929-la-previa

INDEX

Abdala, Alberto 146-7, 163, 353
Acosta y Lara, Armando 255-6
Adair, Charles 157-8, 160-1, 168, 184-5, 198
Agee, Philip 24, 65, 369
Aguerrondo, Mario 66-7, 69, 224-6, 296, 318, 331
Aldrighi, Clara 109, 117, 144, 147, 150, 156, 159, 161, 354
Algeria (revolution in) 30, 53, 233-6, 262
Allende, Salvador 20, 188-9, 202, 223, 225-6, 248, 306, 327, 332, 343
Almería incident, 150–54
Almiratti, Juan 124-5, 187, 205, 208, 223, 242
Álvarez, Gregorio 238-40, 280, 288, 293-4, 296, 300, 303-4, 311-2, 314-6, 318-9, 324, 328-31, 338, 352
Amodio, Héctor 35, 38, 46, 53-4, 79-81, 84, 98, 100-1, 105, 108-9, 111, 118-20, 135, 139, 141, 151-2, 154, 158, 191, 201, 205, 209, 213-4, 218, 220, 223, 247-53, 260, 263, 265-8, 274-7, 281-3, 287, 296-9, 302, 310, 320-1, 344-5, 354
Arce, Líber 74-5, 183
Argentina, 13, 16, 31, 34, 41, 60, 114, 132, 139, 185, 229, 233, 235, 282, 286, 289, 299, 305-6, 308, 331, 343, 369
Arismendi, Rodney 17-8, 23, 65-6, 70, 96, 182, 189, 243, 259, 272-3, 325, 330, 353
armed propaganda, 59, 84-5, 89, 91, 96, 98-9, 109, 112-3, 115, 121-2, 124, 130, 133-6, 143, 152, 161, 174, 179, 181, 191, 199, 218, 227, 241, 288, 336
Arteche, Roque 193-4, 339, 354
Astori, Danilo 349
Báez, Pascasio 260-1, 280, 339, 342, 354
Banco Francés e Italiano heist, 109–12
Bardesio, Nelson 255
Bassini, Ismael 60, 72, 201, 205, 261, 342
Batlle & Ordóñez, José 14-5, 71, 229
Batlle, Jorge 30, 47, 68, 192, 198, 224-5, 295, 301-2, 309, 311, 313, 324, 329, 337, 341
Bidegain, Raúl 98, 102, 122, 127, 128, 135, 151-2, 188, 208, 346

Blixen, Samuel 113, 154, 156, 158, 193, 262, 345-7
Bolivia 41, 69, 86, 99, 114, 126
Bordaberry, Juan María 190, 195, 224-7, 242-3, 272, 293-4, 303, 307, 312-6, 318, 322-4, 328, 331, 352-4
Brazil, 13, 16, 22, 31, 60, 79, 95, 113-4, 116, 140, 142, 144-6, 150, 154, 161, 164, 166, 180, 183, 185, 289, 299, 321, 351
Britain 89, 168, 171, 185, 329
BROU state bank, 24, 100, 102-3, 106, 118, 179
Buenos Aires, 14, 34, 68, 81, 181, 224, 305, 308, 322-3, 327, 329
Cacao (MLN Plan), 173-8, 192-4, 199, 204, 206, 227, 242, 246, 289
Campos, Hugo 151-2, 237, 257
Candán, Alberto 80, 101, 119, 135, 149-50, 152, 154, 157-9, 192, 201, 214, 221, 247, 250, 254, 258-60, 281, 297
Cantrell, William 116, 149
Castiglioni, Víctor 116, 147, 160, 183, 186, 237, 255, 257, 279, 329
Castro, Fidel 32, 36, 70, 161, 188, 192, 226, 248, 258, 270, 338, 343
Chiappe, Hugo 296, 313, 318-9, 331
Chile, 13, 114, 126, 188-9, 192, 194, 223, 225-6, 235, 282, 305-66, 327-8, 343
CIA, 16, 22-4, 26, 49, 65, 78, 116, 139, 143-5, 147-8, 165, 183, 198, 256, 289, 335, 369
CIM naval academy, attack on, 127–30
CNT labor union, 23, 70, 231, 311, 317
Colorado(s), 15, 29-30, 41, 67, 76, 90, 109, 117, 146, 156, 181, 183, 195-8, 225, 229-31, 233, 243, 246, 272, 296, 301, 303, 313, 317, 319, 322, 337, 341
Communist(s), 16-8, 23, 25-6, 29, 33, 36, 48, 57, 59, 62, 65-6, 69-71, 74, 97-8, 133, 143-4, 154, 182-3, 189, 196-8, 224-5, 231-2, 243, 259, 273, 288, 305-6, 311, 317-8, 329-30, 346, 349, 352-3
Coordinador, 29-38, 40, 43, 45-6, 48, 51, 55, 245, 266, 288, 289
Costa-Gavras, Constantin 151, 248
Cristi, Esteban 240, 263, 275, 280, 288, 293, 294-6, 303, 313, 315, 318-9, 321, 324, 328, 331
Cuba, 18, 20, 31, 36, 44, 62, 69-70, 87, 96, 143-4, 182, 188, 226, 248, 257, 306, 330
Debray, Régis 36, 43, 51, 59, 283
Delega, Óscar 151-2, 254, 256
Department of State, 7, 27, 140, 157, 161
Dias Gomide, Aloysio 140, 142, 145, 147-8, 153-4, 156-7, 161, 164-9, 191, 276

dirección (MLN leadership), 49, 76, 78-9, 81, 114, 119, 124, 149, 151, 154, 157, 192-3, 201, 222, 247, 249-50, 257-8, 260-1, 266, 275, 280, 298
Ehrlich, Ricardo 266
El Abuso prison escape, 208–225, 237, 240, 242, 246-7, 249, 251-2, 258, 275, 285, 298
El Pinar incident, 60–61
Election of 1971, 223–26
Engler, Henry 140, 158-9, 187, 191-4, 206, 208, 210, 216, 218-20, 223, 246-7, 249-50, 259-61, 263, 265, 267, 279, 281, 283, 290, 296, 298, 300, 309, 335, 338-9, 355, 359
Erro, Enrique 47-8, 69, 243, 285, 296-7, 319-22
February coup of 1973, 312–19
Fernández Huidobro,
Eleuterio 32-4, 39-40, 43-4, 46, 53-4, 60, 68, 75-6, 81, 84, 92, 104, 106-7, 119, 139, 151, 161, 203, 216, 219, 249-50, 257, 281, 287-8, 294, 296-7, 299, 333-4, 337-8, 340, 344, 349, 352, 354
Ferreira, Wilson 68-9, 117, 147, 196, 224-5, 248, 272, 285, 293, 295, 301, 310, 318, 323, 329, 337, 341, 353
Fly, Claude 155-7, 164-8, 171, 191
foco, 20-1, 36-7, 40-1, 48, 51, 113, 227, 245, 259
France 14, 89, 181, 185, 232-3, 306, 331, 345, 369
Francese, Antonio 164, 312-3, 315-6
Frick, Carlos 83, 191, 273, 275
FUNSA raid, 53–56
Galeano, Eduardo 66, 96, 165
Galula, David 53, 56, 235-6
Gardiol (MLN plan), 187, 253, 265
Garrastazú, Emilio 144, 226
Gatto, Hebert 16, 115, 198, 269, 369
Gavazzo, José 232, 237-8, 280, 282, 292, 309, 313, 315, 320-1
General Motors, terrorist attack on, 96–97
Gestido, Óscar 41, 59, 67, 224
Goulart, João 22, 87
Guevara, Ernesto "Che" 20-1, 25, 27, 32, 36-7, 40, 43, 48-9, 51-2, 59, 69, 75, 86, 91, 97, 102, 113, 126, 136, 187, 241, 270, 369
Gutiérrez Ruiz, Héctor 70, 184, 247, 285, 329
Hevia, Manuel 143-4
Hunt, Everette Howard 16, 268, 369
IAVA, 44, 47, 128, 137
Inteligencia y Enlace (police division) 34, 116
Jackson, Geoffrey 168-72, 178, 189, 191, 202, 227
June coup of 1973, 325
Lacalle, Luis 66, 342, 353-4
Lenin, 20, 182, 198

Macchi, Yessie 32, 50, 88, 95-6, 127-8, 134, 247, 279-80, 345
Mailhos mansion heist, 123–27
Manera, Jorge 35, 38, 45-6, 53, 58, 61, 76-7, 79-81, 90, 95, 107, 124, 139, 187, 201, 212-4, 220, 253, 260, 278, 281, 287-8, 295, 297, 309, 335, 339
Mao, Zedong 19-20, 37, 113, 127, 198, 236, 242, 369
Marenales, Julio 35, 38, 45-6, 48, 53, 57-8, 61, 71-2, 76-7, 79-81, 90, 107-8, 119, 139, 201, 204, 213-4, 216, 219-20, 249, 252, 260, 263, 267, 272, 280-3, 287, 296-7, 299, 308-10, 332-3, 340, 343, 347-8
Marighella, Carlos 21, 113, 164, 175, 369
Martínez Platero, Efraín 31, 36, 39, 46, 59-61, 76, 84, 90, 94, 99, 108, 123-4, 135, 137, 152, 154, 158, 161, 179, 192-3, 223, 249, 251, 253, 266, 298, 306, 308, 343, 359
Mas Mas, Antonio 159-60, 179-80, 281, 309, 345
Michelini, Zelmar 68, 197, 285, 295, 317, 321, 329
Ministry of National Defense, 64, 185, 238, 287, 304, 312, 315-6, 349
Ministry of the Interior, 64-5, 116, 118, 130, 133, 178, 255-6
Mitrione, Daniel 79, 141-73, 179, 192-4, 216, 222, 248, 256, 258, 277, 280-1, 338, 345
Monty investment bank raid, 83–85
Morán Charquero , Héctor 136, 149-50, 182-3, 193-4, 256, 277, 345
assassination of, 121–22
Mujica, José 9-10, 30, 38, 47-9, 66, 69, 71-2, 76-7, 87, 100-2, 104, 107-8, 120, 122-3, 201, 205, 208, 210, 214, 221, 223, 249, 251-2, 263, 265-6, 283, 296-9, 308, 310, 320, 333-4, 340, 342-4, 346-55
Nardone, Benito 23, 195, 295, 313
Nixon, Richard 96, 226
Nueva Helvecia robbery, 34–36
Office of Public Safety (OPS) 26, 64, 143
Operation Pajarito, 71–73
Operation Paloma, 118–19
Operation Rooster, 178, 205-8, 250–54
Operation Star, 205–8
Otero, Alejandro 33-4, 38, 55-6, 64-5, 77, 80, 90, 93, 95, 99, 105, 107-8, 110, 114, 116, 137, 162, 183, 199, 237, 352, 359
Pacheco, Jorge 41, 63-4, 66-8, 71, 75, 83-4, 90-2, 98-9, 113, 116-7, 136, 139, 145-7, 149, 151, 154, 157, 160, 163-4, 173, 181, 183, 186,

190-2, 195-6, 202, 222, 224-5, 242, 255, 272, 285, 294, 312, 323-4, 351, 353
Pando, MLN attack on, 99–108
Parliament, 15, 18, 91, 117, 147, 182-3, 196, 222, 230, 237, 243, 259, 273, 295, 304, 313, 317, 319-20, 322-5, 328, 340, 348
Partido Nacional, 15, 47, 52, 68, 86, 117, 147, 195, 198, 225-6, 285, 295-6, 323, 341, 342
Peirano, Jorge 92, 157, 161, 164, 175-6, 303, 311
Pellegrini, Gaetano 97-9, 135, 142, 193, 276
People's Prison (Cárcel del Pueblo) 142, 150, 154, 167, 170, 178, 191, 194, 258, 273, 275-6
Pereira Reverbel, Ulysses 71, 73, 97, 142, 190-1, 193, 214, 273, 276, 291
Pignorative Loans bank heist, 130–33
Píriz, Mario 190, 247-50, 263, 277, 280-2, 298-9
Plan Hipólito (April 14 incidents), 254–59
Punta del Este, 59, 86-8, 126, 230, 313
Rey, Alicia 46, 79, 101, 119, 150-1, 153, 218, 247-51, 265, 268, 310, 354
Rio de Janeiro, 14, 149, 158
Rio Grande do Sul, 22, 158, 162
Rockefeller, Nelson 93, 96
Rosencof, Mauricio 48-50, 57, 84, 99-100, 124-5, 156, 178, 187-8, 192, 197, 206, 223, 247-8, 250, 255, 258-9, 263, 266-8, 277, 281, 288, 295, 308-9, 333-4, 340, 342-3
Sáenz, Adolph 26, 65, 73, 78-9, 122, 143
San Rafael casino heist, 86–89
Sanguinetti, Julio 63, 66-8, 109, 146, 190, 198, 233, 237, 242, 293-5, 303, 313, 324, 329, 337-8, 341-2, 352
Sarandí radio station raid, 91–93
Sendic, Raúl 30-7, 40, 44-6, 49-40, 53, 57-62, 76, 79-81, 84, 86-9, 92, 95, 98, 100, 102-3, 106-7, 119-20, 127-9, 134-5, 137, 152-4, 157-8, 162, 178, 188, 192-3, 201, 204, 211, 214, 218, 220-1, 223, 241-2, 245-6, 248-50, 260-1, 263, 267, 269, 280-3, 290, 296, 298, 299-300, 307-9, 331-3, 337-8, 340-3, 346-7, 350, 353
Sierra Maestra, 36, 48, 86-7
Soviet Union, 16-7, 23, 44, 48-9, 69, 75, 163, 189, 197-8, 239, 243, 271, 306, 318, 329-30, 344, 350
Spain, 14, 48, 295, 306, 324, 345
Student riots of 1968, 73–76
Tatú (MLN plan), 242, 245-6, 248, 260, 267, 269, 277, 305
Topolansky, Lucía 59, 77, 83-4, 191, 223, 248, 258, 270, 297, 340, 347, 349, 354

Torres, Jorge 36, 40, 155, 262, 346
torture, 52, 108, 115, 142-4, 150, 153, 162, 164-5, 182-3, 190, 240-1, 261-3, 273, 278, 288, 292, 301, 303, 310, 329, 334, 343, 349, 356
Trabal, Ramón 90, 185-6, 238, 240, 263, 277, 280, 287-8, 290, 293-4, 296, 298, 303-4, 310-4, 317-8, 324, 328, 331
Trinquier, Roger 233-6, 302, 304
UJC (Communist youth militia), 17, 25-6, 70, 74-5
United States, 2, 7, 26-7, 33, 64, 75, 89, 93, 116, 127, 140, 143, 145-6, 154-5, 167, 184-5, 232, 237, 255-6, 286, 336
Universidad de la República (University of the Republic) 17-8, 20, 30, 73, 359, 369
UTAA cane workers' union, 31-4, 37-40, 58, 79-80, 87, 117, 211, 242, 245, 307, 347
Vasconcellos, Amílcar 183, 224-6, 312, 317, 323
Vázquez, Tabaré 330, 342, 349
Viet Nam, 26, 41, 59, 97, 113, 142, 157, 160, 176, 189, 223, 232, 234, 333
Wasem, Adolfo 140, 148-9, 187, 192, 204, 223, 247-8, 250, 258, 267-8, 274-6, 287, 290, 295, 309, 335, 337
Washington, 16, 22, 24, 39, 50, 66, 75, 79, 89, 93, 130, 142, 161, 163, 173, 198, 361
Zabalza, Jorge 86-8, 92-5, 103-4, 107, 116, 154, 201, 205, 209, 212, 242, 245, 249, 251-3, 260, 269-71, 287, 332-3, 340, 342, 346-7, 354
Zorrilla, Juan José 239, 294, 296, 314-6, 31

Printed in Great Britain
by Amazon